Augusta Larned

Village Photographs

Augusta Larned

Village Photographs

ISBN/EAN: 9783744652193

Printed in Europe, USA, Canada, Australia, Japan

Cover: Foto ©Thomas Meinert / pixelio.de

More available books at **www.hansebooks.com**

VILLAGE PHOTOGRAPHS

BY
AUGUSTA LARNED

NEW YORK
HENRY HOLT AND COMPANY
1887

Copyright, 1887,
BY
HENRY HOLT & CO.

NOTE.

The sketches composing this volume first appeared in the *Evening Post* of New York, and were designed to depict the varying scenes and changes of nature and some of the aspects of country life.

CONTENTS.

CHAPTER		PAGE
I.	A Green New Year,	1
II.	Some Village Characters,	9
III.	Paradise Farm and Aunt Dido,	16
IV.	Hugh the Druid, Rose Madder the Impressionist,	28
V.	Rastus Thinks of Getting Married,	36
VI.	The Wrens' Nest,	46
VII.	A Mormon Settlement.—Stephen Loses His Money,	54
VIII.	The Hon. Highflyer Visits the Village,	64
IX.	The Village Clubs.—St. Patty and Her Jubilee,	73
X.	The Poor-House Children.—Old Peter's Girls,	85
XI.	The Village Post-Mistress,	94
XII.	Sayings and Doings of Miss Candace,	103
XIII.	The Busy Bees,	112
XIV.	The Doctor's Trouble,	121
XV.	The Boy Almira Adopted,	130
XVI.	One Spring Day in Hugh's Life,	139
XVII.	The Help Question at Fraser's,	149
XVIII.	The Delightful Major,	159
XIX.	A Rose-Bud Garden of Girls,	169
XX.	The Colored Browns,	179
XXI.	The Ministers' Glebe and Hope's Love Story,	186
XXII.	Fascinating Mrs. Bridgenorth,	198
XXIII.	A Stage-Struck Girl,	209
XXIV.	Shiftless Jabez,	219
XXV.	Cupid Among June Roses.—The Little Maiden Sisters,	229

CHAPTER.		PAGE.
XXVI.	Mrs. Legality at the Wilderness Lodge,	238
XXVII.	The "Digs" Boarding-House,	248
XXVIII.	The Old Sweetheart,	257
XXIX.	The Story of Job Bird,	269
XXX.	The Old Tavern Stand,	280
XXXI.	Zip Coon—A Dog Story,	291
XXXII.	A Domestic Tyrant,	301
XXXIII.	The Holworthy Girls,	311
XXXIV.	The Most Popular Girl in the Village,	321
XXXV.	The Mystery of Styles Garth,	332
XXXVI.	John Dean and Oriana,	343
XXXVII.	Hugh gets a Lady in his Eye,	354
XXXVIII.	A Spiritual Experience,	363
XXXIX.	How Bill Fuller was Indemnified,	374
XL.	Jelly Cicero Oldham Falls into Error,	384
XLI.	Strange Disturbances at Stillwells,	396
XLII.	Brother George,	408
XLIII.	The Unearned Increment,	419
XLIV.	Joe Elmore and Bob Smartweed at Home,	432
XLV.	A Bundle of Love-Letters,	444
XLVI.	Loose Ends and Dropped Stitches of Village Life,	453
XLVII.	Christmas in the Village.	466

VILLAGE PHOTOGRAPHS.

CHAPTER I.

A GREEN NEW YEAR.

THE first snow flurry has sifted its white powder from a gray cloud only to be followed by a burst of sunlight chasing the winter gloom from hill and valley until they glitter again in warm browns, gold, and blue, and violet. High winds have whipped the trees naked, and they must go unclad through the cold season owing to the singular inhumanity of nature. But in their nakedness they will contrive to protect the waxy leaf-buds at every point and axis of their being. These buds are babies they dandle and sing to when the wind blows and the snow falls.

The village is too small to have a name familiar to many, but it stands well planted on a small piece of soil which helps to hold the earth together. The grass is faded, but the evergreens are lusty and of a splendid strength. I think I have heard them shout on cold days when all the other trees looked miserable from the whipping of the wind. They were not only born to endure hardness, but to love it. We talk of heart of oak, but give me the heart of a pine or hemlock wherewith to defy misfortune.

Of all the lovely tribes that so lately adorned our woods and fields, we must now content ourselves with a handful of bitter-sweet, and a few ivy leaves, or a branch of cedar and a cluster of the ground-pine. Still the swamp grass is pretty, and the stubble takes on a pale gold like sunshine, and the clean brown fields are good to walk in, yielding a companionship which is very sweet if a little sad.

The long village street is raftered over with the interlaced branches of the elms, and at either end the arcade opens to a pleasant vista such as an artist would love. Eastward lies the old burying-ground, with gently swelling hills behind it, and at the western end is a sharp spire of Saddleback Mountain, and the glade of a wild brook it has sent down into the valley.

The little pools have acquired a crust of ice pellucid and thin like a sheet of window glass, through which one can see the roots of plants at the bottom. By-and-by the ice will thicken on the pond to a blue translucency and get etched in fine lines as the boys try the runners of their skates. The robin sitting on a stake in the orchard fence feels his feathers blown aside showing the beauty of the pale red-breast, while the clinging pink toes look half frozen. The clouds look cold with dark scuds moving fiercely, still letting down sudden gleams of splendor, until at sunset they are blown all away. The heavens then are open and serene, with a fervid glow in the west, against which every object looks black. The earth is a charcoal sketch, lying banked up against that great western blaze, and here and there a mellow lamp throws out its ray from some low window.

The village houses look lower and smaller than they did in the warm days, as if they had shrunk inwardly and had gathered themselves up to resist the winter cold. The front doors are rather forbidding now, whereas they used to stand wide open. You must seek the back way if you would find the housewife and the stove. Still every house feels the dignity of its parlor, if it is cold and cheerless. Many of the houses are well banked with tanbark, and make one think of beaver dams and rabbit burrows. Man's habitation in winter is only an improvement on the fox's hole. He hibernates like the bear, gradually withdrawing his interest from the outer world as the cold advances, and concentrating it on the fireside, the cellar, the cattle-shed, and the barn. It is only in cities where an artificial heat is made by stone and brick walls and the united breath of a great population that people do not go into the winter drowse.

Now the woodshed begins to be a matter of great importance. The village "forehanded" man is known by the neatness of his piles of split hickory heaped up in the sacred repository of fuel. But coal is used in many houses, and the sound of the grimy shoveler is heard as the winter store goes into cellar and bin. The good little maiden sisters in their birds'-nest cottage where the flaming Virginia creeper has lost all its leaves, have been made very happy by two loads of wood, which a kind-hearted farmer drew for them, and the village lads have split it into lengths for the tiny stove and piled it close within the sisters' reach, and they are as snug for the winter as two dormice. Their wise cat looks out of the bright little window, and follows them to church still, although she loves not wet or frosty ways.

The shoemaker hugs his stove, and now works in an overheated atmosphere, such as all shoemakers seem to delight in. He is a crooked old man, with head and beard as white as snow, and a fine pale skin and delicate features, for too much indoor work has spoiled his ruddy complexion. He knows almost every pair of shoes in the village, for his cure of soles is a large one. A curious heap of foot-casings lies in one corner of his shop. They all have a character of their own, from the "stubbed" copper toes of Widow Blair's son to Farmer Grime's great square-soled boots. There are women's shoes, some slender and worn discreetly on the side, some coarse and run down at the heel, some of dainty kid, "storekept," for which the old man has supreme contempt. The lasts upon the shelf are all ticketed: "Old Lady Holt." Yes, he has made for her these past thirty years. Young "Widow Holt," the son's wife, came from the city, and has "notions." How he has stood before that young woman and lectured her in his slow way on the wickedness of French heels! A book lies open turned down on the bench, and there are moments when the old man stops sewing John Dean's "Oxford tie" and takes it up, adjusting the spectacles on his nose and leaning forward with his chin protruding. It is not the Bible. The old man seldom reads that now. It is a book of science, treating of the evolution of the human race. Often the young parson comes in and sits beside him there on the bench, and the two hold weighty arguments together of righteousness, temperance, and judgment to come, but the old man is not convinced. On Sunday the shoemaker goes not to church. All day he is deep in science and philosophy, while his old wife trudges off alone to the meeting, and, coming home again, says, "Oh, father, if you only could have heard that sermon!" But the shoemaker laughs, with a slight touch of contempt, at the idea that the young minister can teach him any thing. He may come and learn of him, if he will, sitting on the workman's bench, but the old man will not sit in the pew to return the compliment. The neighbors think, according to the eternal fitness of things, this obstinate, conceited old man should not be happy, but I am fain to confess that he is, as he sings to his lapstone, in a desperately cracked voice, those old psalm tunes he learned at his mother's knee; not from pious fervor does the old man sing them, but because these have stuck to his memory like burrs, and he knows no others.

Not far from the low shoemaker's shop, where the smoke is pouring in a black stream from the stove-pipe which crowns the chimney, is the doctor's office, with his house adjoining. A square, plain house it is, solid and home-looking, with a great comfortable garden at the back filled with every variety of vegetables, interspersed in the old-fashioned way with such common and hardy flowers as bloom with little care. Hollyhocks, sunflowers, larkspurs, marigolds, tiger lilies, bachelor buttons, and clove pinks grow in pleasant profusion along the borders in summer time, but now the garden is a broken and withered waste. The little drug-shop stands next to the house, and is the doctor's office. The green curtain is drawn, showing the good doctor is at home engaged with a stray patient, who has come in to talk about "rheumaticks," the common village complaint. The old white horse and much-bespattered chaise, still uncleaned from his last round of country visits, stands in the stable ready to be "tackled" and put in motion on short notice. Small peace and quiet has this rough, wise, humorous country doctor, with his gray tousled head, his shaggy eye-brows lowering over the kindest eyes, and his blunt speech giving forth nuggets of sarcastic wisdom for the benefit of his neighbors. Blunt he indeed is, and not too choice in his language when awakened from his first nap after a heavy day's work by a call to go three miles through the dark and cold over miry roads, perhaps through rain and snow, to some hysterical woman.

But who could guess of the deep true vein of poetry in that rough bit of human nature! Often as he bowls along on these errands at night, gently touching up his old nag, who has served him faithfully these many years, he repeats aloud long passages from Shakespeare's plays, or verses from the book of Job, his two favorite poets. He half shouts out the lines sometimes as he looks up at the bright stars through the naked tree branches, or sets the music of those immortal bards to the great sad sough of the wind in pine branches. So he splashes and rumbles away on his visit of mercy, beating his breast with his disengaged arm to keep off the cold, and raising his voice in the highest flights of poetry to warm his soul. How much that old man knows of human weakness, human vanity, human depravity! How much he knows of the sin and sorrow which have entered into so many of the gray, lonely farm-houses scattered over the hills and through the valleys! How often he has acted the consoler and friend with tears of sympathy filling those kindly eyes! How often he has shown himself the stern reprover of vice, even to using his stick upon some delinquent youth who was ushered into the world through his skill, and has lived to disgrace the mother who bore him! I am fain to confess the testy doctor has appeared more than once in court to answer for such breaches of the peace, but a good case has always been made out for him even when he has been forced to pay a small fine. A terror to evil-doers, to profligate, idle, useless people is the old doctor. And have peace, and love, and joy always abode in his dwelling? Alas, no. He had one fair daughter, a wild willful girl who married against his wishes and is lying now in her grave. I hear her child, a flaxen-haired girl of fourteen, just touching the keys of the old piano in the parlor, where her mother used to play and sing in a heavenly sweet voice. The child has brought a great compensation to the doctor and his patient, pale-faced wife. She has reconciled the old man to the world, for he was once cynical and hard, all gone wrong with bitterness of spirit. Now he goes and sits under the preaching of the young parson, his grandchild's hand in his, and says softly under his breath, "God be merciful to me a sinner."

That child of his loves the wild flowers, and the birds, and the clouds, and every sight and form of nature. So in the bleak weather he takes her, well wrapped up, on those long drives to lonely places in the hills. There they go down the road under the big elms, across the bridge by the mill, where the ruby-colored water is still foaming over the great idle wheel. If the north wind still continues to send forth its blasts, the wrinkled, opaque mirror of the pond will grow smooth as glass, and the wheel will adorn itself with thousands of jagged icicles and much fantastic lace-work in crystal pendants. The boys and girls of yonder school will soon be skating and sliding, and sprawling like frogs all over the pretty place where geese and ducks paddled in summer time, while they reared their broods under the pollards. The grists are almost ground for this year. They have made Christmas bread and pies and cake. The earth hath yielded her generous increase. Now she girds herself to endure the cold. Now she lies patient under the flail of the blast and waits for the chastening of the snow.

The road mounts and mounts from hill to hill, as if, like the tower of Babel, it would build itself into heaven. And on the right grows the vision of Saddleback, a long mountain with a hump covered all over with a thick shag of forest. Many little brooks come down from Saddleback and run through the lowlands with refreshing coolness and the earth gurgle of laughter. It is the office of old Saddleback to offer a cup of cool water in the name of his Creator. He is our barometer and our thermometer. When the clouds gather in a certain way on Saddleback it always rains. When he grows dim and ghostly and withdraws into his cloudy tent and shuts the door, it is a certain sign of heat. I wonder the people out on the prairies do not build themselves mountains as landmarks and objects of affection. A mountain need not be very high nor very beautiful to be so intimately inwoven with life that one would miss it like a household companion. It is a good thing to tie up to. It renders the planet stable. It accents the lowlands and gives them emphasis.

The old doctor dearly loves Saddleback. He has wandered all over it with his grandchild in pursuit of nuts, and ferns, and mosses, and autumn leaves ; its top is clothed with pines, and a small spring gushes out near the summit from under the shelter of a great gray bowlder, all embroidered with golden moss and little evergreen ferns, and in spring with wild flowers. Now there is nothing under foot but the red pine needles, and overhead a cloud of dark foliage supported by columnar stems. These serried ranks make a fine contrast on bright mornings to the living blue of the sky. The mountain gathers a deep cerulean, and the purple tree-boughs work themselves out in far vistas with exquisite intricacy. The doctor is quoting poetry aloud as he gently strokes his old nag with the tingling end of his whip, and the solid satisfaction of a day like this beams from his eyes and irradiates his rugged countenance. It is a good open mild day the first of the New Year.

CHAPTER II.

SOME VILLAGE CHARACTERS.

THE village has no manufacturing interests. It is a mere ganglion of inhabitants and houses knotted together, why or wherefore one can hardly tell. Nature holds the little place in its snug hollow like a bird's nest, as if it loved it, as it never can love a smoke-begrimed neighborhood, or one resounding with the discordant noises of much industry. It is pure and spotless these winter days, with the elm trunks and boughs making delicate tracery on the snow, and the sunlight glittering on the clean window-panes in old houses. The snow has not destroyed the charm of little winding footpaths over hills and through bits of evergreen coppice and oak groves, where the leaves still hang, and rattle in the winter wind as if made of stiff paper. Everywhere peeps out the still, white world to the blue of the sky, and the warm gray of rocks, and living green of mosses, with the endless poem of tree trunks, and boughs spotted with white bits of lichen, and colored variously for just this season of the year.

The famous village ramble is Burying-Ground Walk leading to the old graveyard, with its new smart portion called the cemetery—for even the smallest country places have advanced of late years in mortuary architecture, and the idea of what a burial place should be. This path is the favorite in summer, and it is very beautiful in the cold season, owing to the great number of cedars, spruces, and hemlocks, that for a mile and a half line it with their warm fur, while the vista opens to the slope of Saddleback, and the old red farm-houses come so near in view, that you can almost shake hands with the inhabitants. It is skirted on one side by a noisy brawling trout-brook, that runs like a perpetual life current out of the breast of Saddleback, and gurgles under the ice of early winter, making a choice music around its big stones. The fields lie in peace just beyond, their russet brownness showing through the glaze of ice or where the snow has worn away in patches. This rustic aspect is delightful around the graves of the dead. It still holds them in fealty to the soil. The sights and sounds they knew best when in the world are near at hand. The plowman whistles to his team, cows low in the pasture, and idle, truant boys angle along the stream in closest neighborhood to that silent village which is bound by so many invisible fibres to the homes of the living. The brook is lined with violets and anemones in April, and in June the air is loaded with the scent of new-mown hay. In autumn asters and golden-rod make a splendid carpet under the trees, and in certain select spots the fringed gentian opens its blue eyes very late in the year.

This winding path up a piece of gently-rising ground to Burying-Ground Hill has been the scene of more marriage proposals than any other place in the village. An amusing story is told of a village maiden who married and went away to live in that indefinite region known as "out West." Years later, when the husband died, she brought his remains back to the old home, and buried him in the family plot in the graveyard. She could not tear herself away from the sacred spot, and again took up her abode in the village, and spent much time in visiting and laying fresh flowers on the grave. A year or two earlier an afflicted widower had brought the "casket" of his wife back to her native town, and had laid her not far from where the husband was afterward put to rest. This poor man constantly haunted Burying-

Ground Walk to muse on the departed, and, as chance would have it, one golden autumn day he met the widow in her weeds, which, by the way, were very becoming. The village gossips say the match was made that afternoon—struck up in a hurry through sympathy and fellow feeling. But doubtless several interviews did take place in the "walk" or in contiguous parts among the tombstones before matters were settled. Now the happy pair dwell in the village and are sometimes seen going hand in hand, with an artless babes-in-the-wood expression, to visit the resting places of their former partners. As they have a leaning toward spiritism, it is believed they look upon the departed as guardian angels who view their present felicity with extreme satisfaction.

Every week, summer and winter, rain or shine, Miss Milly, the village milliner, walks briskly along the burying-ground path to the old part of the graveyard where the head-stones are decrepit and mossy, and a little cluster of pine trees watches over the country from the highest part of the hill. Miss Milly is brisk and trim and neat; the print of her shoe on the snow seems a work of art. Her father was once thought to be the genius of the village, a young man of brightest promise, but he turned out a spendthrift and profligate, and lies now buried in the graveyard. In spite of his squandered life, his only daughter weeps over him, idealizes him, and adores his memory until the neighbors, who think Miss Milly a bit of a genius herself, are half provoked. In the snowiest days she will go wading to the hill-top to leave some green token on her father's grave, if nothing more, a few twigs of arbor vitæ with a cluster of holly berries from the squire's garden. The earliest wild flowers in spring go up there, and the very last gentians and colored leaves and golden rod. If the path is not cut to the hill, Milly opens it herself, or hires Jake Small to do the work for her.

At home she lives alone (in the little stone house that was once a lawyer's office, and has been enlarged to suit her needs), unless some neat-handed apprentice should find a place by her hearth, with the understanding that she is to do "chores" in return for instruction in the mysteries of millinery. Milly's work-room is so peculiar there is probably not another like it anywhere. It has a case of books, a cabinet of old family china, and the portraits of her ancestors—the wreckage which she managed to preserve when the family fortunes went down. Milly read Latin and Greek a little with her father when she was young. Her school-books are in the case, and a manuscript volume of her father's poems. Spinoza and Plato are Milly's idols, but she reads them now in translations. The young parson sometimes comes in and takes a cup of tea with her, and they talk learned talk, so the village folk say, who have the greatest respect for the milliner's attainments, though, in fact, they do not go very far. Her secret lies in knowing one or two books by heart. Are you surprised that one small village can furnish a shoemaker who reads Huxley and Spencer and a milliner who knows Plato? Such people nowadays are only found in corners. There is no leisure for these things among the masses in great cities, but certain people in the village do still find time to hive up sweetness.

Milly chose to be a milliner when she might have taught school, and the village folk have never done wondering why. But a bleak school-room gave too little scope for individual expression. The learned side in Milly is not her broadest. She is a human creature, a woman to the tips of her fingers. Look at the little shop, adorned as a parlor with etchings and small oil sketches upon the wall and bits of embroidery, such as a woman loves, arranged with an accurate eye to color harmonies. The bonnets are only a part of the decoration.

The little milliner says she is fond of folks. She looks out and sees things in the turn of an eye-lash. In every thing except about "poor papa," she is careful of overstatement, and this makes her pungent little flavoring of dry wit very telling. She is pleasant to the eye, and yet not young, and so plain that every body wonders where her "knack" is.

The judge or "square," as he is commonly called, extends his gracious patronage to Miss Milly or Melissa, the village milliner. It is a rule at the great house that Miss Milly is always to be invited to the Thanksgiving and Christmas dinner. When political dignitaries or literary lights come from a distance Milly is overlooked. But these are not really the nice occasions, like the cozy home meals, when the judge unbends and laughs at Melissa's dry little speeches, of a subacid quality, and she on her part laughs inwardly at his pretensions and corrects his Latin. She has remembered enough for that. But she forgives him in her heart, for he recalls old stories of her father's college life when they were "chums," and speaks gently, very gently, of the dead.

No one knows exactly how the village came to be, but the judge thinks it was made for him. When he walks abroad he has the air of owning the place. He and the clergyman and a few others habitually wear store clothes, which means a certain luster and polish of attire to which the ordinary farmer and mechanic can not attain except on Sunday. The judge would like to be a village autocrat, but his neighbors utterly repudiate his pretensions. "It's a free kentry," says Jake Small, "and I guess human motives is pretty well mixed. The jedge may think he's clean public-sperited all through, but I guess there's some selfishness at the bottom."

Jake can afford to criticise the judge. He is a man of property as solid as a rock. Jake owns a little queer ridiculous gore of land that lies in just between two of the judge's best fields, and cuts off the right of way to a handsome pasture. The village magnate is therefore obliged to drive his cows half a mile round. He has offered Jake a large price for his scrap of soil, and has even condescended to call him Mr. Small; but the old man holds on to his ancestral half-acre with the grim clutch of fate. If he parted with that precious gore of land, all his importance in the village would ooze away. He would be only a shiftless old codger, without power to put in his word anywhere, or to make himself felt in discussions about national politics. The little piece of land came to him from his grandfather—through a disputed title. Jake would rather go on one poor meal a day than think of parting with this miserable strip of soil. When the weather is not good for fishing, or blackberrying, or going to camp-meetin' (Jake is very pious), he often digs and potters about a little in the gore. It puts fat on his bones to know that the "jedge" is looking on from his back window and metaphorically gritting his teeth.

Several times Jake has impounded the judge's cattle for trespass. What makes the situation extremely awkward is the fact that a stream of living water, Willow Brook, flows through one of the judge's pastures, while the other is quite arid. In a dry time there is always trouble, the battle being waged across the gore with terrible pertinacity on both sides. Jake's part of the fence is a ramshackle, ruinous affair, and the judge declares that most of the boards which compose it were stolen from his premises, but he never has been able to bring proof of the fact, for the neighbors refuse to testify against Jake.

Jake lives in a wretched old tenement on the outskirts of the village, that was moved off the Widow Grimes's place, and doomed to destruction. But Jake coaxed the widow to let him have it in return for gathering her garden "sass" and splitting her winter's wood. Then he set to work to patch it up with every old board and piece of tin and bit of rusty iron he could find about the roads and back yards. When the prohibition act was passed, and the tavern had to be closed for want of custom, Jake got hold of the old sign and tacked it over his front door, where it now displays a badly fore-shortened horse and a gig in an advanced stage of dissolution. This he looks upon as the art gem of the place. His unique mansion was crowned with glory by a young painter who came to board in the village last summer. This misguided young person admired Jake's singular abode more than any of the new Queen Annes that are cropping up here and there in the neighborhood, and made a sketch of its picturesque confusion, with children, pigs, and chickens running about in the foreground. Jake says he got five hundred dollars for it down in "York." But nobody believes Jake, and it is one of his good points that he never expects belief in any thing he affirms and is ready to take his Bible oath on.

Jake's wife, unlike the usual type of such unfortunates, is round and fat, and very easy in temper. She is inclined to think that her husband is a pretty smart man, because he manages to keep the "gore," and to get along without any visible means of subsistence. Indeed, she rather admires Jake, and herself, and the children, because they appear to be under the special protection of Heaven. She takes in washing when she can get it, and at other times, the neighbors say, sits right down in the dirt as if she expected Elijah's ravens to come and feed her. Jake says he intends to live to the age of ninety, for if he were to die before Sally, she would surely let the land slip right through her fingers, and then he would "jest turn in his coffin."

Jake Small is a happy man. It is a blessed and enviable thing to be able to hector the judge, to be his gad.

fly, the thorn in his side, the crumpled rose leaf in the rich man's bed, who, when he walks the street, seems to say, "I am the man who planted the common, who built the library, who repaired the church and put in the new organ," as plainly as if he carried so many placards about his person announcing these interesting facts. Then, Jake Small, from time immemorial has been in the love secrets of all the girls and boys in the village. There is nothing he enjoys so much as what he calls a first-class love case, where the old folks are opposed and the young folks "have taken the bit between their teeth." A qveerer Cupid's postman was never seen, but all the billets intrusted to his care are delivered with the utmost secrecy and dispatch. This business, besides being very congenial to Jake's mind, is lucrative. The girls are always ready to bestow a quarter on him for secret service, and the young men of course pay much more liberally.

Although not as instructive as the new library, nor as refreshing as the common, nor as clean and holy as the church, Jake Small is an institution the village could ill afford to spare. There are set, obstinate old folks who uphold him about the land, because they know if they had a gore lying so advantageously for the torment of a rich neighbor, they could not forego the pleasure it would give them. As Jake says, "human motives is mixed." There is a diffused feeling of kindness toward Jake in the village, rather sneaking, but genuine. Even the judge, when all the Small children came down with the scarlet fever, paid surreptitiously out of his own pocket for the needful medicine. The Small children have a characteristic way of getting ill simultaneously, with any infant disease that happens to be about; then the neighbors go in and scrub up every nook and corner of the house. Good, pious women take in clothing and furniture, and fill the larder to overflowing, so that the poor-spirited "Miss Small" has reason to look upon measles, or diphtheria, or whatever the complaint may be, as a blessing in disguise; and she placidly waits until the next dispensation of childish ailments comes along to help her out of her chronic hobble.

There is always a full-blown odor of patronage about the judge which corresponds to his Doric-pillared house, his fine stable, and handsome garden. If there were not people about him to condescend to, life would not be worth the living. For this reason he vegetates in a hamlet instead of living eclipsed and shorn of his beams in a city. Here he is the richest man, the top of the heap. But his vanity is so transparent it passes for a decoration, and his neighbors could not get on without the judge any more than without Jake Small. Both of them are essential to the village.

CHAPTER III.

PARADISE FARM AND AUNT DIDO.

THIS clear, cold winter afternoon the village walks are scraped clean of snow, the roads are packed hard as iron. White barricades rise in all the yards and along the street. The snow crunches and grinds to marble-powder under foot, and overhead it shakes down from the elm boughs in showers as sharp as steel filings. There is a sparkle from the solid blue sky diffused through all the air, and one must adjust the breathing apparatus to new conditions. The mere act of inspiration is a species of excitement; and a great tide of fresh blood brings a bloom like that of youth to old faces.

The ice on the river and pond to-day has that dull semi-translucency, with long reaches of glitter and shine in the distance, that make one's feet ache for runners. Come down the road for a quarter of a mile where it dips and winds so prettily, to the old bridge spanning the river. It was once a toll-bridge, but tolls are taken there no longer; and even the injunction not to drive your horse faster than a walk, under penalty of the law, is disregarded by every old hack and broken-winded jade in the township. The bridge was covered, originally, but the crazy old top blew off in a gale of wind, and it is now the roosting and angling place of all the children and idlers in the village.

The small river curves away through low meadows and gently swelling breasts of hills in the laziest manner. It is like a long narrow scarf of dull blue some gadding nymph has dropped and trailed with her buskined foot. With the thin lines of fences and young trees making small shadows, the world all white, and the sky all blue, one thinks of Luca Della Robbia's altarpieces, the perfection of blue and white glaze. It would be monotonous without the lovely outlines of hills casting such pure shadows on their sunless slopes.

The sluggish river winds about in great serpentine curves through very low grassy banks and groups of trees that in summer time look as if they were made for the poet and artist. But now all the ferns and grasses and wild things are frosted over, and the river's secrets are as open to the eye as a gossip's heart, save where a clump of evergreens, lusty and full of life, breaks in with a soul-warming cheer. The ice is in a perfect state to-day, and half the village folk are on the river. There is the doctor's girl, in her scarlet-trimmed costume, with the light locks floating behind her as she deftly cuts the figure-8 on the ice. And the old doctor has actually mounted skates and is skimming away with his girl's mittened hand in his and his coat tails standing out stiffly in the breeze. With his fur cap and frosty glittering beard, he looks like the Santa Claus of the picture-books. As usual he is spouting poetry at the top of his voice, but at this distance I can hardly make out the lines. They have gone under the bridge, and the laughter of his granddaughter comes up like the twitter of young birds in June. The young clergyman is also out on skates, and he has brought his oldest child, a mere tot of three, and is riding her on his shoulder as he spins along, to her infinite delight. It is just over this part of the river where the doctor, and parson, and Hugh, that young scapegrace of a lawyer, race in their boats in summer, each pulling a mighty oar. Hugh is a back-handed, unregenerate friend of the parson—was in college with him, I believe. The village has as much need of Hugh as a coach has of a fifth wheel, and yet he has a kind of use in keeping things stirred up and getting himself talked about. Milly, the milliner, seeing him stride off on excursions with the clergyman, has slyly named them the Law and the Gospel. Hugh, the lawyer, with his briefless pockets and his Homeric laugh, is a character not to be ignored.

All the village boys are out on the ice either sliding or skating. Their shrill voices echo along the banks as they skylark and indulge in every species of horse-play. The skating-boy comes nearer a tadpole in his awkward sprawl than anything that navigates. But the little girls are all charmingly rhythmical in their exquisite grace of motion. The swish of their skirts has music in it, as they skim over the icy floor, and make a delicate etching on its smooth surface. They follow the curves and windings of the stream to the upper bridge, with arms interlocked and hands hidden in little muffs, moving to the beat of some melody heard only by their ears. Their eyes shine and their cheeks glow with exercise, and when the red sunset shines out from under a low purple cloud it flashes down the river and diffuses a rosy bloom around these happy children, while the snow fields take on the softest blush, like the lining of a sea shell, and the shadow side of their knolls are pure ultramarine, or palpitating violet, or even a delicate shade of green. The evening red strikes boldly on the side of Saddleback and flames among the higher cedars and hemlocks, while the lower ranges of the mountain are plunged in splendid gloom, a kind of blood-shot black melting into a band of blue quite indescribable, for there is nothing else like it in nature or art, unless it be that azure zone of the earth on which the glorified Virgin sits in the imagination of old painters. A fringe of flame runs crinkling along the serrated skeleton trees on top of the mountain, where they stand out so dark in places against the perfect rose of the heavens. But look! the village windows are all ablaze, and the library looms up like a huge castle illumined for a festival; and the top of the church spire sparkles as if it had impaled the evening star.

There is only a quarter of an hour left before dark for a run to the top of Pudding Knoll and a peep down into the little valley below. It is the choicest spot about the village and has been appropriately named Paradise Farm. The house stands at exactly the right angle facing the east, and is a most picturesque jumble of pale, silvery, unpainted buildings. Before it rise two tall Lombardy poplars, like sons of Anak. They are admirably picturesque in the winter landscape, and are so placed they can be seen for miles up and down the river. The barns to the north are sheltered by a sugar camp, where the maple trees grow straight and clean as columns in a temple. This grove is a splendid patch of color in October when it is changed by the finger of the frost. There are snug orchards and gardens and poultry-yards about this farm-house, and the fields slope down to the river in a manner truly Arcadian. Its view opens gently to the principal valley of the local mountain like a decorated side chapel looking into the nave of some stately cathedral, while all around are cheerful little hills perfectly well wooded and watered, and in summer full of flowery nooks and singing birds.

This farm ought to belong to a poet, but it is owned by Rastus, and the mother of Rastus, who is the egg and butter woman of the village. Any fine day you may see the old lady mounted in a high-backed wagon driving into the village a spavined horse, blind of one eye, her baskets and firkins comfortably stowed away beside her. She is still strong and ruddy-looking, like a late Baldwin apple, which, though seamed and shriveled a little by frost, retains its high color. The old dame seems happy enough with Rastus, but still she regrets her late husband, now lying in the burying-ground, who was known to the neighbors as a very handy man. A handy man has no significance in a city household. There is always a workman on the next block, or round the corner, who can fasten a screw, or tighten a bolt, or mend a lock ; but it is very different in a small village or on a farm. There the man, the head of the house, is twice as valuable if he can mend a pump when it gives out, or correct a smoky chimney, or put up a shelf for the women folk. What wonder a village man is esteemed in direct ratio with his handiness! The father of Rastus was eminently a handy man. His jack-knife was a mystic tool, with which he performed admirable works in kitchen and pantry. Every cupboard door had its button, every lock was well oiled before the poor man took that inscrutable disease, located in the pit of his stomach, and extending to the small of his back, until it finally went to his head and baffled the skill of all the doctors, besides furnishing a fruitful subject of conversation to his apple-cheeked widow for the remainder of her life.

Sadly enough, Rastus has not inherited his father's handiness. Rastus is in fact remarkably slow and "pokey," with a moderation of ideas and movements, and a blundering way of doing things eminently original. He is tall and rather shambling in his gait, while his nose describes a very strange angle not set down in any of the geometries, and his mouth has a tendency to stand slightly ajar. Oddly enough, Rastus, though in no sense a comic character, always excites mirth. The whole village bursts into an unrestrained roar of laughter when Rastus begins to narrate his adventures while at the war. He was taken prisoner by the enemy, and shut up over night in a henhouse, with nothing to eat. In the morning the "rebs" were obliged to beat a hasty retreat, and they forgot all about Rastus, and left him in the henhouse, from which he escaped by a series of thrilling adventures. There is nothing really funny connected with this story, and Rastus is very fond of telling it. He likes in his slow way to "wave the bloody shirt," but now for a good many years he has been greeted with such unseemly signs of mirth when he has tried to narrate his hairbreadth 'scapes connected with the late unpleasantness, that he has grown very shy of drawing the long-bow in the company of an irreverent villager. He generally reserves his war stories for the ear of some patient stranger who happens to be staying in the neighborhood. Last year he found a summer boarder who was remarkably long suffering in this regard, but it turned out that he wanted to buy Paradise Farm. Rastus took a week to think over the proposal, which was an excellent one, and after a great deal of chewing of straw in the barn he repaired to his new friend :

"I 'low I can't sell the old place anyhow," said Rastus ; " mother won't part with her thirds, and without the thirds the land wouldn't vally much. And then, you see," scratching his head, " dad, he lived here, and granddad, and great-granddad afore him, and if I live long enough I expect to leave the old place to my son."

"Oh, you do," said the stranger, dryly looking at the incorrigible old bachelor with a twinkle of his eye.

"Yes, I do. Mother's getting stiff in the j'ints, and I shall have to provide for the future."

The stranger did not renew his proposal, but the idea which had taken root in the mind of Rastus worked like a very slow process of fermentation. Rastus is a very forehanded farmer, and secures some of that kind of consideration which money always brings.

On the road to the "Hollow," quite at the other end of the village, is a little brown house that seems to cling to the earth like a ground-bird's nest. It is the home of Aunt Dido (an absurd abbreviation of Diadema), the sister of Rastus's mother. She differs materially from her close-fisted relatives, and is, in fact, a survival of a vanishing village species—the good-natural cook, the old-fashioned housekeeper, a person who before the days of cooking schools was supposed to take as naturally to all the mysteries of the culinary art as a duck takes to water. Such a person enjoys heartily the pleasures of the table, and herein, perhaps, lies the secret of her genius. No nervous, thin-blooded, narrow-chested woman who lives by the week on tea and toast ever became a great cook, with local fame resounding far and wide, for flap-jacks, crullers, spice-cakes, pumpkin and mince pies, and all the endless variety of New England concoctions. Aunt Dido especially prides herself on her exquisite bread and biscuits. Any fool, she says, can make a good cake after a recipe, but only a woman of genius knows how to turn out a fine domestic loaf of bread.

Aunt Dido is large and broad and glowing with vitality. When she walks she makes a breeze, and when she runs, as she sometimes does, just to work off her superfluous vigor, she creates a whirlwind. Her throne is her kitchen rocker, and her scepter is a great iron spoon which she flourishes in the most artistic manner while engaged at one and the same moment in conversation and cookery. She is more than a cook—she is a woman of ideas. She threw herself into the abolition cause, into the temperance reform, and a few years ago she became a religious free light. There is generally some very "advanced" book, rather shocking to the ideas of her more conservative neighbors, turned down on the corner of her kitchen table, to be picked up and read at odd moments. You should see her kitchen, more beautiful than any parlor in its spotless, immaculate niceness. No one ever intrudes there irreverently, not even her small, meek husband, who sometimes asks the privilege of wiping his hands on the jack-towel. The odors that proceed from that kitchen are enough to warm the cockles of the heart. It is said that you can smell Aunt Dido's coffee 'way down in Saw Mill Hollow, half a mile from the brown cottage.

Aunt Dido is by no means forehanded. She is far too generous and large-hearted to lay up an excess of goods anywhere but in heaven. Her penurious relations say that she might fatten two pigs and keep a cow on what she gives away every year to tramps and children. She does fine baking for the richer neighbors, there being no bake-shop in the village, and Mrs. Judge Magnus often bespeaks bread, and cakes, and pies, and even cooked meats which are to furnish forth the feast for some dignitary at the great house. She is childless, but she deserves to be called the mother of the village, for all the idle, vagrant, ill-conditioned urchins that hang about the place get a vast amount of coddling, petting, and feeding from her hands. The mother of Rastus has solemnly warned her sister that if she should ever come to poverty, she must not look to her for help. But Aunt Dido goes on spoiling the rising generation to her heart's content. She has an amount of sympathy for the so-called bad boy that is perfectly disreputable in a person of her years, and by people of grave and severe virtue is looked upon as a demoralizing influence in the community. For years she has constantly kept on hand in her buttery a large jar of caraway-seed cakes of a most delicious and toothsome variety, which she gives to the village children when by mere accident they happen to pass her door on the way to school. When her prudent sister suggested that she might turn a pretty penny by selling her cakes to the ever-hungry urchins, she was scandalized by the mere suggestion—she who had always been the village almoner.

Last summer she noticed a small black-eyed urchin, with several varieties of soil on his face and hands, who came more regularly for the dole than any of the other lads. He would set up a most piteous wail just at the moment of reaching her gate, and exhibit wounds which seemed to have been made by barking his little brown shins on a stone wall, or scratching "hisself," as he said, in a bramble-bush, much to the detriment of a very ragged pair of trowsers. He was a cunning little rascal, and Aunt Dido knew in a general way that he was one of Jake Small's numerous brood. She could never forbear taking him in and comforting him with goodies. But the same appeal to her feelings was made so often by this pertinacious youngster, as he exhibited the gory stains on his feet and legs where he had "hurted" himself, that Aunt Dido began to suspect he was playing on her very tender heart by staining those nut-brown feet and ankles with pokeberry juice or something else of a vegetable nature. The wounds certainly did look suspicious; so one day she seized the boy with her firm, large hand, and hurrying him into her woodshed chamber stripped off his poor little duds of things and buried him in a great tub of warm water, while she administered a plentiful lathering of strong soap—in perfect silence. Bill, when he described the operation later, said: "First it was kerswish, and then it was kerswash," and then he had to "holler" because he was "drownded." But the old lady wouldn't "let up on him" until she had scrubbed every inch of his skin. Later she placed him on a chair, done up like a mummy in a blanket and proceeded to cut and comb his gipsy locks. She even scrubbed out his mouth, and then put him to bed until she had mended his clothes.

When Bill again went forth into the light of things, he was a changed boy. His own father and mother scarcely knew him. The nearest neighbors had always supposed that Bill was dark "complected," but after that vigorous scrubbing he came out exceptionally fair. The boys teased Bill unmercifully over this adventure, and for three days he was strongly inclined to take to the woods and hunt wild Indians the remainder of his life. He will never make sham wounds and scratches on his legs again with pokeberry juice, and he now fights very shy of the little brown cottage. Since this occurrence Aunt Dido's "stock" has risen among the boys of the vicinage. They now know she keeps her weather eye open, and respect her accordingly. Aunt Dido did get a great deal of satisfaction out of her bout with little Bill, and she is ready to own it any day as she laughs over the story until the tears fill her eyes.

CHAPTER IV.

HUGH THE DRUID, ROSE MADDER THE IMPRESSIONIST.

AUNT DIDO has one regular boarder—the young lawyer known as Hugh—a tall, easy, unconventional young man, a local antiquary, an excellent oarsman, and a great walker. He is always ready to attend to anybody's business but his own—indeed, his own personal business is an unknown quantity. His mouth is generally seen stretched from ear to ear in a huge laugh over his own joke, or at the expense of somebody else. The fun bubbles up in him from a consciousness of the latent comic elements lying all about in the neighborhood which nobody sees but himself. It must be confessed that Hugh sometimes carries his jokes too far and makes enemies for the time being; but it is impossible to remain long angry with a humorist who perpetually feels the laugh tickling his midriff and rising in him as little jets of gas dance about in an effervescing mineral water.

He lounges in all the village parlors—comes in and goes out like a cat, without ceremony, and takes liberties which in any one else might seem offensive, but with Hugh are rather graceful. The villagers say that Hugh is "a case." The pretty girls say it with a little smirk and blush; the old maids say it with a certain bridling touch of self-consciousness, as if they had now and then encountered the young man's impertinence; the nice old ladies say it with a half-smile of relenting, indicative of a soft spot in their hearts for the scapegrace. He pretends that he is busily engaged looking up a law business more difficult to find than the traditional needle in a bale of hay. He has in vain tried to excite a little legal irritation by rubbing the neighbors the wrong way, and artfully stirring up lucrative discord. But he can not show even one cow case for his pains. Most of the village folk are too shrewd and close-fisted to be drawn into what they call "lawing," with its concomitant bill of expenses. They generally "fix things up" by arbitration. The doctor has probably done more arbitrating without pay than any other man in the United States.

Hugh, having no active business in the legal line, interests himself in the titles to estates, in old deeds and wills, and the bits of local history bedded in such musty parchments. This useless kind of erudition is very much to his mind. He has up in his queer attic chamber at Aunt Dido's a collection of old seals—impressions in wax and plaster—that is very curious. He is deeply engrossed, too, in black-letter literature, and seldom cares to read any thing less than 150 years old. His room is an interesting museum of old books in various languages. He has discovered that several of the farms in the neighborhood are held under the original grants from English sovereigns in colonial times. Although he reads almost nothing that is modern, he writes for some newspapers and magazines, and has been heard to say that he intends to produce the great American novel in an autobiographic work with himself for the hero. But Hugh could never be as effective in print as he is in person. When he takes pen in hand he becomes rather heavy and solemn. His fun must froth out at the moment of production, and it is impossible to preserve it in printer's ink.

The old maids, as I have hinted, regard him rather kindly, his taste in women being somewhat omnivorous. He keeps an eye out for all the pretty girls, and will run half-a-mile to peep under a smart hat at a blooming face, but his impudence is only the unquenchable vivaccity of young spirits, and really means nothing ; if the girls take him too seriously, that is their lookout. He is always on a " lark," and instead of finding the after-effects vapid, his appetite seems to grow with what it feeds on. It is pleasant and surprising to discover a human being who has such an insatiable interest in the mere act of living. Some people say Aunt Dido has spoiled Hugh with her good cooking and her much coddling, and that if he never amounts to a " row of pins," it will be entirely her fault. But this is doing Aunt Dido great injustice, who gives Hugh the best of advice, which he takes great pains never to follow.

He is intimate with Milly, and often appears in her little parlor of an evening with a black-letter folio under his arm. In summer he comes in his slippers, though the road be damp, wearing his big-flowered dressing-gown, without a hat, and smoking a long-stemmed brier-wood pipe. He is the only human being who would dare to smoke in Milly's sitting-room ; he has never asked her permission, and she tacitly allows it. At one time it was thought by the villagers that things were looking rather serious between the two, although Milly has a few years the advantage of Hugh in age, but within a year a young lady artist has come to the village and set up a studio, who is considered the most inexplicable young person ever seen in the neighborhood.

Rose Madder lives over Peckham's grocery store, and has hung out a little sign which says that there pupils are taught crayon and water-color drawing and china-painting. Rose wears little artistic skimpy gowns, a high-crowned Tyrolean hat, and a bag like a pilgrim's scrip slung over her shoulder by a long strap. The small sleeves of her gown have queer little puffs about the elbows, and the embroidery on her skirt looks like a distracted landscape. Under her hat she is all hair and eyes with a white moon face gleaming out in dreamy melancholy. The villagers know not what to make of her, while she only looks at them with a view as to whether they will " compose." I am sorry to say most of them will not ; they are too angular, weather-beaten, crooked, and hard-visaged. It is suspected that she has taken up her abode in the village because she can live here on next to nothing.

Hugh made no end of fun of the Madder phenomenon when she first appeared, but one day he lounged into her studio over Peckham's grocery store, as he lounges in everywhere, and caught her making her solitary luncheon on bread and jam and a Japanese pot of tea, eating the jam spread on the bread, in child fashion. The picture of Rose, backed by a sage-green Canton flannel curtain topped by a bunch of peacock plumes, touched the sensibilities of Hugh. He became slightly " spooney," and has since maintained relations with Rose very different from those he keeps up with Milly.

Rose has not the remotest conception of the meaning of his jokes, but she thinks if he would only be serious, and cultivate a certain cut of beard, he would do very well in a sketch as Launcelot to her Guinevere. The neighbors speak of her as if she were an exotic bird that has lit by accident under the village elms. Deacon Hildreth's wife says she " s'poses she hasn't got any folks, and she don't seem to possess a conscience any more than a katydid, for she goes off sketching on Sunday when the rest of the people are in church." Rose is always looking out for " effects," and she dabs away industriously at little bits of wayside weeds, thistles, and mullein-stalks, and pins them up against the sage-green Canton flannel curtain, and waits for somebody to buy them. Her contempt for the inartistic world about her is so profound that it seems to frame her off in a perpetual frozen calm. She talks very little, and Mrs. Judge Magnus has not found her a success when she has tried to introduce her at her evenings. She has posed a little in a languid way at the village tea parties, but as there is no one to know when she gets in a good light and becomes effective, it is time thrown away.

Milly has bought one or two of her sketches, which she has hung very high that they may be properly viewed from across the room. This is the way Hugh described one of Rose Madder's most celebrated pictures, before he became, as I said, slightly "spooney": " Sky : a splash of white and a larger splash of blue. Middle distance : a streak of intermediate dirty yellow. Foreground : a pretty large daub of lightish green, with several black serpents wriggling on end intended for trees standing about in a field. Then a spot of brown to indicate a pond with five vague daubs of white for geese, and under all, the legend :

"'Oh, what is so rare as a day in June.'"

Hugh is a tremendous walker. He makes nothing of a tramp of twenty-five or thirty miles a day. His legs are long, and he naturally falls into a kind of Indian "lope" which carries him over the ground with great ease. The parson often joins him on these rambles, and then Hugh is apt to take himself seriously, and they fall into those close and confidential talks which sincere and sensitive minds seldom indulge in except in the open air, when sitting to rest on stumps or mossy stones or the sharp angle of a rail fence. Nature is so confiding to her lovers she leads even the reticent to breathe their inmost convictions out in her confessional. Hugh calls himself a Druid. Stretched under some great pine or oak, with the sweet air caressing him, he will often indulge in an exposition of his religious views, which are of a curious nature and lead to heated discussions with his friend the theologian. Hugh believes the sentiment of worship is best excited out of doors, under trees, in view of hills or mountains, or beside running or still waters. He thinks the face of a flower or the call of a bird can awaken deeper religious sentiments than any temple service ever excited. This is a simple spontaneous offering of the heart to its maker, unpolluted by turbid systems of theology—the clear crystal through which we see eye to eye with Him who made us. Nowadays, since the old creeds are so much shaken, he thinks this out-of-door worship is almost the only pure religious sentiment left in many callous, worldly, or faithless souls. In view of the exquisite beauty of the universe, the confirmed skeptic even must feel a thrill of childlike trust and love toward the Author of the day, the night, the stars, the firmament, the wonderful and supreme order that reigns around us. Out of this species of modern nature worship he thinks will come the foundations of a new faith, more simple, direct and unclouded, than those that have gone before. It will be the natural hymn of the creature to the Creator in this exquisite world, thrilling with the profound revelations of loveliness and beneficence. Beauty, he holds, is the stumbling-block of the materialist. He can not account for this spirit-bloom spread over the face of nature. Jaded, overwrought minds, burned out with excitement, nauseated with folly, and the pursuit of unreason, or blinded and dazed by vain ambitions—even these can come still to the old service under the sky, and like Faust can weep again to find the world so sound at the core.

The minister, of course, can not accept this queer kind of Druidical worship as sufficient for the needs of sinners. Hugh's faith is entirely too easy-going to secure safety for the imperiled soul of man. But the influence of his friend has been stimulating in many ways. It has modified his preaching more than he would be willing to admit. Hugh never goes to church, for he says he fears he would be obliged to get out an attachment to recover his stolen ideas. So they tramp about, these two rather interesting young men, and preach to each other in many wild and lovely places.

Their walks almost always tend due east to the large tract of woodland which lies about the foot of Saddleback and climbs the slope of the mountain, with here and there a small rent made in its verdant garment by rough clearings for pasture land. In an old settlement like the village there are myths of that extensive tract of woods. The children delight in the story of a bear living on Saddleback within the past twenty years. One very cold winter night he trotted down to a lonely farm-house on the hillside, crept into the store-room and ate up the Christmas turkey nicely trussed and stuffed for roasting. That bear has given rise to a great many charming stories, and has produced a large family of cubs.

There are foxes in this piece of woods, and many rabbit burrows. The local ornithologist says we have over twenty-five species of birds which live here and in the adjacent farm lands, among them the splendid red oriole. Squirrels, gray and red, abound, and the drum of the partridge is often heard in October. The brook coming down from Saddleback makes numerous shady pools, where the shy woodland creatures resort to drink. These pools in winter are mirrors of frosted silver set in brown carven frames. Paths, made by boys and cattle, run in all directions. When the snow is on the ground, Hugh makes his own path, guiding himself, as the Indians do, by the moss on the trees. He has the genius of woodcraft in his blood, and his eye and ear are as delicate and sensitive as a wild creature's. He often strikes a bee line for the top of Saddleback, where in winter the view is very extended. It looks into a series of pocket valleys, with its congeries of villages, its checker-work of farms, and boundary lines of fences and stone-walls. You can trace the windings of the river for miles and miles, and many smaller streams running into it, and many belts of woodland wedged into home fields or descending the hill-slopes like platoons of soldiers. All this is a story to Hugh, for he knows more about the farms and their titles and history than any body else. Every blue smoke wreath curling up in the still winter air becomes garrulous to him touching what has gone on under the roof.

CHAPTER V.

RASTUS THINKS OF GETTING MARRIED.

CERTAIN matters of importance have been going on in the village, which if related in a novel would probably not be believed. I only ask credence for them on the ground that truth is stranger than fiction.

One winter day, just at the beginning of a thaw, when all the elm boughs dripped, and little pools of ice-water stood collected in the snowy road, Milly sat in her work-room trimming a new hat for Rose Madder. It was one of the high-crowned affairs; and Rose had sent her a sketch to show just how she wished it to look when finished. It was placed on a block in front of Milly while she bowed up a large quantity of parti-colored ribbon for its adornment. Enter Jake Small in an overcoat two sizes two large for him, which Grandfather Andrews had given him out of his store of old clothes for a Christmas present. The collar of this garment was turned up above his ears so that he seemed buried alive. Milly often employed Jake to carry bundles and band-boxes to distant farm-houses and the more remote village homes: "I haven't any jobs to-day," she called out without turning 'round.

But Jake didn't go. He hemmed and hawed, and stood first on one foot and then on the other. "But I've a leetle job of my own," said Jake at last mysteriously behind her back.

"Well, what is it?" quoth Milly, still intent on pinning snips of ribbon on the hat before her, and cocking her head this way and that to study the effect.

"What du you think of Rastus B.?" Jake hitched a little nearer, and emitted the words in a loud whisper that they might not reach the ears of the small apprentice at the other end of the room.

"I don't think any thing of him," Milly replied calmly, but now she did look 'round.

"Wa'l he thinks a sight of you."

"Does he?" said Milly, with a touch of surprise in her voice. "I'm very much obliged to Rastus."

Jake drew near by another hitch or two, twirling his old hat between his hands. "I told him he'd better write. I advised it strongly; but he said he wa'n't no fist at writin', and as he knew I'd had exper'ence he put the case in my hands."

Milly had now suspended her work, and her lips began to quiver slightly. "Oh, I see, you have come to make a bargain between me and Rastus—a delicate negotiation."

"Jess so," broke in Jake, eagerly forgetting to whisper. "You know Rastus is a rich man; has money in bank, and twenty head of fine stock on the place, the very best critters in the town."

"I am very fond of critters," interposed Milly, whose back was shaking a little.

"I knew you was," put in Jake eagerly, "because your head is level. Then you know all about the farm—a sightly place and so well watered. Got in ten acres of winter wheat in the fall."

"Oh, yes, I know all about Paradise Farm. You need not go into an inventory of crops and stock. I am just in love with the farm."

"Glad to hear you say so," returned Jake judicially. "You know the old lady can't last long, and if any thing should happen sudden-like to Rastus, you might be left a widdy with a snug place."

Milly did not try to repress her laughter, and her face

was full of attractive little dimples. "There is nothing in the world that would suit me better than to be left a widdy with Paradise Farm."

"I thought you would view it in that 'ere light. I felt sure on it from the start. So I s'pose I have your leave to chirk up Rastus a bit."

"You haven't my leave to do any thing of the kind."

"Then I shall tell him to come and speak up for hisself. I shall report what you've said verboatim." This was a word Jake had picked up at public meetings, and of which he was very proud. He hung about Milly's shop sometime longer, but as he could gather no more crumbs of comfort for Rastus, he finally disappeared.

The interview he had held with the village milliner was the result of a great many interviews with Rastus in the barn, and behind the hay stack, and down by the creek, due to the fermentation of ideas set up in Rastus's brain the previous summer. Rastus had confided in Jake, because he knew he was experienced in affairs of the heart, and in this regard Rastus felt himself more out of his element than when he had been a captive to the Confederates in the hen-house. He knew Milly only in a general way, as all villagers know each other, and had often heard it said that she was as "smart as chain lightnin'." His only conception of smartness in a woman was of the kind that washes, mends, and bakes for the stronger sex. He had perhaps been slyly egged on by Hugh (who divined what was brewing) to make this perilous venture.

Rastus allowed a day or two to elapse after hearing Jake's report of Milly's sweet reasonableness before making trial of his own powers as a lover. She had been on the lookout for him, and when he came was rather grimly pleased at the idea of a bit of fun. Rastus had put on his best clothes, as he understood courting business always demanded this kind of homage. He was rather high-colored, and his mouth had more of a tendency to stand ajar than usual. Milly's perfect self-possession was very upsetting to Rastus, who proceeded to forget every thing in which Jake had carefully " coached " him. She looked like a Sunday-school teacher who is receiving a new pupil, and is prepared to give him a wholesome lesson. Rastus fumbled in the crown of his hat, and a peculiar embarrassed grin overspread his features : " I suppose Jake has told you what I've been thinkin' on."

"Oh, yes," said Milly promptly. "Whatever put it into your head, Rastus ?"

Here was a chance for a pretty speech, one of those he had thought over, but had forgotten, and he lapsed into a shocking literalness. " You see mother ain't what she was ; she has gone deaf and her hands are growin' out of j'int with rumatiz."

"Oh, I see," said Milly briskly. " You will have to hire help in the house unless you make other arrangements."

"It's natural to suppose," nodded Rastus, who was getting more at his ease as the conversation took a strictly business turn.

" What work did your mother do when she was well and strong ?"

" Well, she allus milked the cows and made butter, but now her hands——"

"Oh, of course ; and I suppose besides, she swept, and washed, and made beds, and cooked, and mended your clothes ?"

"Yes, mother has allus kept things pretty snug. She's one to look out for all that's goin' on."

" Then she raises chickens and turkeys, and sells eggs, and poultry, and butter to the village people. You would expect your wife to do that too ?"

" Natural to suppose," assented Rastus ; and then he bethought him, and pulled himself up with a jerk—" not unless you liked it. Some folks like to drive 'round in the fresh air. It's real healthy. If you lived up at the farm you might live to be ninety. You never will, here, shut up in a shop—good air and water on the farm, the very best."

"Oh, yes, I know all that," murmured Milly, musing deeply, "but I was thinking what I should get for all my work. It would be your society, wouldn't it, as you would never think of paying wages to your wife?"

"Natural to suppose," muttered Rastus, quite losing his head again.

Milly got up and faced him with perfect candor and sweetness. "Well, I should love to live to be ninety, and I don't mind the work a bit, not even peddling truck around the village; but I couldn't endure your society all those years. I'm afraid I should get tired of your conversation, especially the war stories. Therefore I must respectfully decline, with thanks."

"But," stammered Rastus, "you encouraged Jake Small."

"May be I did encourage Jake, but I haven't encouraged you. But I shall deal with your mother," she added, "just the same. Don't be afraid of losing my custom." She made him a little courtesy, and then she moved to the door, opened it, and shut it again softly behind her.

Rastus stumbled out into the open air, and Jake was obliged to fight quite shy of him for several weeks. Milly never told the story, but somehow the little stone house leaked, and it was presently known all over the village.

The story of the village is a story without an end. It deals with the homely facts of life, and, unlike the novel, has no ulterior aims and no great respect for the literary unities. There is never a pretense made of bringing fascinating people together solely that they may fall in love, marry, and live forever after in a state of bliss. Love is an episode, always, of course, the most interesting and exciting that can occur. But marriage is not the be-all and end-all of a considerable section of village life. There are several of both sexes who do not marry, and who appear to get along about as well as their mated neighbors. They have fewer cares, and they are not a bit more given to gossip than other people ; indeed the greatest gossip in the village is a blind man who has reared a family of twelve children.

The story of the village does not attempt to finish all lives with a round turn. It recognizes the fact that most lives remain unfinished and are deplorably raveled and ragged at the edges. Many people show fine romantic possibilities which never come to any thing, and yet they are not blighted beings. They visit and amuse themselves, and read books and magazines, and eat and sleep, just as if they never had been nipped by an untimely frost. Village life is hard, like all life, but it is ameliorated by those touches of humanity which make us all akin ; it is lubricated by that divine humor which plays like lambent flame over the surface of existence. The people enjoy the privilege of social criticism in select circles. They enjoy each other far more, I think, than they would if they were all perfect characters. For it must be confessed that although they understand the value of friendship, they also tacitly prize their spites and animosities. There is nothing that will keep a tough old person so long alive as avarice and a neighborhood enmity. The asperities come in to help as well as the amenities, with that blessed feeling that one is superior in virtue to some other folk. If you get to the point where you can not pay your debts, then you are accursed. Any thing else of a venal nature may in time perhaps be forgiven. Married experience is not altogether a romance in a little hamlet. It has its large, sober, practical aspects and its absorbing economic side. It is the best way devised of getting on in a difficult world, but by no means ideal. The old maids talk a good deal about the æsthetic side of married life, and the true way to bring up children, but the married people do not moralize so much. They know the hard facts of the case. They try to slip along between uncompromising conditions with as little friction and heartache as possible. Their wisdom is embodied in that excellent practical maxim, "Make the best of things."

There are not many of the purely ornamental kind of women in the village, and those are criticised rather severely. The practical feminine virtues are still held to be very important. Even Mrs. Judge Magnus, who has figured in Washington society, puts up her own jelly and jam, and is a notable housekeeper. To be sure she keeps two or three maid-servants and a man, but she is a bustling, busy kind of person, with sufficient good sense to make her neighbors feel that she is one of them, and not an alien. In all small villages there is a certain distrust of strangers and strange ways. When new persons come in the approaches may be a little slow unless there is a good introduction, but if your great-great-grandfather ever lived in these parts, you are of the elect.

The village man most honored and beloved is the man very good to his "women folks," which means that the women run over him and have their own unbridled way. He is a man regular at his meals, who doesn't complain of the food, and talk of the dishes his mother used to cook when he was a boy, even if the steak is burned and the coffee a trifle muddy. If he would be truly popular, he must be easy about money with his wife and his girls, and not keep the purse-strings too tightly drawn. He does not make any unnecessary work about the house, but is nice and catlike in his customs. He will go in his stocking feet to prevent waking his wife when she has a headache, and he thinks of the extra washing when he takes out a clean handkerchief. He must above all things be a good provider, with not the smallest taint of slackness or shiftlessness clinging to his skirts. He must have a nice square pile of wood all split and seasoned, and a fine bin of coal provided against the cold weather. His ten commandments are written all around on his fence, his garden-patch, his roof and chimneys. He must get in provisions freely by the bag and barrel, and see that every thing is done that can be done to make the life of women less laborious. Then if he is willing to arise at night and walk the floor several hours with a fretful teething child, he is considered truly angelic.

In the household where there is no servant employed, the man who will allow his wife to get up in the morning and build the kitchen fire is not looked upon as much of a Christian. He may write fine poetry and entertain the most beautiful moral sentiments, he may even pray well in the weekly meetings, but this thing is always spoken of disparagingly at the tea "fights" and in the Dorcas Society, where women put their heads close together, and talk low and confidentially. A selfish man can never hide himself from censure in the village. He is known and marked for condemnation. A shiftless or unpractical woman, who neglects her family, is also open to severe criticism. But I do not know that I have ever heard a woman called selfish who made her husband wait on her and the children to an unreasonable degree. It would be dangerous to admit the possibility of that form of feminine selfishness, and it never has been admitted.

One of the former village saints was a little, slim, pale minister who preached here at one time, and who had a bed-ridden wife. He was always seen when out of the pulpit carrying an air-pillow, two shawls, and a hot-water bottle. It was well known that his constant care of his wife, who suffered from an inexplicable nervous complaint, had made him quite bald before the age of thirty-two. Yet, although it was shrewdly suspected that this complaint was at least partly imaginary, never was a word spoken concerning the selfishness of the minister's wife. I may add that some years later, while he was preaching in a neighboring town, the parsonage took fire on a cold winter night, and the invalid lady, who had been unable to do more than walk across the room in five years, arose in her fright, and, in a pair of slippers and very thin garments, ran through the snow for half-a-mile. Since that time she has been a perfectly well woman, doing her own housework, and the minister has grown a new and fine head of hair. But I am afraid his prestige as a moral hero is somewhat dimmed.

The doctor, who has been such a power for good in the community, and withal so open-handed and public-spirited according to his means, is a masterful person with a strong will, and a natural tendency to domineer. The neighbors know his value, but they suspect that his wife is a little too meek, a little too much given to that perfect feminine submissiveness which, though enjoined by Scripture, is not the village ideal. She has a saintly face, as pure as a snowflake, and almost as pale. The silvery hair has still a golden sheen and is puffed at the border of a white lace cap of the old fashioned variety. Her dress of worn black silk seems never renewed, but has an indescribable refinement about it like all her delicate belongings. Her voice, with its soft, low intonation, and her rare smile, repel all undue familiarity. She finishes the pretty tea-table like some very rare family portrait—a Sir Joshua or a Van Dyck. I like to look at her in church, she is such a perfect picture of a time when manners were more ceremonious and courtly than they now are. The neighbors say that she has never dared to say her soul is her own in the household. But she is intimate with only a few of them, and it is perhaps her superiority to them all which leads them to try and pick a flaw in her character. She is a great student of the old Bible, and has found much comfort in the most consoling Psalms and the beautiful portions of Isaiah. She holds with perfect simplicity and true-heartedness to the religious doctrines of her youth ; and even Hugh, with his farrago of fantastic notions, is alway deferential in her presence.

CHAPTER VI.

THE WRENS' NEST.

THE range of farms lying in close order form a rustic fringe to the snugness of village life. The place is in part made up of retired farmers, too old to labor, who have left the homesteads to their sons. Thus the village tendrils run out into the country in all directions. Mill Farm lies south, and is one of the most picturesque places anywhere about. The old mill, with its flume and water-wheel, its floury interior, its humming grinding-stones, and revolving hopper, is joined to a farm-house, with a flower garden in the half-inclosed court, and at the back commands a view of the wild mill-brook glen, where picnic parties come in summer. The brook feeds the mill-wheel and falls into a rocky ravine down a few gigantic stone steps. In the freshets of spring and autumn it becomes a charming waterfall. The rocks below the fall are cushioned with brilliant green moss, kept continually fresh by the spray of the cascade. The young birches, and maples, and witch-hazels which lean over the water, take the most graceful forms in the delicate tracery of their boughs. There are two or three lower pools, where the trout blink in lazy motion in the sunlight as it slants down the dewy wooded bank, and lights up the very heart of the glen, flickering on the moss and wet stones, and the purple tree trunks. Now that the season of frost has come the mill-wheel is still and the fall is bearded with icicles—the most beautiful frost-work is gathered on stone and bush and tufted moss, where the spray has frozen, making miniature caves with fairy work of ferns, and grasses, and weeds all covered with powdered silver, glittering in the sun.

On the road to the flume, as this ravine is called, is a stone cottage, low-browed, with broad porches, and a huge outside chimney. It has the oldest sycamore tree in the town standing before its door—a patriarch among the tribe of trees; a Methuselah that seems to have lived a thousand years; it shades the whole house and the front yard, and throws its nourishing summer dews over the roof into the kitchen garden. Every body in the village and neighborhood is proud of this tree. It is one of the curiosities of the place, to be pointed out to strangers. I will not attempt to give its measurements. A party of twelve young girls once tried to span its girth with their united outstretched hands, and it is suspected that the old tree was as joyful over this embrace as was Tennyson's Talking Oak over having love secrets poured into its ears. For several years the largest limb of the old sycamore had been weak and decaying. It was bandaged with iron, and carefully staid with a kind of framework which served the double purpose of support and rustic summer-house. The three maiden sisters who lived in the cottage, if they heard a noise in the night, would get out of bed to see if any thing had happened to the tree. They were excellent women, who had received, I suspect from Milly, the name of the Three Wrens; and the cottage under the sycamore was known as the Wrens' Nest.

There was also a male wren, known as Brother, who lived in this snug and tidy establishment with his womenkind. Morning, noon, and night the conversation of the three Wrens turned upon Brother. You would have supposed to hear them talk of the way he slept and ate, and from the account of his habits, that he was a weakling, and chronic invalid. But, on the contrary, Brother was a large, well-colored, rather fine-looking man who went away regularly to his business by the morning train and who never seemed the least in need of being taken care of; still he was taken care of by his doting sisters as if he had been a helpless paralytic. I do not know whether he liked so much attention from those adoring females, but it was bliss to them to adore; and if they all could have been taken in a picture kneeling at his feet, it would have fitly expressed the way in which he was regarded by these good little Wrens.

His room at the Wrens' Nest was a perfect museum of masculine comforts and luxuries. It was reported in the village that he slept in worked bed-slippers and that certain of his under garments were ruffled and fluted. That room was the shrine of the house, a place the sisters never entered irreverently. They took turns, as a great privilege, in doing it up and airing the mattress. The bachelor shrine was probably the prettiest bedroom in the village, for the Wrens would have gone without tea rather than deprived Brother of any little charm their purses could buy or skillful hands devise. It was never known how Brother liked it. Hugh threatened to ask him whether he did not sometimes kick off the crazy-quilt, and throw the worked foot-stools and tidies out of the window, but even Hugh's impudence would not carry him quite so far. Brother presumably did like it, for he treated his good sisters with great respect, and was always most kind and attentive.

One night in spring there happened to be a terrible blow from the north-east. Brother was away from home on business, and the Wrens scarcely closed an eye all night, thinking of the weak limb of the mighty sycamore, which was groaning and laboring so piteously in the blast. There they were in their night-caps peering out of the chamber window, and suffering with that poor dumb thing which had thrown its protecting shade over their whole lives. Before morning the great limb came down with a crash, burying the front yard under its ruins and just missing the roof, which would certainly have been crushed beneath its massive weight. The Wrens wept as they thought of the sad welcome Brother would receive, and looked at the dismantled old tree, which, now shorn of its chief ornament, stood up gaunt and black and wounded in the morning light. Moreover, they regarded the catastrophe as an omen of trouble to come to their house. They set down the day and hour of the fall in their little note-books; and the story goes that on that day the widow and her six children moved into the village. But this important event did actually happen a month later.

The widow was the niece of somebody who formerly had lived in the village, and in her girlhood she was in the habit of visiting her relative. But she had been lost to view for many years, now appearing on the scene with six small children, the youngest two girl-twins of tender age. She had married a good-looking young man who turned out to be dishonest and bad in every way; and now he had departed to another world, leaving her with naught to thank him for but a very flourishing, healthy, handsome family of little ones. As she sat in her poor home after the funeral, dressed in her scanty mourning gown, she wept bitterly, not because of the demise of one who had caused her great pain and humiliation, but from the consciousness that there was scarce a dollar in her purse and but small store of food in the house to feed the children. The loving little twins crept into her lap, and clasped their arms about her and pressed their soft cheeks to hers, and administered the love and consolation that come from baby hands. Neighbors were kind, and within a few weeks remittances began to come from some rich relatives at a distance; and finally the widow moved to the village, as a few others had done, because it was cheap living there and because of the library and the high school.

The advent of such a troop of bright-faced children was of moment, for the best village people do not have large families now. The time grandames tell of, when the old district school was in existence, and the eldest child of a family was expected to shout out the number of his brothers and sisters present at roll-call, has passed away. Then one of the Stockton tribe often sang out "Thirteen"; but the Stocktons are no longer found in the village. Many houses have no children; some, like the doctor's, have a grandchild, or a nephew, or a niece; a few quite poor people, like Jake Small, are blessed with a quiver full. The pair of twins, called respectively Goody Twoshoes and Baby No One—why, I am sure I do not know—became very popular. They were lovely little Kate Greenaway creatures, so exactly alike that no one but the mother could tell them apart when they slept. Their frocks and sun-bonnets and worn shoes had a touch of something idyllic. They were much given to running away, when they would fall captive to some childless woman and be carried into her house and fed and entertained with playthings for hours. The mother, with six to feed and clothe, and only one pair of hands to do every thing, was often obliged to let the twins run wild. Goody Twoshoes was the most enterprising and adventurous, but Baby No One always followed where Goody led, and copied her sister in every thing. Hand in hand, chuckling in their dear little hearts, and ripe for mischief, they slipped out of the back door and were off down the road as fast as their winged feet could carry them. Several times they had been picked up a considerable distance from home by the butcher who distributes meat to the villagers daily, and once, to their infinite delight, they came home in the band wagon of a circus. But no harm ever came to the twins. They were in a measure adopted by the whole village. The doctor often took them in his wagon when he went on his round of visits, and young men and boys swung them on gates and carried them off on the most delightful excursions, and altogether they had a jolly good time and were veritable sovereigns of the place.

The mother, I should have said, was a remarkably pretty woman, in spite of her many cares and troubles, and now that the little sums came quite regularly from her rich relations, the roses began to blossom in her cheeks. She was at work at the sewing machine from morning till night, making and mending for those six little ones, but still the roses would begin to blossom again. It was a long time before Brother made her acquaintance ; indeed, he hardly knew of her existence until one lovely June day he encountered the twins in a shady lane not far from his own house. They had gone in a very naughty way and pulled Marcella Hildreth's finest roses, superb Jacqueminots and Maréchal Neils she was saving for the flower show, and had gathered a great quantity of ox-eyed daisies and buttercups by the wayside, and were planting them all out together in a little garden made of soft brown dirt just in the middle of the road. They had brought water in plantain leaves from a brooklet close at hand, a few drops at a time, mostly spilled upon their pinafores, already much soiled with the soft earth. They had stuck in all the roses and the weeds together, and were patting down the ground with their four little hands, and looking like very industrious golden-headed chicks. They were quite fluffy and heated, with locks of hair hanging in their eyes and their sun-bonnets bobbing sociably together.

It was thus that Brother found them, naughty and soiled, but O, so lovely. He came upon the scene just in time to save them from the dreadful consequences of the wrath of Miss Marcella, who, discovering her loss, had come forth to seek the culprits in the spirit of an avenging Nemesis. I know not what would have happened had not Brother arrived on the scene to shelter the two little miscreants in his arms. He carried them all the way home, and handed them to the grateful widow over the front gate. He must have noticed then and there that the widow's pretty forehead was corrugated just in the middle by three little anxious lines. Being a benevolent man, the desire may have arisen in him to smooth away those tiny wrinkles. At any rate it appeared soon after this encounter that Brother had less urgent business abroad, or his summer vacation may have fallen at this time, for he was often seen in the neighborhood of the widow's cottage. He sometimes invited the twins, with whom he had fallen in love, to drive out with him, and of course the mother was obliged to accompany her darlings. It dawned upon him at last that in order to possess the twins he must marry the widow and the other four, and in spite of the prayers and remonstrances of the Wrens, his sisters, who had devoted their lives to making him selfish, and gloried in their work, the inevitable was accomplished.

The poor Wrens have always attributed their misfortune to the broken limb of the great sycamore. If this had not happened the widow would never have had power to cast her spell about Brother. They have done just what they always said they would do if Brother ever married. They have moved out of the cottage, taking their personal belongings with them, and have departed on the railway, with veils down and handkerchiefs pressed to their eyes. The thought of giving up Brother to one was intolerable; but now that he has married a family of seven, the case is one of unparalleled atrocity.

Brother, though he looks a little older, seems to take kindly to family cares. He drives a smart little bay horse harnessed to a two-seated buggy, which he had made on purpose to accommodate himself and the three Wrens. You may see him almost any day driving about, with the twins on the front seat, and the other four packed indiscriminately in the back of the wagon. As to Brother's shrine, I leave you to imagine what has happened to the crazy-quilts and the foot-warmers, and the embroidered stools and cushions. A certain pathos clings to their memory.

CHAPTER VII.

A MORMON SETTLEMENT.—STEPHEN LOSES HIS MONEY.

THE shortest days have come, and the darkest, those days when it requires some active faith to believe the world will ever emerge from its own shadow. If ghosts ever walk, it must be now, when "chaos and old night" seem to have things all their own way, and the belated sun comes laggingly over the frozen shoulders of Saddleback at an unseemly hour in the morning, and with a faint, pale gleam, as if half inclined to turn in again to his warm bed in those blessed islands where his steeds are stabled over night. The new daylight lies bleak along the village highways, and makes the old houses look more gray and gaunt than ever, and lights the piles of snow with a hopeless kind of glimmer, as if the task of dissolving them were entirely out of its power. The scene is desolate in spite of the snugness of many trees, and the effort made by door-yard evergreens to keep a spark of hope alive in the numb breast of the vegetable world. Sad winds blow at night, bringing bodeful creakings out of the old elms, which whistle, and whine, and sob as if living creatures were whipped by the blast. The huntsman of the German forests clatters with his troop over our Puritan village roofs. Old doors and windows are dismally rheumatic on such nights, and groan piteously in all their joints. Spirits jabber, and mutter, and laugh down the big chimneys, and bang the window-shutters. Sick people lie and listen with vague foreboding, and children tuck their heads under the coverlid.

No healthy person here suffers from the cold. Fuel is cheap, and people would be horrified at the thought of actual need. Even old Betty Speer and Jake Small are perfectly snug in their poor houses, and there are people who save cats' meat for Betty's two felines, Arnica and Malaria, to whom Betty gave these titles because "they are real pretty soundin' and she don't care what they mean." Several of the village homes are luxuriously warm. They have double sashes, and portières and thick rugs and big open fires, as well as furnaces and heaters. Mrs. Judge Magnus preserves a summer warmth throughout her large mansion. The conservatory is full of blooming plants, and the rooms wear a delightful aspect of welcome and good will. Houses have faces like people, and this house is always smiling out of its large windows which glow with crimson curtains.

The boys collect with their sleds on Pudding Knoll with perfect indifference to the cold. If the mercury drops 20° below zero, so much the better for them. Some of the little fellows have their ears bound up in mufflers and handkerchiefs. They stamp their feet and clap their mittened hands, and try to talk big as if their voices had already changed. Their trowsers are tied at the bottom with string, which indicates that they are prepared for serious business. The slide on Pudding Knoll is almost ideally perfect, starting from a small clump of trees on top of the knoll, and running down the smooth side of the hill free from snags, until at the foot it strikes a little duck pond of smooth glare ice. Across this the sleds glide until they touch the opposite shore and the momentum is spent. The boys grow red to the tips of their ears as the fun waxes fast and furious. They tug uphill their own sleds, and perhaps a girl's besides, for there are plenty of girls on hand, though sometimes they are not wanted, and are simply endured as a necessary evil in a difficult world.

The larger boys have to tolerate the girls, to take a kind of grudging care of them, and to give them bits of rides. After all, they are not as exasperating as the smallest boys, little tots all done up like round dumplings by the hands of careful mammas. They have all brought something to eat in their pockets, which gives them a peculiarly bulgy and amorphous appearance. These ambitious infants are apt to cry and get babyish when they hurt themselves, and they often have to be dragged up hill. They have also a " nasty " fashion of tying their miserable little sleds, named " Blue Bird " or " Robin Redbreast," in a sly way to the tail of a big bob-sled, thus adding a samll boy accompaniment to the more exclusive fun of their elders and betters. Besides, these small boys are apt to tell tales at home of the way they have been abused on Pudding Knoll, at the same time showing their wounds, and then there is what the big fellows call a " row." But in spite of persecution and hindrance of this nature, owing to the absurd need there seems to be for the existence of girls and small brothers who will " tag," the big boys still do have a glorious time on that beautiful little knoll. Of course they never look at the far-stretching landscape, with Saddleback in the distance, shading to a soft blue and purple, and the whole valley ready to tell its story to a seeing eye, if there should chance to be one. But the air is delicious, and exercise even in these bitter days in a nipping wind sets the blood dancing in the veins and the heart beating to a merry tune.

Unfortunately youth and its tastes and pleasures last but a short time. There are not many in the village who care greatly for outdoor exercise or for the beauties of nature. The lovely setting of the little town has its effect on them. They are proud to hear strangers praise it ; but most elderly people live indoors, and know not that winter has its charms. The hard, grim facts of our

New England life produced a stern type of Puritanism, which, though much effaced about the edges, still has an undissolved core. When people endure much hardness they naturally come to believe in an inexorable and limited God and a pitiless fate. With better circumstances God grows more loving, and the doctrines of election and predestination loosen their grip. This process has been going on a good many years, and has led to interesting results. Here in the village you may study in small the whole religious history of the land, and mark how " isms " and strange doctrines have arisen and faded. Even in times when people found comfort in an angry God and a lurid background of condemnation, the crotchety eccentric spirit lived here, and brought forth ideas which have shocked or softened the religious sensibilities of the place.

The village is not more prolific of these new lights than other places, yet we have had a number of Second Adventists, Spiritualists, Mind and Faith Healers, and other independent thinkers. Many years ago a small company of Mormons lived in some detached tenements about a mile from the place, on the old plank road. No one knew whence they came or why they did not at once move on to Utah. They were always talking of their land of Canaan, but still they lingered, and in spite of their faith were respected as peaceable and upright citizens. They were forever on the point of departure, with their loins girt about and their lamps trimmed and burning, but the money to transport them to Brigham Young's paradise seemed a long time on the road. Occasionally an apostle came among them, and then a great preaching and exhorting was held. Some of the village children would steal into the conventicle in the hope of hearing or seeing something extraordinary. It was rumored that " Mis' " Hyslope, one of the Mormon women of the neighborhood, could speak with tongues ; and she was looked upon with a certain awe by the children, though in fact she was a rather untidy, red-haired woman, always carrying about a heavy baby in her arms. One day little Harry Holt, who had run away from home to the Mormon meeting, came back with his eyes very large and in a high state of excitement.

"Oh, mother," he exclaimed, " the vials is going to be poured out."

" The what ?" asked his mother, naturally thinking of her medicine bottles.

" The vials of wrath is all going to be poured out on the heads of us Gentiles. Mis' Hyslope says so ; and she danced right up and down in the middle of the floor."

The vials were poured out on the head of poor Harry, for running away and disobeying orders, but that was all that came of Mis' Hyslope's dreadful prophecy. The Hyslope family had one beautiful child, a little girl named Jane, very gentle and lovely to look upon, with large blue eyes and the most perfect curling golden hair. Jenny was a great favorite with the neighbors, and just before all the Mormons in the village received the word of command to march to Utah she sickened and died. Her little grave was made close to the roadside in an open field, as the bigoted father did not wish to lay her body among the bones of the unbelieving. When her people marched away there was nothing left to speak of them but the little grass-grown grave with its rude headstone. But the tradition of Jenny Hyslope's loveliness has lingered in the neighborhood, and up to this time, though her very name is forgotten, the school children are accustomed in spring-time to lay flowers on the " Mormon girl's " grave.

Even in these days of relaxed discipline there are village lines dividing the goats from the sheep. Every family takes a religious newspaper, and nowadays all shades of theology are taught by the religious press. Some of the more attractive papers, well filled with pictures, stories, and secular items, meet with a good deal of favor, but they are not looked upon as quite sound. To be both safe and sound a paper must be rather dull and absolutely untainted in its doctrine. As Deacon Hildreth's wife says : " You want something to tie to in a newspaper, and a good many that look attractive are theologically as slippery as eels." The village families who take the *Watch Tower* and who swear by it are considered a little more respectable than some others who have run off on to side tracks in regard to their Sunday reading. The *Watch Tower* has gone on in one straight groove for fifty or sixty years, never veering to the right or left. All its little stories and its editorials are of one piece. Some of the old families have in their garrets files of the *Watch Tower* going back to the first number issued. They are like so much good doctrine stacked and corded for winter use. When a village boy goes wrong it is very apt to be said that he was brought up on the *Brazen Trumpet* or the *Religious Chromo*, and then every thing is explained. Laxity of doctrine, it is thought, has crept in with the *Chromo* to an alarming degree ; but it is so bright, newsy, and sparkling it gains the largest number of subscribers, and there is a painful rumor that Mrs. Deacon Hildreth has been caught reading it in the back kitchen when she thought "folks" were not 'round.

I am fain to confess that many of the best people in the village were educated by the *Watch Tower*, but of course there are exceptions to every rule. Stephen imbibed its doctrines with his mother's milk. His parents were very careful to exclude all kinds of doubtful literature from their only son. But Stephen soon took matters in his own hands; and has been more or less perturbed in his orbit by the motions of other heavenly bodies. Stephen is eccentric, but there is no danger of his ever going wrong unless spite and malice should overcome his prudence. Did such danger exist, there would be more hope of him. He is so shut up in conceit of himself and his own virtue that I do not suppose any least little sin will ever penetrate his coat of mail to bring him to a better frame of mind. He goes about preaching abstinence to people who are already too abstinent, and have never in their lives taken any thing stronger than a glass of old cider. He has opinions on all subjects, and he thrusts them in with his raucous voice where old and wise people would fain be silent. He is an extreme example of the ill-effects of a small neighborhood on a narrow, sharp, and acute mind.

Stephen is very clever. He has studied the birds of the vicinity, and made a collection, which you may see in a large glass cabinet in his mother's parlor, worthy of a skilled taxidermist. He has corresponded with learned societies, and written articles for scientific papers; and probably the only two men in the village you would ever hear spoken of at a distance are Judge Magnus and Stephen. But some people dwindle perceptibly as you draw near their homes. The judge's good opinion of himself is an exuberant, interior satisfaction, and an amiable desire to patronize all the world. It can be endured, and almost liked. But people wish to run away from Stephen as from a pest. His irritable mind stirs up the most peaceable to an indignant protest. He tackles most indecently quiet folks who just wish to be let alone to serve God, and do their duty in the walk in life to which they have been called.

The weekly prayer-meeting is open to every body, and it is considered an excellent sign of spiritual awakening when a young man or maiden is willing to take a part. At one time Stephen invaded the prayer-meeting regularly every Wednesday night, and if he had carried a hornets' nest into its subdued atmosphere, he could not have created a greater commotion. He holds literally to the doctrines of the burning lake of Gehenna, and of election and predestination, tenets which some of the best Christian people have blinked for a long time, feeling that it is well to play the part of the ostrich and hide one's head in the sand when such disagreeable questions are uppermost. But Stephen never blinks any thing; he comes out with a sharply defined literalism quite shocking to sensitive minds, and yet not all of his doctrines are of the most strict sect. Mixed up with extreme "orthodox" views are notions he has picked up or evolved from his own consciousness, such as the idea that all souls are not immortal—that through extremity of sin some may perish utterly. These things he proclaimed in a brazen manner at the meetings until the old people, who mainly resort there for an hour of spiritual repose and meditation, were driven nearly wild by his fluent, rasping talk, which came under the head of " giving experience." Old Miss Withers, who in her way is almost as eccentric as Stephen, rose from her seat very angry one evening, and with her face quite scarlet, said in a shrill, piping voice: " Ef you think you can teach folks twice your age, and cram things offered to idols right down their throats, why don't you move to a bigger place ?" Then she sat down fanning herself hysterically, and Stephen answered with solemn sententiousness : "Because I think the village needs me." There was a ripple of laughter all over the room, and Deacon Hildreth was obliged to dismiss the meeting.

At one time Stephen took up violently against banks. Consequently he took to hoarding his money at home. By trade he is a cabinetmaker, and one of the best. His manual dexterity is such if he had the poetic feeling he would be an artist. The summer boarders have bought a great many of the little writing-desks which he makes of native woods, and at the time of which I speak

Stephen had hoarded two hundred and fifty dollars. As he would not patronize a bank, he looked about anxiously at home to see where he could place his funds in safe-keeping, and finally he hid the money in the watch-pocket of an old pair of trowsers, which he hung behind some lumber in the garret. Stephen did not mention the matter to his mother, but kept the secret locked in his own heart. To tell the truth, his mother is afraid of him. Naturally, she would be a gossiping, lively, kind-hearted old lady, but her child has forced her into a home-staying, brooding sort of person, who is always on the lookout in a furtive way for the opportunity to do little deeds of kindness without being detected. Stephen does not believe in feeding the hungry or clothing the naked. He is one of those horrid economists who carry out their principles to the letter, and can not be made to feel that any form of human misery is undeserved. But his mother is made up quite differently. It would pain her dear old heart to have any being, however unworthy, gnawed by the pangs of hunger. She has, I fear, helped to fill the alms-houses and inebriate asylums by giving away part of her slender income to tramps.

Stephen having the smallest opinion of his mother's mental capacity, had refrained from telling her where he had hidden his cash. One day a poor man with his draggled wife came begging to the back door. He was suspiciously red in the nose and watery about the eyes, but his clothes were miserably poor and thin, and the day was cold, and the woman told a piteous tale. Stephen's mother, therefore, actually with tears in her eyes, trotted up to the garret and pulled out an old gown of her own, and then rummaged about until she laid hands on that identical pair of old trowsers under the lumber-pile which her son had so carefully concealed. Well, the result, though fearful, was unexpected. Stephen treated his mother so abominably that she roused herself to confront him, and for a time was far less meek and timid than before the event occurred. The villagers, I must confess, were all secretly glad. The sheriff got out a posse and raised a hue and cry, but the two tramps had utterly disappeared before the loss was discovered.

CHAPTER VIII.

THE HON. HIGHFLYER VISITS THE VILLAGE.

HUGH has now concluded to write a history of the town—an employment for which his talents and attainments are admirably fitted—and to leave the composition of the great American novel to a future day. He has made local research the excuse for invading most of the village homes and prying into old trunks, escritoires, and bureaus where yellow documents lie concealed. He is more troublesome than the book-agent or the lightning-rod man, but then he is far more insinuating and persuasive ; and it is quite a picture to see him at the village tea-tables, discoursing about the ancestors of the family. There is scarce an old love-letter in the place into which he has not taken a peep, and he has gathered up odd bits of domestic history sufficient to make a volume, a vast amount of rubbish out of which he hopes to extract a few grains of gold.

His antiquarian research has been the pretext for hobnobbing with all the old maids and flattering all the old ladies in the town. He has brought each one round to the belief that she is descended from a famous old English family, with nothing less than a baronial seat, dating back to the Crusades, or possibly as far as the Norman Conquest. He has even hinted at sums of money in chancery to which some of them may be entitled ; and has thoroughly stirred up that pride in descent from a long-lived and distinguished race and that greed of inheritance which is latent in us all. You should see Hugh in confidential confab with some ancient dame who has little left to her but family pretensions and cracked china, going over all her bits of things with solemn seriousness, and delivering a lecture on ceramics, to which she listens as if it were law and gospel. There is not an old cabinet, or spinning-wheel, or chest of drawers, or colonial clock, or brass warming-pan, which Hugh has not taken in hand and descanted on profoundly to the delight of the owner.

All this rummaging and tea-drinking is in the interest of the town history which is to place a halo of light about our hamlet, and let the world know the great number of distinguished families it contains. The town has no particular history, being of that Arcadian sort that nothing of note has ever happened in it. The great people have all been greater in their own estimation than in the opinion of the world at large. But Hugh is bent on inventing a history of the town if one can not otherwise be obtained. He thinks he can create a batch of revolutionary heroes with the pen as easily as the queen makes knights with the flat of the sword.

Hugh is not at present on favorable terms with Milly. She has accused him most unfairly, as he declares, of taking a hand in the Rastus adventure. That painful affair has, however, brought its compensation. The mother of Rastus, now, when she halts her old horse before the little stone house, and Milly comes out bareheaded to do her "trading," smiles on Milly benignly, and gives a peculiar cluck far down in her throat. She deals her out now invariably thirteen eggs to the dozen, which, considering her penurious disposition, is a very high mark of approval. The old lady is still spry and vigorous, and does not care to be "sat upon" by a daughter-in-law.

A more unfortunate alienation exists between Hugh and Judge Magnus. When the judge is over attending court at the county town Mrs. Magnus sometimes lets him slip in to dinner or tea, as she can not wholly deprive herself of his society. But the judge has taken a severe cold in his shoulder and now turns it invariably on Hugh. The trouble all arose last fall when a very exciting political campaign was opened in the state, in which Judge Magnus took a leading part. Most of the villagers are opposed to the judge in politics. Jake Small came out very strong against the Judge's candidate for governor, the Hon. Mr. Highflyer. As one of the landed proprietors of the town, he thought he had a right to be heard. Perhaps the judge did not exactly try to corrupt his neighbors and to win votes by favors, and what Jake called " inflooence," but he was determined Highflyer should be heard in the village where he lived, and should receive such a rousing " ovation " as was never given to any other man in that vicinity. Consequently a flaming poster appeared on all the fences, trees, and dead walls announcing the near advent of the candidate. There was to be a dinner at the judge's, to which all the principal men of the village were invited, including the parson, Hugh, and Stephen. A meeting was arranged at Library Hall, where the Hon. Highflyer would speak, and the judge had engaged a brass band to come from the nearest large place, that there might be a parade with music, and later in the evening a serenade to his candidate. The judge also procured some torches and waterproof capes to array the loyal rabble of boys for a fitting turnout, and it was rumored in the village that he had laid in a considerable store of pinwheels, rockets, and Roman candles to illumine the line of march.

Every thing was in order for Highflyer; Aunt Dinah had been commissioned to prepare the fatted calf. The judge was in his glory. He went swelling up and down Main Street, and stopped every body he met to talk of Highflyer:

"A big man, sir; the biggest man in the country.

And you will see, sir, we shall roll up an overwhelming majority—yes, sir, an overwhelming majority, on election day. Take a cigar, sir, and when you can, call and see Mrs. Magnus. You know you are to be on hand for the reception and dinner."

And thus with immense expansiveness he paraded the little place, filling its smallness oppressively full of his self-importance and the reflected glory of Highflyer. The morning of the great day had arrived, and all was in perfect order for the ceremonies to follow. Highflyer was to be welcomed at the station as he never had been welcomed in all the days of his life. But at three o'clock in the afternoon the judge received news from Highflyer which gave him a stunning blow. The great man was at home ill of a sore throat, and the reception must perforce be postponed indefinitely. It was pitiable to see the collapse of the judge, and Mrs. Magnus, with that great dinner on her hands, was not less to be commiserated.

There was no time to lose, as the band would soon get on board the train at R——, on its way to the village. Hugh, who happened to be lounging about in the judge's library, was commissioned to go and dispatch a telegram which would keep it at home. He was also asked to affix a hasty notice to the door of Library Hall conveying the heavy news of Highflyer's sore throat. The small boys of the village were about to receive a crushing blow, and Hugh naturally felt for them. However, he says he did notify the band not to come, by means of Mr. Diggs' "ticker" and private wire. By this means Mr. Diggs transacts business in stocks in a secret manner with a distant city, and the general opinion in the village is that his business is not respectable. Mr. Diggs' ticker, it seems, did not work well on this particular occasion, and within an hour some one who in size and figure much resembled Hugh, well wrapped in an ulster, and with bag in hand, boarded the four o'clock western train.

The judge shut himself in doors, and Mrs. Magnus pulled down the front parlor shades, which always indicated that she was not at home to visitors. The notice on the door of Library Hall, if such existed, was not visible to the naked eye. Apparently, the fact of the Hon. Mr. Highflyer's sore throat had not leaked out in the village. At six o'clock a little sputter of yellow and red fireworks was observed about the station. The east and west trains came in almost at the same moment. Suddenly there was a clash of brass instruments, and the boys began to hurrah and throw up their caps for Highflyer. Oddly enough, the judge was not on hand at the moment to welcome the great man in person. But the sheriff of the county, a very active, even offensive partisan, scheming for re-election, was present on the platform with several of his henchmen. He had seen Highflyer at a state convention some years before, and thought he knew him well. Therefore, when a tall stranger well muffled about the ears and mouth, with his hat somewhat drawn down over his brows, stepped from the western train, the sheriff pressed forward, seized him by the hand, and welcomed him in as neat a little impromptu speech as had ever been heard in the village.

The Hon. Highflyer, who was suffering from a hoarse cold and a sore throat, answered briefly, but much to the point, and was at once escorted to the best livery hack in the village. The sheriff immediately formed the procession in line; the band struck up "Hail to the Chief." The lads with torches and capes ranged themselves behind the band. The rabble fell in at the tag end, and all moved onward to Main Street amid a fizzing and sputtering of fireworks, shouts for Highflyer, hisses and groans for Lowlander, the opposition candidate, cat-calls, cheers, and other outbursts of enthusiasm. The villagers all rushed into the street. A few had prepared to illuminate in a modest way, and some of the house-fronts began to blaze with tallow dips. The judge in the retirement of his library heard that fatal blare of brass and the cheers of the crowd. He rushed bewildered out of doors regardless of his hat. On came the procession, the band now tooting forth, "See, the Conquering Hero Comes." The judge waved his arms wildly and ran to the front gate crying, "Stop! stop!" But that triumphal procession had neither eye nor ear for any thing but the matter in hand. It marched on past the house with the dreadful effigy of Highflyer streaming to the breeze on a broad banner carried by the vanguard—the din of brass and shouts of the multitude. It marched to the extreme end of the village, as far as the old bridge, and back again to the judge's door. And on its arrival the hack was thoroughly examined. But the Hon. Mr. Highflyer had evaporated, and refused to materialize again.

The judge was in danger of apoplexy from the terrible state of wrath and mortification into which he was thrown, and Hugh, when discovered, was found in his dressing-gown and slippers quietly sitting at home in Aunt Dido's chamber, inditing a page of his history. Aunt Dido, though torture screws have been applied to make her confess, will say nothing except that Hugh was home at supper-time on that fatal night; but as to the exact hour of the supper her memory fails her. The judge was obliged to pay the band full price for time and trouble, which was but the smallest part of his humiliation. Mrs. Magnus, who is always practical, gave the dinner which had been prepared for the next governor of the state to the men of brass, who were very hungry. But the worst feature of the case is the fact that Highflyer was most shamefully defeated by Lowlander in the near election—so cut up, horse, foot, and artillery, in fact, that he now says he shall never again run for any office, but intends to devote the remainder of his life to the composition of his great work, "What I Know About Politics." A coldness quite down to zero still continues between Hugh and the judge; and that nicest, most hospitable house in the village is unfortunately closed to the young historian on all public occasions. The sheriff lost his re-election, and this sad fact is attributed to the handsome little speech he made on the station platform the evening of the Highflyer ovation, scraps of which have been used to his disadvantage in the miserable little opposition sheet published at the county town.

Accounts of this election incident flew far and wide, and for weeks the village was quite famous. Hugh looked upon it as valuable material for history. It is not to be supposed that he has ever "given himself away" and confessed he personated Highflyer on that memorable evening. The sheriff declares that the person he addressed was a taller and stouter man than Hugh, and wore a dark mustache, and there are other credible witnesses ready to swear to the same facts.

The boys, however, have pitched upon Hugh as their benefactor. They feel grateful to him for the good time they enjoyed swinging about the judge's torches and shouting themselves hoarse for Highflyer. They have named their snow redoubt on Sampson's Hill, near the school-house, Fort Hugh, and the opposing parties are known as Highflyers and Lowlanders. The battles fought there during the noon recess are of a terrible ferocity. They have even placed Quaker guns on the top of the fortification, and bodies of infantry can be seen rolling downhill pursued by a shower of balls.

Sampson's Hill is on the road to Mill Farm, a charming walk in summer. The path runs over a stile and trickles along through meadow-grasses, and under tall trees, and finally strikes the road to the ravine. The fields thereabout are speckled with ripe strawberries in

June, and the village children resort to them in their by-hours. Here, too, young lovers come to walk under the trees at sundown and listen to the song of the evening thrush.

Old Betty Speer lives on this road, in a picturesque hovel half covered with vines and creepers. She receives out-door relief from the poor guardians of the town, and there is a tradition that she has money hidden away in old tea-pots and tomato-cans all over the premises. But these tales are entirely unfounded. Betty has tried hard to cultivate a good paying reputation as a witch and fortune-teller, but has made a dismal failure. As every well-regulated village should have an old woman seeress to act in this capacity, it is disappointing that Betty Speer should be quite unable to inspire awe in the smallest child. She occasionally wheedles a dime out of the pocket of some country bumpkin who resorts to her to find out where lost or stolen articles are concealed. For this purpose she pretends to look in a rather curious pebble picked up somewhere about the fields. She also keeps a pack of greasy cards to reveal to young girls the very important fact as to whether they are to marry a light or dark "complected" man. Beyond this her simple magic can not go. She has picked up the art of distilling simples, and now makes a slight addition to her income by the sale of a quack decoction put up in small black bottles, which she affirms "is good for rheumatiz if rubbed on at the change of the moon."

Her two cats, Arnica and Malaria, are not even black. Arnica is a pretty Maltese and Malaria is white, with black nose and boots. Sometimes the boys in the fort on Sampson's Hill turn their missiles against Betty's queer little habitation, from which the smoke of the chimney always streams forth in a long vaporous feather. But nothing ever disturbs the old woman's equanimity save the need of eating a poor dinner. She is short and sturdy, with a black wary eye set deep in her head. She is generally done up in an old serge cloak, and over her shoes when the weather is snowy she draws on a pair of heavy woolen stockings. In this guise she trudges all over the town. Betty has an unerring nose as to what may be cooking in the neighbors' houses. Each fair day she elects to dine at some favorite place, and regardless of an invitation, ensconces herself in the easiest chair in the kitchen. Her eyes follow all the operations of the housewife with anxious scrutiny. She has a weakness for dumplings, and can scent them quite a distance off. For what is known as " boiled dish " she has as great an aversion. When her favorite viands are preparing she is always glued to her seat like a dumb thing, watching with wistful eyes for her portion of the feast to be placed on the corner of the kitchen table. But if " b'iled victuals " is the order of the day old Betty steals out sorrowfully, shaking the dust of that kitchen from her shoes.

CHAPTER IX.

THE VILLAGE CLUBS.—ST. PATTY AND HER JUBILEE.

THE days of quilting-bees, apple-parings, and spelling-schools appear to have vanished. A new order of entertainment has sprung up in the village, which, if not more enjoyable, is more select. The mania for clubs has reached our quiet precinct, and a number have been organized both for profit and pleasure. Of course, we have lectures and concerts during the winter in Library Hall. We have also symposia, a kind of parlor discourse, established by a philosopher who was raised in this town, and who returns to his native haunts for a few days or weeks during the year. The symposia are only held among the cultivated few. By the uninitiated crowd they are sneered at and unmercifully ridiculed. Still the advent of the philosopher makes a decided ripple in the rather sluggish currents of village society, and creates an appetite for reading and speculative thought which, on the whole, is profitable. When he is with us we all try to appear as learned and profound as we can. The men, as a rule, keep clear of him with the exception of one or two, but there are a number of women who sit devoutly at his feet. Some of these very women, who have heretofore enjoyed a dish of gossip over their tea, and have been so little regardful of the improvement of their minds as to compare notes on bonnets and gowns, as soon as the philosopher appears, put away the vanities of life and take to serious studies. The library is ransacked for the works of German philosophers, of Locke, Mill, Descartes, and a variety of other profound authors. It is always impressive to have these books lying around on the parlor table even if one does not read them ; and the philosopher feels the compliment to himself, as he should. He is perfectly happy when, as Deacon Hildreth's wife says, he can get in the midst of a " passle " of women and have them all listen to him in open-eyed wonder as they try in their inmost souls to understand the philosophical terms, such as " cognize," " concept," " percept," " self-conscious personality," and a great variety of other well-sounding words and phrases.

As I have hinted, the men of the village generally turn up their noses at the philosopher, because they are incapable of understanding him, and are jealous of his influence over a certain clique of women. The young parson meets him on that happy neutral ground which he has chosen for friendly controversy, where he gleans new ideas and gathers fresh inspiration. He is cordial to all who bring grist to his mill, let them call themselves what they may. Hugh, on the contrary, looks askance at the invader for poaching on ground which he feels belongs of right to himself—the domain of female influence—and consequently, as he has no special bent toward speculative thought, he generally goes on a long tramp when the philosopher is around. The old shoemaker, with his long white hair and complexion like old ivory, is the only man in the village who thoroughly understands the history of philosophy, but he, faithful to his lapstone, is never lured away to any of the parlor symposia. When the philosopher lectures in Library Hall, as he sometimes does, to a select few of his admirers, the shoemaker, much to the speaker's annoyance, stations himself on the front bench with a smile childlike and bland wreathing his countenance. Milly, who has always been a devotee of Plato and Spinoza, because of their affirmative spiritual side, is no general student, still she has a strong leaning toward speculative studies, and has been known to lock her shop when it was full of spring work to go and sit at the philosopher's feet in Miss Drusilla's parlor.

The philosopher is a short man with a very large head, covered with bushy hair. He wears spectacles of course, and a great beard and mustache give him a leonine aspect. But he is the most approachable, gentle, kindly-mannered little man in the world when he is not lost in abstractions. Then the light seems to go out behind his spectacles, and he will sit in one position for hours together. But he is a human creature with a heart which vibrates to the awed attention and the homage of his coterie. It has been queried whether he ever looks at a woman's face, or knows whether she is young or old, well-favored or ugly. But I suspect that the beautiful face draws even him, and that barred up somewhere in the " Ego " is a living man.

Of course, it is quite a strain on our intellectual women to have the philosopher with us for a fortnight or three weeks, the usual length of his stay. It is very taxing to the brain to try to appear profound all that length of time, to abandon one's usual low altitude of thought and feeling and mount of a sudden into the clear, bracing but rather chilly realm of abstract ideas. For a week after the philosopher has taken his departure little is heard in some of our parlors, but the reverberations and echoes of his lectures on the philosophy of religion. Such words and phases as " Socinian," " Arminian," the " sensational school," " the spiritual school," " the soul entity," seem to roll and mutter in all the corners like half-spent thunder. But presently we give a long sigh of relief ; we recognize the fact that we have been under great cerebral pressure and need a little wholesome recreation to let us down with safety to the ordinary flats and shallows of real life.

A fortnight after the philosopher's departure the village is a scene of wild dissipation. "Tea fights," whist parties, club meetings, crowd upon each other's heels. The heavy tomes which have weighed down our tables are sent back to the library shelves where they belong, and out of corners come creeping the despised fancy work which was shoved aside to make room for them. The crochet bag, the knitting basket, the Kensington art work, of which we should have been ashamed in the philosopher's presence, again resume their sway. Women enjoy themselves immensely talking over family diseases and the gossip of the neighborhood. It is as if they had been away on a long journey and had come together for the first time to hear the home news. Even Drusilla is more active and energetic in town affairs than ever. Being intensely practical, Drusilla is not of the philosophic cast of mind, but she has taken to patronizing philosophy because it is neither frivolous nor petty. Drusilla wishes to emancipate herself from feminine limitations. She rejoices in not being troubled with any of the weaknesses of her sex. As I said, there are several clubs in the village embracing all ages and conditions. The high-school girls have one in which they talk of archaic Greek art and early Assyrian pottery; but exactly in proportion as you recede from the high-school age you will find the clubs growing lighter in character, until with the old ladies nothing but pure amusement and recreation is intended. They call themselves the Wintergreens, and their insignia is a little sprig of that plant pinned into a kerchief or adorning a dress-cap. The Wintergreens meet semi-occasionally, when the old men are engaged at town-meeting or have a monthly session of their Saturday-Night Club. Part of the regular programme is an old-fashioned supper where tea-cup fortunes are told. The frisky performances of the Wintergreens and their inextinguishable fun and laughter are the delight of the town. Very comical stories leak out in regard to their secret sessions, for the greater part of their meetings are held with closed doors. Occasionally the old men are invited to be present, and once or twice a general town invitation has been given out. But the private meetings are the most enjoyable. As the Wintergreens are particularly secret and silent about their doings, public curiosity is whetted to a keen edge. It is known that they sometimes play old-fashioned games, and tell ancient love stories, and rehearse the triumphs of their girlhood. A prize has even been offered for the best love tale, and to judge from the peals of laughter which ring out when this pastime is going forward, it is one of the most enjoyable.

No old woman can become a Wintergreen until she is willing to tell her age and take her Bible oath thereon. Sixty is about the limit for admissions, and several have not gone in until past their seventieth year. Drusilla, who is only a few years past fifty, proposed herself for membership, but she was blackballed on other grounds. The old ladies were afraid of her genius for management; and, as Mrs. Deacon Hildreth said, they wished to "boss" their own affairs. Drusilla would speedily have transformed them into something else. When the weather is unfavorable, a carriage or sleigh goes out as far as Mill Farm and picks up the Wintergreens; and the secret conclave invariably breaks up at ten. It is thought this club has had something to do in preserving in the beauty of age a number of our bright-eyed, fresh-complexioned, cheerful old women, who continue useful in their own sphere, and give a certain dignity and grace to village life. Aunt Dido is a leading spirit among the Wintergreens.

The young parson encourages wholesome, innocent amusement among all classes of people. He has joined an athletic club, and is one of the best wheelmen and oarsmen of the town. He has of late given a sermon on dancing which has offended a few of the tender consciences. It was thought at one critical moment there might be a division in the church on this burning question, and the young parson stood to his guns and confessed himself ready to resign. His pretty wife was in tears, and the women of the neighborhood came in and put their arms about her and declared they could never love another clergyman's wife so well. Then they went home, and decided if the breach was not healed and the poor thing was obliged to go from them, they would present her, as a parting gift, with a handsome black silk gown, which, I am fain to confess, the poor thing needs. But the breach was healed through the diplomacy of Deacon Hildreth, who is known in the village as the Town Clock. He always walks on the same side of the street, rises and goes to bed at the same hours, and offers the same stereotyped blessing at table, and the same prayer in the weekly prayer-meeting. Some of the children, hearing him called the Town Clock, have actually believed that he possesses wheel-work inside his plethoric body which can be wound up and made to tick. Happily the deacon knew nothing of the modern theory that our games and pastimes are the survivals of old heathenish religious festivals. But he knew his Bible; and, like the famous man who said it was a pity the devil should have all the good tunes, the deacon was ready to do battle with the same potentate for some of the good amusements. It was a great surprise, therefore, when at the next stated meeting he rose slowly from his seat and gave his testimony in favor of the parson. It was an incontrovertible fact, he said, that David danced before the ark; dancing was not therefore *per se* a wicked act. The fate of the young woman who mocked David out of the window was also judiciously touched upon, and the fine lesson educed that even our amusements may be holy and worshipful if indulged in the right spirit. As the deacon, the central pillar of the church, had gone over to the enemy, the case against the clergyman broke down, but the ladies, I am sorry to say, forgot to present that black silk gown to his pretty wife.

Drusilla also supported the parson, and she is a power in the parish. There are women doomed to rule a petty hamlet who only need a wider sphere to make themselves famous. Drusilla is one of this variety. Formally she was known all over the village and surrounding parts as Miss Drusey, but she abhors the name and refuses to turn the light of her favor on any one who indulges in its easy colloquialism. Drusilla has the Roman matron in its sound, and she has the Roman in her blood. Ordinary women she looks upon with contemptuous pity, and is half ashamed that the fates have denied her that manhood she might so nobly have honored. But Drusilla is politic, and knows how to conciliate. She has gradually drawn into her hands all the work of the parish a woman can do, and some that no woman has ever aspired to do before her time. She has re-organized the Sunday-school and straightened out the choir. She attends to all the festivals, fairs, Lady Washington teas, Christmas trees, and ministers' conventions. She could do it single-handed, but that is not allowable, and her coadjutors have become mere clay and putty in her strong grasp. It is said that the young parson is afraid to fall ill of a Sunday, for fear that Drusilla would mount into the pulpit and preach in his stead. He knows her worth, and values it justly, even while he is struggling to keep her out of his place. The only rival she has to dread is Mrs. Judge Magnus, who is of an energetic and unquenchable spirit. But the judge's wife is absent in Washington during part of the year, and she never regains during the summer and autumn what she loses in the winter.

I have always suspected that Drusilla was born with her bonnet on, the strings untied and thrown over her shoulders. She is large and fair, and could easily be handsome if she paid attention to dress. But her clothes are always of the same plain cut and pattern, and are known as Drusilla's business suit. Though neat, she would scorn to condescend to any of the fripperies of fashion. Her hair has a pretty ripple and gleam upon it, like sunlight on running water, but it is always brushed behind her ears with severe simplicity. She wears no ring nor jewel of any kind, and when she is invited out to dinner or to an evening party she invariably appears in a stuff gown. Of course she has no wish to conceal her age, since she tried to get into the Wintergreen Club, that she might reform it from the inside.

We have, as I have said, a number of nice old people among us, but Drusilla's mother is the gem of the collection. She lives in a real old colonial house which has come down to her through several generations. The sword of a brave ancestor is suspended in the wide, spacious hall against a tattered set of colors carried, it is said, at the battle of Saratoga. Her presses, and drawers, and cupboards are full of relics and mementoes of other days, and her memory of things that occurred half a century or more ago is vividly bright. Hugh intends to work up several chapters of his history from the old lady's reminiscences. All her own boys, now stalwart men, are away in the far West, where they have made their fortunes. One of them, a great ranchman, has been governor of his territory. When he comes home to see "mother" he always brings a band-box containing a new dress-cap which he ties about the dear old face with his own hands, and tells her she is the belle of the village.

Drusilla's mother is unlike her capable daughter. She is fond of dress and takes a great deal of pride in her appearance. And indeed she is beautiful, with soft chirpy ways, like an aged canary. A touch of gratified red flutters into her cheek over a compliment ; her eye brightens, and she straightens up and quavers a merry laugh exceedingly pleasant to hear. The children and young people are in the way of bringing her small presents, wild-flowers, the first strawberries, roses from the early bush, small works they have wrought and embroidered—a kerchief for the neck, a bag to hold the snuffbox. I am fain to confess she does snuff just the least bit, but she is so neat the white muslin on her neck never bears the least stain, and her delicate old hands, with the wedding ring, grown so small, are like faded lilies.

An intense rivalry has sprung up among the small towns in our vicinity as to their very old people. The local papers are constantly inserting paragraphs about aged women over one hundred, who rise in the small hours, pick up a basket of chips, build the fire, and milk a few cows before breakfast. They can all see to thread a cambric needle without glasses, and several of them have cut new sets of teeth in their second childhood. Of course the laudable desire to possess the oldest and smartest person of this kind has developed in our village. We do not in this respect wish to kootoo to River Junction, Slabville, Smith Forks, or the Barrens. Now a very singular thing happened to Drusilla's mother. Her family archives were accidentally burned a long time ago, and for many years she seemed to have forgotten the exact year of her birth ; and there was no one in the neighborhood who could remember so far back. Drusilla's mother has always been accustomed to dress up things with those pretty touches which lend themselves so readily to an imaginative mind. Not that she deliberately falsifies. Such a suspicion would shock the sensibilities of her neighbors, who have always felt that they must take her narratives with a pinch of skeptical salt.

Years ago Drusilla, who is entirely devoid of imagination, whose clear dry-light intellect is marked off like a checker-board into accurate squares, was constantly in the habit of correcting her mother, but now that she is so very old, much to the relief of the family friends, Drusilla lets her twitter along without interruption. We have known for a number of years that Drusilla's mother was past ninety, and some few seasons since we celebrated what was given out in an indirect way by the old lady herself, to be her ninety-fifth birthday. Since so much has been said in the newspapers about centenarians, and the luster they shed on a small town, Drusilla's mother has been fired with the laudable ambition to become the oldest inhabitant of the whole country-side. She has received a kind of canonization while still alive because she has been so very good-natured as to live to be almost a hundred. She is called St. Patty, a name which exactly suits her, although the idea of St. Patty being the mother of Drusilla is supremely ridiculous. Well, we did intend to have St. Patty's portrait painted by subscription at the time of her centenary and hung among the pictures of our local worthies in the library bookroom. We already have a bust and two large photographs of the judge which he has presented to the town. Of course, as St. Patty celebrated some years ago her ninety-fifth birthday, we have of late been planning what we would do on the great anniversary close at hand. The old lady entered into our scheme with enthusiasm. The young clergyman was to deliver an address on the honor she had done the town. Hugh was to give an historical survey of St. Patty's ancestors and their deeds, bringing the narrative of the family down to date. Our literary young lady, who contributes to the magazines, had promised an ode, and the local glee club had been practicing some time for the great occasion.

It was noticeable that when the jubilee was talked of

Drusilla immediately left the room. We all set it down to family modesty, and felt that Drusilla had acquired a notion of good taste quite new and surprising. Happily, the anniversary would fall in May, at a time when there was abundance of flowers to trim the house and adorn our St. Patty. But as the time approached we noticed the old lady began to languish and droop. She lost her appetite, her eyes grew dim, her hand shook, and she would sit and brood an hour together—so unlikely a thing for St. Patty to do that the whole village became alarmed, and the doctor was called in. He found the old lady wiping away a furtive tear-drop, but he could discover no marked symptoms of bodily ailment. Something was weighing on her mind. Her memory was a little confused, and she mixed up people's names, and brought in some of neighbors long dead. The doctor prescribed a soothing mixture and went away. A week passed in this unsatisfactory manner, the whole village dreading to hear that St. Patty had taken to her bed. But at the end of that time her spirits did not seem to improve, and one day she sent for the young clergyman, which we all took for a bad sign. When the parson entered her room, she was holding a cambric handkerchief to her eyes, and there was a half audible sob in her throat.

"I wanted to see you to make a confession," she began brokenly. "I'm afraid I am a foolish, vain, wicked old woman. You know the family Bible was burned in the Hadley fire twenty-five years ago. Well, Drusilla was my youngest, and she says she's going on fifty-three, and of course she knows. I must be a few years younger than I thought, just a few years, you know; I can't make out how many, more or less. I wanted to oblige the folks, they were so set on celebrating, but I've been going over it in my mind, and allow it wouldn't be right."

And then St. Patty broke down and shed all the tears

which had been pent up in her heart. We had the celebration just the same, but our village on the score of the oldest inhabitant has been obliged to bow its head to Slabville, which is very humiliating.

CHAPTER X.

THE POOR-HOUSE CHILDREN AND OLD PETER'S GIRLS.

ONE of the prettiest drives out from the village leads to the poor-house. The road runs through a tangle of wildering lanes and old farm roads, skirted by stone fences and abundant trees. In early spring, when the grass is of a uniform tender green, an Arcadian sense of quiet hangs over these lanes. Once or twice you come to an old cellar-place, or broken chimney, with a circle of straggling bushes, indicating an extinct family life. Stray sheep nibble about in these places and crop the wild herbage. The lanes are bordered with cherry and plum trees. Early in the season, before they have put forth a single shoot, the grass grows tufted around the old roots, and blue-birds flit through the empty branches and make the scene softer with their notes.

The poor-house is a long, low, unpainted building, with a faculty of looking ugly which institutions of the kind always possess, even when planted in the most enchanting landscape. During the summer it is rather thinly tenanted. The clean rooms, with their poor-house odor, a smell of some kind of strong soap, their high beds covered with old-fashioned blue spreads, their meager little wash-stands and board presses, are often empty, swept and garnished. The place fills up in the fall when the tramping season is over, but there are a few decayed old people, regular boarders, as Mrs. Tripp, the matron, calls them, who remain the year round. They are too old to go tramping in summer, and their greatest change is a move from the stove-heated rooms of cold weather to the summer porch.

They are gray, shadowy, crooked old folk, who look rather discontented, though they are treated with great kindness. Mrs. Tripp is a round, jolly woman with a good face. She knits perpetually, even while she is walking about the house overseeing and giving directions. She says they have little to complain of, but it is a necessity with them to grumble, if of nothing else, on the size of the dole of tea and "baccy" they receive every week. We have a society in the village to furnish them with flowers and little delicacies and reading matter. The oldest of them like children's story books, with bright colored pictures. There are young girls who come out once a week to read to them, or write letters, but very few have friends or kindred they remember as living. They have forgotten most of their joys, hopes, and affections, and retain only voracious appetite and other enduring bodily sensations.

The parson goes out occasionally to give them a Bible reading and a talk, but the ungrateful, pampered old creatures are not much edified. Thaddeus, the oldest of the inmates, generally grunts and says he "hain't no stummick for parson preachifying; what he wants is suthin' to wet his whistle," meaning whisky, which now he never gets. The old creature has been preserved in spirits. His toughness and tenacity of life sheds a kind of luster on the poor-house. His much enduring wife bore many a cruel beating from his hand. Thad, who is a humorist, said it was because she was "so poor spirited; if she had once showed fight he never could have found the heart to strike her." Well, the poor sodden creature went out like a smoky candle, and Thad in his old age came heavily upon the town. Now he is forced to be sober and virtuous. He hates the authorities who built the poor-house, and have converted him against his will into a harmless old person. His chronic growl "ag'in government" and the laws of the land is a constant support to his declining years. Mrs. Tripp calls Thad her pet lamb. She is rather proud of him as a show-person who may be induced to get up his growl for visitors, as a dog is taught to bark for a reward.

There are generally one or two mildly insane people confined in other portions of the building. One of them imagines herself the Virgin Mary, and sits veiled most of the time. Another thinks he is a quart bottle and gurgles in his throat when he speaks like a full flask. There are also a few weak-minded children who have come upon the town by the death or poverty of their parents. These children are the pets of the establishment, and, in their way, form an interesting little group. In pleasant weather they spend most of their time in an open courtyard where there is a grass-plot and a few trees. A shed in one corner gives them shelter from the sun and rain. Here they keep such little possessions as have been given them or they can gather for themselves. One possesses a tame chicken that pecks about on the gravel; another is the happy owner of a rabbit and a little hutch. One or two possess hideous rag-babies, mere bundles of straw or sticks covered with old cloth, which they tenderly cherish and take to bed with them every night.

A kind lady has given these children some of the colored figures, globes, and disks now used in the instruction of the weak-minded, and they have been taught a little, so that it is plain to see that with care their rudimentary intelligence ought to be considerably developed. All of them are bodily infirm. The strongest can scarcely walk alone. Some have learned to walk several times, and have forgotten how in the end, or lost all control of their paralyzed limbs for months together. Still they manage to move a little either by means of hands or feet, or both, with ingenuity quite surprising. Watch them when they think themselves unobserved, and you will see there is a certain method in their pathetic little attempts at play—a shadowing forth of the instincts of healthy child life.

Mick, who is perhaps twelve years old, though stunted and withered about the legs, is not feeble-minded in the ordinary sense of the term. His defects came from an injury to his head received in early infancy. Mick is a feeble-minded child of genius, if you can imagine such a being. His face is that of an old man, and his eyes have a shrewd twinkle, showing how much he knows. Though he can talk very imperfectly, Mick readily understands every thing that is said, and picks up even unfamiliar ideas with marvelous quickness. He is invaluable to Mrs. Tripp, for she gives him the general charge of the other children during the day, and he is so excellent a disciplinarian that she seldom finds fault with his rule unless to scold him for over-severity. Mick has a keen sense of justice. When the bread for the eleven o'clock luncheon is given out, not one of the little creatures dares take more than his share, knowing that the eye of the tyrant is upon him.

He has an intense love of color. He would perhaps have been an artist had he attained a normal development. He has covered his clothes with patches, tags and ends of bright cloth which he has picked up, and he worships his clothes as devoutly as an Indian his totem. In summer, when the fields about are full of daisies and buttercups, the other feeble little creatures will manage to pick a few only to drop them from their nerveless fingers, but Mick trims himself all over with the posies, and is as proud as Punch. You should see Mick exercising authority over the others when, as he tries to say, he keeps school. School is held on a long bench under the shed, where Mick ranges the scholars with an accurate eye to size. Then he mounts a little stool in front of the row, and with a long stick and a vigilant outlook keeps the most tyrannous order. If any child ventures to wink or yawn while school is in, down comes the switch with a sharp tingle. Mick possesses a large glass marble, which he sometimes allows a very good scholar to hold in its feeble hand as a reward of merit for a few minutes. If it has not been given out during the session, it is certain the class has been unruly, and has suffered more than usual from the switch.

When one of the old people dies it is an event of great interest in the poor-house. Those who are left of about the same age congratulate themselves on their greater tenacity of life. The good rule, Speak no ill of the dead, is not strictly observed. Bill or Jimmy, or whoever the departed may have been, is generally criticised as a " dretful meechin', no-account kind of creeter' thus to give up so long as the poor-house exists as a home for onfortunits." Mick by some means or other gathers, through his imperfect senses, the whole significance of the event. Before the funeral he keeps even a more strict rule than usual among the little ones, and cuffs any child disposed to make a noise. Around the wrist of each he ties a shred of black rag as a proper token of respect to the departed, and wears the same himself. No one ever told Mick that black is the symbol of death. It is a notion he has picked up of himself, and woe to the unfortunate little one who dares pull off the mourning badge before the funeral. But after that event has taken place Mick forgets all about it and turns to some new idea.

On the road to the poor-house stands a picturesque but rather dilapidated stone dwelling with an upper gallery reached by an outside flight of steps. In summer the place attracts the eye because of the ragged wildness of its garden, overgrown as it is with bushes and weeds and tall grass. Old Peter lived for many years in this house with his two hoydenish girls, whose pranks were the talk of the town. He was a well-to-do miserly old curmudgeon, who allowed his aged mother to die in the poor-house. She was a notorious scold and backbiter, but the whole village reprobated the conduct of old Peter, and has never found a good word to fling after him. His wife died when the girls had just entered their 'teens, and he dispensed with hired help and strove to make them do the work of the house. But the old man found his hands full in trying to tame these irrepressible tomboys. If he tied them up in the barn and whipped them cruelly, it did no good. Their spirits triumphed over every obstacle. There were hours when he stood over them switch in hand to make them sweep and wash; but the greater part of the day, when he was necessarily absent about his affairs, they devoted to the pure unbridled spirit of mischief. Like *Lady Teazle*, they rode the old dock-tailed plow-horse around the pasture barebacked and boy fashion, one behind the other, making the poor brute gallop furiously, until one day she stumbled, and the youngest girl fell off and broke her arm. Old Peter set the bone himself, being what is called in the country a natural bone-setter. He did all the doctoring in his family with roots and herbs which he gathered in the fields and brewed in his own way. He had never been known to call in a physician, except at the last moment of his wife's existence, when some of his neighbors insisted on his securing medical advice, and then it was too late, and he had the best of reasons for not paying the bill.

When Vinnie was laid up with her arm, Betsy, or Peg, as she was called, used the interval of unwonted quiet in making over one of her mother's old gowns. Dire necessity drove poor Peg to this effort, for she was literally in rags. It was almost the first time in her life that she had seriously tried to wield the needle. She had grown all out of such tattered things as she possessed, and was urged to diligence by an aching desire to get into long dresses—skirts sweeping the ground and trailing off like a queen's. The gown was only basted together, and was probably the most remarkable piece of sewing and fitting ever seen. But Peg was delighted with it. She put it on her back the earliest moment possible, and then went through all kinds of strides, attitudes, woven paces and measures, to show off the long-tailed gown to Vinnie, who lay envious and helpless in bed. But, being so lightly put together, the garment had a way of bursting out in the most unfortunate places, and was soon reduced to tatters. Every nail, and bush, and bramble about the place had some token of Peggy's long-tailed but short-lived glory. A relative of the mother, who came at intervals to set the house to rights and look a little after the girls, found Peg clothed, not in sack-cloth and ashes, but the next thing to it—in one of old Peter's linen dusters.

Peter tolerated the presence of this woman because she worked without wages or hope of reward. She was a patient creature, and the girls could do with her as they chose. They had not passed entirely out of the doll period when their mother died. They still kept a closet full of rag infants, mostly boys, and one night, while playing in this closet with a lighted candle, they contrived to set fire to the house, and came near burning it to ashes. After this prank old Peter tied them up in the garret, and kept them a day or two on bread and water. But they managed to escape through a little skylight to the roof of the main building, and by making signals of distress to a neighbor's boy he let them down on a ladder, and they escaped to the woods and wandered about and lived on blackberries—sleeping one night in an old barn —until hunger drove them home.

But the girls had the best impulses, and might have been tamed but for their father's intolerable harshness. They gathered into their poor, starved affections, all the stray, hungry, homeless cats they could find, and kept them in a room in the barn until old Peter discovered the cat hospital, and sent all the felines flying from his premises by means of a savage dog. They were naturally fond of flowers, as all women-kind are ; and one summer a neighbor gave them seeds and they planted a little garden, taking great delight in the labor. The flowers were mainly hollyhocks ; and they came up in great profusion and blossomed heartily after their kind. But old Peter did not believe in rubbishy flowers, which have no money value and are not good to eat. He desired to use the space where the little garden bloomed so pathetically in a wilderness of weeds, for a bed of late peas, so he pulled the hollyhocks up by the roots and threw them over the fence into the road, where they sowed their seeds, and the next season, to revenge his grudging stinginess, the road was like a path through paradise—a waste of rose and white bloom. The young artist who summers in these parts made a pretty sketch of the road and the house and the neglected garden, which I have seen in a city exhibition. The girls cried over their flowers so ruthlessly torn up and thrown out into the sun to die. It was a symbol of the good impulses and instincts in their own natures uprooted, nipped off, and ruined by a brutal, ignorant old man.

But a great change was coming to Peter's wild girls. One night he had been violently angry with them over some small waste he had detected in the kitchen, and going to bed in a passion, died before morning from a sudden stroke. It had long been surmised that the old man was possessed of considerable property, but the extent of his riches had not been suspected. On search being made by the public officers, bonds, stocks, and gold were found hidden in the bed-tick and in odd corners. Suddenly it was discovered that Vinnie and Peg were likely to be accounted heiresses, and kind friends soon came forward to take them in hand. They were speedily dressed in civilized black garments, their elf locks brushed out and neatly braided, and their gipsy skins washed to perfect cleanliness. They were both pretty girls, and "pretty behaved" they became in time when they had been sent to school for three years in a distant city. We now learn they have turned out fine young women. Vinnie is a belle, much admired for her beauty, and Peg, of all things in the world, has become literary.

CHAPTER XI.

THE VILLAGE POST-MISTRESS.

THE village is an exceptionally good place for the few workmen it can support. Living is cheap, rents are low, the people are friendly. The library and public school and lyceum course are open to every body. It is the pride of the village that it has an excellent small class of Irish citizens who live in comparative comfort, possess a degree of self-respect, and are not too much given to bad politics and worse whisky. Politically they are all of one complexion, but as yet there are no rings, no bosses, no corruption fund. The whisky, if obtained at all, is taken surreptitiously, and though some is undoubtedly consumed in the town, the Irish are not the only thirsty souls who break the laws and fall into the deep disgrace of "jim-jams." The younger generation of Irish boys and girls have had great influence over their parents. Many of them have been educated in the public schools. Some of the girls have learned trades, some have gone into the best families as house-servants, have been helped and taught by kind mistresses, and have proved valuable factors in the political economy of the village. One or two of the prettiest and smartest have married young farmers and gone west.

Tim McCoy was a soldier in the war of the rebellion. A red-haired, freckle-faced lad of eighteen, he shouldered a gun and marched away south, where he was wounded in the battle of Antietam, and sent home on a furlough. Tim married and reared a large family. He could earn about four hundred dollars a year as a stone-mason, and the little pension swelled his income to near five hundred dollars. Tim bought and managed partly to pay for the small bare house and garden-plot where he lives down near the railway. There was still a small mortgage on the place, and with his strong shoulder to the wheel, and his good wife's help, he expected season after season to lift it off. But that last rise of ground was always too much for him. Sickness or slack work came repeatedly to bowl him down. But Tim always kept a light heart in his bosom and a whistle on his lips, on his homely face a ray of Irish sunshine, and his speech well larded with the mother wit of his nation. Tim never drank whisky. He was always content after his day's work to sit in his shirt sleeves on the small porch of his house, minding the baby (there was always a baby) and smoking his clay pipe. The "childers" played in the dirt, and his wife bustled about among the pots and pans in the kitchen. Mrs. McCoy took in washing when there were summer boarders in the village, and with the little sum thus gained she could subscribe for a newspaper and dress the children better on a Sunday than some other folks dressed theirs.

Mary McCoy, the eldest girl, was very pretty—tall, with rosy cheeks, free from freckles or sunburn, and dark hair curling in small close rings about her temples. Mary's clothes, though of cheap material, fitted well, and they had a certain style some richer girls might have envied. But, more than all, at fourteen, Mary proved to be the best scholar in the public school. She was quite a mathematical prodigy, and had gone ahead of a large class of boys in algebra. The village always took an interest in the best scholar; and when it was known that Tim McCoy's girl was going to carry off all the prizes that year, there was quite a little stir even among the most refined and aristocratic families. On exhibition day the school-room was crowded to overflowing. Tim

McCoy was there with a great spread of cotton shirt-collar up about his big ears, sitting quite on the front bench, his elbows well squared, feeling he had a pretty tough job of work to get through with in spite of the pride in his heart. His wife was sitting beside him in her best shawl and bonnet, quite nervous for a woman who never knew she had nerves, and all the little McCoys were ranged along in a row, just ready to burst their buttons to think of the honor their family had attained. Mary appeared in a white cambric gown with a blue sash, and was so pretty, and discreet, and modest, and wise withal, every body was loud in her praises. She was undeniably the best scholar of the school, one of the best the village had ever turned out. The parson noticed pretty little Mary most affably. The judge, who was one of the school examiners, condescended to beam upon her. But the doctor, as usual, was the one who bestirred himself to render efficient help.

He obtained a place for Mary in the State Normal School, first as a kind of servant and pupil, and later as under-teacher; and Mary in a few years was educated far away from the little house on the railroad, with the hennery and the pig-sty. Poor Mary! she found her life at home terribly dislocated and incongruous when she had acquired seeing eyes and a new consciousness of her family and surroundings. There were times when in her bitterness of spirit she felt that it would have been kinder to have left her in that sphere of life in which she was born—left her just to drudge along with her mother and the children in that stuffy little house, until she had married a mechanic or farm hand, and begun the ceaseless, hopeless round of toil in her own poor home.

But she was now completely out of that sphere. The only thing left for the best scholar in the high-school was to go away as far as possible from the village and the humble relations whom she loved, and strike out for herself.

So she accepted a position as teacher in another State, and for a time we saw her but seldom. Tim McCoy was a modest fellow. He was never heard to boast of his achievements in the war, where he got an ugly wound. But he did brag a little about his clever girl, who was to pay off the mortgage on the house, and educate the children, and lift the family of McCoy to a high notch on the social scale. Mary had ceased to be a Roman Catholic, and that was a grievance to her mother. There is a small chapel in the village, but no resident priest. Mass is celebrated once a month, by a priest from a neighboring town. Tim and his wife Bridget were devout worshipers in this humble place, where they knelt on the floor before the altar, crossed themselves, counted their beads, and said their prayers in meekness and lowliness of heart. Poor old Bridget, in her dim way, thought education like playing with fire—delightful but dangerous; if it upset the worship of the Holy Virgin and the blessed saints in the soul, it ought to have great compensating advantages in the way of worldly prosperity. She believed as firmly as Tim did that Mary was to make the fortunes of the family.

And so she might perhaps if ill-luck had not struck the little house on the railroad a staggering blow. Bridget caught a bad fall and broke one or two ribs, and she finally died of internal injuries. Tim was seized with inflammatory rheumatism and could not turn over in bed, and the oldest boy Dennis had run wild and was in danger of taking to bad courses; so Mary was sent for to come home and take charge of her deeply-afflicted family, and one day there stepped out of the train at the station a tall, trim, handsome girl dressed all in black. Aside from the natural grief which Mary felt for her mother's death, it was sad for so nice a girl, who had imbibed all the refined and delicate feelings of cultivated life, to be doomed to suffer imprisonment in that house on the railroad, with the children and the pig ; but she behaved nobly, and took the tenderest care of her sick father, and reformed the domestic economy of the whole place. The village admired and pitied her, and, more than all, our doctor felt that something must be done for her. Mary's social position was very equivocal, not to say painful. The girls she had known in school could not meet her now on equal terms, and therefore shunned her. The best families had never taken up Irish mechanics' daughters for pets and intimates ; it was against all the traditions. Mary might have taught in the highschool, but the school children knew her little Irish brothers and sisters, and might not have the grace to respect her authority. So the best scholar the village had turned out and the most unfortunate person in its bounds was left pretty much to herself and her crushing troubles.

About this time a new administration had taken the reins of government at Washington. There had been a great political revolution quietly wrought, and a new-old party had again come into power. Petty officials who had been warm and snug in their berths a great many years now began to tremble and shake in their shoes. Tim McCoy, both by birth and tradition, belonged to the party now in the ascendant. A few of his friends, seeing the straits to which he was reduced, began to agitate for a change in the village post-office, and the name of Mary McCoy was brought prominently forward for the place. She was a soldier's daughter, an excellent accountant, and a worthy woman with a large family of helpless relatives on her hands. The doctor, though ranged on the other side in his political affiliations, was supposed to have given Mary McCoy all his influence. A petition was numerously signed in the village begging that she might be made post-mistress.

There was nothing to be said against Ferdinand Wilkins, the incumbent, except that he was an offensive partisan. If that means any thing, it did not weigh with the villagers. He was well-to-do, had a nice place free from debt, and had held the office for ten years. It was felt that he ought to make way for a soldier's daughter, a much burdened, needy woman. But Wilkins had no idea of yielding without a struggle. He had grown to the place, so to speak, and felt he had a sacred, inborn right to retain it for the rest of his life. Wilkins was a poetaster and somewhat of a dandy. He kept growing plants and a canary bird in the post-office, and was an authority on gloves and perfumes. When St. Patty celebrated her birthday Ferdinand composed an ode for the occasion, which increased his local fame. His wife had died a year previous to the time of which I write, and Ferdinand, urged by the pressure of grief, composed an elegy called "In Memoriam," which, however, did not in the remotest way suggest the great work of the Laureate. It is probable that Ferdinand, carried away by poetic frenzy joined to great grief, did breathe out vows of eternal fidelity to one dead idol, but few men are capable of fulfilling. Ferdinand published the poem at his own cost in a neat pamphlet, and handed it out of the little window in the post-office with the mails to all the villagers.

There was a person living in the village, an opinionated, pragmatical, well-to do old gentleman named Spengler, who was very much affected by "In Memorian." We all have our hobbies, and Spengler's hobby was that it is irreligious, immoral, and wicked to marry twice. He was so bitterly opposed to second marriages that the village had a standing joke that if Spengler could find a nice widow as much opposed to them as he was, he would probably propose to her. We named him the perpetual widower. A man of this kind, who has hugged his loneliness and solitude for twenty years, and gloried in it as a work of supererogation, by which he is laying up treasure in heaven, is of very little account for romantic and exhilarating purposes in a small village, and the women voted him a hopeless old fogy. When the burning question of the post-office came up, Spengler espoused Ferdinand's cause with ardor. Although he had always stood on the side of the Irish contingent, he now headed a petition in favor of the incumbent, and actually set off to Washington carrying the petition in one pocket and "In Memoriam" in the other, to bore the representatives of his district on the subject of the local post-office.

I suppose there was no name on earth Ferdinand Wilkins hated as he did that of Mary McCoy. He had not seen her since her early girlhood, and had forgotten all about her, but he hated her on general principles. Mary, on the other hand, knew him very well by sight, and one day she chanced to meet him exactly in the middle of the walk in front of Drusilla's old house. He saw only a pretty girl in a very neatly fitting black gown, and with such a figure and face as scarcely could be matched in the village, and not dreaming of Mary McCoy, he half stopped from curiosity and admiration. She stopped wholly, blushing and half afraid, but longing to tell him how sorry she was that any trouble had come up concerning the post-office—how she would withdraw if her friends would let her. Then, in an instant, when she began her timid little speech, he knew it was Mary McCoy. He probably did not hate her a bit the less for being pretty, but he did seize the opportunity to reason with her, to show her how wicked and wrong it was of her to wish to oust him from the post-office, which he had reorganized on a strictly civil-service principle, the principle that a good man once in should stay in until he dies. He even walked with her a half mile or more out of the village as he went on in his tonguey, fluent way to show her the enormity of her position. Poor Mary had little to say for herself, but the next day she wrote Ferdinand a few lines, saying she had about made up her mind to withdraw from the contest, to which he replied that on thinking of it over night he had concluded to get out of the office before he was thrust out by the ingratitude of a cold world in general and of the villagers in particular. He also conveyed a hint of the fact that he was an unappreciated genius.

So the two enemies rested for a time, but they met on several occasions, and took long walks on Burying-Ground Hill and out toward Saddleback, that Ferdinand, who had now assumed the pose of the generous, self-devoted martyr, might instruct Mary in the duties of the office. A great deal of instruction seemed requisite, and, strange to say, no one in the village gained an inkling of what was going on. Ferdinand never entered Mary's home, but they both needed long rambles to work off the suspense and excitement of the situation.

One night they were walking under an umbrella just at dusk. It was a soft-dropping spring rain that brings the odors forth from the grass and swells the buds moment by moment. They had not yet heard from the capital, but a great reconciling idea had come into Ferdinand's head, striking well through the pomade and the glossy locks. He proposed a compromise. He said, although he had once disliked the idea of her very much, he now hated to look on Mary as an enemy. It was an anomalous and strained position. Naturally they ought to be allies and the dearest of friends. If she had been in the wrong, he was willing to forgive. If Mary felt she had a grievance, he hoped some ground of amity and mutual good will might be reached. After awhile he proposed a plan.

Mary did not answer directly. She gently turned into another road, and going down to the poor Irish quarter of the town, they stopped under the flare of an oil lamp, where, through the soft shadows, could be seen the open door of Tim McCoy's house. Tim was still feeble and bent, but he had crept out to breathe the fresh air, with his youngest boy on his knee. His head had dropped on his breast, and the fire had gone out in his pipe. He was thinking of Bridget, and he looked broken and old.

Mary's voice was very husky and sounded strangely in her own ears. "No one can take me who does not take him and the children. You would be ashamed of them. Good-by."

He caught her hand and kept it. "I will be good to them, Mary. They shall be like my own." For once Ferdinand rose to the height of a moral hero.

They had been married a few days when old Mr. Spengler came back from Washington. Mary was in the back office with the plants and the canary bird making up the quarterly account. Old Spengler looked weary and travel-stained, and he said, softening his voice to a touch of sympathy, when he met Ferdinand: "We have lost the battle, my boy, and I am very sorry. The president, you know, has sent in her name for confirmation. Come and stay awhile with me, and I will try to brace you up."

Ferdinand blushed to the roots of his pretty hair, feeling himself to be an awful fraud. He said faintly: "We—that is, Miss McCoy and I— we have gone into a kind of partnership and I shall keep the office after all."

Old Spengler shut himself up in his house for several days and made an *auto-de-fé* of "In Memoriam," and now there is a rumor abroad that he is looking out for a wife. The village women generally pity poor Mary. They say she has thrown herself away on a milksop. But is it not in accordance with a great law of nature that clever women do generally throw themselves away on milksops?

CHAPTER XII.

SAYINGS AND DOINGS OF MISS CANDACE.

THE growing light brings a new sense of breadth and largeness out of doors. The sky stretches to an unexpected size and finer constellations seem to burn in the evening heavens. The elm trees sway in the dry wind tempest, and great shadow giants flicker over the tops of the houses, and climb the steeple and mount the sky. The sunrises are red behind the fir-trees on our solemn eastern slopes; and at evening the fading light draws a long sanguinary finger and splashes warm on the dullest gray wall. A thought of spring, inchoate and vague, tingles in the twigs of the lowland willows until you seem to see their yellow and brown stems through a quivering mist of green. At noon, for a single relenting hour, the earth stretches itself like a yawning Titan. The crusted snow, dwindled to belts and patches, breaks loose from the clay banks, and little rivulets begin to trickle down, making hieroglyphs older than those of Rameses.

The cackling of hens is now an original sound, suggestive of budding hopes and the early resumption of business. The house sparrows at work in our elms begin to cheep out the information very early in the morning that spring has taken the air line for the village. At night it still freezes hard, but not as vindictively as of old. A fresh, frosty tingle nips fingers and ears, and makes you think of getting down the sap-buckets and tapping the sugar maples. The winds still caper wildly around old chimneys and casements, but they seem to pipe in quite another key.

We wait many weeks in the bleak North for the first wild-flower and the first bluebird. But they are getting ready in the great workshop. Long before they come the essences of flowers seem free and floating in the sweet, cold air; and there is a prophecy of song in the empty woods that is worth more than the song itself.

There is a small holding of land, not more than ten or fifteen acres, just outside the village, where the spring seems to come first. The few old peach trees in the garden get up a show of blossoms before any other spot has thought of a bud; the grass breaks out into a sudden glow of crocuses and lilies of the valley, when scarce a dandelion has put forth elsewhere. The early sun seems to exhaust itself in nourishing the cherry trees along the stone wall until they are all a flutter with white flowers, and only brings to us its later guerdon. This warm slope of land, with the little brown house attached, by several small industries, such as the raising of early vegetables, small fruits, eggs and honey, has supported a large family for several years. The father and grandfather is a microscopic economist, such as can only be found in New England and among the French peasantry. Not a stick or straw ever goes to waste on his domain, consequently he is as forehanded as any of his neighbors —always ready to pay his doctor's bill and his pew-rent when due—signs of special grace in a small neighborhood.

His wife died years ago, and he has been ably seconded in all his efforts by his daughter, Candace, his housekeeper and general manager. The old man has reared two families, his own and the children of his daughter Rachel, who died young, a widow, leaving five small children. Every one in the village knows Miss Candace, and every one likes to welcome her ample person and homely, honest face—so kind and open it has been many times said she would be properly named Candor. Every wrinkle and crow's foot and hollow and line, even to the mole on her left cheek, is filled with wisdom, goodness and benevolence. She is so wholesomely plain she is positively attractive, and may well be likened to mignonette or lavender, unobtrusive but loved products of our gardens. Miss Candace by birth belongs to the Society of Friends, but she does not speak the "plain" language nor wear the dress. She was not educated after the manner of the schools. She reads very slowly and peruses the same books year by year. These are the Bible, "John Woolman's Journal," "Pilgrim's Progress," and a few others to which very late in life she has added "Emerson's Essays." Miss Candace is a great authority on the rearing of children, the raising and care of fowls and the cultivation of flowers. No one in the town has ever had half her success in the mysteries of egg production. When people try to discover the secret, they find that she has only an ordinary hen-house, with no patent laying-boxes or special arrangements for coaxing the wary, unwilling fowl to lay out of season. Neither does she pride herself on rare breeds or costly varieties. The barn-yard hen, clucking in comfort and security, is good enough for her. She shows every process of feeding in winter—tells you to keep your fowls warm, to give them plenty of fresh water, gravel and lime, and that is all. You go home and do just as she directs, but her eggs are always the first in the market; they are larger and of a more exquisite pearly tint than yours. Her spring chickens are the best, and will command a higher price even than those raised by Rastus and his mother.

Go in when Miss Candace has done up her morning's work, and is resting in her favorite rocking-chair, knitting in hand, and sit down cozily with your knees close to hers, and she may let you a little deeper into the secret "Folks don't think hens have feelings," she begins, "but they have, and they talk together a good deal, and I

We wait many weeks in the bleak North for the first wild-flower and the first bluebird. But they are getting ready in the great workshop. Long before they come the essences of flowers seem free and floating in the sweet, cold air; and there is a prophecy of song in the empty woods that is worth more than the song itself.

There is a small holding of land, not more than ten or fifteen acres, just outside the village, where the spring seems to come first. The few old peach trees in the garden get up a show of blossoms before any other spot has thought of a bud; the grass breaks out into a sudden glow of crocuses and lilies of the valley, when scarce a dandelion has put forth elsewhere. The early sun seems to exhaust itself in nourishing the cherry trees along the stone wall until they are all a flutter with white flowers, and only brings to us its later guerdon. This warm slope of land, with the little brown house attached, by several small industries, such as the raising of early vegetables, small fruits, eggs and honey, has supported a large family for several years. The father and grandfather is a microscopic economist, such as can only be found in New England and among the French peasantry. Not a stick or straw ever goes to waste on his domain, consequently he is as forehanded as any of his neighbors —always ready to pay his doctor's bill and his pew-rent when due—signs of special grace in a small neighborhood.

His wife died years ago, and he has been ably seconded in all his efforts by his daughter, Candace, his housekeeper and general manager. The old man has reared two families, his own and the children of his daughter Rachel, who died young, a widow, leaving five small children. Every one in the village knows Miss Candace, and every one likes to welcome her ample person and homely, honest face—so kind and open it has been many times said she would be properly named Candor. Every wrinkle and crow's foot and hollow and line, even to the mole on her left cheek, is filled with wisdom, goodness and benevolence. She is so wholesomely plain she is positively attractive, and may well be likened to mignonette or lavender, unobtrusive but loved products of our gardens. Miss Candace by birth belongs to the Society of Friends, but she does not speak the " plain " language nor wear the dress. She was not educated after the manner of the schools. She reads very slowly and peruses the same books year by year. These are the Bible, " John Woolman's Journal," " Pilgrim's Progress," and a few others to which very late in life she has added " Emerson's Essays." Miss Candace is a great authority on the rearing of children, the raising and care of fowls and the cultivation of flowers. No one in the town has ever had half her success in the mysteries of egg production. When people try to discover the secret, they find that she has only an ordinary hen-house, with no patent laying-boxes or special arrangements for coaxing the wary, unwilling fowl to lay out of season. Neither does she pride herself on rare breeds or costly varieties. The barn-yard hen, clucking in comfort and security, is good enough for her. She shows every process of feeding in winter—tells you to keep your fowls warm, to give them plenty of fresh water, gravel and lime, and that is all. You go home and do just as she directs, but her eggs are always the first in the market; they are larger and of a more exquisite pearly tint than yours. Her spring chickens are the best, and will command a higher price even than those raised by Rastus and his mother.

Go in when Miss Candace has done up her morning's work, and is resting in her favorite rocking-chair, knitting in hand, and sit down cozily with your knees close to hers, and she may let you a little deeper into the secret " Folks don't think hens have feelings," she begins, " but they have, and they talk together a good deal, and I children. Look at my plants there filling the windows with their great stocky shoots and healthy leaves. I've a notion they wouldn't grow where there's envy, hatred, and malice, and all uncharitableness. I guess backbiting and evil speaking would kill 'em as soon as coal gas; but they ain't half as sensitive as the mind of a child. We must get into the nature of roses and geraniums and try to learn the best conditions for them, and that's about all there is in raising hens or children. The method requires a deal of patience, a kind of divine unselfishness strained and clarified like the best honey. If you've got a weakly plant, nurse it and give it richer earth, more air and sun. It may in time bear blossoms that will take the prize at the flower-show. Don't ever be discouraged with an unlikely boy or girl, but study out what it needs, and try, and keep trying, and by and by you will hit on the right thing to bring that weakly one along where he can begin to grow. If you love him enough, he may some day stand at the head of the life class. I always say folks are like pitchers: there is a handle to every disposition if we only knew how to take hold of it. Plenty of folks fail to influence their children because they get tired searching for that handle."

I have gathered up a few of Miss Candace's miscellaneous sayings which are scattered among the neighbors, and these not the best:

"There are some folks like a hill of potatoes: all the green part and the blows must die away or get killed by frost-bite before you find there is any thing worth digging for underneath."

"There are folks like the scrub oak: they never know when to shed their leaves. I hate to see dried-up youthful follies and vanities hanging on to old people."

"There's some sugar in a corn-stalk, and I expect there's about as much sweetness in the dryest stick of a human being. It's our loss if we don't know how to extract it."

"I hear a good deal said about living with the saints and angels, but when I go to the other world I want to go to my own folks. I can feel with humanity, but I don't know nothing at all about angelmanity."

"If you believe in your work, your work will believe in you. If you are a sham, your work will kick like an old rusty gun."

Miss Candace believes in the licensed order of women preachers and in the custom among the Friends of bearing testimony against certain things which call for reformation. Her testimony, borne vigorously against intemperance, has had a great deal to do with driving the gin-shops from the town. She is never exigent; her voice is placid and pleasantly modulated. She never has been insulted or rebuffed even by rough men under the influence of drink. She is always guided by high motives, and her words go directly to the point. It is her conviction that we must not let "folks" alone; that we have no right to ignore the spiritual and temporal needs of our neighbors, or to shut ourselves up in a cold sense of isolation and superior virtue, when we may have a message hidden in the heart that is needed by some fellow-being.

From time immemorial there has been a class of exhorting women in the village, who at certain seasons have felt called upon gratuitously to attend to the spiritual interests of their neighbors. They have grown less in the course of years, but there is always some one left to assume the mantle of prophetess and itinerant religious preacher. Mother Embery is an old, bent woman of vinegar aspect, who for a great many years has believed herself in a state of sanctification and incapable of committing sin. This happy immunity from personal guilt has left her free to sit pretty heavily in judgment on her neighbors.

She lives in a lonely little hollow outside the town, and long ago, before she was "sanctified," she believed she saw the Evil One, horns and all, looking in at her sitting-room window. In recent times the anthropomorphic Satan has grown rather unpopular among us, and Mother Embery is shy of talking about this remarkable experience. But she occasionally makes house-to-house visitations of personal inquiry as to the spiritual condition of the family, talking with each one of the inmates, and offering prayer if it is allowed. Some resent her interference and shut their doors against her, others tolerate her presence though it be unwelcome, and a few receive her as a chosen vessel of grace and an inspired ministrant. On one occasion, immediately following a revival in the village, when Mother Embery's brain was a good deal exalted, she went into Aunt Dido's to inquire after the state of her soul. That invincible optimist replied pleasantly that she hadn't heard from her soul for some time, she was sorry to say; she had been so busy taking care of the bodies of other people. She presumed, however, it was all right. Mother Embery was not well pleased with this practical answer from a person whom she felt to be in the very gall of bitterness. She therefore poured forth warning and admonition in an impetuous stream of words, delivered in a high key, and finally wound up by asking Aunt Dido what she would say when she came into a dreadful place where the fire is never quenched. Aunt Dido was busy making mince pies, weighing and portioning out the fruit and meat, the raisins and citron, and spices, and did not wish to be bothered. So, standing at her kitchen table, she turned her head over her shoulder and said good-humoredly:

"Don't know what I should say, Mother Embery, under those circumstances. Guess I should warm my hands and remark, as an old lady did I once heard of, 'What a particularly nice fire to broil a steak!'"

Mother Embery flung out of the house, shocked by such unpardonable levity, and since that day she has had the utmost satisfaction in consigning Aunt Dido to the place where Dante bestowed all his political enemies.

CHAPTER XIII.

THE BUSY BEES.

OUR spring high water and freshets are always periods of great interest and excitement, especially to the children. The river is sure to rise at about the same time every year. There comes a warm, impetuous rainstorm and then an ice-break. The snow melts rapidly on the mountains. The brooks rush down and pour into the larger streams. A rush and roar and trampling of waters fill the world with a new spirit. For a few days there is great anxiety lest the dams should break and the bridges be carried off. People are set to watch day and night at different points while the crisis lasts, for fear the village, which lies on a low plateau, should be invaded by a mountain torrent. But this has never happened within memory. In a short time the river ceases to rage and boil, and spreads out peacefully in lake-like expanses over the meadows, where fresh-water birds come promptly to feed.

Mill Farm is always a point of attraction in freshet time. Then the wine-colored and golden-brown water rushes over the wheel and through the race, and churns along the stony brook in foam until it finally makes a leap down the three giant steps of rock, clearing them at a bound with a shout. The fall throws off spray in clouds, which cling like lace webs to the rocky slopes of the glen, and when the sun shines are shot full of rainbows. Mill Farm, with the old gray stacks of buildings, the busy wheel, the water-course and the cascade, is the most picturesque place about the village. The miller and his wife are both round, jolly, homespun people of the true miller type. When the miller emerges from the dust raised by his wheel, his rosy face beams like a full moon. His wife is of the same build, short and cherubic, and is noted for being dressy and wearing the gayest old-lady caps in the village. The little court between the mill and the house in summer is filled with the brightest flowers that blow, such as fish-geraniums, nasturtiums, scarlet beans and poppies. Even now the sitting-room windows make a fine display of hyacinth glasses.

But there are other flowers looking out from the windows and smiling into the bland spring air. They are the bright eyes and blooming faces of the "Busy Bees," three young girls, nieces of the miller's wife, who come frequently from a neighboring town to visit their aunt. The old miller is uncommonly fond of these pretty girls. He has no children of his own; and it is shrewdly suspected that if they marry to please him, he will make them his heirs. They are orphan girls, and already well endowed for the country with this world's goods. Indeed among the simple minded inhabitants of the village they are looked upon as great matrimonial prizes. They bring with them Saratoga trunks full of bewitching clothes in which they array themselves; and all about the glen, and the fields, and the mill they pose to be admired. Each of the "Busy Bees" has her fad, which she pursues with ardor. The eldest is practical and active, ready to do anything in the house or on the farm, from concocting a pudding to riding on the mowing machine, provided some one of the male kind is by to admire her vigor. The second is decorative. She brought old china and art work into fashion in the village before Rose Madder opened her studio above Peckham's grocery store. She first showed the villagers how to compose nocturnes and symphonies in plush and satin, Berlin wool and floss silk.

The youngest Busy Bee is an entomologist, to the extent

of catching butterflies in a green silk net and looking very pretty while she pursues science out in the daisy-decked fields in a bewildering little Mother Hubbard and a big straw hat. It is very instructive to her young admirers to see how deftly she jabs these poor winged creatures, and puts them up as specimens with a lovely smile on her innocent, rosy face. The "Busy Bees" all unite in adoring and patronizing the country. They dote on sunrises and moonlight nights in the glen, on horseback excursions to Saddleback, and walks to the wildest parts of the neighborhood. They have a gipsy camp down by the waterfall, where they spend whole days in picnic existence and give audience to the most favored of their male friends. They are rustic in a way very surprising to the country girls. In their best gowns they hunt hens' nests in the barn, or ride on the hay load, or go out, holding up their dainty skirts from the reek of the farm-yard, to pet the horses and cows and calves. They are affable and pleasant to every body. There is not a creature living they would not like to make happy if they could do it in a picturesque and effective manner.

When the Bees appear there is constant stir and bustle, accompanied with cackling, and laughter, and fun. Of course, the advent of these rich, attractive, and desirable damsels creates a commotion in the village. The atmosphere changes, and all winds blow toward Mill Farm. The young men, old bachelors, and widowers "spruce up," and turn their longing eyes in the direction of the glen. In some quarters, hair dye is in brisk demand. The tailor notes quite a perceptible increase of orders. The bootmaker laughs and says he never sells any patent leathers unless the "Busy Bees" are in town. As a spur to trade and a quickening impulse in dull times the Bees are always welcomed with open arms. When they go chattering through the village, showing their fine feathers, and tripping along on the toes of their French boots, with a following of attentive gallants, window-shades fly up, old people hobble to the door, and excellent girls who have been allowed to hang upon the bush unsought many a year gaze with mild asperity, feeling in their inmost souls that the Bees "ain't such a great sight better looking than other folks!"

Hugh has flirted impartially with all three of the Bees, as he has found himself in perfect accord with all their tastes. He might possibly like to marry one of them if the other two were not just as nice and just as alluring as any given member of the trio. Aunt Dido has advised him seriously to pay attention to the eldest, who she thinks has more sense and is less volatile than her sisters. She has set forth the advantages of matrimony to her boarder while wielding her large iron spoon over the kitchen stove, while changing his plate at his solitary dinner, and even while tidying the house in her whirlwind fashion with broom and duster. It is strange Aunt Dido should think so much of the married state, when her own husband is such a small, insignificant man, it almost takes a microscope to discover him. But she has the weakness of her sex, which judges a man married a man made, and tells Hugh with commendable frankness that if he settles down into the well-worn groove of domestic life he may turn out a steady man; otherwise she very much fears he never will amount to any certain sum. Hugh objected very much to having, as he said, a bee put in his bonnet, but once there he could not help its buzzing. He has tried to look upon the eldest Bee as a possible Mrs. Hugh, but for the life of him he can not help regarding all three in an impersonal affectionate manner. To quiet the importunities of Aunt Dido, about a year ago he planned to give the sisters a serenade at the mill on a lovely moonlight night. The serenade was charming, but it did not turn out just as it was planned, as I shall show later.

There is one old bachelor among us who lives in perhaps the snuggest, tidiest place we have, just below the grand mansion established by Judge Magnus. This man has furnished more food for harmless gossip and matrimonial speculation than any other man ever "raised" in the town. He is a very shrewd business man, and has amassed a large fortune, which it is his ambition to increase. His thin, keen visage appears to have been ground fine on hard bargains and doubtful transactions. All the village spinsters know that he dyes his hair and whiskers, which are of a splendid sable, glossy and rich beyond the power of nature to produce. When the Bees are in the village his locks take on an added luster beautiful to behold. He is mathematically exact in dress and deportment. His silk hat shines as if just taken from the counter, and his gloves fit to perfection. Impossible is it to describe the glitter of his linen. He has been called Mr. Worldly Wiseman, though some who know the smoothness of his tongue and the grip of his hard bargains think Mr. Facing-both-ways would be quite as appropriate. His house always appears to have just received a coat of new paint. Every thing about it is kept in perfect order. The most voracious insects never dare to attack his trees and vines. His roses are all full-blown ones with just so many leaves to the corolla. His grapes form in the most absolute perfection, resembling those mouth-watering clusters you see in agricultural papers. The walks in his garden and door-yard are accurately cemented, and no weed, be it dock or pusley, dare show its impudent head along his borders. His trees grow according to a pattern. The elms bend with precision, forming the same regular curve on both sides, and his maples shoot up into thick pyramids. If any one tree on his premises should venture to lean or crook it would probably be removed, as nothing but mathematical symmetry can satisfy the soul of Mr. Worldly Wiseman.

It was at one time thought he might marry his housekeeper, who keeps his house in the perfect order of the multiplication table—getting out her " wash " by the rule of three, and serving up everything on the beautiful principle of vulgar fractions. But within the last year or two he has cast his eyes on the middle Bee, who is as decorative as she is pretty, and the question has been busily canvassed in the village as to whether Miss Bee will have Mr. Worldly Wiseman. There are some who think that, although she has such a gushing fondness for nature, this young lady will take an urban man, and never seriously think of bestowing her charms and her fortune on a village magnate. There are others who think she might go further and fare worse ; as that perfect place on Main Street is a lure to feminine eyes.

The bachelor's attentions had been going on for some time when Hugh, prompted by Aunt Dido, devised the idea of a serenade to the three charming sisters at Mill Farm. Mr. Worldly Wiseman plays the violin in a sufficiently feeble manner to accompany some of our village girls on the piano. Hugh invited him to join the serenaders, and although much older than the young fellows who compose the glee club, he consented to be of the party. Stephen has a fine command of the flute and is a skilled performer. When Hugh approached Stephen and opened the little affair of the serenade with all the inducements he could throw around it you should have seen that young man's face. At the moment he happened to be preparing for the stuffing process old Mrs. Holt's pet canary, which had died of the pip. As he held the bird in his hand he just turned short about to shout a terrific " no " to Hugh's request, and then resumed his work, the hair bristling straight up on the top of his pugnacious head. Stephen has become a dreadful misogynist since the loss of his cash. His mother has now gone away to visit her sister for an indefinite length of time, and Stephen does his own cooking, makes his bed, and, for aught I know, washes his own clothes. He puts his tin can outside his door very early, and locks it with a vicious snap that he may not be forced to speak to the old milk-woman when she comes round of a morning. Hugh was obliged to dispense with Stephen's flute; but the Glee Club boys were all willing, and after a great many rehearsals in private, a beautiful moonlight night in spring was chosen for the serenade. The "Busy Bees" were, of course, fully informed of what was going forward, and were in a flutter of pleasurable anticipation. The mill was stopped, the bulldog was chained up in the barn behind the house as a necessary precaution, and the miller warned not to get up in the night and point his old rusty musket out of the window if he happened to be aroused by unusual sounds. The young ladies had prepared beautiful bouquets wherewith to pelt their admirers, and these were all ranged along the old-fashioned bureau under the dressing-glass which often reflected the three charming faces.

A moonlight night at the mill is a bit of paradise regained. The old irregular pile of buildings, with the race and the great wheel and the many trees grouped at the entrance of the mossy glen, make a witching picture. In furtive fashion the moonbeams steal about the court, glimpsing upon the windows of the chambers where the "Busy Bees" repose, and quivering down in sparkles on the many-hued flower beds. It was here in this court under the windows that the Glee Club was ranged, with Mr. Worldly Wiseman a little withdrawn, shrouded in his inky cloak, and suffering some sharp rheumatic twinges from the night air. It was past one in the morning, and all nature was deliciously still and dewy, when the spell was broken by the melodious sound of voices with a violin accompaniment. Hugh let out the full volume of his rich tenor. The bachelor as first suitor bowed away with commendable energy. They heard the casement softly open. They could catch faintest glimpses of those lovely Bees in light raiment, and the sound of suppressed laughter. The "Glees" had sung in their best style "Come into the Garden, Maud," and had given a bird song with prolonged trills and cadences, when from behind the muslin curtains came a soft sound of handclapping. A shower of nosegays flew out of the window, which the happy serenaders managed to secure as they pattered down in the flower-beds. But Mr. Wiseman sank to the ground with a suppressed groan which sounded like a muffled imprecation. Something much heavier than a bunch of flowers had struck him on the side of the head and demolished his violin. For a moment he believed he had been shot with murderous intent. The windows of the girls' chamber were hastily closed. Hugh ran to the assistance of Mr. Worldly Wiseman, and the other boys, with consternation painted on their faces, gathered around and helped him out into the road, where he continued to groan, while they examined him all over for injuries; but no wounds or abrasions could be discovered. Hugh was bent on rousing the house to demand an explanation of this mysterious assault. But the bachelor sullenly restrained him, and after giving himself a shake, said he could walk home. His personal pride and self-love had been terribly wounded, but otherwise he appeared to be sound. His hat and violin, however, were both badly damaged.

In somber mood the young men took their way back to the village. There was but little said, but they all kept up a desperate thinking. Mr. Worldly Wiseman in his battered state was sulky to the point of rudeness; and as soon as possible sought the repose of his own immaculate abode, where he nursed his wrongs in silence. Why the pretty Bees should have peppered their serenaders with missiles harder than bouquets or billetdoux remained a profound mystery for some time. The offended Glee Club would not go near them to demand an explanation. The old miller when taxed with having fired his gun out of the window could remember nothing of the kind. He had slept soundly during the whole fracas, and now took counsel with his equally befogged wife. The girls were very reticent, at first, and when any thing was said of this nocturnal adventure, blushed and hung their heads, while stories went through the village to the effect that the "Busy Bees" had of late been practicing with a pistol for their own amusement, and had fired on the whole pack of their lovers assembled under their windows from pure wantonness. Mr. Worldly Wiseman had been dangerously wounded, according to their account, and was lying in a critical condition. But Mr. Wiseman in order to check the tongues of the myth-makers soon appeared on the street in his usual health.

Behold how great a matter a little fire kindleth. After a few days it came out just how Mr. Worldly Wiseman happened to be assaulted at Mill Farm, to the damage of his hat and violin. The youngest Miss Bee, that volatile butterfly girl, had been suddenly awakened from a profound sleep by the music of the serenaders under her window. Her nosegays were all ready, tied with celestial blue ribbon, but in a half-waking somnambulic state she arose, fumbled about to find her flowers, and seizing instead, by accident, a cut-class scent bottle, hurled it from the window with fatal aim, because she took no aim at all. She and her sisters have tried to appease the wrath of Mr. Worldly Wiseman by many unobtrusive attentions, but the village Achilles still nurses his offended dignity in his tent. Thus many a budding and incipient romance is spoiled by a ridiculous little accident for which no one is really to blame.

Hugh has made it up with the Bees, and goes on flirting with all of them just as usual.

CHAPTER XIV.

THE DOCTOR'S TROUBLE.

THE ties which bind a small community together are many and subtile. You may dislike your neighbor in the village; you may envy or distrust him, or feel contempt for his ability or his pretensions, but when he is ill or in trouble, or when death comes knocking at his door, you can not ignore him. Human fellowship is still found to be strong and active. The trained nurse has not yet come in to prevent neighborly offices performed by the gentle hands of good women. Housewives still cook little delicacies to tempt the appetite of the invalid across the way or in the next street. Bonny girls and children carry flowers to sick chambers. When death comes, the undertaker does not do all that is required. Experienced women enter the house of mourning with a kind of authority and perform the last kind offices for the dead.

Many a poor creature has passed away with a certain sense of comfort in her heart from the thought of kind neighbors who would not let the family suffer, who would see all things done decently and in order at the funeral. These customs are good and humanizing. In prosperity the people may bicker and backbite, they may nurse their jealousies and piques and divisions, but when trouble comes they are united. They see the solemn fate bringing all to equality of lot, and they stand together in a closer sense of brotherhood.

The doctor, as we know, has had poignant experience of other people's sorrows. He has experienced living and dying troubles by the score, and taken a multitude of human griefs into his own breast. He has felt for his fellow man and woman in a humble sphere with the tenderness, charity, and compassion which might have made a saint, and yet how far is he from being a saint. Into his ear have been poured the troubles of lowly lives, the discouragements of poor farmers and mechanics, the griefs of over-worked, dispirited women, the heartaches of maidens and young men whose aspirations have been crushed out, the struggles of lonely and saintly souls of whom some still remain in the foldings of our blue hills.

The doctor has never betrayed a secret in his life. He does not talk about his bad cases at home, thus to find relief from mental strain. When he has a very sick patient on his hands, he betrays his anxiety by swallowing a great many cups of strong tea, which his wife knows to be bad for him. If things are getting desperate, he sometimes braces up on a small glass of brandy, which he takes from a side cupboard in his office stocked with some choice old liquors kept for medicinal purposes. The doctor is so strictly temperate in all his habits that when his grandchild sees him take a drink of clear spirits from the decanter, she always knows there is something disastrous in the wind and watches him with wistful eyes, though even she has learned it is never safe to question him about his cases.

The doctor has a hot, passionate temper. His growl is something terrific, and not to be encountered with temerity. Miss Candace laughs, and says she rather likes it, it is such an honest and sincere sound. There is no cant in the doctor's growl, nor is there any concession to false conventionalities. He has a lightning-like directness of speech and action, and it is never safe to beard him in the wrong mood. But like such violently contrasted natures, when he is genial nothing can exceed the warmth and brightness that rays out of his being. Like a central sun he seems to light the world, and the amount of beautiful poetry he recites gives evidence of his prodigious memory. To his poor patients who can pay nothing but thanks, and to whom he often gives the medicine he prescribes, the doctor frequently shows this beautiful side of his character. He is worshiped by crippled children and wretched women, as if he had been canonized and held a place in the calendar.

When any thing happens to the doctor, a tocsin rings through the village, and people are aroused. Even the people who have fought with him, and have denounced his violence, stand aghast at the thought of any calamity overtaking the principal institution of the town. The thunderbolt has struck his roof more than once, as you can read in the pale, saintly face of his wife, whom the neighbors are apt to think is altogether too submissive to her lord and master.

It is known to but few that the doctor's grandchild will inherit a small fortune from a distant relative when she comes of age. This legacy was much exaggerated by public rumor and before the end of two years the larger part of it was lost by bad investments. The girl herself was unaware of the fact, as the doctor and his wife have carefully sought to conceal it from Effie until she is older and has received a thorough education. But the villagers do well remember all the painful, harrowing circumstances of Effie's birth and early childhood; how the father absconded to Europe with a degraded woman, and the broken-hearted mother and little child were taken into the doctor's household. Effie's mother faded away in two years, and the child, though still very young, was deeply impressed by the wrongs and sufferings she had endured from a dissolute father. It was this trouble which aged the doctor and whitened the brown locks of his wife. But years passed on. The child was growing up to take the place of the daughter they had lost. The doctor recovered his firmness and poise. His eyes grew keen and bright again. In a year or two now Effie could go before the court and choose her own guardian, and all danger from the renegade father's claim would be at an end. Secret terrors lest Philip should come back to try and get possession of the girl, now that she had inherited property, were always afflicting the soul of the doctor's wife. At times she would not let Effie go out alone through the village streets. The doctor knew just what it meant when he saw one of these nervous tremors taking possession of his wife; I believe she dreaded the blandishments of the handsome unprincipled Philip and the power he might gain over the mind of the child more than any thing else.

But as they saw Effie growing taller and more womanly each day, their fears were quieted, and their vigilance fell asleep. One afternoon in April or early May, I know the tulip beds were all ablaze in the Squire's garden, Effie rushed quite pale and disheveled into her grandfather's office, and threw herself sobbing into his arms. In broken words, when she could command her voice, she told him of a dreadful fright she had received coming home from school. Two men on the old turnpike had tried to force her into a carriage. But she screamed loudly, and resisted with all her might, and was heard by an old man, Eben Tripp, who was driving along in his "democrat" wagon. The men seeing him so near let her go, and whipped up their horses. Her books had fallen into the dirt in the road, and she was trembling so she could hardly stand, but old man Tripp gathered up the books, and put her into the wagon, and brought her home. And then Effie asked under her breath, her large eyes strained wide with fright: "Was it that man that used my mother so? Oh, grandpa, don't let him get me." The doctor grew rigid as stone. He clinched his hands until the nails were driven into the flesh, but he tried to soothe the child, and finally he put her to bed and gave her a sleeping potion, and then he told his wife the evil days had come upon them. The next day very early Effie was sent away to a safe place.

In a day or two it began to be whispered about the place that strangers were abiding at Saw Mill Hollow, a little hamlet two miles away. Who they probably were and the purport of their visit filled the air with conjectures and vague disquiet. The old doctor's face was a study at this time, and many watched it, though none dared to question him. He went doggedly about his business, but all his leisure he was locked up in his office busy with secret matters, while his wife sat anxious and alone in her own room, or moved about the house with her soft, still tread. One day, the week after Effie was sent off, she slipped into the office; the doctor, as she supposed, had gone into the country to visit a very sick man. After searching a long time in various corners she came upon a pair of old pistols newly polished and carefully oiled. But the doctor had not gone to the country, it seemed, for he surprised his wife with one of the weapons in her hand. As he stopped at the door and looked in: "Judith," he cried, sternly; "what are you about?"

"John, John Rivington, you are going to murder him." It was all the answer she could make, for her heart was constricted and her tongue parched.

"I am going to have it out with him, that's a fact. And mind what I say, Judith; you must keep still and not try to interfere."

She was still as a statue of despair, and as she slipped down in his old office chair he thought she would faint. Seeing that great anguish in her tearless face, the doctor by a sudden impulse took the pistols out of the drawer and laid them in her lap.

"Here, you may take these things away. I won't do it with firearms, I'll use my fists. But I must have it out with that man, for life is not worth a brass farthing to me while he skulks around here with his cursed detective, and goes unpunished."

That was all that passed between them, and a few days later the doctor met Philip on the road to Saw Mill Hollow. It was just at dusk, when soft brown velvet shadows filled the spring twilight. He had not seen his son-in-law for twelve years, but he knew him at a glance of his old eagle eye, and instantly he leaped from his wagon and grappled with his enemy. The doctor being a more powerful man than Philip, with the heavy horsewhip he carried gave him a terrible punishing. There in the brown shadows, where the birds were softly calling to their mates, the two men clinched and fought, rolled over on the grass, or rising to their feet took a new life-and-death grip. The struggle went on until some laborers in the fields, hearing groans and stifled cries, ran to the place and found Philip lying deathly white by the roadside, with the old man, his clothes torn and muddy, standing over him like a lion at bay.

No one molested the doctor. He got into his wagon and drove home. In spite of the terrible condition of his clothes, he looked excited and almost young as he burst into his wife's sitting-room. The lamp had just been brought in. She sat there still and apprehensive, listening to every sound. "Well, Judith, you see I've done it," looking down at his coat.

"You haven't killed him, John?" "Pretty nigh," he said curtly. "Not many whole bones left in his body, I guess. It was a long score, Judith, and it had to be cleared off. You must make haste and put up a few things in a bag, for as soon as I have cleaned myself and changed my clothes I am going to drive over to ——— (naming the county town) to give myself up to Sheriff Dawson." She stood up to obey him silently, but her limbs refused their office, and the doctor put his arm around her and drew her close to him. It was not an habitual thing with these two. Perhaps he kissed her. "Judith," he said, "I haven't been a very good husband to you. I have been too obstinate and self-willed to make you very happy; but if any thing should happen to separate us, I want you to believe this thing had to be done."

That night the doctor gave himself up to Sheriff Dawson—routing that functionary out of bed in the small hours to tell his story and to put himself in the power of the law. The sheriff was an old and tried friend, and much troubled by the necessity. He gave the doctor a room in his own house, and turned the key upon him. It would be impossible to describe the excitement that simmered, and bubbled, and boiled in the village when the fact was made known that the doctor had thrashed Philip Hadley within an inch of his life on Saw Mill Hollow road. The little town seemed hung in black, for now he was in trouble the people were to a man, woman, and child loyal to the old man. He had great faults, of course, but who was there like him for grand virtues?

In the morning reports came that Philip was dying. He had been carried to his lodging in Saw Mill Hollow, and the local doctor had been called in. Some of his ribs were broken, but the worst feature of his case was concussion of the brain. His antagonist had given him a heavy fall on stony ground. The people were feverishly anxious that Philip should live. A messenger came every hour from Saw Mill Hollow to report. It would be impossible to get a jury together in the county to convict the doctor of murder, for the story of Philip Hadley's rascality was too well known, but the anxiety lest Philip should die was none the less agonizing. In a day or two, when a slightly favorable turn had taken place in Philip's state, it was known that the doctor would be released on bail, and half the men in the village crowded the first train down to the county town to offer to go on his bond. There was the judge, and the minister, and the old shoemaker, and Hugh, and Peckham, and Mr. Worldly Wiseman, and the postmaster, and even Jake Small and Tim McCoy, whom the doctor had brought through that bad illness.

When the village delegation squeezed into the sheriff's office it was a remarkable sight. The doctor had been very cheerful, indeed, in the best of spirits since he gave himself up, but this demonstration almost unmanned him, and he could only grasp the hands of his old neighbors, for his voice was entirely too husky to attempt a word. All the property in the village might have been pledged for his prompt appearance at this trial, but the signature of Judge Magnus was all-sufficient.

When he found himself a free man once more the first thing the doctor did was to inquire particularly after the condition of Philip and the mode of his treatment. When told the latest news, that Philip was wandering in his mind and in a high fever, the old man muttered to himself: "It's that ass of a Dodds." Well, I know not how it happened: when the neighbors reached the village escorting the old man, they found the flags flying from all the houses that possessed flags and the big banner from the liberty-pole. By a spontaneous movement of sympathy everybody crowded into the street to welcome him, and some of the lads got into the belfry of the church and rang the bell as they always do on Fourth of July morning, and somebody fired the old cannon on the common. Philip Hadley was still in danger of death, but he was two miles away, and the people did not care to think of him, or if they did think of him, it was with the feeling that he richly deserved his punishment. He had ruined the life and broken the heart of the doctor's only daughter, and he had tried to steal his grandchild to get possession of her little fortune.

The doctor was serene as a May morning. He had

performed an ugly task, but it had been laid upon him, and he had not flinched. Now that he was at home again, however, his professional conscience began to work. He felt almost sure that Dodds by his blundering would let the fellow die; and now that justice had been meted out to him he did not wish him to die; indeed, he desired to save him. So one dark night, he stole down the Saw Mill Hollow road, and paid a clandestine visit to his precious son-in-law, whose bones he had so recently broken. Philip was still wandering in delirium and did not know him. The doctor of course decided that the treatment was all wrong, and in a day or two he arranged with Dodds, and openly took charge of the case; and so rapidly did he heal the wounds he had made that in two weeks Philip Hadley was on the road to health.

This thing was so characteristic of the doctor that it caused a great deal of laughter in the village. But there were other important consequences which grew out of this anomalous position of affairs. Philip Hadley, during his convalescence, professed great penitence, and made the doctor believe he was a changed man—that the drubbing he had received had been to him a means of spiritual grace and renewal. And when the doctor saw him off on the railway train he actually gave him a considerable sum of money to set himself up in morality and good behavior. The case against the doctor is what Jake Small calls "squashed." No one thinks less of him for what he did, and I am afraid he has risen in the estimation of many. "'Taint Christian doctrine, is it?" asked Mother Embery of the parson. "Scriptur' says, if you are smote on the right cheek you must turn the left." "Perhaps he isn't a Christian," returned the young clergyman thoughtfully, "but we must all admit that he is a fine old pagan."

CHAPTER XV.

THE BOY ALMIRA ADOPTED.

THESE spring evenings, when the light begins to linger on the growing grass pied with dandelions, and the buds to pout on the lilac bushes, the children play in the streets with unwonted vigor, and their sports take on an epic beauty and grace I never remark at any other time of year. Their choric dances are like pictures on old classic vases, and unconsciously they assume the most beautiful and unstudied attitudes, especially the little girls, when they throw off their hats and let the tresses float free on the wind. From all lanes and by-places come those sounds of children shouting, as much a part of the opening season as the cheep of nestlings or the great bum-boom of the bullfrog's bass-viol in the pond.

Now come into the fields, where the farmer's boy in the early plowing turns the rich brown furrow with a pair of red oxen. The sky is so soft and vaporous with broken lights and large luminous clouds, the humble scene appears to breathe the poetry of one of Millet's pictures. A black skurry of clouds comes over to drop a sudden sharp shower into the newly turned clod. Then it moves frowningly off, and the sky comes out in such dazzling bursts of splendor—the king-birds and thrushes shake the drops from their wings and trill forth in sudden ecstasy, until you deplore your own dumbness, and long to join in that chorus of nature: "Praise the Lord, O my soul, and all that is within me praise His holy name." A flash darts across the sky, and thunder cracks over the woods, and goes rumbling along Saddleback in a grand surly growl. It seems to shake the forest trees to their deepest roots, and to open the lids of the flowers with a start of surprise. The furrow is good and fructuous, and sheds abroad that terrene smell we notice on warm spring days, when the earth seems to purr with content.

In many parts of the country the farms are practically abandoned or leased to the Irish or to French Canadians. But it is not so here, where the land has come down through generations in unbroken lines of inheritance. The farmers are not all hurrying and eager to get rich. Some of them are content just to live along in comfort, making both ends meet as their fathers did. There is generally one son who is willing to stay on the old place, and sometimes it falls to a daughter's share to take the laboring oar and keep the ancestral farm in the family. There is a pretty walk to just such a farm through a piece of woods that lies not far from the town. These woods begin to look social again on a pleasant spring day. Their elegant openness gives one a new sense of light and space. They remind one of royal saloons in the grand old Italian palaces frescoed with the sky and heavenly bodies. No columns of porphyry or marble can exceed the beauty of the tree trunks spotted with moss and lichen and so richly colored and carved. It is good to get among them after a winter spent in the village streets. You feel as if you were moving into nature. The hepatica and wind-flower, and the trailing arbutus, betray themselves in spite of the brown leaves where they are hidden. Scrape away the rubbish and you will see where they are pushing up buds in knots and clusters. The waxy leaf buds that tip the twigs of forest trees are as yet very backward-looking. Cold spring storms come to repress all the aspirations of the growing world. But a delicate beauty clings to the first movements of spring, and lights familiar fields and hillsides with a gleam out of some new source of beneficence. The soft brown landscape mellows into smiles of greeting where it touches the blue of the sky. There is a clean, wholesome look about the world. Its face has been thoroughly washed, and all things are ready for a new revelation of beauty.

The old farm-house I mentioned stands near this woodland, where the villagers come in spring to search for arbutus. It stands close to the road, with a horse-trough a little way beyond under a wide-spreading balm of Gilead. The house is nearly a hundred years old. A long shed is attached to its southern side, and the gable is ornamented with an angel trumpeter surmounted by a vane, which has steadily pointed north-east for the last ten years. The ancient rooms are furnished much as they were at the beginning of this century. The old chairs, and tables, and presses, and chests of drawers are still intact. Braided mats and strips of rag carpet cover the floor. The high clock ticks in the corner of the sitting-room. The loom holds its place in the garret. A spinning-wheel and two little flax wheels are nicely kept in a chamber up stairs. All the bedrooms are furnished with high-post tested beds and dimity curtains trimmed with knotted fringe. The old brasses of the fireplace, the warming-pan, and the quaint bellows are all in place. The outer door still has those quaint holes furnished with flaps—a large one for the cat and a small one for the kitten. The ancient book-shelf is furnished with its pictorial Bible, its New England primer, Cotton Mather's "Magnalia," Michael Wigglesworth's "Day of Doom," the works of Jonathan Edwards, Baxter's "Saints' Rest," and the "Holy Living and Dying." The keeping-room has a few modern additions in the way of rugs and curtains to make it comfortable, but it is mainly unaltered. The front door, with its worn granite step, opens directly on a smooth unfenced bit of

Almira turf, with a little footpath trickling down to the wagon-track. A pleasing prospect lies before it of the lazy little river, the intervale, and distant hills.

This old house has come by direct inheritance into the possession of a fashionable city woman, who was married in the keeping-room on the very spot where her mother stood up to be married some twenty-five or thirty years earlier. It is the story of the mother chiefly which is interesting, for though the daughter is brilliant and attractive, she is not, so the old people in the village say, endowed with more than a tithe of her mother's talent.

Almira, as I will call her, was one of those maiden farmers who hereabouts occasionally take charge of the old place when there are no men folk left, or when, if there are, they prefer some other occupation. She had been brought up on the farm, and a few years away at school was all the change she had ever known. Almira was intensely, absorbingly pious, and at an early age, as she recorded in her journal, she determined that she would never marry, but would devote herself to the service of God and the education of the young. She let most of the land on shares, and then she took in a pair of decrepit relatives and kept them in comfort till they died. But this and the general management of the household did not interfere at all with the great object of her life, what she had called in her journal the education of the young. Teaching was Almira's absorbing love. It is acknowledged that she laid the foundation of the excellent school system of the town, and her name is still mentioned as that of the most remarkable woman this part of the country has produced. But her fame is purely local. It does not extend beyond the shadow of Saddleback.

Almira's studies went on with all her varied interests and occupations. She took a deep interest in the religious controversies of the day, and was listened to with much deference and respect by clergymen, many of whom were her friends. One winter, it is said, while studying Bible exegesis, she knit a large number of woolen stockings for the poor of the town, as she could contrive to turn the heels and toes by instinct without giving much heed to work. The little stone schoolhouse, resembling a juvenile penitentiary, where she began her teaching, was preserved for many years as a kind of relic of Almira. She opened and closed her school invariably with fervent prayer, and labored in season and out of season for the conversion of her pupils. She taught for some time in this jail-like building, until the fame of her great ability and acquirements caused her to be elected preceptress of the village academy. She fitted many youths for college, and her mathematical and Latin instruction, in those days, was considered second to none. Almira's pale, serious face was bordered by brown hair, brushed behind the ears with Puritan simplicity. Her dress was always severely plain in cut and make, her forehead high, expanded, and broad, was the home of a royal intellect. The girl had never been young. From her tenderest years she had been weighted with a sense of the awfulness of sin and the burdens of the moral law. In her eightieth year, for she lived to be a very old woman, she was really young, gentle, sportive, and possessed of a pleasant humor.

It was while Almira was still teaching in the stone school-house, that she chanced one day to meet a little lad of ten who was looking for some lost cows on the hill-side. He was a bright-faced, handsome boy, as she discovered in spite of his bare feet, patched trowsers, and torn straw hat. In his perplexity he had caught a "daddy long-legs," and with a country boy's formula was invoking its aid to discover the strayed cattle. He held the insect in his hand and said aloud, "Daddy, daddy, which way have the cows gone?" Thereupon daddy pointed with his feelers in the right direction, or was expected so to do.

Almira was pleased with the lad. When she questioned him he looked straight in her eyes, and answered with promptness. She found he was a charity boy "bound" to a neighboring farmer for five years. He had never received any schooling, indeed, was as ignorant as a little savage, both of science and the Westminster Catechism. This was a state of things Almira could not abide. She tried to induce his master to send him to school, but failing in this, she finally offered him a sum of money to break the indenture, that the boy Eben might be given up to her. In time she carried her point, and Eben was transferred to the old farm-house, where he became Almira's pupil and helper, indeed, her adopted child. She took hold of him with the joy such a woman feels in having a human being all her own to try her theories upon. At night, after school hours, he did "chores," drove the old horse, split the fire-wood, or with a feminine apron tied about his neck churned the butter. She brought him up in the strictest creed, instilling into him all the rigors of the Old Testament law, while she taught him all the profane learning she herself had mastered. She did her utmost to educate the boy as a model of learning and Christian character, and to consecrate him a chosen vessel to the service of the Lord. And if Eben did not take as kindly to theology as she wished, it was soon evident that he was the brightest boy in Almira's school. She fitted him for college at sixteen, and entered him at old Harvard. At a time when the college course was not as expensive as it is now it was no light task to pay all her boy's bills with the result of her school-keeping. Her colony of old people and poor relations at the farm had grown somewhat of late years, and the farm itself hardly paid expenses, having no energetic man at the fore.

But Almira worked on incessantly, taking no rest, glad to sacrifice health and strength for the boy Eben, and rejoicing in his brilliant progress. All his bills were promptly paid when he was graduated with flying colors at the end of four years; but Almira was older and more careworn than she ought to have been for a woman but a few years past the first corner of old maidenhood. Indeed, she looked upon herself then as an old woman. Eben had developed into a stalwart, handsome man, of great stature. He spent his vacations at home, and could mow in the hay-field, or break a wild colt, equal to any young farmer in the country. There was a profession to be thought of, and in spite of all Almira could say he decided against the ministry and chose the law. He worked his way through the law school by tutoring and the usual grind of student life.

It was during this period that Almira thought constantly of Eben's future and prayed over it not a little. With his brilliant parts and great promise, she saw the prizes of life ready to drop into his hand. He would live in a large town, mix with men of talent, and marry some charming girl and rear a family of children; and she would necessarily grow to be less and less to him, and at last drop out of his life. So she prayed for pure self-abnegation. Some of the most interesting human relations are like the delicate vapor of water, so unstable there is always danger of their turning to rain, or frost, or snow. They can not remain long in suspense, and it is while in suspense, like the rose-cloud of heaven turned toward the evening sun, that they are most beautiful. The thought that Eben was going from her was exceedingly painful to Almira in spite of her religion, which came in as a prop and stay, and she secretly formed the plan of looking out for another smart boy to educate. No girl could ever prove as satisfactory as Eben; she must take another boy.

It is said that the very day Eben left the law school with his parchment in his pocket he came straight home, and the very first thing he did was to offer his heart, hand, and prospective fortune to his benefactress. It seems he had been thinking of this for some years, while Almira had been praying for the strength to give him up. If the heavens had fallen, her consternation could not have been greater. She thought the boy had gone mad, and when he convinced her he was perfectly sane, and had long cherished the purpose of making her his wife, it is said that she boxed his ears roundly and turned him out of the house. But Eben came back, not once, but many times, determined to win her. There is a deeply-rooted belief in the human mind that any woman can be won by persistent effort, and, of course, Almira did yield in the end, although that boy Eben was twelve years her junior.

Nothing has ever made a stir in the village to be compared with the marriage of Almira and Eben. The only explanation she could give her friends was that she could not live without Eben because she had brought him up, and Eben vowed he would never see her again unless she would have him. It was a feeble excuse, every body felt, from a woman who had written solemnly in her journal at the age of sixteen that she should never marry, but devote her whole life to God and the education of youth. Almira would have despised any body else who might have made it. They were married at a certain spot in the keeping-room, just in front of the old fire-place, with its brass andirons, which on that day was full of apple-blossoms.

The village tried to adjust itself to a sense of its loss, the loss of its invaluable school-mistress, the cleverest woman ever " raised " in that part of the country. But they always felt she had taken a foolish step, and lowered herself from the high pinnacle of a perfect school ma'am, until Eben began to shine forth in the councils of the state and nation, and then a new theory was formed, which has lasted to this day—*i. e.*, that Eben's wife had made him; that she wrote all his speeches, and without her he never could have become a distinguished man.

To the imagination, of course, this marriage was not ideally perfect, but it turned out an ideal marriage all the same. The judge and senator revered his wife to the last day of his existence, and treated her with a mingled respect, deference, and affection beautiful to behold. Their home life was pointed out as a star-like example among the homes of the world. Almira began to grow young from the day she was wedded. Her children thought her the most delightful of beings. She softened her creed and added to the fullness and richness of her gowns. It was true she did *make* her husband. He was her creation, and he knew it.

Well, it was pretty in the daughter to come back to the old farm-house and be married on the exact spot in the keeping-room, the same day of the month, and the same hour, when her mother had stood up to marry Eben.

CHAPTER XVI.

ONE SPRING DAY IN HUGH'S LIFE.

HUGH has made up all his quarrels and differences with his neighbors, and as a result of this closing of the temple of Janus he is a little melancholy and low-spirited. Perhaps, however, it is nothing more than a disordered liver or a touch of spring fever. He has worked quite steadily most of the winter on his local history, which is now approaching completion, and will be published by subscirption during the year. With the opening of spring a restless wandering fit has seized the young man, and he starts off on what he calls round-about journeys, interminable rambles to the distant hills to find the first catkins and tree blossoms and listen to the earliest note of the wood thrush. In those deep solitudes he indulges in his Druidical worship of nature, and does not even care to have the young parson along.

Once or twice this spring he has taken Milly on a long mountain tramp, and Milly has carried with her the MS. volume of her father's poems and has read to Hugh the verses, " To a Lone Tree on Saddleback," sitting on a mossy log near where a spring trickles out just beneath the roots of an aged oak. The landscape lay soft as a dream below them in the blue and violet haze of early spring. They could hear the patter of sheep among the rocks and the cries of young lambs. I think Milly made up her difference with Hugh after the Rastus affair, when she found he had inserted a handsome notice of her father in the local history, blinking all the specks upon the man's character and making him shine as a poet and a gentleman.

He has also reconciled himself to Judge Magnus by stopping a runaway horse attached to the phaeton of the judge's wife; and the judge, in his gratitude to the young man for saving that excellent woman from injury, has forgotten all about the little unpleasantness which had separated them for over a year. Now Hugh again has the run of the house, and can make himself pleasant to the young lady visitors, can carry off books of reference from the library, and drop in any time to dinner or tea.

Now that almost everybody has tried a hand at settling Hugh and making a man of him, the judge thinks of taking hold of the job, and setting him up in a law office in the county town, where he can throw a great deal of business in his way. Poor Hugh has received the proposal almost like a warrant for his execution; and in order to indemnify himself for future privations, he now spends most of his time in those roundabout rambles of which I have spoken. He loiters about old fields and cow lanes in the mild urbanity of spring sunshine, hangs over bars and gates, sits and whittles on old stone walls, watches the frisky calves as they consort with their staid mothers, talks to the men who are mending the road, or goes and smokes with the quarrymen in Saw Mill Hollow. One of his favorite tramps is to Cedar Glen, where a little red school-house is situated, of which Hugh is uncommonly fond. It is a genuine country school, not graded, or degraded, by modern fashions, furnished with hacked benches and with walls defaced by successive generations of bad spellers. About a score of country urchins are gathered here during six months of the year—three months in the spring and three months in the fall. The school-mistress is not at all pretty, nor is she young. She has an acidulous voice and talks through her nose. Her hair is Titian-red, but the scholars do not admire it; they take it for just what it meant in the old days. Hugh likes her because she is a remnant of a past age. She keeps a bundle of birch switches hung upon the wall over her desk, and makes the urchins empty their pockets regularly every morning before the classes open. This juvenile *omnium gatherum* is almost as great a delight to Hugh as a collection of flint flakes and hatchets from the stone age.

He is sometimes allowed to sit on the visitors' bench and listen to the recitations, and he has picked up a lot of boys' compositions which he prizes highly. But Hugh disgraced himself the other day by laughing out in school at the wrong time, and there is danger of his corrupting the scholars by slyly giving them various small tips. The occasion of the disgrace was at a moment when the teacher happened to ask the history class, "Who was Xerxes?" and a boy's hand went up quick as lightning. He happened to be an inveterate stammerer, but his mind was so congested with accurate knowledge the words came tumbling out of his mouth pell-mell all together: " He was a gen-er-al—a very gre-gre-at gen-gen-er-al, but I d-d-don't 'member whether he f-f-fit for the Union or the 'fe-fe-federates."

The teacher gave Hugh a severe look, and he stumbled out of the school-house and allowed his laughter to explode in the soft spring air. Cedar Glen was so still no sound came to his ears, save the drone of children's voices through an open window of the school house and the caw of a solitary crow, hanging like a little black speck over a newly plowed field. Hugh made up his mind the next time he visited that school he would slyly reward the urchin who knew so much about Xerxes with a twenty-five-cent piece. He had secured a composition from Tim Long, the best composer in school, which he was reserving for a treat when he sat down to rest in some shady nook by the way.

Cutting across the hills that day, Hugh made a great

détour, and came out far below Burying-Ground Hill. But by sturdy walking, as the sun declined westward, he reached a little evergreen bower on the far side of the brook, where, through loopholes in the boughs, though himself well hidden, he fully commanded Lovers' Walk, and could see and hear all that passed on the other side of the stream. Hugh often resorted to this place; and he had made for himself a seat of stones, backed by the sturdy stem of an old oak. It had occurred to him that here, undiscovered, he could take a sly peep into the little romances of the village, but up to this moment nothing but the most prosy commonplace facts had ever leaked through the crevices of his bower.

Now Hugh, when he had comfortably stretched himself out to rest, drew forth Tim Long's composition. It was written in a terribly cramped hand, the worst schoolboy pot-hooks and hangers, on a soiled half-sheet of paper. Here it is:

"ON MY BROTHER TOM.

"I thot I would chose to rite about Tom 'cause they say he is a blood relation of mine on my father's side. Mothers as I've ben tole ain't no blood relations, but they is suthin nearer they is kin. Tom is a small boy a good sight smaller 'n I be but he feels awful big and sassy. When he got his new boots on he was jest ready to bust with innerd pride. You ort to see Tom when he is choke full of importance. It would make you sick. There ain't no more disgustin' sight than a small one horse boy as don't respeckit older folks. Tom don't respeckit me as he ort. He don't look up to me wuth a cent. When I want to put my chores off on Tom, as is proper, so as I can play ball with the older fellers, Tom he don't see as how he ort to look up to me and mind 'bedient, but he runs to tell mother and she bein' no blood relation only nearest of kin ginerally takes his part. I think there is no more disgustin' sight than a small boy as runs to his ma or his pa to tell on a big feller like me. I never did it 'cause how I was the oldest brother of the fambly. They say in the Sunday-school as how brothers ort to love each other. I should love Tom a great sight more if he respeckit me as he ort. This is all I can think of to say about my brother Tom only he had mumps and measles one winter and had to take nasty-tasted stuff. I didn't ketch mumps and measles. When I do ketch 'em an' have to take nasty doctor's stuff—Tom won't be very sorry. He won't go round all day with his finger in his eye. He's a hard-hearted little chap is Tom. This is all about Tom except as he has got a bull-pup as can siccum jest like an old dorg."

Hugh had been enjoying this composition in the shade of the cedars, when who should stray down "Lovers' Walk" that delicious spring afternoon, actually hand-in-hand, like a pair of babes in the woods, but Rose Madder and the young artist, Mr. Hubert Milletseed, who won so much glory last season by drawing Jake Small's eccentric domicile. He carried Rose's hat on his arm half-filled with ferns and spring flowers, and his eyes were turned on the down-cast orbs of the young lady impressionist in a way to show how true it is that—

"In the spring a young man's fancy lightly turns to thoughts of love."

He has come back to the village and taken up his abode for another season, and it is now known that Mr. Milletseed recommended Rose Madder to Peckham when she secured the studio over the grocery store. He has turned out to be an old friend. Milletseed is poor but courageous. He has worn the same artist's coat and slouched hat—which gives him the air of a retired bandit—for several years. Rose is also very poor. But two poverties when united make only one. Thus there is a distinct mathematical gain in getting married. Between them they can save the hire of one studio. He will always have some one to pose for him without paying a model by the hour. He will also secure a life-long admirer of his pictures, who will enter into all his artist's quarrels, condole with him when his works are badly hung in the exhibitions, and sympathize with the most secret sentiment of his breast, the belief that he is unappreciated.

Rose, on her part, will always now have some one at hand to know at once when she makes a good pose, and gets into a proper light, and becomes effective about the hair and eyes. Moreover, he likes those puffed elbow-sleeves, and big hats, and skimpy skirts embroidered with distracted landscapes and flights of birds. He sees a great deal, too, in those pathetic bits of mullein stalk and thistle-head stuck up on the sage-green Canton flannel curtain in Rose's studio. He thinks she has improved since she began to sketch the wayside weeds of the village under a white cotton umbrella. Milletseed can see the divine in a thistle-head as easily as in a whole Yosemite Valley. And oh, what sketching excursions they will take together in the blissful time to be, when one white umbrella, if large enough, can be made to answer for two! They were talking softly of even more blissful things than these as they passed down Lovers' Walk.

Hugh was the first to discover the pretty secret, and it made him rather blue there in his little tent of closely woven evergreen branches. Rose had gone from him. All the nice, desirable girls, to whom he had been impartially attentive, would be taken from him. Like *Ko-Ko*, he would at last be forced to wed—

"A most unattractive old thing
With a caricature of a face"—

perhaps the Titian-red-headed school-mistress at Cedar

Glen. He felt savage toward Milletseed for taking Rose away from him, yet never for a single moment had he thought seriously of wedding Rose Madder.

The unexpected always happens, and as Mrs. Deacon Hildreth says, " Things happen in a bunch." Hugh had scarcely roused himself from his somber mood, as he watched the birds carrying sticks and straws to their nests, conscious that he had too long neglected to build his own nest, when his attention was attracted by the sound of a man's step crunching the little stones of Lovers' Walk, and the heels of a light womanly pair of boots clicking in unison. Suddenly at a little turn in the path appeared Mr. Worldly Wiseman in spotless dress, looking down with a happy air of ownership on the eldest Miss Bee, that nice, practical, utilitarian girl, who had been especially selected for his (Hugh's) wife. She was clad in a new spring costume, and wore a large bunch of yellow flowers in her hat, while her hands were filled with hot-house roses, the gift of Mr. Wiseman. Great heavens! it was now plain Mr. Worldly Wiseman had not been after the middle Bee, that decorative maiden assigned to him by common rumor, but had cast his eyes upon the eldest sister, set off and apportioned to Hugh if he cared to put forth his hand and take her. In regard to the unfortunate affair of the serenade, a reconciliation had been brought about through the kindly offices of the old miller. Mr. Worldly Wiseman lost no time in bringing the affair to a business-like conclusion. It has turned out that Miss Bee always admired that fine place on Main Street, and has had an ambition to light a candle in our social world that shall outshine the wax taper of Mrs. Judge Magnus. As to Mr. Worldly Wiseman himself, she says girls can't be quite so particular when they have passed the age of twenty-five.

This new revelation left Hugh quite stunned and dazed. Two of his old flames had been taken from him, and in the case of Mr. Worldly Wiseman, he felt like at once sending that gentleman a challenge. To be sure, two other delightful Bees remained unappropriated, and there were many other uncaught fish in the sea, but the sense of injury still remained and rankled in his breast. The climax of the afternoon, however, was yet to be reached, and it brought Hugh back to his usual exuberance of spirits. It was the most delicious little mystery, and the clew was thrown into his hands like a ball tossed accidentally over the fence.

For, coming down Lovers' Walk, in the soft spring checker-work of light and shade, he saw no other than Drusilla, the village's only and own Drusilla, dressed in her usual brown stuff gown, with the strings of her bonnet untied and floating on the breeze. She looked quite flushed and handsome in spite of her avoirdupois and the strictly business air she carried into all the affairs of life. Beside her walked a tall, black-habited thin-chested clerical person, with long hair combed very sleek behind his ears, and a prominent pair of eye-glasses. He appeared weak about the lungs, and stooped slightly as he peered into his companion's face, with an anxious, deferential, beseeching look. He had put his hand under Drusilla's elbow, although she in her abounding vigor could easily have picked him up from off the ground. They were in deep and earnest confab, and Hugh, hidden behind the clump of evergreens, could not help hearing a few words that passed between them:

"I can not desert my mother while she lives, and she is now too old to leave her home."

"I would not ask it, dearest Drusilla; we will both stay beside her and soothe her declining years."

These were the words Hugh heard: "Dearest Drusilla!" He rolled over on the moss and dead leaves, and nearly choked in the effort to suppress his laughter; and as the evening shadows gathered, he crept out of his bower and took his way home with his old spirit of mischief all in arms. In a few days Hugh had gathered as much information about Drusilla's little romance as she herself possessed. For a long time the village looked upon it as an impossible joke. Drusilla being a rich woman, of course malicious things are said. The consumptive-looking thin-chested parson is now out of a parish, and is much in need of a nurse. To Drusilla a husband will be only another bond slave and subject menial. She is already regulating the diet, in fact, the whole course of her *fiancé's* existence, on her own theory of hygiene. He will henceforth only be allowed to eat each day so many ounces of highly nutritious brain food. Drusilla has ordered in dumb-bells and a lifting-machine. She intends that he shall lift so many pounds morning and evening until he can heave a thousandweight. The mild cigar he was want to smoke in the evening, rather under the rose, has been sternly prohibited. The tea and coffee which, as a man of studious habits, he has always taken in considerable quantities, have been interdicted. He is not to drink any thing but hot water, quarts of hot water, deadly hot—hot enough in fact to scald his midriff. His meat is weighed out to him, just so much a meal, and no attention is paid to his sensations of hunger or thirst. He is obliged to eat gluten bread, a dreadful compound which Drusilla sends for to a neighboring town. Saint Patty is rather glad Drusilla has taken up a new reform in the shape of a prospective husband, as it leaves the dear old lady more freedom to indulge her own individual weaknesses. She likes the Rev. Arthur Meeker, and calls him, with a sly little laugh, "Drusilla's tame cat." She rather hopes that after they are married and Meeker gets plump and well on Drusilla's system of training, he may assert himself and put down his domestic tyrant.

Of course Drusilla will not abdicate as village manageress when she marries. Her great mind is equal to half-a-dozen villages,—and shall I venture to say it?—several husbands. Our young clergyman now hopes that, as Drusilla has a parson of her own, she will let him alone. But he hopes against all probability. As soon as the presence of Mr. Meeker was accounted for, and Drusilla's romance made known, every body was saying, "Where did Drusilla pick him up?" Hugh alone has ferreted out the whole story, and he chuckles over it, and keeps it to himself to tantalize the neighbors.

It seems that some months ago Drusilla was taking a night journey alone on a river steamboat, when a collision occurred in the darkness of the early morning, and a large hole was stove in the steamer's side. The wildest confusion ensued at once among the distracted passengers, but Drusilla was up and fully dressed, bag and bundle in hand. In the dark saloon where the lamps had gone out a man ran against her crying piteously, "Who will show me how to put on my life preserver?" "I will," said Drusilla, with promptness and dispatch, although in the dim light she could scarcely see his face. She buckled on his life preserver, helped him to gather his things, and finally assisted him into the boat which took them off from the sinking steamer. He confessed to Drusilla that he was nearly scared to death, but she was perfectly cool and collected, and showed no nervous tremors on the occasion. Rev. Arthur Meeker someway believed Drusilla had saved his life. She was just the prop and support he had long been seeking; and Drusilla—well, Drusilla after all is a woman.

CHAPTER XVII.

THE HELP QUESTION AT FRASER FARM.

PEACE over the farm lands, peace in the deep valleys, peace in the forest, where scarce an opening leaf stirs in the wind. The pale spring dawn is breaking over the still world, and the light spreads faint and tremulous on the trunks of the trees and blanches the sky to a pure white pallor. The young blossoms coming out in the orchards and gardens seem a part of the pearly, dew-bespangled whiteness of the dawn. The stars glide back into infinite depths. The walking ghosts, if there be any, flee to the graveyard. The village houses look into each other's curtained eyes like strangers. The farms on the distant hillsides come out in luminous patches. The mist rolls up from the river, making a long, milky serpent, as it winds through the valley, solid like marble. The flowers open their cups, and the grass glistens faintly. Still it is a silvery world, strangely denuded of color, though clear and solemn. Hark! there is a bird singing a solo. It is a catbird; it balances itself on the top of a young maple and sings until all the place about seems flooded with delicious melody.

Now the sun is fairly up, and has dipped its beam as low as Fraser's Farm on the intervale, where the white veranda shines eastward with a pleasant invitation to enter. Fraser's is one of the best farms hereabouts, and Fraser himself is very forehanded. To be sure, he is somewhat bent, and looks older than he ought to for a man of his years. But the soil in our part of the world takes toll of youth and good looks in return for the gift of good harvests and independence. Fraser has much fine imported stock in his pastures. He went into choice cattle-raising before it became the fashion, and his stock-barns and yards have long been a show for the village. Fraser went to California during the gold fever, but he found there was more money in farming than in gold digging, and he came home and invested what he had saved in his parental acres on the intervale, to which he has largely added in the course of years.

He did not marry young, and when he chose a wife he took a town-bred woman, who has proved more practical and efficient than most country girls. She is buxom, cheerful, and merry, a real lover of country life, and not averse to the management and work of the farm. She loves flowers, books, and music, and has aimed to blend the enjoyments of her early girlhood with the inevitable cares of her married state. Her children are still young. The boys can not yet be of any service to their father, and the little girls are only just beyond babyhood. The labor problem is the vexed question in this prosperous household, as in so many others. Farm life is somewhat easier for the farmer's wife than of old, for the milk is now sent to the creamery. There is no making of butter or cheese save for the family. But with the heats of summer come haying and harvesting and a great increase to the household. The farmer can obtain his extra hands when he wants them, but the farmer's wife finds herself overburdened with a multitude of new cares, and often no helper can be obtained for love or money.

The American-born country girl seldom goes out to service now, or if she does she is comparatively worthless. She is generally a frail creature, with a weak chest, who can do no heavy work. She must sit at the family table and "eat with the rest of the folks," and she not unfrequently addresses the head of the house, with easy familiarity, as "John" or "Henry." She has a beau who comes to take her out riding in a smart new buggy once or twice a week, and she dresses a great deal better than her mistress. Camp-meetings, picnics, and platform dances come in to disturb the mind of the rustic American maid. She stipulates that she is not to milk or wash, or do any heavy lifting. Besides, she expects to get married soon and has gone out to service mainly for the purpose of making up her wedding clothes on the family sewing machine. She is unhealthy and eats little but pie and pickles. She wears a rose in her hair, and a hole in her stocking, and when she goes out to pick peas she puts on a small hat and a nose veil. She reads the *Ledger* and the *Family Newspaper* up in her bedroom by a smoky kerosene lamp, and she principally dotes on pop-corn balls, prize packages of candy, soda water, and one plate of ice-cream with two spoons. Her biscuits are speckled, like Cairngorm pebbles; her bread is of a grayish white, solid as lead and warranted to keep in all climates. Her fried steak and boiled coffee are enough to make St. Jerome get up and use mildly profane language to his old toothless lion.

Mrs. Fraser knows all about American "help" in several of her moods and most of her tenses. When the American "help" has done her best to imbitter Mrs. Fraser's sunny temper, and to spoil her sweet reasonableness, and when she has summarily got rid of the latest specimen, she tells her husband that she is going to do the work alone for a time, or with Uncle Hiram's help, and her eyes sparkle and her cheeks are quite rosy with excitement. She is so happy to have done with the "help" she goes singing all over the house, and the way the windows fly open, and the beds are shaken, and the rooms swept and dusted, is quite delightful to behold. Mrs. Fraser renews her youth. She forgets that she possesses a back or ever had a touch of neuralgia in the head. Uncle Hi, too, shares in the excitement of what he calls "the great clearing out sale of American help." Uncle Hi is perhaps a distant relative of John Fraser. At any rate, he has lived with him a great many years, refusing wages, and letting Fraser and his wife buy his clothes for him, and even provide him with tobacco. Uncle Hi is such a delightful oddity, the farm people think if he had not been born it would have been necessary to invent him. He is a plain little man, with a queer face full of puckers that slowly fill with sunshine when he laughs; and a humorous quip comes as naturally to the end of his tongue as a rose to the tip of its stalk. Uncle Hi seldom wears a "boiled" shirt except on Sunday. Other days he appears in flannel, with a bright blue gingham necktie, which exactly matches the color of his eyes. He is scrupulously, charmingly clean, like a marigold or a hollyhock. His hands are big, knotty, malformed by labor, exaggerated at the joints, brown as a berry, with a little white hairiness about them, but they are the best and kindest hands in the world. Children love the feel of them. Uncle Hi has brought up all the Fraser children thus far—has rocked them to sleep many a night in his arms, when the mother was ailing and the father tired out with a hard day's work; has even taken them all away to his own chamber, which is just as odd and just as scrupulously clean as Uncle Hi himself is, where he tells the children those marvelous, impossible tales that make the eyes bulge out of their heads, while they suck in their breath with a sound of awesome delight. He has a world of sentiment in his soul. Up in that queer chamber, as in a museum, he has preserved mementoes of the children's babyhood—little shoes and broken playthings. He has so many things of the little one who died Mary can scarcely ever bring herself to go in there.

Such is Uncle Hiram, the farm stand-by. Mrs. Fraser says if every thing else fails, she knows Uncle Hi and the ice crop can be depended upon. As soon as the last "help" moves out Uncle Hi moves in. Fraser has only to say to him, "Mary wants you," and he drops his hoe or his scythe and starts for the house. They begin by shoveling the débris of the last domestic out of the kitchen. Then they sweep and scrub and finally put on the fine touches. Mary is happy, and Uncle Hi is full of his odd sayings. He sticks that last help's character as full of jokes as a toilet cushion is full of pins. Mrs. Fraser has been wonderfully helped over the rough places of life by Uncle Hi's fun, and he almost enjoys having the " help clear out " so that he can cheer up Mary.

When the house has been cleaned from top to bottom Hiram brings in blossoms, cherry and apple blossoms in the spring, and Mary embowers the chimney-pieces, and every thing looks so bright and charming she is in love with her home, feeling that once more it is her own. She brews delicious tea and coffee, and the warm bread and feathery cakes come sweet and fragrant out of the oven. All the cookery smells good, and is so appetizing the men and children eat more than they otherwise would. So it goes on for a time until Mary breaks down with one of her neuralgic headaches, and Uncle Hi "goes off his head." Without her he can do nothing. He is only high private; never was born to be captain, so he says. He must always be under somebody, and as he loves Fraser and his wife and the children, he is glad to be under them. So when Mary is ill the web flies out of the frame, as it did with the Lady of Shalott, and Fraser is quite lost. Of course, help must be got into the house.

Mrs. Fraser has tried the Irish in all their phases. Uncle Hi says if Gladstone had as much practical experience of the Irish home rule as they have had on their farm, he would know a thing or two. A raw Irish maid on a farm is rather a queer animal. Although Ireland has always been an agricultural country, she has but the slightest conception of the use of implements and the meaning of rustic processes and procedure. Her propensity to blunder causes her to put the cart before the horse until she has painfully been taught better. There is a certain good humor about her which makes it pleasanter to have her in the house than the hysterical gum-chewing American " help." But she is always " kilt entirely " by the deadly loneliness of the place. She sees nothing companionable in nature. The sound of the bull-frogs and the cheep of the birds at sunset bring no hallowed associations with the bogs and the bog-trotters of her native Erin. If there is an Irish hired hand on the place, she may console herself a little chaffing him in the stable or in the garden. She does not spend as much time as her American sister crimping her hair or reading the *Ledger* in bed, but she must attend the Roman Catholic church, distant three miles, at least once every Sunday. The man is obliged to drive her over, while the master stays at home from church and does his chores, and the mistress works hard all the morning to cook the Sunday dinner and have it nice and hot by the time Bridget and Patrick return.

The graces, especially the goddess of handiness did not stand by and bless the cradle when the average Irish maid was born. Her work lacks finish, and has that raggedness, which sets the teeth of a nice housekeeeper on edge. Her bedclothes are pitchforked on to the bed, her tablecloth is awry. The glass and the knife stand on the wrong side of the plate. The soup plates are brought on when dessert plates should be handed. The clothes are ironed wrong side out. The night-shirts are starched and the day shirts left limp. All the photographs are put upside down on the chimney-piece. The best vase is fractured and the cracked side put to the wall, in hope the mistress may not see it. The crockery soon begins to look as if it had been along with the bull in the china shop. Every thing in the house feels the heavy hand of the fair maid of Erin. She breaks the stove-covers and smashes the flat-irons. She wrenches the clothes-horse apart opening it the wrong way. The dog is given his dinner in the best glass preserve dish. There isn't a sound chair left to sit on. Her lovely countenance cracked the looking-glass before she had been in the house a week. But she is a good-natured creature, and there is much in her to like, only, as Uncle Hi says, it is necessary to turn her adrift or the house would be hopelessly wrecked. It takes a year to replace what he calls her " tare and tret."

Well, Mrs. Fraser has tried the German maiden, that slow, flaxen-haired, ox-eyed fraulein. She came one summer day in a woolen cap and a thick jacket fastened with clumsy metal buttons, and carrying an old country carpetsack of immense weight. She was the most peaceable and the most quietly obstinate person in the world. She loved animals and would have been happy to spend all her time among the calves, and pigs, and cows. She had no objection to a lonely situation, and being a Protestant, was quite indifferent to church services. Her plodding, quiet, patient nature would have been invaluable on the farm but for an ineradicable tendency to greasy cooking and the onion flavor. Her baked beans swam in oil ; even her fruit-pies bore the effluvia of garlic. Uncle Hiram, who is a mystic worshiper of the New England national dish, has adapted a sentimental stanza to describe the fragrance of Gretchen's culinary art :

"You may break, you may shatter the dish if you will,
But the scent of the onion will cling round it still."

So Gretchen, with all her stolid virtues and negative excellences, had to go, and Mrs. Fraser and Uncle Hiram, having cleaned the house as usual, and made themselves happy with the blessed consciousness that they owned the premises, and were free for the moment from the plague of hired servants, began to look in the newspapers for one of those companionable, nice, educated women who advertise their grateful services in return for a home and a modest stipend. Such a reduced lady they thought would at least have nice refined ways. She would never leave kitchen and cellar in the condition of a pigsty, and her cooking, if she did any, would be dainty and delicate. It would be pleasant to take in a companionable person, who loved the country for its own sake, and could find something social in nature when human society was not at hand. They would make her quite at home. Mary Fraser, who is rather imaginative, pleased herself picturing a decayed gentlewoman whom she could make her friend; how pleasant to do the work together, and then to sit down and read some congenial book in company.

So, after looking over a great many advertisements of ladies in search of a country home, who would be glad to take a position as housekeeper, Mrs. Fraser entered into correspondence with some of them, and the result was that on a beautiful May day Uncle Hiram drove the lady help and her trunk over from the village. This decayed gentlewoman was of an uncertain age, occupying the debatable ground somewhere between thirty and fifty. But as she was well made up, with false hair and teeth, and a suspicion of rouge on her cheek-bones, time's ravages did not count for so much. She wore a large bustle and quite a gay hat, and appeared to be supplied with considerable jewelry for a person in distressed circumstances. She was painfully ungrammatical, as Mary noticed at once, and her little dream of self-culture in company with the new assistant tumbled into dust.

The next morning she came down with her bustle and her jewelry on, as if she were a guest in the house. Mrs. Frazer, in her clean gingham gown and freedom from jewelry, cosmetics, and cheap perfumery, began to feel herself quite put in the shade by the new-comer. Mary watched the effect she produced on the other members of the family. They all called her Miss Pinchback, and Uncle Hiram, she could see, brushed his hair up a little more on top of his head, and even John Fraser thought he must be more particular about his dress when he came in to meals. Miss Pinchback, in her rings and bangs, offered to work the day after her arrival, and the mistress of the house set her to dusting rooms and making beds. But in the middle of the forenoon Mary found the beds unmade. Miss Pinchback was lonely, and had gone out to talk with the men. In less than two days she knew every male creature for quite a circuit round; and in her frank devotion to the other sex she soon began to ignore the mistress of the house. She waved her handkerchief out of window to the butcher, and blew kisses to the peddler, and kept the hired man from his work, hanging over the gate to talk to him. She followed Uncle Hi all about the place, and insisted on driving off with him in the farm-wagon when he went to the store or the mill. Uncle Hi, modest old bachelor that he was, said he didn't like Pinchback's free ways, but it was evident to Mary Fraser that the simple soul was rather flattered by her attentions.

One day the mistress of the house had occasion to step out into the barn, and there she saw Pinchback, in all her finery, sitting on an overturned bushel basket, and talking very amicably to John Fraser; as she said, making great eyes at him. John was leaning on his pitchfork, looking at the woman with some curiosity, and it must be confessed not without a certain air of interest. Still, like Uncle Hi, he has always said he could not bear the sight of her. Well, Mrs. Fraser did a very unreasonable thing for a woman who declares she never has felt a twinge of jealousy in her life. She stole back home and sat down in the rocking-chair and shed a few bitter tears. She resolved that Pinchback should leave the house that day, but how to get rid of her was the question. She resolved to search her room for a clew to those nice, lady-like letters she had received from town signed with her name, for she had discovered that Miss Pinchback wrote a villainous hand and spelled like a Hottentot. It was while searching her chamber that Mrs. Fraser discovered quite unexpectedly a few of her own possessions—her mother's wedding ring, a locket with the picture of her little boy who died, and various pieces of wearing apparel marked with her name. Miss Pinchback went away quite suddenly that afternoon, and since that time Mrs. Fraser has been a strong advocate for the introduction of Chinese cheap labor.

CHAPTER XVIII.

THE DELIGHTFUL MAJOR.

THE cherry trees are already casting down little showers of white petals every time the wind sways them. They snow down into the grass and drift in the ruts of the road. The gnarled apple trees in some neglected orchards of natural fruit are bossed all over their warty arms with bright nosegays. If you search in the grass beneath you will find clusters of deep blue violets mixed with buttercups and dandelions.

Every hour brings out something to admire along the village street. The maples are casting down their pale green and bright red keys. The poplars are shedding fringy blossoms. In every flower-bed something is abloom ; here the lily of the valley ; there the hyacinth and bright tulip ; over the wall daffodils, jonquils, and snow-drops. The past few days have spread a tent of gauzy green over the street, and brought the delicious sense of virginal freshness, peaceful growth, and expansion conveyed in the odors of plants, and the cooing of doves in the sun, the clucking of hens, the peep of young birds, the skimming of swallows as they wheel about old barns and make slim shadows on the sunny ground.

I think of dear Major B. now, when the trees are in blossom and the door-yard shrubs are out in their glory. He was as fresh and breezy as the lilacs, as full bloom as the peonies, as innocent as the snow-balls, and as welcome as the new-mown grass. You ought to have seen him in his white waistcoat—he always preferred a white waistcoat when the day was the least warm—twirling his little cane and dangling his eye-glass. He nearly ruined himself in gold eye-glasses and white waistcoats, but they were his only vices. He did not drink, or smoke, or use profane language, except in moderation, and yet the major had seen much rough service on the frontier. He was almost as expansive as the judge—not quite, perhaps, in the way of omniscience—and his self-conceit was less aggressive. He loved so artlessly to be admired, his vanity was like that of a young, kittenish woman.

You should have seen him engaged in controversy with the judge as they strolled together down the village street, taking up all the sidewalk. The judge's right hand grasped his gold-headed cane in the middle and performed all kinds of figures and flourishes in the air. The major's hand clutched the hook of his little cane and performed an equal variety of extraordinary antics. Their voices were both loud and penetrating, and as they strolled along much of their talk flew into open doors and windows. Except for a great hearty laugh which burst forth now and then, the people would have thought they were quarreling.

The major was strenuous on the increase of the United States Army. That a great and glorious country like ours should be represented by a mere handful of regulars seemed to him the result of the most shameful cheese-paring policy. The judge, on the other hand, contended that large standing armies are a menace to a free government, and backed his opinion by quoting familiarly from Senator This and Governor That. He even cited the head of the government on this subject, intimating that the great man had, in a moment of confidence, said things to him he never would have spoken to any other human being. The major, on the other hand, had seen service, had smelt gunpowder, sir, and heard the bombs and cannon balls whizzing about his head. He had the proper military contempt for the opinion of any civilian, however high in place and power.

Hotly as the contest might rage over this moot point, the major never failed to see the pretty face of village maid or matron if one chanced to appear at a window or on the street ; and he would dart away from the side of the judge or whoever he happened to be engaged with at the moment, to investigate the phenomenon a little nearer. " You know," he would say apologetically, and with the most perfect candor and naïveté, " I have been so long away on the frontier among the Indians, where the women are all hideous, I am starved for the sight of female loveliness. It isn't my fault that I was made a devotee of beauty. I do not drink drams or smoke expensive cigars, but I must occasionally indulge my penchant for the sight of a pretty woman."

The fact that the major was starving for the sight of female loveliness, because he had been so long on the frontier among the Indians, went all over the village, and was commented on by the gossips with varying degrees of spite, acrimony and uncharitableness. A few saw its humorous side, and judged that the major was perfectly simple and guileless. Others remarked that having no female beauty at home, he was forced to enjoy the sight of it where he could. The poor major contended that he was just what God had made him, and not personally responsible. Some men are fond of music, others have a passion for painting and sculpture ; for his part he worshiped the living art that lies in the ruby lip, the rosy cheek, the sunny locks of adorable womankind. Most of the pretty girls and handsome matrons came in time to take the major's part. They judged rightly that there was no harm in the creature, and certainly he was very amusing. No wonder he was a little weak in the upper story, having lived so long among the Indians, poor thing. They voted not to mind his monkey-shines, but to get as much enjoyment out of him as they could.

The major's wife was a tiny woman, coming just up to his shoulder, not, in fact, a bit higher than his heart. She was undeniably pale and plain, except for a pair of soft brown eyes and a trim little figure, which was itself a kind of beauty. She always dressed in dark shades of gray or slate, in a little straight skirt and a small tight-fitting jacket. Her hats were devoid of the least ornament. No touch of brightness came to their monotonous mouse-color—not a bud or flower even in the spring, when all nature is so exuberant. It was certain the major could not find local color in his *ménage* save what he provided in his own florid person. And yet how he loved it! No man ever adored beauty as he did. Why had he chosen this little gray mate, who beside him looked like a tiny ground-bird beside some tropical songster?

There were always three little care lines in the middle of her forehead, and she commonly looked as if she were mentally calculating the amount of the week's washing, or doing some other little domestic economy sum in her head. The major's white waistcoats, and gloves, and canes had to be paid for out of rather a small income, and this was no doubt one reason why the major's wife dressed in slate-color. She was soon known all over the village as "Hetty," for thus the major habitually spoke of her, and when he was not talking of his great deprivations among the Indians, and the criminally absurd condition of the United States Army, he generally did talk of Hetty. Sometimes he met the little woman face to face, when he was escorting a whole bevy of pretty girls on a walk, and was up in the seventh heaven of bliss. It is rather trying to be confronted by one's lawful better-half at such a moment, but the unembarrassed major was always equal to the situation. "My dearest Hetty," he would cry out, "where are going in the heat (or the damp, as the case might be)? You ought to be at home this minute, taking care of your sciatica." Mrs. Hetty's sciatica became another village joke. She did not at all take good care of it. When she met her husband and the girls in this manner she was generally going with some little comfort in her hands to visit a sick child or a poor, tired woman. Probably because she had a fancy for paying these little visits to humble folks and leaving a thin wake of light behind her, was another reason why Hetty always dressed in that old slate-colored gown.

The major's wife had one great friend and advocate in the village. There was at least one person who believed in her wholly, and sounded her praises among the neighbors who seldom saw any thing in her to admire. This discerner of spirits was old Dr. Rivington. He became almost as fond of Hetty as if she had been his own child. But in proportion as he admired her he disliked the poor major. The æsthetic side of the doctor's nature not having been well developed, he could not appreciate the cruel privations the major had suffered among the Indians, nor the necessity for indemnifying himself which the major so keenly felt. When he would pass some village house where the major's loud frank voice came through the open window, mingled with the laughter of girls, the doctor would grasp his knotted stick, and look tremendously fierce and pugilistic. He wanted to make the fellow who neglected such a gem of a wife feel the weight of that bit of oak, he said to himself, as he strode on his way.

Of course every body talks in a small village, and soon there came to be floating specks and wisps of gossip all through the air about the major and Sibyl Pringle. Miss Pringle was one of those handsome, rather wild and fearless maidens, who have a faculty for getting themselves talked about in country society. She had been engaged to a young man who was obnoxious to Pringle, apparently for no other reason but because old Pringle was an obstinate, hard-bitted old man, who had contrived to make the most of his large family of children quite miserable while they remained at home. Sibyl, at her father's command, had broken the engagement, but on good ground it was supposed that she was still secretly attached to the man she had sent away. Owing to her disappointment, perhaps, Sibyl had grown rather reckless, and unmindful of appearances, and did things the staid village matrons who had outgrown all their young impulses and errant fancies, looked upon askance. Miss Sibyl was decidedly handsome, with large black flashing eyes and a damask rose complexion. She was a style of beauty the major particularly admired, although being a distinguished connoisseur of female loveliness, he enjoyed any thing good of its kind—a golden blonde almost as much as a sparkling brunette. Old man Pringle took an unaccountable fancy to the major. He liked his bold martial air, and felt his house honored by the visits of a military man. Miss Sibyl, too, was evidently pleased to receive him, and the major's hearty voice was heard issuing from the cracks of the Pringle mansion more frequently than from any other, and the major's martial form was seen escorting Sibyl Pringle up and down the street in open daylight, quite without shame, as the people said who peeped from their windows in hope of catching their neighbors in the commission of sin.

Of course the major's wife could see a great deal for herself if she kept her eyes open. But there were kind people who felt it their duty to inform her of what was said in certain houses in the village, and one day on coming home from a delightful stroll with Sibyl through Burying-Ground Walk, the major found his wife prostrate on the sofa, suffering from sciatica or something worse. She may have been crying; at any rate, her eyes looked suspiciously red. She was a gentle little woman, and long suffering, as we know, but now she opened her batteries upon the major without giving him time to look to his ammunition. She laid the terrible charge directly at his door of paying entirely too much attention to Sibyl Pringle. He had set the neighbors talking and destroyed his wife's peace of mind. The poor major was terribly scandalized. He felt his honor as an officer and a gentleman impugned, and his first impulse was to go out and shoot somebody; some one of those gossiping people who had allowed their tongues to wag to the injury of Hetty's peace. "Haven't I told you," he exclaimed, "that a beautiful woman is no longer a person to me? She is a cult, a worship. Think of Dante and his blessed Beatrice. In certain moods of the mind she becomes an abstraction," he went on, waving his hand as he stood over Hetty, prostrate there on the sofa. "I have convinced you, Hetty, how crude it is to cherish a feeling of jealousy."

"Then I am crude," moaned the major's little wife, "and I don't believe that Pringle girl is one bit more of an abstraction than I am."

"Hetty, Hetty, you are as suspicious as these backbiting neighbors; and you know very well how long I was obliged to endure the sight of those hideous Ind—"

"Oh, don't mention *them*," choked Hetty. "I wish we were out there now, away from this dreadful Pringle girl with all the village folk tattling. I wish you had to look at squaws for the remainder of your life."

The major picked up his little wife from the state of moral and physical collapse into which she had fallen, and he contrived to make it up with her, and to convince her that she had been very much in the wrong, while he on his part promised to observe a little more discretion in the pursuit of his devotions at the shrine of female beauty.

But things went on much the same as ever. The exuberant major escorted the ladies with strict impartiality, but he did not entirely discontinue his visits to Sibyl Pringle, because it would look too marked after all that had been said ; and besides old Pringle kept inviting him to come to his house. The people watched Hetty, and they were at a loss to know whether to admire or to despise her, when they saw that she went about her little affairs quite unconcerned.

However, one morning in mid-May, when the trees were out nearly in full leaf, there was a great commotion in the village. Sibyl Pringle had disappeared on the previous day. She had taken a ticket on the railroad to the county town to do some shopping, promising to return at night, and the discovery had been made later that all her clothes had disappeared. The major, it turned out, also was missing. He had hired a horse at the village livery-stable, and leaving it at the next station to be sent back, had also taken the train. In a few hours news was brought to Hetty that the major had eloped with Sibyl Pringle. The depot stage was passing at the moment, and Hetty hailed it, and hastily tying on her bonnet with cold, trembling fingers, she put herself in the vehicle, and rode over to the station. There she found old Pringle telegraphing for news of his lost girl in all directions and swearing most horribly. The doctor was also there, as he happened to be attending the station-master's wife ; and when Hetty stole into the waiting-room, where a number of villagers were talking excitedly, he went up to where she sat pale and calm in her corner, and stood before her to partially screen the poor little thing from observation, and to give her a chance to relieve her feelings if she should wish to cry. He tried to get hold of some appropriate word of consolation, but his tongue blundered, and he merely muttered to himself, "The scoundrel ! He isn't fit to live !"

"What—what do you mean?" and Hetty's clear eyes

looked up out of her pale face in a way that staggered the doctor.

"What do *you* mean? You don't wish to say you still believe?"

"Indeed, I do," cried Hetty, her eyes ablaze with righteous indignation. "It is all a ridiculous mistake. He has never dreamed of running away with that Pringle girl. I tell you he can not live without me. I am as necessary to my husband as the air he breathes. These people with their spiteful tongues have tried to make mischief. They are always thinking evil of others," and she waved her hand in an inclusive way hard for the doctor to bear. "I tell you," she went on, getting quite angry, "he will come back to me on the next train, and all will be explained."

The old doctor looked at her with mingled awe and reverence and pity. If she were not demented, she was certainly worthy of worship. The next train would not arrive from anywhere for an hour and a half, and the waiting-room gradually emptied. The people cast curious glances at Hetty as they went out, but she sat quite composed, without heeding any of them. Presently there was no one left except old Pringle, who was watching the clicking telegraph instrument, the major's wife, and the doctor. Hetty ignored them both, and as for old Pringle, she hated the very sight of him, without the least touch of sympathy for him as a fellow-sufferer. The doctor paced up and down the platform, keeping his eye on the motionless little woman in the corner. She might need his services before all was over. It was a long, tedious time, but it did end at last. The train rushed down the track, slowed, then stopped, with many a snort and whistle. Only a few people alighted, and the last to step out was a stoutish, beaming gentleman in a light overcoat, with a rose in the buttonhole. Well, Hetty fell sobbing and laughing into the major's arms, as she gave the doctor a terrible look of reproach. Old Pringle rushed up to the major, brandishing his clinched fist, and crying out excitedly:

"What have you done with my girl?"

The major paid no heed to any one but his wife. "My dear, why are you so agitated? Have the neighbors been filling your head with foolish stories? I had to go away on a little private business—nothing less than seeing two worthy young people who love each other dearly united in the bonds of matrimony. I promised my old friend, Frank Drummond, I would help him in this business, and pledged myself, on my honor as an officer and a gentleman, not even to tell my wife. Miss Pringle is no longer Miss Pringle; she is Mrs. Frank——"

Old man Pringle would not let the major finish the sentence. He danced up and down with rage, and would have assaulted him if the doctor had not restrained his violence and taken him home by main force.

In a few days Hetty called at the doctor's office to say good-by, looking bright and happy. The doctor took her hand and gazed with paternal kindness into her good little face.

"And are we to lose you, my dear? I am sorry, very sorry. Where are you going?"

"Oh, the major has been ordered back to the frontier among the Indians. Of course it is very hard for him, poor fellow, but I rather like that kind of life."

CHAPTER XIX.

A ROSEBUD GARDEN OF GIRLS.

THE wistaria is hanging its purple clusters high on the chimneys of the old Myers house, which stands on the turnpike just outside the village limits. The garden and grounds look neglected; of late years the old house has not been occupied. But great bushes of the spirea trail their white wreaths through the grass, and the syringa and althea hedge has overgrown the palings, and the snowball is now in full perfection. Great clusters of the blue iris and striped grass struggle through the wild growth. The climbing roses are getting ready to push out pink buds. There is a corner given up to the delightful barberry, with its sprays gemmed with tiny yellow flowers, and near it stands a large dogwood tree, brought thither from the woods, covered thickly with white flowers.

All things look celestial now, and yet how fleeting is the delicate tracery and flutter of young leaves, the exquisite unspoiled green, so tender and fresh it seems to have been made for better and happier beings than any this workaday world produces. The delicious bloom and fragrance, the beauty of blossoms so delicate, spiritual, and affecting, is very short-lived. We seem always to miss the best of it, because we do not get out in time to catch nature at her prettiest revels. It belongs to the youngest and fairest creatures—happy children, merry maidens, nestlings and lambs, and to the few old and middle-aged people whose hearts are entirely innocent and uncorrupted.

This freshness of the spring-time brings back that quintette of charming girls who lived once at the old Myers place, when the doors and windows stood wide open all day long, and the old garden, with its tall shade trees and bright flower beds, was like Armida's enchanted grounds. The professor's five daughters, with their sunny heads and fluttering skirts, seemed always flitting about under the maples and elms and buttonballs. The sun glanced lovingly down on them as they picked vivid handfuls of petunias and nasturtiums and morning-glories, and the trees threw soft shadows on their white gowns. They lifted the edges of their petticoats out of the dew and showed delightful little slippers and clocked stockings. The place, so silent now, was then always full of a subdued murmur of sweet voices, of chat and laughter and snatches of old songs and little airs played impromptu on the ancient piano which had been their mother's.

The father of these charming girls, companions of the spring, had been for many years in a theological seminary in one of the staid New England towns, where every house was as prim and orthodox as the Westminster Catechism. When some years past middle life the professor retired from his post, and bought the old Myers place, a property which had once been in his wife's family, and where he had courted her twenty-five years earlier. He brought with him this bevy of five daughters. Only one of them was at all plain, and she was the housekeeper, good little Lois, named for her mother. The others were charmingly, irresistibly pretty. How such rare blossoms came to flower on the professor's rather dry family tree it is impossible to say. But there they were, indubitable facts, delightful, unaccounted-for phenomena, like tropical birds singing in the cell of an anchorite, or little love poems inserted between firstly and fifteenthly of an old yellow sermon.

The mother had been dead only a few years when the professor moved back to the village with his family of girls. On the mother's side there were wealthy relatives, who lived in nice, lively towns, where there were plenty of eligible, or, as Mrs. Deacon Hildreth would say, "'legible" young men. These relatives were always inviting their cousins and nieces to stay with them weeks and months at a time. They were fashionably clothed by this loving bounty, and taken off on delightful trips to the mountains and the seashore in summer, and to Florida in winter. The result of all this was that the four young beauties were all engaged when they first came to live in the village, three of them to town men, and the fourth and youngest—a little blonde, with curly hair and gray eyes, with dark eyebrows—to a young theological student at the seminary where her father had taught for nearly a quarter of a century.

Lois was still heart-free, and it happened that though nice-looking and such a good girl, she was not a decided beauty. Therefore, however illogical it may seem, she was expected to be practical and to take to housekeeping. The question, such a burning one in New England, "what shall I do with my girls?" had been easily answered for the professor. They were all, or nearly all, soon to enter that holy estate of matrimony which was the primal solution of the problem, and in spite of modern improvements, is still by the majority of mankind considered the best. It is a terrible piece of work having four engaged girls in the house at one time, as poor Lois found to her cost. It is not necessary to mention that engaged girls are good for little or nothing in a practical way. They are always writing and receiving interminable letters. The day's mail puts them in the seventh heaven of bliss, or sends them to bed with a headache. Nothing can be done but to count the hours before *he* will come (in this case it was *they*), to curl hair, and try on becoming gowns and sashes, and gather nosegays in the garden—to improvise sentimental strains on the old piano, to cry over a novel, or to dream in the hammock, utterly distraught as to the every-day things of this life.

Poor Lois had experience of all kinds of lovers' moods. She had so many confidences poured into her ear she forgot sometimes whether it was Frank who had last quarreled with Jane, and then kissed and made up, or Paul with Grace. She took to wearing her rings on different fingers in order to keep the secrets separate and distinct in her mind. She was expected to sympathize with every body, and to enter into every body's feelings, because she was not supposed to have any feelings of her own. If she was ever a little slow or obtuse in unraveling the webs of love's diplomacy, the remark was made with rasping emphasis, "you would know just how it is if you had ever been engaged." The poor girl was nearly distracted, for the economic problem was of even greater difficulty than the entanglements of the heart. There were always one or two lovers on hand to be lodged and fed, and others might arrive at any moment. Lois discovered to her cost that being in love does not injure the male appetite ; however much engaged young men may disregard an unengaged prospective sister-in-law, or look upon her as an object of covert pity, they fully appreciate her batter-cakes and waffles, her tender steak and fragrant coffee.

The case of the old professor seemed even more pathetic than that of his eldest daughter. He moved about in a cool remoteness, feeling at times terribly alien to love's young dreams, and then again, catching the infection of the house, his old heart would begin to beat with a strange flutter. The girls were all very fond of papa. They petted him a great deal, and called him an old darling, and sat on his lap, and curled his gray locks over their pretty fingers while they coaxed out of him all manner of little favors. Still he could never quite overcome the feeling that these lovely bright beings ought to belong to some one else. It was simply ridiculous that he, an old seminary professor, who had made a great deal of dry wood in the long years he had taught theology in an ugly little town, mainly to young rustics, and with one sole and only hobby, the freedom of the will, should be the father of such a group of sirens. The professor was spare in flesh, and wore his gray locks rather long. He was excessively short-sighted, and had a way of peering at things common to persons thus afflicted. He was rather absent-minded, and now that he found himself away from the routine of seminary life, with no college bell to guide him, he would have forgotten to eat if his daughter Lois had not recalled him to the necessity. He was gentle and slow of speech, and no great talker, but with that habit of iteration and reiteration to the point of tediousness so common to life-long instructors.

The professor had formerly made for himself a study in the old seminary building, and here, abstracted and apart from all family cares, he had written his various books on the freedom of the will, which gave him a very solid, substantial reputation in clerical circles. Though I have never chanced to meet any one who had read them, the professor was considered a most sound authority, and was spoken of with great respect in learned treatises and theological conventions. He had not been shelved; he had simply retired from the professorship, that he might have unlimited leisure to shed ink upon his great theme, which looked as beautiful to his eyes as the principles of perspective to that old Italian painter who would stand musing for hours, and then exclaim, "How beautiful is perspective!" So when they all moved to the old Myers place that spring, the question at once arose among the girls as to where papa would have his study. The house, with its quaint gables and outside chimneys, looked large on the exteiror, but within it was badly cut up into little odd rooms, opening upon blind passages. Steps led up here and down there, and bedrooms communicated with each other like a nest of boxes. The windows were put into corners and placed too high, and there was not a private nook for a scholar in the whole house. The old man went dreamily over the house with his girls, living over again in some dim way the hours he had spent there in his youth when he, too, was a lover. But it all seemed very vague and shadowy. There were only two rooms in the badly contrived place that were at all adapted to his needs, and these the girls had previously appropriated for spare chambers. For of course they must have some place to stow away Frank, and Harold, and Paul, and Edward when they came. And they would always be coming; some lived near and some at a distance, but the house could count on at least one resident lover in perpetuity.

The girls of course could not tell dear papa there was no place for his study, but he understood it well enough, and yielded tacitly in his own gentle, uncomplaining way. He wandered out in the garden under the tall trees, where he had walked with his young bride so many years ago; it seemed all to have happened in a pre-existent state, and he tried to recall those vivid emotions and the flush of happiness when the birds sang in Paradise. Then he stepped on into the barn. It was a clean, water-tight, sweet-smelling barn, with that homely cheer and pleasantness that belongs to such places. It was empty, swept and garnished. The professor felt himself too poor to keep a horse, and the barn was practically useless. He climbed up a ladder into the mow, and looked out of a high window. The view was glorious over Saddleback, the intervale, and the winding river, all dressed in the living green of May. His dim eyes, accustomed to the close quarters of an ugly paved town, devoid of scenery, beheld this lovely prospect as something new and surprising. It was a revelation of the beauty of the world, and seemed to blend with those vague visions of his old self, of the time when he was not a professor, absorbed in the freedom of the will, but a young man pleading ardently for a fair girl's love. He determined then and there to build a study for himself in the vacant barn. A roughly plastered room, warm and light, was all he wanted. Here he could insure perfect quiet in which to pursue his great theme. So the room was built, and all the professor's books and papers were carried in, as well as his desk and study chair. He was furnished with a student lamp for night work, and Lois laid down a carpet and rugs, and hung some old prints on the wall. The window stook in that exquisite mountain and valley and river view in the first flush of spring, and the old man felt as if scales had fallen from his eyes as he sat watching the changes of the landscape—the play of light and shadow over the sky, storms gathering and moving off the mountain, bursts of sunlight on distant fields and woods, the dart of lightning, and the flush of sunrise upon the hills. For a quarter of a century he had been immured in brick and stone, and there had written a great deal about God's universe. Now the universe was before him, and new aspects of the great free-will problem presented themselves to his mind. He felt himself in primitive and child-like relation to God, and a fresh, original scheme of doctrine and argument warmed his heart and animated his intellect. When he wrote now it was with a kind of inspiration that surprised and delighted him. He became reverent and religious in a new and unexpected way.

Of course, no one knew of the wonderful hours the professor was spending in his barn study. He was reticent of all that went on within him, and his own girls were as ignorant as his neighbors. One of the windows of his study commanded a corner of the old garden, just a little hidden nook with a green bench set in the shade. Here one or other of the engaged couples came sometimes for a quiet talk, and the old professor would have felt guilty in watching them if they had not seemed to him so like a picture or a vision—a help in that odd psychological process by which he was getting back his lost youth and revivifying his heart and brain. The neighbors pitied him because his large family of giddy girls had pushed him out into the cold. A few spinsters and widows who were looking for husbands tried to let him know how well prepared they were to sympathize with a lonely gentleman unappreciated by his own daughters, and obliged to live with the bats and owls. But it was all lost on him. He was too happy to think of changing his state. He spent more and more of his time in the repose and solitude of his new study, and when he failed to come to his meals they were carried out to him by one of his girls, who, it must be confessed, saw but little of their father at any other time.

The summer holidays had come, and the lovers were all there. The windows were wide open, and roses and honeysuckles bloomed around the old porches, and the trees threw thick, cool shadows. Every corner of the yard and garden was consecrated to love and romance, and the house, too, was appropriated in every part by these happy young people. If the professor entered unexpectedly, he was apt to find Frank and Jane installed in the parlor, Harold and Hatty in the library, while Lily and Ned pervaded the reception-room and Grace and Paul held possession of the veranda. There hardly seemed a place inside the house where he could sit down without intruding on lovers' rights, so he fell into the habit of asking his friends to come and see him in the barn. His old clerical companions and fellow-professors were always asked out there to see the view when they called. The professor, in his simple-mindedness, thought nothing of it. The repose and quiet of the barn had been so much in his spiritual experience, of course it must be pleasant to his friends.

The villagers made jokes about the professor's hobby on the freedom of the will, he who had no freedom in his own house, and had been driven out by a pack of selfish girls to seek refuge in a stable. Poor Lois heard it all, but so long as papa seemed happy and contented she would not let the gossip come to his ears. Her sisters would all be married in a few months, and then she would devote her life to making papa comfortable. Meantime the professor was writing a book that was destined to be very popular among all classes of religious people, though he did not know it. It was an Indian-summer poem, called out by the aspiration and the new life he had found in the summer solitude. His cramped thoughts expanded and became winged and caught the motion of the swallows as they skimmed round his windows. His mind, he felt, had always been in a straight-jacket, and now he was free, and the ideas came like spring torrents. So the days went on, those idyllic barn days, when the old man's one popular book was getting written—all the dry arguments transfusing themselves with a glow of new life—when one morning Grace, his youngest daughter, came into the study.

"Well, what is it, my dear?" putting out his fatherly hand, without looking at her, as his head remained bent over the writing-table. "Papa, I want to speak to you if you do not mind." "Of course, my dear, I am always ready to attend to you." He turned about at once, and she perched herself on his knee, looking like a depressed canary bird with its feathers a little rumpled by mental agitation. There were two or three diamond drops twinkling on the long lashes of her gray eyes.

"Well, my dear; well, what is it?" and the hand

kept on smoothing her hair half-abstractedly. "Oh, papa," and her head suddenly buried itself on his shoulder. "I have qua-a-r-reled with Paul. He is going away."

"Quarreled with Paul?"

"Yes, papa," she sobbed, "and about you. You know he was in your classes in the seminary, and he always looked up to you; and now he says we girls don't treat you with respect—our own dear father. We don't honor you as we should, and the village people know it. We have thrust you out in the barn; we neglect you shamefully, and you such a great, and learned, and distinguished man."

The professor drew his little weeping girl closer in the bend of his arm, and tried to soothe her as best he could. "My child, how your heart beats! You are ill. I have been engrossed with my own thoughts. I have neglected you, and it is all my fault. You must go and send Paul to me."

Well, Paul went to his old professor and had a long talk with him, and of course it was all made up with Grace. But the old man would not leave his barn study. In the autumn the four sisters were married, and the beauty and charm of those weddings are still talked of in the village as something to date from. But the old Myers place looked deserted after the lovely quartette of sisters had departed. The professor came back to the house to live with his good home-staying Lois. But the wonderful inspiration of the summer never returned, though he tried to woo it. It was his brief Indian-summer, and it left him broken and old. His book made a noise in the world, and brought him the pleasure of an afternoon success, but the rare mood which produced it was gone forever. One day, with a gentle, placid smile on his worn face, the old man was found lying dead on his couch, where he was taking his midday rest.

CHAPTER XX.

THE COLORED BROWNS.

WE have only one family of colored people in the village, and we are rather proud of the possession. It was by a mere accident that Mandy and Sambo Brown came to live with us. They were both born into slavery, and were taken by their parents to Canada by means of the underground railroad. Having grown up in the bleak North, they met and married in the Queen's dominions, and started back toward the old home a few years after the close of the war. They stopped one day at our village with the thought of resting for a time, but as they were made welcome by Aunt Dido, the great friend of their race, and work was procured for them, and a place to live, they finally settled down into citizens of the town, and have become by their sobriety and industry as much respected as "white folks," and more than some. As Aunt Dido was the first to take the Browns under her wing, she has always been rather proud of them as specimens of "likely" black people, prophecies and hints of what the race may become with proper culture and favoring circumstances.

But the merits of Black Sambo and Mandy shine brighter than they probably would in a community where negroes abound. Here they shine alone—black diamonds, among the contrasting jewels of the village. Sam, with the peculiar genius of his people for jobbing, gets plenty of work to do, but it is not what may be called regular, steady employment. He makes gardens for the single women and widows, helps in house-cleaning, whitewashes, paints, and "paper-hangs" a little, runs errands, chops wood, doctors sick dogs, and "teams it" to the next town. He knows, too, a little plumbing and carpentering, and can tinker at several trades. There is always something to keep Sam going; and he is so faithful, pleasant, and happy-tempered that people like to have him around.

Sam is up with the dawn in spring, and you will hear him singing snatches of old plantation song, as he digs and hoes in his little garden. That garden is the pride of his life. The dew is sweet as it falls into his beds and nourishes the tomato plants and the succulent sweet corn. Sambo has what many a poor man might have by taking a little pains, a bed of asparagus and a patch of fine strawberries. He grows a little okra to give the children a taste of it in their broth, and is careful to put in plenty of crookneck squashes, cucumbers and melons. He kills the potato bugs and roots out the vermin, and waters his plants in a dry time, so that, whether the season be wet or droughty, warm or cold, Sam Brown's garden is a beautiful example to his poor neighbors.

There were but two children in the Brown family when they came to the village some years ago; now there are five of them, pretty, bright-eyed and neat. You would not ask for a kink the less in their frizzled black heads. But Mandy Brown is of an entirely different temper from Sam. There is but little of the happy-go-lucky about her. She seldom sings the old plantation and camp-meeting songs Sam is always whistling. The iron of slavery seems to have entered into Mandy's soul when she was very young, intensified by her experience of the cold Canada winters, and the hardships of exile she experienced when her mother died from privation. But Mandy has a far better intellect than Sam. She is the elect head of the family, keeps all the money they jointly earn, buys all the supplies, plans every thing, and gives Sambo just so much change to spend each week for fish-hooks and tobacco. She is a high-class laundress, and is regularly employed by three or four families in the village, who know what nice work is and are willing to pay a good price for it. Mrs. Judge Magnus employs Mandy to do up all her fine bed and table linen, her damask of the best, her lace-trimmed and embroidered pillow-shams, also her own dainty gowns and dressing-sacks and petticoats, frilled and fluted to perfection. You should see these beautiful things drifted like snow-banks into Mandy's exquisitely neat sitting-room where she irons. The clothes smell as fragrant as a field of clover or sweet grass, and shine with the gloss of a strong elbow, and on the window-sill stands a mug or pitcher full of flowers the children have brought in. It is a picture to see the black face at the spotless ironing-table bending over the snowy linen, while the deft hands crimp, and flute, and shape, with a real love for the work. You would know a good deal about Mandy by looking at her clothes when they lie heaped in the great basket, or are hung for the last drying on the horse. She is tall, and trim, and neat, in her dark calico gown, with a graceful turn of the waist and shoulders not uncommon to her race. Mandy never wears bright kerchiefs or head-gear, but she shows her tropical nature in her love of red poppies and scarlet geraniums and vivid salvias, which she cultivates by the door of her little house.

The house stands on the edge of a small field and garden, with a few pear and plum trees at one corner, and all the bright flowers Mandy can crowd into the narrow space between the door-step and the front gate. A tiny stable made of slabs and cast-off boards shelters the cow in winter. Chicks, and hens, and kittens run about at will in the grass, and a lean-to shed with a rope swing makes an outdoor nursery for the children. Sam and Mandy own this snug little place. They have been able to pay for it in small installments, and there are no people in the town more independent, and, I may say, more self-respecting.

But Mandy, in spite of her love for the scarlet flowers, still has something of the Puritan sternness of temper. The old sense of wrong rankles at times in her soul. Her conscience is uneasy and inclined to be morbid. She goes over and over the old slave days and her early sufferings, and dwells upon them—contrasts them with these piping times of peace and prosperity. She reads the old Bible—for she can read and write, too—with all its ancient curses, and wonders in her soul whether she and Sam and the children are vessels of wrath too worthless and unfit for salvation. She feels her own heart to be rather hard and cold, when there is no living being who ought to be more tender and thankful. She teases herself with the idea that as a family they are not as grateful as they should be for the mercies of the Lord, that perhaps some day they may be punished because they don't have enough thankfulness in their souls. She can not enjoy with careless light-heartedness, like Sambo, the goods the gods provide, but must be digging up her blessings to see how they grow before she has tasted the sweets thereof.

It must be confessed, Mandy, with all her good qualities, is at times rather saturnine and ill-tempered, with something of the old African seeress in her blood. Sam, so easy-going and sunny, attributes her bad temper to the fact that she is "powerful smart." All smart folks, in Sam's estimation, are high-strung, quick, and touchy. It is a penalty that smartness pays for the privileges it enjoys; therefore Sambo reveres even his wife's temper and looks up to her as a superior being. The children are all like Sam, easy-going, careless, light-hearted little types of their own race. Sam secretly regrets that Mandy's high qualities have not been transmitted to some of the "pickaninnies." He says, "They're peart enough, the Lord knows, but not so peart as Mandy, fo' sho." Mandy keeps them as neat as wax and they go to school and sit on benches with the white children, and study out of the same books. But the rollicking nature of the Southron gleams out of their bright black eyes, white teeth, ebon faces, and knotty curls. Even the little dances and plays they improvise together all carry Mandy back to the old hated plantation days, and she sees them with pain. She wishes her children to get "shet" of all that, to be like northern folks—good little Sunday-school children, learning their text-cards and minding just "beautiful."

But Sam delights in the children just as they are. He "totes" the little ones when they "play 'possum," and pretend they can't walk, until his back aches. The moment he comes home they are swarming all over him—taking liberties with his pockets, climbing up on his shoulders, and begging for stories. So Sambo "nurses" the children, gathering as many of them as he can into his arms, while the others hang on anyhow, and tells them interminable yarns while he smokes his pipe. Sambo always goes back "Souf" for those marvelous tales, and shows the little ones in his rude, figurative speech, between pulls at the pipe, the cane-brake, and the cotton-patch, and the solemn pine forest and cypress swamps, and the great red oaks clad in long gray moss. He shows them "ole mas'r" and "little mas'r and miss" riding on their ponies or in the "kerridge." He shows them the fine old plantation-house, and the negro-quarter as he remembers it before the "wah," and describes the banjo playing, the dances and songs and break-downs, the revivals and love feasts, and how the darkies pray and shout. He shows them the strange flowers, the magnolia, and jasmine, and myrtle tree, the creepers and wonderful blossoms hidden in "de swamp," which he knew in his boyhood, and the fascinating serpents and wild animals, alligators, catamounts, 'coons, and 'possums. He imitates the call of the mocking-bird in a long, low whistle until the kinky hair kinks a little tighter, and the eyes roll up and show the whites, and the absorbed look is most charming in that dusky group of little ones, who have never seen the wonderful, fascinating "Souf," with all its mirthfulness and wealth of color.

Sambo never threw any dark shades into his pictures. Mandy, when she caught snatches of his stories as she went to and fro about her work, wondered if he had forgotten all the oppression and wrong of the old slave days, and remembered only those sunny pictures, that careless life of dance and song when the long day's work was done. It must be confessed Mandy had a kind of contempt for light-hearted Sambo, who had endured so much unscathed in soul, and now felt no touch of bitterness, rebellion, or revenge for the past. Perhaps now in these blessed days of freedom he hardly remembered there had been any wrong.

The children did not love her as they loved the father. Her high temper brought a word and a blow. She often instructed them about old slave times, showing how they had no sénse of gratitude for what they enjoyed, only a powerful all-dominating love of play and mischief. They were idle ne'er-do-wells, unworthy of the liberty so dearly bought. It almost seemed a grievance that her children had not known the sufferings of the old life, the escape from bondage, the underground railroad, the Arctic exile in Canada. It was at such moments, when administering correction for little trespasses and idle ways, errands left undone, and lessons shirked, that Mandy recounted these things.

"Yo'se no account, you is (cuff). Yo' don't know noffin' 'bout what it is to be a slave, to have some bad man crack de whip over you and make you work when yo' is fallin' in your tracks (slap). Yo' never tinks of de bless-in's of born freedom, nor what y'r moder endured in de ole days. Yo'se dat no account, you 'fuses to learn your lesson when your moder had no schoolin'—wasn't let to learn any t'ing—was kep' in ignerance (slap), had to steal away in de night time to get a little instruction in de Bible and de hymn-book. Yo'se don't care much 'bout de word ob God, nor de wraf of God, nor how de bars come and eat up de bad children as mocked. Yo'se don't want to learn about Abram, and Isaac, and Jacob, dem just men, and de land ob promise, and all dem pious t'ings. You'se no account—dont know what it means to be livin' in a land of liberty—don't know nothing 'tall about de oppression of ole slave times, don't care to hear 'bout dem t'ings, when yo'se fader tells ob de cake-walks and de break-downs on de Miss'ippi. I'se ashamed of my chilluns as don't 'preciate der blessings, and ain't t'ankin de Lord every bref dey draw for bein' free." (Here a sharp series of slaps.)

"Yo'se just spilin' dem pickaninnies," Mandy would say to Sambo, " teachin' of 'em to be plantation darkies 'stead of 'merican citizens as read de newspapers, and votes to shut up de rum shops, and goes to meetin' Sunday neat and respectable. You is puttin' all kinds of fool notions in dere heads, and settin' 'em ag'in' me."

Sambo laughed in his easy way at the notion of setting the children against their mother, who was probably the " peartest " woman that ever lived, while he was only an or'nary darky, without any thing specially bright about him. But still the fact remained that the children loved him best, and liked better to be with him and listen to his desultory talk, given forth with unctuous, easy voice, than to hang about their mother at the risk of getting their ears boxed for every little misdemeanor. It was also true that Mandy knew while she sat up nights to make them nice clothes, and denied herself much that they might go as well dressed as the children of her white neighbors, they loved their father best, and was jealous of his influence.

Sambo had put up a swing for the children out near the shed, and there they built their play-houses and held their little revels. One day Mandy heard a great groaning and shouting out in the shed where the children were at play. So she slipped unobserved into the stable, and peeped through a crack in the board wall to see what was going on. Most of the children were holding a " 'sperience meeting " such as their father had often described. They were down on their knees in the straw, clasping their stomachs, and waving back and forth in great distress of mind as they groaned over their sins. Now and then they broke out into snatches of negro hymns, or fell down in the straw with the " power." When seemingly quite stiff and stark, one would cry out, "I'se dead fo' sho'," and another would answer, "I'se deader," and then they would leap to their feet with shouts of laughter, and begin a plantation clog dance or a cake-walk. They had improvised a banjo with some string wound over a wooden box. The banjo accompaniment was given with all the dances, and even with the prayers and hymns.

One little girl sat nursing her colored rag-baby in a corner of the shed, where a log table was set out with bits of broken crockery. She wished the child, who was afflicted with rag-baby colic, to take paregoric peaceably out of a teaspoon, and without any resistance to maternal authority. But as the infant was rebellious, she gave it several sharp cuffs and shakes, thus apostrophizing it while the process went on : " You'se a low-down no-account little nig. I'se ashamed of you in dis land of liberty ; you don't sense what it is to be free and to enjoy de pribliges ob schoolin' and churches. Yo'se dat worthless yo' o'ut to be a slabe all yo'se bo'n days," and then after another quick series of slaps she threw the luckless infant down into the straw, and gave it a hearty kick. " Let's all be slaves," cried the children simultaneously, and then they tied their hands and feet loosely together with string, and went hobbling around the shed singing an improvised ditty suitable to the occasion :

> "I'se gwine to ole mas'r,
> I'se gwine to de Souf,
>   Glory, glory, hallelujum,
> I's gwine to ole Virginny,
> 'Cos I'se a pickaninny,
>   Glory, glory, hallelujum.
>
> "I'se gwine to ole mas'r,
> To dance in de cane-brake,
>   Glory, glory, hallelujum,
> I'se gwine to ole mas'r,
> A walkin' for de cake,
>   Glory, glory, hallelujum."

Mandy stole back to her bright, clean kitchen, and for the rest of the day she was very quiet and thoughtful. She had seen a picture of herself, and such self-revelation is always profoundly instructive. She was suffering from that reaction in her children which accompanies the violent, harsh teaching of all good doctrine. She had tried by blows and strong language and sarcastic appeals to make them devotees of liberty and above all things "'spectable," and now, God help them, they were sighing for the flesh-pots of the Egyptians—"ole mas'r and de Souf," that land of easy jollity and careless pleasure.

When Sambo came home he found Mandy quite meek and subdued, dressed in a new blue gingham, with a spotless white necktie. He thought he had never seen her so nice or so kind. That night when the children were all in bed and she sat patching little Jim's breeches by the lamp, she even allowed Sam to smoke in the sitting-room, a privilege not often accorded. She had been snipping away with her shears a long time in silence, communing with her own thoughts, when she broke forth :

"Sam, I'se goin' to try and be a Christian after this. I reckon I'se been a big heathen all my life."

"Dat's the one t'ing needful for us all, I reckon, Mandy," said Sam, as he shook the ashes from his pipe.

CHAPTER XXI.

THE MINISTER'S GLEBE AND HOPE'S LOVE STORY.

I REMEMBER with the greatest pleasure some walks through the "minister's glebe" on the old post-road, about a mile and a half from the village. The path winds through the farm and home fields, to the stone parsonage or manse, which has long been disused as a parish house, and is now turned into a boys' school. The land is a high plateau framed in blue hills, with vistas of valley and river gleaming through chance gaps in the woodland. On such land one has almost the same sense of being launched off in the sky as on a mountain-top. Clouds assume the grandest forms in such open spaces, and the chasing effects of light and shade bring back those inimitable Flemish landscapes where the nimble play of the sun fills the mind with that sense of expansion which I can imagine is the first and most immediate effect of death.

The little twisted path through the glebe takes you close beside fields of wheat, oats, and rye, and other growing crops, and through the grass and clover fields, which are now lusty and of splendid promise. The sheen of those young, glossy crops bending under the morning wind, and spotted with sunlight, is not soon to be forgotten. What wonder the bobolink loves these places with all his passionate little heart, and pours out a series of trills that seem to run all round the still leafy world, mounting at last into the very sky?

The oldest people of the village remember the Rev. Dr. Abijah Manners, the last of our old Puritan ministers of a former generation, who lived on the minister's glebe and occupied the old manse, and they talk of him still almost as if he were alive and moving about among us. The old clergyman was such an upright, downright, positive man, he made an indelible impression on his generation, and even the children fancy they have seen the swing of his strong, active figure down the village street as he strode along, taking great steps, dressed in the single-breasted coat and shovel hat of his order. He carried with him everywhere a kind of paternal authority. Brusque, quick, and active, the doctor was not given to long harangues on the state of the soul, but he often spoke the word of admonition and warning which went directly to the point, hitting the nail on the head with marvelous accuracy and precision. He carried the same prompt, clear manner into his religious ministrations. He never shirked a duty, nor did he allow any of the old dogmas to waver and grow weak in his mind, thus invalidating the potency of his instructions. He took his doctrine as straight as the swath he mowed in the nine-acre lot. The edges were not blurred by modern doubt or critical inquiry. All was clean, and direct, and true in the doctor's mind. Indeed, it was a much simpler age than ours. When he prayed for rain, the people trusted implicitly in his power to change the laws of nature. All up and down the valley Doctor Abijah was depended upon in a dry time.

Once after a great drought Dr. Abe, as he was called by the profane, prayed powerfully for the windows of heaven to open, and that night a heavy storm of wind and rain set in, which lasted three weeks and nearly spoiled the corn crop. The village tavern-keeper of those days, who was inclined to Universalism, called infidelity by the neighbors, met the doctor one morning on the road driving his old white nag in the clerical "shay."

"Don't you think you overdid it just a leetle this time,

doctor?" he asked, with the rain streaming down from his garments.

"Manifestly I did so as far as you are concerned," returned the doctor testily, "for you need fire more than water."

Dr. Abijah was an excellent theologian, sound as a nut on all the doctrines, and he was moreover an admirable farmer. His sturdy figure, with the clerical hat laid aside, and his big orthodox head cased in an old straw tile, could be seen taking the lead in the haying-field, where he cut a broader and cleaner swath than any of his men, and always led them by several rods. It was the same in the wood-lot and the plowing and harvesting; Dr. Abijah could hold his own against the best farmer in the county, nor did he think it at all derogatory to his cloth to be seen thus mixing spiritual and temporal interests. The earth is the Lord's and the fullness thereof, and the doctor thought it perfectly right that he should have a good portion of that fullness stowed away in his barns and stacks. His energies demanded something more than a little sermon-writing each week, and it was often remarked that the harder he worked on the six days the more powerful he was in prayer and exhortation on the seventh.

To be sure, when the weather was very "ketching," as it often is in these hills, the doctor had been known to wander a little in his discourse as his thoughts strayed off to his exposed crop. He had even on occasion rushed directly from the pulpit to the haying-field without changing his coat, hurrying his men to get out the wagons, and with his own strong arm pitching great cocks upon the mountainous load, while the heavens grew black and the thunder growled overhead. With all his strenuous orthodoxy he was a firm believer in the truth of the words of Jesus, that the Sabbath was made for man. Indeed, all practical farmers, whether priests or laymen, are obliged to accept in their most literal interpretation the words of the Master. If any of the old women of the congregation, whose duty it is to watch the pastor, complained of this laxity of practice in keeping the Lord's Day, the doctor quoted the parable of the sheep fallen into the pit, and drew the conclusion that a field of good grass is as well worth saving as a sheep. As in those days most of the members of the First Parish Church were farmers, with hay and grain of their own to look to, this was accepted as a comfortable doctrine, worthy of all honor.

Doctor Abijah kept a dining-room sideboard well stocked with good liquor. All the well-to-do people in the parish did the same, and as the parson was more forehanded than any one else, he was of course justified in laying in a stock of good old fourth-proof brandy and venerable port. When he wished to incite his men to unusual activity in the field, he sometimes dealt out to them portions of old rye with his own hands; it was well known all over the parish that the doctor's liquor was of the very best quality. This was before the days of the Father Mathew and Washingtonian societies, and the doctor died before cold water, the sparkling and bright, came much into fashion. He was a man who carefully guarded himself against every excess. The "creature," as he called it, was for use, not abuse, and he preached that doctrine, hammering the pulpit cushion with his strong fist until the dust flew out in a cloud.

In the old stone manse the doctor kept open house for all his clerical brethren who came that way, and they did manage to come in a pretty steady stream all the year round. There was good eating and drinking in the manse; ministers have always been known to have a cultivated taste in the culinary line. The doctor's oldest daughter, Ruth, was the housekeeper. She had "put up" a great number of the clergy, and she was wont to say that she liked to see the poor brethren go away from the manse door looking a little less gaunt and thin than when they came. The manse kitchen was a reservoir of bounty to the whole neighborhood. All the tramps and itinerant beggars, all those who plied wandering trades, the essence-man, the pack-peddler, the clock-mender, the poor tinker, knew their way to that door where free grace flowed out in the shape of liberal meals of good, plain, wholesome food. For years a table was always duly spread in that vast kitchen, with its great fireplace and brick oven, for these chance guests, and not one day in the year were they wanting. He who giveth to the poor lendeth to the Lord; Doctor Abijah's lendings were very large in this way, and seemed to bring in a good interest, judging from his productive fields, and bursting barns, and the fat cattle in his pastures.

This kitchen, in its way a special New England institution, was well ruled by Ruth Manners, the Martha of that family. The doctor's invalid wife occupied a large upper chamber, where she was moved daily from the bed to the couch, but never passed the door. Ruth, though she was tall and stout, had incisive ways and a certain subacid in her temper, which reminded one of the flavor of her favorite summer pippins. There was also a twinkle of humor which recalled the old man, and she could give a hard thrust and administer a needed lesson in a joke. Ruth said if she could not jest sometimes between the ministers and the beggars, she would get the "hypo," and the "hypo" above all things was the malady she abhorred. She was endowed with all her father's indomitable energy and took her theology in the same strong unadulterated way. She was accounted a housekeeper of unrivaled excellence. Her worldliness and other-worldliness were mixed in equal parts exactly like Dr. Abijah's. She always took the lead in the female prayer-meetings, and was considered to have a gift in petitioning the throne of grace second to none. Ruth kept an eye on all female delinquents in the parish, and prodded their sins, great and small, in a way the customs of our time would consider intrusive, if not indecent. She made inquisition into consciences, and let the giddy girls and foolish young matrons know that her sleepless eye was upon them. She was, of course, disliked by some, but the admirable way in which she seconded all her father's endeavors to further the material and spiritual interests of the community were gratefully acknowledged.

The Mary of Scripture was not wanting in the doctor's family, although her name happened to be Hope. She was the youngest child, the flower of the flock. Several little ones had died between Hope and Ruth, and therefore, even in her grown and matured state, she always seemed a child to her energetic elder sister. Hope was slender and fair, mild of speech, and with a still tongue. Her life, much of it, had been spent in her mother's sickroom, where she read aloud books of an exclusively pious tone. Though devoutedly religious, Hope had none of that taste for leadership, the public display of piety, for which her sister was so well fitted. A touch of sadness and dreamy melancholy clung to Hope from having grown-up in that shaded sick-chamber and imbibing large doses of low-spirited religious literature, such as Hervey's "Meditations Among the Tombs," a favorite book with her invalid mother. Her active sister meantime faced all the difficulties of the farm, and kitchen, and dairy, and kept her weather eye out on the parish with salutary results.

Hope perhaps had hardly dreamed of a lover. The heavy hand of duty pressed down all the impulses of her young nature, and she yielded without complaint. But one season there came to the manse a young minister who had just completed his course of study, and being slightly run down in health, had been invited by Dr.

Abijah to spend a few weeks on the farm, and breathe the pure air of the mountains. This young man was entirely unknown to the family, but he soon became domesticated in the great spare chamber where Ruth put him to lodge. He had the run of the old doctor's library and study, and the family found him a pleasant inmate. He preached a few times in the parish meeting-house, and some of the long-headed people even then predicted for him a great career. To the old doctor, who plowed, and harrowed, and top-dressed, and sub-soiled his sermons much as he did his land, this young man's enthusiasm and strong convictions seemed a little too fervid and high-colored. Still he liked him, and in time came to look upon him almost in the light of a son.

The young man saw less of Hope than of other members of the household, but the glimpses he caught of her pure young face and slender form tantalized him, and made him desire to know her better. It was a little strange that Hope, in that distant shaded chamber, so unearthly in its quiet, always knew when he entered or left the house, and learned to distinguish his step from all others. It was before the days of muscular Christianity and athletic training, but the young minister did occasionally take a turn in the field along with his father in Israel, and manifestly to the improvement of his health, and it was then he began to preach to Hope about fresh air and the necessity of out-door exercise to bring roses into her cheeks. The pale blush roses were already there while she listened. Then began those walks in a far-off old-fashioned summer time, when the birds sang as sweetly as they do now—walks through the woods, along the river, and over Saddleback to the cascade and the glen. He taught her a beautiful theology spelled out of the flowers, and clouds, and sunbeams, and one day in a pretty avenue of old trees, still known as "Hope's Walk," he asked her to be his wife.

But a terrible struggle had arisen in Hope's breast. She was skilled in the morbid anatomy which belongs to her peculiar phase of pietism and has always prevailed in the Puritan land. Self-dissection had been for years a favorite religious exercise with her nervous invalid mother, and Hope knew all its torments. Could she erect a mere mortal in the place of her God, when he had heretofore ruled alone in her heart, and if so was it right or possible to leave the ailing mother who had lived on her affection and sapped her vitality from childhood? Poor Hope said no, said it with tears and tremblings and unutterable pain. But after the young man had gone away the futile passion of grief which swept over her for weeks and months came near shattering her life. It was after the physician had declared that he could do nothing more for her that Hope, thinking she was about to die, told all the sad little story to her father, how she had learned to know her own heart, and how she loved his young friend with all the intensity of her nature.

Dr. Abijah, with his usual promptness, cut the Gordian knot by sitting down and writing frankly and freely to his young friend. He recounted the whole case up to fifteenthly, and bade him come back. The mother, too, sent him her blessing from her sick couch. It had been borne in upon her soul that she must give up Hope to the chosen servant of the Lord, and she, though a poor broken reed, was ready to obey. It was all couched in rather stiff old-fashioned phrase, but it had a true heart-beat in it. The letter was sent off, and it was a long, very long, time before the answer came—the young minister had been traveling about, preaching in different places as "candidate"—and poor Hope's sufferings were hard to bear. At last it came. Dr. Abijah, a strong man, with no knowledge of such a thing as a nerve in his body, was visibly shaken when he took the letter from the post-office, and carrying it out into the field with him sat down on the stone-wall under a wide-spreading walnut tree, and opened its ample sheet of foolscap, sealed with a great splash of red wax, and read.

His young friend had been placed in a terrible position. His letter was kind, brotherly, Christian. It bore all the marks of pain and deep feeling, but the truth must be told : Before the doctor's letter had reached him he had engaged himself to a dear friend of his sister, an early playmate of his own. The doctor had done many a hard stint of work, both in the home acre and in the pulpit, but the hardest he ever had to do came to him that day when he was forced to carry the news to his girl. But Hope, after a sharp attack of nervous prostration, was apparently resigned. She grew more active in her habits from that day, and went and prayed in the female prayer-meeting, and paid visits to neighbors she had seldom called upon. She even offered her assistance to Ruth in the kitchen and dairy, and took some interest in the animals on the farm.

Well, the old minister died, then Ruth, and finally the weakly mother, and the "glebe" and the old manse were left to Hope. She was a comparatively rich woman now. There was no need of exertion, and she rented most of the farm, reserving only the home-fields and "Hope's Walk." Sitting in the shady old manse in those days, Hope Manners heard echoes of the fame of the man whom she had loved. The long-headed farmers had been right. He had turned out a great preacher. She sat and wondered in her gentle heart if she could not secretly, in some humble way, help forward his cherished aims. She longed to strike hands and keep step with him, though he knew it not, in his life work. Stealthily she poured out her bounty for that work, for she had striven to find out all that he was doing, thinking, and planning in the city where he lived. At last, when she died and her will was opened, it was found she had left him her fortune to further, as she put it, "some great and good object of humanity on which his heart was set."

The villagers knew Hope had had one great chance in life, and had lost it. They knew she was what the world calls "disappointed." A tender romance clung about her as the first love of a distinguished man. But she was more than calm as she grew old, she was merry and bright in her own gentle way. Always beautiful, she grew more so as life advanced. Love had brought her great suffering, but it had developed and ennobled her nature. She had drunk of the wine of sacrifice, but she had also tasted the bread of life, and her afternoon was golden.

CHAPTER XXII.

FASCINATING MRS. BRIDGENORTH.

WE are all very sensitive about the standing of our village, and despise nearly every other town within a radius of fifty miles. We have a great deal of public spirit, and when a proposal was made to organize a fire department and provide the village with a small engine and hook and ladder company there was great enthusiasm among the young men and boys. They soon formed a fine company, with a pretty bright blue and white uniform and shiny helmets. A fire very seldom occurs in the village, not more than once or twice a year. But the boys, with their new and exciting toy of an engine, naturally loved to see it work, and desired to run to a fire at least once a week. The result was that hay-stacks, old sheds, and some tumble-down barns and outhouses on the borders of the town mysteriously burst into flames every few nights, and the rush and hurrah boys of a fire alarm became so frequent that delicate women were thrown into hysterics, and a few people with heart disease went off with frightful suddenness. The magistrate was at last obliged to lock the engine, hook and ladder and all, in the engine-house and put the key in his pocket, in order to save the village from utter destruction by fire, and to prevent the people from going mad.

But this was all owing to the exuberance of youth. We wisely shut our eyes to such boyish scrapes, and still cherish the belief that we are a very moral, good sort of people. But the sad fact remains that now when a real fire breaks out in the village our engine refuses to spout water, our hooks and ladders are practically useless, and we are obliged to send off to a neighboring town for aid. Still, as Providence loves to protect the innocent, and virtue, as we know, is always rewarded in this world, fires very rarely occur, and we have come to feel in our unprotected condition that we are special favorites of Heaven.

Outwardly we are a very decent people. No gin-shops, no disorder manifest, and if an intoxicated man appears on the street we always know he came in on the railroad. This is an idea cherished fondly by the old people of the town. Every thing evil—small-pox, diphtheria, measles, extravagance, vanity, impiety, even the seven-year locusts —came in on the railroad. So, Heaven be thanked, most of our intoxicated and disreputable persons, like stray gipsies, organ-grinders, beggars, and tramps, do come in on the railroad, and are 'jugged' by the watchful selectmen, who put them in a kind of human pound on the confines of the village, where they are made to saw wood in payment for a night's lodging and a meal or two, and then are sent packing about their business or no business, as the case may be. Did you ever think of it—what an admirable invention this is of getting rid of the evils of life, just to send them packing, with a devil-may-care indifference, until all the roads and lanes of the countryside are filled with irresponsible tramps, and lonely women and feeble old people quake inwardly with the fear of being murdered in their beds? In spite of the "no license" vote in our village and the closing of the rumshops, there are more than ten places known to the initiated where liquor can be obtained. This knowledge has crystallized into a kind of secret society, whose members give and take the grip and countersign. They nod, wink, smile, and it all means one thing. Yet every thing is outwardly quiet and orderly. People speak of these little blemishes under the breath — in a half whisper.

With other evils which came in on the railroad must be classed our summer boarders. The villagers have a slight distrust of city people, and they think New Yorkers a little more "dubious," than other tribes of urban folk. I hardly know why, for a few persons from the metropolis have brought a good deal of money into the town, and have been generous in contributing to the repair of the church, to the library, and other public objects, and are personally much respected. It is a vague feeling not easy to define, and has been somewhat intensified of late by a circumstance I am about to relate. The summer people, in spite of our heavenly-minded innocence and purity of manners, have their own complaint to make. They say that when a stranger comes to the village with a reputation for riches—and all city folk are supposed to be rich—he is set upon by the neighboring Bedouins exactly as if he were in the Arabian desert. Two prices are charged for every thing he buys in the town. Every bunch of asparagus, head of lettuce, and box of strawberries, raised under his very eyes, is shamelessly put up far above what they would cost in the city. The butcher and fishman raise their wares fifty per cent. The livery-stable keeper merrily elevates his charges to a fancy figure for the worst old "plugs" ever seen. He would be called a bloated monopolist, perhaps, as he is the only liveryman we have, and, poor soul, his season is short. But the blinded city man says he can get no idea of what the natives pay for any thing. He is supposed to have a gold mine in his pocket, and is a miserable object of prey, and must betake himself to less primitive, pure-minded, and bucolic neighborhoods in order to preserve a shred of his faith in human nature. But these stories are mainly exaggerations. We are an extremely good and honest people; and if the New Yorker does not know how to take us, it is his own fault.

Mrs. Martin is our best known boarding-house lady.

Her house, though comfortable, has not been much modernized. She clings with faithful affection to her penitential hair-cloth sofas and chairs, her big-patterned ingrain carpets and slippery oil cloth. The most trying thing about her Lares and Penates, which Mrs. Deacon Hildreth calls "lairs and peanuts," are the photographs of her dyspeptic, aggressive, low-spirited looking relatives which in their black frames break out all over the walls, and give a kind of measly look to the ugly wall paper. Mrs. Martin is very bland. She has a slightly stuffed look, from being puffy, and short of breath, and wearing her dresses too much girt in at the waist. She dresses her hair in the old-fashioned way—brushed smoothly over her ears as if glued to her skull, and fastened with side-combs. The good woman talks about her boarders as if she had boarded them as infants in arms, and had brought them up by hand. She calls the ladies "my dear," and pats the men on the back in a truly maternal and encouraging manner. Though not the superior cook that Aunt Dido is, she keeps her house in better order, and is not troubled with any of the eccentricities of genius which do sometimes perturb Aunt Dido's orbit.

Mr. Allibone, the cashier of the village bank, is Mrs. Martin's pet boarder. She shows his room to new-comers as a model of all that a boarder's room should be. The walls are decorated with numerous chromos. It is, in fact, a chromo paradise. Mr. Allibone also has a fancy for clocks, and he has six in different parts of the room, all ticking away for dear life. The little gifts of his sisters, nieces, cousins, and aunts are all ranged around his bureau, and dusted daily by his own careful hands. There are pen-wipers, shaving-paper cases, pin-cushions—painted, frilled, and embroidered—scent bottles tied up in ribbons, handkerchief-cases, and glove-boxes, all dear to the good little man's heart. He is an excellent bank officer, and would be trusted with untold sums of money, but he is mildly laughed at by the girls, and as he has, until of late, for a good many years evinced no intention to marry, little romantic or sentimental interest has attached to his small, neat person. His little feet and nice hands are as pretty as a fine lady's. His hair sets up brusquely from his head in front, and there is something clerkly and exact in all his movements. A self-importance attaches to his walk and gestures. He feels the bank to be the center of the village, and he, as the cashier of said bank, is the hub toward which all the spokes of the wheel converge. He carries the bank around with a certain dignity, and does not like big, loud-voiced men who have no respect for under-sized people; for there is always the present fear that these rough persons may jostle the bank from off his shoulders, and leave him in his own native insignificance. He is painfully methodical and always uses his white handkerchief with a certain explosion, called by the village people "trumpeting," just as he reaches Mrs. Martin's gate.

I think Mr. Allibone had always been a good deal afraid of the lady boarders until Mrs. Bridgenorth came early one spring, and she was so seductive in her manner, poor Mr. Allibone succumbed to the charm almost without a struggle. No one knew just who Mrs. Bridgenorth was, although on her arrival early in March she had mentioned a certain Hon. Mr. Farrington, member of Congress from another state, as her brother-in-law. Farrington was pretty well known by reputation, and Mrs. Martin was very glad to let her best room to so distinguished a "party" long before the opening of the regular season. Mrs. Bridgenorth dressed in deep black, with a good deal of heavy crêpe on her gown and a long sweeping veil pinned to a little close bonnet, within which she wore a very becoming widow's cap. She often tied a large quantity of crisp white illusion under her chin, and placed a large bunch of violets in the beautifully fitting bodice of her gown. As Mrs. Bridgenorth's complexion was fine, this mode of dress attracted more attention than brilliant colors. Without being strictly handsome she had many of the elements of beauty—an elegant small figure, fine eyes, and perfect teeth. Her nose, however, was somewhat sharp, and her light hair under the widow's cap had a lifeless, towy look, with a suspicion of the bleaching process. She was much younger at a little distance than close at hand, and though our villagers are so simple-minded, some of them thought they detected traces of rouge about the lady's cheek-bones.

The widow had the purring, caressing, kittenish ways of a small woman, who has enjoyed no end of admiration and petting. Her dear Rolf, as she called her departed husband, had spoiled her, and made her shamefully dependent. She ingratiated herself with good Mrs. Martin, fashioned for her a new cap from lace and ribbon, and fairly bewitched the old lady out of all ordinary prudence. At that early season there were no other boarders. Mrs. Martin set out a charming little round dinner and tea-table for two, and across this small board Mrs. Bridgenorth made eyes at good little Mr. Allibone. She told him how she had lost a fine fortune by the speculations of a rascally trustee, having saved out of the wreck only a paltry hundred thousand; how her two children, Paul and May, were at boarding-school, and what sweet creatures they were. She had come to the village, she said, because she needed rest and quiet. She was an ardent lover of nature, and her hope was to hide herself and her troubles far away from people, among these restful hills, and here she had found such charming society—"Oh, so charming," and she clasped her hands impulsively, as she gazed into poor little Allibone's face. He was near-sighted, and wore spectacles, and although he was considered an excellent judge of doubtful currency, how could he tell that Mrs. Bridgenorth was not all pure gold as she sat there weaving her little spell, and every now and then throwing in a word or two about the Hon. Farrington and her other distinguished connections? She looked young and charming when her eyes sparkled, and the sinister lines in her face and the meaning curl of her lip were not as easy for an experienced cashier to detect as the false ring in a counterfeit dollar.

Mrs. Bridgenorth pervaded the whole house. She arranged flowers in the clumsy old-fashioned vases; she taught Mrs. Martin how to make salads and sauces; she re-arranged the furniture in the sitting-room and parlor, and skipped and chirped and rustled up stairs and down. Poor Mr. Allibone was living an enchanted life in those days. The rows of figures in his bank books danced before his eyes, and seemed to be set to music, while they tied themselves up into true lover's knots. Mrs. Bridgenorth was so assured and self-possessed, so much the mistress of the situation, she always knew just what to do, while he grew ever more timid and backward. She took him out walking at times as if he had been a lap-dog tied to a chain, and when they came back she always wore the wild flowers he had gathered for her in a great breast-knot on her black gown. Being the most methodical of men, when he mislaid a paper one day a clerk asked him if he were ill. He had not lost many hours' sleep at night for twenty years, but now he was often tossing about in the darkness, with broken visions floating before his eyes, in which he saw the widow in all her attitudes and expressions, the glance of her eye, the way she used her hands, and the glitter of her rings; her voice and accent came back, and those charming confidences, when she told him of her loneliness, her need of sympathy, her dependence, and how ill-fitted she was to go through life without a protector. For so staid and orderly a man his dreams and visions were of the wildest.

Mrs. Bridgenorth went to church every Sunday, and when the plate was passed she always folded a crisp new greenback with her beautifully gloved fingers, and dropped it deftly within. In time all the best people called upon her, and she was freely invited to the mild dissipations of the village. If she yawned a little behind her fan over these rather diluted excitements, she was still gracious. She was not "bookish," and she had not much conversation certainly with women, but it was a study to see how she dressed and moved. Judge Magnus pronounced her a fine woman, by Jove, and passed one or two evenings with her talking over Washington life, where it seemed she spent a part of each season. He thought it very odd he had never met the delightful widow, but then you know she had been in deep mourning for a few years past. Mrs. Magnus patronized her, took her out driving in her carriage, and made a dinner-party especially for her benefit. Mrs. Magnus prided herself on her penetration. The feeling was pretty general that Mrs. Bridgenorth had come excellently well recommended. It was one of those social myths which, though foundationless, are easily spread abroad.

The widow occasionally dropped into the bank, and offered checks drawn on a city bank where she kept an account. Her checks, though generally small, were always duly honored.

It was about the middle of April, and Mrs. Martin had gone to spend the day with a sick relative, and had left the house entirely at her lady boarder's disposal. It was just at this time that poor Mr. Allibone had decided to take a great step in life. He had slept but little for the past week. Mr. Allibone said to himself that it was his duty to take this step, for had she not told him she was alone in the world, that she needed a protector? Had she not asked his advice, in the sweetest way, about the education of her children and the management of her estate? Allibone felt it would be unmanly not to come to this charming woman's aid, even at the sacrifice of all his bachelor habits. On this particular morning she rose early, and when she had kissed Mrs. Martin good-by with effusion, she went to her room, and stealing about on tip-toe packed her trunk swiftly and carefully. This business completed, she put on her bonnet, locked the door of her chamber, and walked down to the bank, where, with an easy and confident air, she offered the paying teller a check for one thousand dollars, drawn by the Hon. Mr. Farrington to her order. The clerk looked at it with some curiosity. It was a different kind of check and for a much larger amount than any she had ever offered before. He scrutinized it a moment, and then handed it to the cashier. " I suppose, of course, this is all right." Allibone, with his heart in his mouth, came to the window. The widow smiled on him enchantingly. " You know," she said lightly, " Mr. Farrington is the guardian of my children. He has sent me this quarterly check to pay for their education." She was wearing the flowers he had given her the night before. It did not occur to him to show the least doubt, or to make an inquiry even, and with his own hands he counted out the money in bills of a large denomination. She thanked him and said expressively :

"Mrs. Martin is absent to-day. Come home early, and we shall have a *tête-à-tête* dinner." His heart gave a leap ; it was then he meant to take the step.

Mrs. Bridgenorth strolled out of the bank and crossed the street to the livery-stable. She engaged one of Haines's easiest carriages for a morning drive. Haines promised to have the carriage at the house inside of ten minutes. She went home and sat down by the parlor window waiting with her things on. Haines was late as usual, and her hands closed with a nervous effort at self-control, and her face grew pinched and old and sharp with anxiety. The carriage came at last, but Mike the Irishman was not driving; young Haines had taken his place. However, she went out to the gate and said in her easiest way: " I am sending off a small trurk by express. Won't you be kind enough to bring it down from my room, and then drive me over to the station ? " The cook in the kitchen with some surprise caught a glimpse of Mrs. Bridgenorth just as she was shutting the hack door. Mrs. Bridgenorth had intended to bribe Irish Mike to drive her at double-quick to the station. She dared not attempt such a thing with young Haines, so she sat in a state of cold, benumbed dread until the station was reached. Then she leaped out of the carriage and rushed forward. The twelve o'clock train was just on the point of moving out. An instant more, and she would have lost it. To his utter bewilderment young Haines saw the conductor and brakeman lift Mrs. Bridgenorth on to the platform of the car, while two baggagemen ran and seized her trunk and dashed it on board.

In less than three hours poor Mr. Allibone was going wildly about with his hands to his head, dazed and lost. The teller, who had had his suspicions, applied to the telegraph, and it sent back the dreadful news that the one thousand dollar check was a skillful forgery. There were no funds in the bank belonging to the Hon. R. Farrington. " Well," said Judge Magnus when the excitement was seething, " we are all in the same boat." She had left an unpaid board-bill of six weeks with Mrs. Martin, she had run up an account with Haines, and had neglected to pay her washer-woman.

But they were not all in the same boat. Poor Mr. Allibone was in a little boat of his own. He was hit very hard, and was obliged to go away on a six months' leave of absence to recruit. When he came back he was but the shadow of his former self. It did not affect him much, at a later day, to learn that Mrs. Bridgenorth had been arrested as a notorious confidence woman. His little world of illusion and dreams had been rudely shattered to pieces, and to a middle-aged man of steady habits that means disaster.

CHAPTER XXIII.

A STAGE-STRUCK GIRL.

THERE are days, though we know not where the mysterious influences come from, that restring every nerve and fiber in the body ; and we tingle all over with pleasurable excitement and energy. The west wind blows and our mountain breezes join merrily in the fray, bringing the scent of fir woods, the perfume of meadows, and the honied sweetness of clover fields. Small violet clouds float high in the air and melt into ether, as soap-bubbles vanish before the eyes of a happy child. All the trees rustle like innumerable fine ladies in stiff brocade, turning up the white edges of their leaves, while the light is thrown off in sparkles from the green surface, and the shadows lie cool and long on the dewy grass shaven by the lawn-mower. The village street is a beautiful arched bower woven close with leaves and boughs, and through gaps in the covered roof birds fly in and out. The brown road is dappled with great patches of light and shade, and some of the denser trees look black in the sunshine. Saddleback and the lesser hills have come out of the spring haze, and glow with resplendent azure and rose, that breathing color that appears to envelop a living form, and seems to wave and change under the movements of a soul.

On such a morning, when the honeysuckle and white cluster roses are just ready to bloom around the low windows and brown porches of her little house, Mrs. Maria Dalrymple loves to work in her garden early in the day before the sun gets 'round to the great horse-chestnut that shades the rear of her house, and throws its protecting coolness over the garden and flower-beds. Mrs. Mariar, as her friends call her, has a great taste for roses, and cultivates with success some of the improved fashionable varieties, with which she has made acquaintance through the newspapers and florists' catalogues. You should hear her talk learnedly of her "Catherine Mermaids," and "Marshal O'Neals," and "Jack Motts." For Mrs. Mariar has not the remotest idea how these names are pronounced nor what they mean.

Her old garden is a charming place, turfy and cool, with straight rows of currant and gooseberry bushes, and a delightful mixture of new-time and old-time flowers. It has clumps of trees in the corners, and the bushes are picturesque in contrast with the neatly-kept vegetable beds and the brilliant flowers. Mrs. Mariar, when she is working in the garden, looks singularly tall and gaunt. Her cotton dress-skirt falls in straight parallel folds, and she appears to have a patent hinge in her back, about the lower part of her spine, very convenient for digging with trowel or garden-hoe. At church and tea-parties, and even at home, when dressed for company, she is quite a different looking person. Then she puts on what she calls her "vanities and falsities," consisting of a "front" and "switch" of false hair, stays, a bustle, starched petticoats, and other inventions by which a gaunt female form is ingeniously padded and shaped into the approved ideal of feminine comeliness. There is a fiction in the mind of Mrs. Mariar that no one ever sees her without her "vanities and falsities," except her own folks and her nearest neighbors, who, of course, don't count, while the fact is she is hardly ever seen by any one except as that vision of long, meager, unpadded womanhood in a straight calico gown, and with skimpy gray locks brushed behind her large ears. She keeps up the same illusion about her mourning for her last husband (she has had two, neither of them good for much). When she goes to meeting or abroad on visiting duty, she wears her crêpe and bombazine. But during the greater part of her work-a-day life her widow's weeds are laid aside in her bedroom along with her other "falsities and vanities."

Mrs. Mariar keeps a cow on her little place and sells milk to some of her neighbors. The milk is carried about by her nephew Alick, the boy of her dead sister whom she has raised. Alick's sister, known to every body in the village as Sissy, has also lived with her aunt from childhood. Sissy needs none of those vanities and falsities which Mrs. Mariar uses to produce a youthful appearance. She has a charmingly plump little figure, well filled out in every respect, and a pretty face, framed in curly hair, which she wears boy-fashion. It must be confessed Sissy has always been something of a trial to her aunt, for she has as much spirit and independence as most American girls, and is rather pert from being over-praised and petted. Moreover, her head was turned a year ago by what Mrs. Mariar calls the play-acting mania. Sissy once, on a visit to some relatives in a distant city, was taken to the theater a few times, and being young and very impressionable imbibed a passion for the stage. She also read of Mary Anderson and other "stars," who have come up from small beginnings to be the darlings of the footlights. So on her return home the old pleasures and duties of life had lost their charm. Sissy dreamed waking and sleeping of those enchanting scenes in the theater, and the idea for the time took possession of her soul that she was destined to become a great tragic actress. Poor Mrs. Mariar, moving in her narrow domestic world with treadmill steadiness, thought the girl was bewitched. For Sissy put on grand airs, walked with a stage strut, and, like Mrs. Siddons speared an innocent potato as if she were stabbing a perjured villain, and spoke in deep chest-tones. She also took to practicing elocution in the barn, to the surprise of the hens and chickens, and the disapprobation of Betty, the cow. Moreover, she had persuaded Alick to learn parts and practice with her in tragic pieces, and had almost upset the poor lad and made his school studies seem perfectly flat and distasteful. They sat together in the barn-swing at moments when Sissy deigned to put off her high tragic buskin, and with arms intertwined, and taking alternate bites out of the same apple, while the light stole in dimly through the high barn window, they talked of "starring" it together all over the country, of making heaps of money and crowning themselves with deathless fame. Poor Mrs. Mariar, when she found out what was going on, scolded and stormed terribly. She boxed Alick's ears and sent him to bed without his supper; but she could not do the same with Sissy, who was stronger than she was, with wrists like steel, and who openly defied her. Finally, after shedding floods of tears, she sent for her brother Silas.

For a girl like Sissy, blessed with an ardent, devoted, constant lover, such conduct was certainly reprehensible. Her bond slave, Rufus Clover, was a young farmer, independent in maens, and belonging to the old farm aristocracy of the country side. He was very good-looking, and had received a fine education. His sisters could see nothing at all admirable in Sissy, and could not understand his infatuation. But then, brothers do not marry to please their sisters. Sissy played with Rufus as a frisky kitten plays with a mouse. At times she threw him off with a cuff of her velvet paw, and then she drew him quite close to her with gentle and captivating coyness. But one in watching her maneuvers could hardly help believing that in the end she would scratch his eyes out.

Brother Silas lived in a neighboring town, but he did most of his trading, bartering, and dickering in the village. Horse-dealing was his main vocation, and he might often be seen speeding through Main Street, a new colt attached to a sulky wherein he sat with his feet braced wide apart, his whole being, to the rakish set of his old slouched hat, redolent of the horse-jockey. His nags always kicked up a terrible dust as they rushed past, and the clatter of the sulky wheels warned every one to keep out of the way. This speeding of a new colt at a two-forty pace was a piece of swagger, a direct challenge to timid buyers, like the brag of old Homeric heroes when they came out in front of the lines and defied the cowardly foe with endless self-vauntings. It was a method very exciting to rash people who wished to "swap" or purchase a horse, and before night Silas was almost always able to sell his new animal at a pretty large advance on what he had paid for it. Sometimes he took another horse with good "boot." He had a way of casting a glamour about horse-flesh peculiarly his own. It was even said he could make an old rackabones look plump and youthful by some sort of magic known only to himself. A spavined, halt, wind-broken creature would under his manipulations come out for the time being as sound as a roach. Kickers, shyers, and balky nags beneath his hands were like lambs. When people had been bitten by Silas in a bargain they generally said nothing about it, for we all know misery loves company. And in this way he continued to drive a flourishing trade in the village long after his character was perfectly well understood.

Aside from the tricks of his own trade, Brother Silas was a very exemplary man, a "professor" and church member in good and regular standing, and a thorough teetotaler. His word could be trusted about almost any thing except a horse. He knew no more of vain and worldly amusements than an infant in arms. He was red-haired, and his two eyes never seemed to focus properly; due, I suppose, to squinting around all kinds of horses in his double-dealings. When he came to visit Sister Mariar he always tilted his chair back against the side of the kitchen, and rested his head upon the spot it had made on the wall-paper on former occasions. After a few minutes he stealthily took out his jack-knife, a huge, murderous-looking instrument with a horn handle, and on the sly began to cut notches in the edge of Mariar's old wooden kitchen chair upon which he was seated. The edge of the chair-bottom looked like a fine-toothed saw, owing to the little bits he had furtively taken out of it when Mariar was not looking. She never appeared to notice the way Silas carved up her furniture, but she seldom allowed him to sit in the parlor, for fear that in a fit of absent-mindedness he might begin to work on the mahogany.

Silas was a good brother and an affectionate uncle, if he did leave his mark on the chairs. Now, when Sissy was brought in to receive his admonitions he sat tilted back as usual, with his sanguinary-looking jack-knife in his hand. "Why, Sissy," he began, in a soft, coaxing voice, as he gazed fondly at the pretty delinquent before him, "I've knowed you ever sense you were knee-high to a grasshopper. I've knowed you like a book, Sissy, and I can't believe what I've heard tell, that you want to take to play-actin', Sissy. It's out of all natur', and it's ag'in' Scriptur'. The ministers preach ag'in' play-actin' regular as they do ag'in' intemperance. There's always been horsemen in our family as far back as we've knowed, but there never was a play-actor. We take as natural to the horse business as a fish takes to water; but as to this play-actin', Sissy, it beats all, it beats all;" and Silas, unable to express the enormity of his niece's turpitude, shut his eyes and leaned back against the wall, with his red head exactly in the middle of the spot he had made on the paper.

Sissy looked defiant and just ready to cry. She was undeniably pretty, and pouting did not detract from her charms. Silas in his soft heart felt the penetrating feminine influence. He could not be harsh with Sissy. He had named his best roan colt after her; how could he?

"It all comes from Aunt Mariar," cried Sissy, breaking into sobs. "She's been making a time because I want to —to—im-p-rove myself in el-el-ocution."

Mariar was already in tears, with her apron to her eyes, quite oblivious of her "vanities and falsities." "You don't know how she's carried on, Silas; you can't ever imagine; and she has bewitched Alick with this fool business. I caught her twice in the barn, dressed up in a pair of my best sheets, acting *Lady Macbeth*. She was telling Alick to stab somebody, and I thought there would be bloody murder."

Silas opened his eyes. "*Lady Macbeth?* Who is she, Mariar?"

"Why, don't you know, Silas?"

"Oh, yes, of course," Silas replied; though he had not the smallest conception. He remembered reading of a Kentucky horse named Lady Macbeth, but this only served to muddle his brain worse than ever.

"And there's that *Hamlet*," resumed the lamenting Mariar, as if the melancholy Dane were an obnoxious neighbor. "She's filled Alick's head with him, and he goes spouting verses all over the house."

Silas was terribly befogged in regard to *Hamlet*, but he thought it best not to say any thing before Sissy, only he opened one eye and shook his head dismally, at the same time taking a furtive notch out of the chair and then clicking the blade of his knife with a sharp explosive noise. "Don't give way, Mariar; brace up," he did venture to remark soothingly, as if "giving way" referred to her stays or possibly to some part of her bony structure.

But Mariar did give way, and quite in a new place. Seeing Sissy look obdurate and hard, she broke forth with a touch of spitefulness Silas could not approve.

"And there's Rufe Clover—as forehanded, good-principled a young man as there is in the country. She has treated Rufe like a dog; beckonin' him on, then shovin' him off at her pleasure—smilin' and frownin' for a whole year; and Rufe is sich a soft-hearted fool he keeps a following her, whether she gives him a cuff or a pat on the head."

"Most of us are durned fools some time in our lives, Mariar. Jest so with horses. The stiddiest of them will have a flounce now and then. I wouldn't give a red continental for a man who hadn't made a fool of himself once or twice in his life. Wasn't it old Solomon as said there's a time for every man to make a fool of himself?"

"I don't take no stock in Solomon," remarked Mrs. Mariar gloomily.

Sissy, though sulky and in a semi-showery April-like condition, looked more charming than ever, and Silas felt his heart giving way under the influence of her beauty. He puckered his lips to whistle, though he made no sound, and occasionally he clicked the blade of his jack-knife to keep himself up to the right pitch as a moral monitor.

"Well," said Mrs. Mariar, breaking silence, "the first thing we know she will run off on a play-actin' spree, and like as not she will take Alick with her. I think I shall have to lock her up for a few days in the store chamber, until she gets some of this nonsense out of her head."

"No, no," said Uncle Silas deprecatingly. "Don't do that. Come here, Sissy," and he took the little, soft, plump hand in his own big brown one, while his heart felt ridiculously weak. "Now, Sissy, you ain't agoin' to do any thing rash, and your Aunt Mariar she ain't agoin' to do any thing ha'sh. I ain't agoin' to do any thing ha'sh either. I'm opposed to ha'shness. I always say you can do more with a fractious pony by rubbing its nose and ears than you can by pounding its back."

A smile began to peep out of Sissy's bright eyes, and Silas winked back, as much as to say, "We know how to manage that old filly Mariar, excellent old creature that she is."

"We ain't going to tie you up in the stall," Silas resumed, "or hopple you with a log of wood, or any thing of the kind. We are jest going to treat you kind and give you your six quarts of oats regular, until you get over this play-actin' nonsense, and treat Rufe Clover as you should."

"I guess Rufe won't suffer," said Sissy, with a pretty toss of her head, and she went out of the room.

In less than three weeks Mariar, who, as Silas said, was by nature always in hot water, sent over in great distress for her brother. He found her, like a female Jeremiah, in the midst of lamentations. Sissy had run off sure enough, and had taken Alick with her, and the house was in a terrible state. The breakfast things were standing on the table in the middle of the floor, and it was past three in the afternoon. Mrs. Mariar had missed them both very early in the morning, and since that time she had enlisted the neighbors' aid, and had done what she could to get on the track of the fugitives and have them brought back. Her fears of late had been much allayed by the constant visits of young Clover, whose affair with Sissy seemed at the time to be progressing to a happy conclusion. All this Silas learned between floods of tears and the outpouring of a torrent of reproaches on his own head. Poor Silas had counseled moderation and gentleness, and now see what had come of it. He forgot even to take his accustomed place by the wall or to get out his soothing and companionable jack-knife.

But just at dark a neighbor riding by brought a telegram over from the station. It read thus: "Mr. and Mrs. Rufus Clover will be home by the eight o'clock train."

"I vum," cried Uncle Silas, starting up joyfully, "if she ain't gone and married him on the sly. She jest did it to give you a turn, Mariar; and she took Alick with her as a blind. The plaguey little jade! She's a smart one, Mariar. Chain lightnin' ain't nothin' to Sissy. A colt with that there cunning disposition would be worth a thousand dollars. Come on, Mariar, let's cut a pigeon-wing. Were both of us 'professors' and church members, but the folks will never know it."

When the newly-married couple arrived the first words Rufus Clover said were: "Well, Mrs. Dalrymple, Sissy made me run away with her and get married. She said she would not have me otherwise."

And yet I don't suppose Sissy had ever heard of *Miss Lydia Languish.*

CHAPTER XXIV.

SHIFTLESS JABEZ.

BURNT PIGEON is a semi-deserted hamlet a few miles from the village, at the termination of one of the most beautiful drives in the country. The road ends there. Civilization ends there. It is the jumping-off place of life, enterprise, and good living. The hamlet clusters like an aggregation of cells in a wasps' nest round an old abandoned iron mine. At one time, some twenty-five or thirty years ago, it was thought we were to become a vast iron-producing region, and visions of suddenly-acquired wealth rose before the minds of the quiet villagers. Land rose to fabulous prices and village real estate was quoted at a large advance. Misguided people dreamed of a miniature dingy, smoky Pittsburg on the borders of our lazy little river. But, thank heaven, there was no available water-power for smelting-furnaces and rolling-mills; the ore proved very stubborn and hard to work; and the distance from a large market rendered its transportation too expensive to make the working profitable. So, after some years of experimenting, after digging shafts, and throwing a great deal of money into them, the Burnt Pigeon mine and Burnt Pigeon mining village were abandoned by the owners, and we shrank back into our native blissful state of insignificance, with only five or six lines in the gazetteer.

Why the mine was called Burnt Pigeon nobody knew. The name has now been degraded to Pidgin. After the miners went away their miserable houses were taken in possession of vagrants and tramps, those loose elements of gipsydom, which gather about such places like crows in a newly-planted corn-field. Occasionally the sheriff makes a raid upon Pidgin to look for a stolen horse, or a petty thief, but though the hamlet bears rather a hard name, being lawless, godless and schoolless, like all such nests of wandering folk, the truth is, that the Pidginites are far better than could be expected, considering the communal freedom they enjoy. Now and then the doctor or minister is called up there—the one to heal the living, the other to bury the dead. Some religious young men in the village tried to establish a Sunday-school in Pidgin, but it failed, partly because the population is always shifting, and partly because the place is difficult of access in bad weather.

The road which runs curving about the mountain-flank washes easily in heavy storms, owing to the friable nature of the soil mixed with loose stones. There are several water-courses and small cataracts on the mountain-side, and an impetuous thunder-shower in the spring or autumn sets them foaming and tearing down into the valley, uprooting trees and moving large bowlders in their course. Occasionally in the winter, Pidgin has been literally dug out of snow banks like sheep buried in the Scotch Highlands. The wretched handful of people would certainly suffer for food at times if some of the men were not skillful hunters, very successful in snaring small animals, and in fishing in the remotest brooks, the secret of whose wild deep trout-pools is known only to themselves. The road to Pidgin gradually lifts you up to a higher plane, the air becomes sweeter, the sunlight more joyous and youthful. You smell the sweet-fern mingled with the perfume of balsam, and up and up you go until you feel like a fly on the ceiling. Great hemlock boughs sweep abruptly down and brush across the wagon top. Giant pines arise with their columnar stems over yellow earth carpets, framing in long galleries of pictures. You hear the tinkling of cow-bells just below you. The grass meadows are so close to the base of the hill their perfume comes floating up the wall of rocks. Large bowlders beautifully colored and moss-grown, lie close to the steep descent, and between them grow juniper bushes, sassafras trees, arbor vitæ, bunches of feather-fern, wild raspberry and blackberry bushes, the wild honeysuckle and azalea, and great colonies of hedge-roses. The whole road, all the way up to Pidgin, is bordered by a natural garden, with here and there a gadding grape-vine, which clambers into a tree to make the picture more like the Italian Apennines.

Probably the doctor knows more about the ways of life at Pidgin than any one else. Children are born up there occasionally, and several of them have been named John Rivington, much to the amusement of the doctor's friends. The name is generally sandwiched in between others more or less high-sounding and absurd. The so-called Christian names of the Pidginites are among the stock stories the village people always tell to strangers. One of the girls up there is simply called Queen Victoria Columbia Alleluia—the last name not given from irreverence, but from sheer ignorance. Another child is doomed to bear about with her the heavy weight of Guy Fawkes Dunleath Howard Sarsaparilla Jones. Where Guy Fawkes was picked up it is impossible to say. A boy, in the fervor of patriotism, is entitled Brave Gen. Grant, William T. Sherman Fish. To each one of his namesakes the doctor presents a Bible, with name inscribed on the fly-leaf, and a small sum of money. It is known that he buys the Bibles by the dozen of the American Bible Society, and of late he has taken to giving out the new version, as he wishes the little John Rivingtons to be brought up on the pure milk of the Word.

Last year the doctor was selectman, and he had his eye severely on all tramps, beggars, disreputable and lawless persons. The mixture of hardness and tenderness in the doctor's nature is very marked. He will not bate one jot or tittle of right, or allow any miscreant to go unwhipped of justice, but he will share his last crust with the unfortunate, and will enter into the innermost lives of those about him with a sympathy so intense that it becomes the rarest kind of genius.

One summer day, when the doctor was driving his old white nag in a venerable chaise down toward the red bridge, he saw approaching him at a crawling pace a miserable broken-winded, weak-kneed horse drawing a meager load of household stuff which shook and rattled at every step. Sitting perched on a washtub turned bottom up, framed in by a broken rocking chair, a clothes-horse, and the posts of a rickety bedstead, sat a lean, brown man, long and limp, with face, beard, and hair of the same dirty clay color, and out of this countenance looked a pair of singularly winkless prominent light eyes. He was clad in the shabbiest of nether garments and a tattered shirt, and his feet, destitute of stockings, were thrust into a pair of old slippers trodden down at the heels. His rimless straw hat had a bit of white rag pinned in at the back to preserve his neck from the sun. Beside the wagon, garnished on the exterior by a few miserable pots and pans, walked a woman miserably pale and troubled with a hollow cough. A handkerchief was tied over her head, and from the way her poor old gown flapped about her feet it was evident that she had on no underwear. In her arms the doctor at once recognized the latest John Rivington, a helpless red infant not more than a month old, so limp about the neck that the poor thing's weak head, with a suspicion of black down upon it, hung helplessly over the woman's shoulder, like the head of a young lamb when carried by the shepherd. By the woman's side trotted a lean, tanned, ragged girl of ten or eleven, with eyes surprisingly large in her thin sharp face. Her straight legs and arms were like bundles of sticks. Her bare feet made splashes in the soft dirt of the road, with ten little depressions for the toes. She carried a black and white kitten, held with a nervous grasp in her bony arms.

The doctor jumped out of his wagon, at the risk of hurting his rheumatic knee. The sight of this family on the road, moving with the whole of their earthly possessions, gave him a sensation like nostalgia. He wanted to pull that man off the load and thrash him within an inch of his life for allowing the sick woman to walk and carry her baby. But the doctor restrained himself, and the man at sight of him began to duck as if with the intent of putting up an umbrella to screen himself from the storm of wrath he felt was about to descend on his devoted head.

"What are you about?" said the doctor sternly, as he stood in the road, his long carriage whip in his hand, while the woman looked up in his face with her weary lack-luster eyes.

"Wal, you see, we had ter move. The folks up thar kinder took a prejudice, and they lent me a hoss and wagon to move my stuff."

"Oh, they made you clear out, did they?" returned the doctor, while a grim smile spread over his face. It tickled him to think there was some righteous wrath up in Pidgin, and almost restored him to good humor.

"Yes, I b'l'eve they did. I don't know why. I was allus peaceable, me and my folks. I hain't no idea why they took a prejudice," he went on in a whining tone. "But they did, and they hinted at tar and feathers."

The sunshine of laughter spread over the doctor's face. Really there is balm in Gilead, there is hope for Pidgin, he thought. "Do you think the village folks will like to have you quartered on them any better than they liked it up in Pidgin? Do you expect to go to the poor-house?"

The man lifted the edge of his rimless hat, and scratched his head. "I 'low not. There's that old house off the turnpike in the woods they call haunted. I ain't afeared of ghosts, and I thought I'd move my folks in there until I could get in better shape. Hayin' is coming along, and I 'low I can get a job of work then; and there's my wife and the girl, they can pick berries at odd times."

"We don't propose to harbor vagrants," said the doctor sternly. "I know you won't work. You are a perfectly hopeless case. If I had my way, there would be a whipping-post set up for just such louts as you are."

The man looked down and wiped his face on the sleeve of his ragged shirt. "I ain't no vagrom, and I don't propose to beg. And I know you can't jug me unless I do suthin' ag'in' the law."

The doctor knew it too, and at that moment he caught sight of the woman's white face, the baby that had gone to sleep on her shoulder, and the great eyes of the child fixed on his face.

"Here," said he, half jerking the man out of the wagon. "Now put your wife and baby in there, and do you take those reins and walk alongside, and guide the horse." He helped the poor woman up to the seat on the bottom of the wash-tub, and lifted in the little girl, who was painfully light—like a bundle of hollow bird's bones—and then he stood and watched as the load moved down the road, swaying from side to side, the man shuffling along in his old slippers.

The haunted house in the woods off the turnpike had long been an object of intense awe and curiosity to the village children. It had lost its doors and windows and part of its walls, and was in a ruinous condition. The plaster had dropped from the ceilings, and a rickety stairway led to a dilapidated chamber, where, it was said, spots of blood could be seen on the floor. As the legend of the house ran, a peddler had been murdered in that room, and nightly came back in search of his pack and a bag of gold. When the nomad Jabez and his family took up their abode in this old shell of a house, the children all rushed over to see how a family looked living without any front door or glass windows. Their domestic life certainly had a very open expression, and for a time the fascination of watching what went on in the very inside of the Jabez household, where a ghost was supposed to be one of the inmates, kept the children glued to the spot.

Jabez meantime would stand in the doorless doorway, his ragged nether garment held up by a tow string, and monotonously reprobate their presence. Mrs. Jabez, poor soul, did what she could in that dreadful open-work house by pinning up newspapers and hanging the only pair of sheets she possessed at some of the orifices to secure a little privacy. In a few days Jabez put out a shingle sign: " Ginger Pop and Spruce Gum sold here. Also Ginseng and Pepper root." He gave it out that he was busily engaged in searching the woods for roots and herbs, and intended to invent a patent medicine and call it the Jabez Elixir of Life. But his wares were all frauds. The boys who invested a portion of their pocket money in his ginger pop found it was nothing but colored water, and the spruce gum was in no way chewable. They threatened to mob him if he did not take down his shingle, and Jabez, the victim of circumstances, was forced to withdraw from mercantile life. But the boys did not cease their persecutions. They crept round to the rear of the ruinous cottage where Mrs. Jabez had left things all open to the universe, and there they made remarks on what the Jabez family had for dinner and supper, and watched the whole of the internal domestic economy as if it had been an absorbing play. This continued until the village schoolmaster came out, clothed with authority, and drove the boys home at the point of a sharp stick.

Meanwhile the burden of feeding the family in a manner, however inadequate, fell almost entirely on the little ten-year-old girl. She was known in the village as the chippie bird, because she was so slender and light; she could creep through the smallest opening in a hedge, and almost seemed to fly over stone walls and fences. Chippie had that indefatigable energy possessed by some nervous children, and a most patient, angelic temper. She performed the labor of a girl twice her years, and never complained of being tired. She collected sticks in the woods and carried great bundles to furnish fuel for the fire. She pulled greens in the meadows and gathered wild berries for miles around to sell in the village from door to door. It seemed as if the little creature never rested day or night, and her brown legs, and feet, and hands were cruelly torn by the brambles. When the mother was ill, and she was always ailing, Chippie took care of her nights, tended the baby, and cooked such food as she could procure.

The village people soon came to recognize the rare spirit of the child. Her wonderful old eyes troubled them and touched their hearts. They gave her more than conscience warranted, knowing it would go to feed lazy Jabez. They took her into their houses and fed and dressed her, but in a few days she appeared again in the old rags. Where the good clothes went to they never knew, but it was conjectured that Jabez sold them to procure tobacco and whisky. He was known to have taken his wife's strengthening medicine for the sake of the spirits it was put up in. The doctor would have given a considerable sum of money to rid the neighborhood of Jabez, in such a humane and perfectly satisfactory manner that he need never think of him again. He offered to take the little girl and find her a good home, and have her taught, but the father refused.

"What's the use of bringin' up children," said Jabez argumentatively, "and havin' all the worry, and fret, and bother, if they don't help their payrents when they are weakly and unable to help themselves? You folks can't have that little gal nohow. I'm an affectionate father, and I should be pinin' for her society. No use talkin', you can't have my gal."

When the cold autumn weather began to pinch the inmates of the doorless and windowless house, and there were no berries or wild fruits to gather, and the grain fields and apple orchards had been pretty thoroughly gleaned, Jabez grew very fretful and morose. He raised his hand against his miserable consumptive wife, and the village officials warned him that they would lock him up in jail if he did not behave better. He was worse than a pest in the neighborhood, and pity for his wretched family made it all the harder for charitable folks who could not in conscience feed and comfort this miserable shiftless being. One day Chippie came home from a foraging expedition looking quite blue down to the tips of her pathetic little toes. "The doctor says I must go to school," she began in her piping, childish treble. "He says its compulsilatory, that's just the word he used; and I must have a new frock and a pair of shoes."

"Compulsilatory!" repeated Jabez, as he lay half stretched out on a truckle-bed in one corner of the room. "I don't approve of this community at all. It's the meanest place I ever got into. There ain't no fishin' and there ain't no huntin'," he went on bitterly, as if nature had contrived the deficiency especially to spite him. "Leastways if there was huntin', I couldn't hunt, cos I hain't no gun. There ain't no whisky to be had nuther. When a man feels weak and all gone, a thimbleful of whisky sets him up amazing. Wife, we shall have to move on to the pine barrens, where there ain't no talk about this compulsilatory eddication—takin' a man's children away from him and shuttin' of 'em up in a schoolhus' when he needs them as a prop and a stay in time of trouble. We will pack up to-murrur and be off, and then where will their compulsilatory eddication be? Farmer White said he'd let me take his wagon to move any time and glad to do it."

The next day, when all the wretched Jabez household was packed into Farmer White's wagon, some one asked Jabez what there was to live on in the barrens and what he expected to do there.

" Dunnó," said he, scratching his head, " what I shall do, and dunno what there is to live on in the barrens unless it is turpentine. And turpentine for a stiddy thing is better than nothin'."

CHAPTER XXV.

CUPID AMONG JUNE ROSES. THE LITTLE MAIDEN SISTERS.

THE rose season brings with it every thing beautiful. To Italy it brings the nightingale, to Persia the bulbul. But as we can have neither nightingale nor bulbul, we must content ourselves with the bobolink, the robin, the cat-bird, the song-sparrow, and the evening thrush. The meadows are in their glory. Some hillsides have a milky froth of ox-eye daisies which the farmers behold with displeasure, while young girls gather them in great clusters to deck the bodice. The timothy and herdsgrass have gathered a delicate pinkish dust of flowers. The clover is rounded to a crimson globe, inviting the bee. It is a time of enchantment, when young hearts and simple unworldly old hearts think of love, the adjustment of the inner world to the outer vision.

Roses, new-mown hay, honeysuckle, and strawberries are associated in one's thoughts with wedding bells, wedding favors, bride-cake, and happy pairs whirled off into the blissful honeymoon. We have had our village weddings. They have been rather frequent this year for a community not much given to matrimony, and now that they are all over we regret that we must settle down to the prosaic hum-drum of ordinary life. The wedding of Mr. Worldly Wiseman and Miss Busy Bee was of the purely conventional sort. The village church was handsomely trimmed with palms and exotics, and there was a great abundance of white satin, tulle, and orange blossoms. The town was filled with the bustle of visitors who came from a distance; and our village paper devoted two or three columns of its valuable space to a description of the trousseau and the wedding gifts. Hugh cheerfully acted as best man to show that he had no grudge against the lady for taking a richer lover and slighting him. Mr. Wiseman's house would now be one of the most agreeable in the village. He could not afford to be on bad terms with the pretty young mistress. The groom slipped a wedding fee of a hundred dollars into the parson's hand, and, soon after, our young clergyman's wife appeared in a new black silk gown, which became her amazingly. Mr. Wiseman's old housekeeper sat in a back pew crying and sobbing during the entire ceremony, but when the happy pair drove off amid a shower of rice and old slippers, she sent a pair of her old shoes (number tens) flying after them for luck, and raised a shout of laughter.

But Mr. Milletseed and Miss Rose Madder could not think of being married in that style, which they considered horribly ugly and inartistic. They were wedded under a blooming apple tree, which made a pretty bower for their young heads. Rose was clad in artless Swiss muslin made rather scant, and tied about the waist with a white satin sash. She wore a high shepherdess hat, trimmed with a great deal of fluffy white lace, and she hoped she looked sufficiently like a Whistler or a Burne-Jones to be æsthetically interesting. Milletseed had procured a new velvet coat for the occasion, and was married in knee breeches and buckled shoes. He was a Walter Crane all over. The artists and students who had come up from the city danced about the apple tree, and poured libations to Hymen and sang French love songs. When the young couple went away so poor and so happy, with the future an unknown x or y in their reckoning, a great many tender good wishes, like a flock of doves, flew after them, and a few sentimental old maids shed tears because they looked so young and so little able to cope with the hard facts of life.

The nuptials of Drusilla took place at home, in the great drawing-room, where a wealthy ancestor had formerly given fine banquets. It is one of those handsome old colonial rooms, white and gold, with a great tiled fireplace and high chimney-piece, which modern decorative taste has again brought into vogue. There are two white and gold pillars at the east end of the room framing a mullioned window. Drusilla's friends wished to adorn these pillars with vines and flowers, to make a kind of bower where she and the Rev. Arthur Meeker were to stand. But Drusilla would not hear to such nonsense. She allowed only two large clusters of red and white roses to be placed in the tall blue china jars on the hearth by the great chimney-piece. Neither would she have the new-fangled marriage ceremony with a ring taken from the Episcopal Service-Book. She insisted on being married in the plainest way. There was not even a bride-cake. Her idea was just to stand up and have it over with as quickly as possible. But a few friends would come in, and our old St. Patty was brought down in her invalid chair and ensconced in the place of honor. She was dressed by her friends and lovers in her tabbinet gown, and those dainty laces and clear-starched muslins which became her so well. She allowed the girls to pin white flowers in her cap and in the breast of her gown, and though nearly a hundred years old, she looked much more like a bride than her matter-of-fact, strong-minded daughter.

Drusilla was married in a good stout serviceable traveling dress of a color that would not show dust. She wore a bonnet and gloves of the same hue, and her air was prompt and business-like. It had taken considerable energy to get the Rev. Arthur Meeker in trim for the wedding journey. It was necessary to brace him up with two eggs beaten in half-a-tumbler of sherry. He was obliged to wear a mustard paste on his chest during the ceremony, and was well padded all over with new and thick red flannels, which Drusilla had selected for his use. It seemed cruel to pelt so frail a person even with rice, and this ceremony was omitted by request. When the newly married pair went to the carriage, which was in waiting to take them to the station, the Rev. Arthur carried a light summer shawl for his wife's use over his left arm. But she came loaded down with his two coats, a pair of umbrellas, a walking-stick, a hot-water bottle, and a flask of new milk. It was a significant symbol of the respective burdens they would bear through life. The people tried to hide their smiles while they whispered to each other that Drusilla had at last got her hands full. But it was what she had married for. She had taken him up as a vocation—a home-mission enterprise—and although he was a smaller one than her natural ambition would have chosen, he was better than nothing.

In a small community weddings leave a ripple of excited feeling behind them, and stir up the feminine fancy with new and pleasing hopes. After Drusilla went off, " at her age," all the single sisters looked in the glass with a certain feeling of encouragement. It might not be too late after all, and small flutterings of pleased anticipation lent a vague charm to the summer days. As for the young girls, their innocent hearts were filled with the cooing and soft twitterings of the dove of promise; and the young men's eyes sought theirs with new meanings, and blushes came more readily than their wont. Even the most wooden of the old bachelors felt growing pains and slight twinges of romantic impulse, as if their sober affections might yet put forth new shoots, and the Indian summer bring a blessing they had missed in the spring.

The two maiden sisters, who live in the cottage nearly opposite the great gate of Judge Magnus's mansion, under one of the largest elm trees in the village street, belong to those tender souls who, though unwed, never pass the prime of romantic sentiment, sacred to love's illusions. They are small women, who have gone off a good deal in figure with the advance in years, and they both have the same curious little stoop of the shoulders and the same way of wearing the hair, with feeble attempts at girlish curls and frizzes straying out from under their black head-dresses. Miss Henriette is supposed to be very lively and waggish, while Miss Sophie is more serious in her cast of mind, and occasionally writes poetry as a pastime. They are both as innocent as babes, though they imagine they know a great deal about the wickedness of the world. They are apt to think the same thoughts, and speak the same words simultaneously; and when the lively Henriette leads the conversation Sophie nods and smiles approval, and repeats after her the end of each sentence.

The little sisters take great care of their health, and have a number of pet diseases, of which they are as proud as if they were rare plants or vines. They are homœopaths on principle; but when they are seriously ill the doctor comes in unbidden, throws the little pills and mixtures with which they are continually dosing themselves out of the window, and treats them as he pleases. Strange to say, the little sisters are hardly ever ill one at a time. If one takes to her bed, the other is sure to follow very soon. They have lived so long together, they have the same motions, the same sensations. If one feels a twinge in her right thumb, the other feels it in exactly the same place. The only difference is that Henriette sometimes sees a joke when Sophie does not see it, and then she has to make an elaborate dissection of the joke for Sophie, which is very trying to a humorist.

When they go to church on fine Sundays their old fat tabby cat always follows them like an enchanted maid, and waits outside the sanctuary until they emerge.

Every boy in the village knows this old tabby, and a youngster who should venture to shy a stone at her would be considered hopelessly depraved by the whole community. They have two canary birds which make a music-box of their little cottage ; and as seems perfectly right and natural, Henriette's is a livelier and sprightlier bird than Sophie's. The little sisters are certainly poor, and for many years their frugal housekeeping has been helped out by the gifts of kind friends. All sorts of fictions are devised to make the delicate, refined old women believe they are not objects of charity, but, as some one has well said, objects of amity. It would hurt their sensibilities to discover that their small economies are known to the neighbors—the fact that the old gowns are turned and turned, and dyed with their own hands, to look perfectly ladylike and respectable. When the judge's wife comes home from Washington, she brings them little gifts ; and at Christmas, of course, presents are allowable. The kind farmers are always asking them to taste their vegetables and fruits, their butter and eggs ; their wood is mysteriously laid in for them when they go away on visits. Some one for ten years past has regularly paid their tax bill, and although it is an open secret in the village, they have never been able to discover their benefactor. Thus they are kept in perfect comfort, while the fiction of their independence is maintained.

They take the most innocent lively interest in the affairs of the neighborhood. They are fond of gossip, especially the love stories, but they are free from malice and most ingenious in finding out the good points of people generally considered immoral and worthless. When a villager is caught in any overt act of wickedness which appears to admit of no excuse, the neighbors are always eager to hear what the little sisters will say about him, in what good quality their charitable souls will take refuge from the general turpitude of the delinquent. The country-side has its myths and legends, and one of the most frightful of these clings to a notorious character, Hank Hayrick by name, who over twenty years ago kept a low tavern on the side of Saddleback. Hank was a hard drinker and very quarrelsome and profane in his cups. During the war of the Rebellion he was a blatant, shameless secessionist and copperhead; and in the midst of a most loyal community was considered a standing disgrace and infamy. At the time of President Lincoln's assassination, so the story runs, Hank openly rejoiced, loudly declaring his gladness. For three days he held an orgie with his boon companions on the mountain, drinking and carousing, and uttering horrible blasphemies. The road from Hank's house leading down the mountain, is steep and dangerous, as for more than a mile it flanks an abrupt precipice, along which some brush and trunks of trees have been thrown as a slight guard. In the spring the danger is much increased by ice and washouts. Hank, in the afternoon of the third day, while still under the influence of drink, started with a pair of half-broken colts to drive down the mountain, the road being in very bad condition. As he was alone, it was never known just how the accident occurred, but at night he was found at the bottom of a gorge a hundred feet deep, he and his horses stark dead.

When this dreadful story was told to the little sisters they sat in pained silence for some time. They had been crying over the death of the good president, and their eyes were red and swollen. "Well," said Sophie at last, with a great sigh, "I often and often saw Hank Hayrick drive past here. He may have been a dreadful wicked bad man, but I never saw him no ways intoxicated. He always sat up straight in his wagon and managed his horses well. And once when sister Henriette was trying to pick her way across the street in a muddy time he stopped to let her get past without spattering of her,"

"So he did," said Henriette, brightening up wonderfully. "I am so glad you remembered that, sister."

The little sisters cherish the harmless fiction that if they had not been so devoted to each other, they might have married. But they never could bear the idea of living separated. Perhaps no one ever asked them in marriage, but that makes no difference. The small speck of possible romance keeps their hearts soft and young. Of course, they know it is too late to think of such things for themselves now. But they can enter into other lives and sympathize with all lovers most truly. Within a year a distant relative has come to pass some time with them. She is considerably younger than either Henriette or Sophie, but still she is a spinster pretty well advanced in years. The little sisters regard her as a great deal younger than themselves, indeed, quite a young person, and on the score of her youth would excuse any folly or indiscretion she might commit.

The sisters have woven a little romance about their friend from the fact of her once having been partly in love with a young man who paid her a great deal of attention and then went off and married her most intimate friend. It would appear that the young man had been so very attentive because he wished to talk about her friend, the lady with whom he was in love; but in the eyes of the little sisters his conduct is none the less reprehensible. They could find excuses for Hank Hayrick sooner than for "that man," as they always call him. Miss Crayshaw dresses nicely and does not in the least despise those arts of the toilet by which the ravages of years are repaired. She has quite a pretty income for a single woman, and has brought a large increase of comfort into the household. But the little sisters never think of what they would lose in her marriage. Their tender souls are only alive to her felicity. They are sure that in the scheme of divine goodness the transgressions of "that man" toward the comfortable well-to-do Crayshaw will be repaired. They have formed in their fancy the very image of the man who is coming to make her happy.

"I am sure he is coming soon," says Miss Sophie, as she looks out of the window, gazing up and down the village street in search of this not impossible he. "And then when he comes we shall have a wedding here. How delightful that will be! We have never had a wedding in the family; for you know sister and me are so bound up it wasn't possible. But it will be so pleasant for you to say *we*, my dear. *I* is such a chilly, cold, dismal little word. Sister and me never say *I*. If we had been obliged to say *I*, possibly we might have married long ago. I feel in my bones, Mary Crayshaw, that *he* is coming soon to make it all up to you for what *that man* has made you suffer. We shall have to lose you one day, sister and me. But then if we know you are happy with *him*, it will console us. We should hate to be selfish, sister and me."

He has not come yet, nor are there any imminent signs of him on the horizon. But if faith can move mountains, he will certainly appear.

CHAPTER XXVI.

MRS. LEGALITY AT THE WILDERNESS LODGE.

TWO or three enthusiastic devotees of the rod and gun have built small shooting-boxes within a few miles of the village, and have been in the habit of coming out to them from the city at any and every season when they felt the need of rest or recreation.

One of these, known as the Lodge, is charmingly situated among the oak timber in the upper valley. An extensive pine forest stretches away on the hillside behind the house. The river purls peacefully along within a stone's throw, and here spreads out to a greater width, and clears itself from the water-weed in broad silver expanses. The place is as solitary and sylvan as the forest of Arden. One wanders about in the open glades carpeted with soft turf and spotted with sunshine, expecting to come upon *Touchstone* and *Audrey*, or even fair *Rosalind* in her boyish disguise. A little clearing and garden-patch for the sake of those savory herbs a sportsman loves with his game and fish dinners invite the wild bee and the song-bird.

The Lodge is a quaint little affair, planned by an old bachelor to his liking, with half-a-dozen rooms, each furnished with a fire-place to burn logs of some size, on cold days. It is shingled nearly all over with yellow cedar shingles, and the veranda is broad and pleasant, looking westward. The lower rooms are ceiled and wainscoted with Georgia pine, and the chambers have received one rough scratch-coat of plaster. The Lodge is owned by a celebrated city lawyer, who, at home an elegant man of society, with a just estimate of the *convenances* which lie in dress-coats, crush-hats, gloves, white neck-cloths, and other tokens of the humanities, as soon as he arrived at the Lodge put on a dreadful old hat and a whole suit of flannel both within and without, allowed his beard to grow untrimmed, and appeared in old boots and shoes, of which he kept a large collection at the Lodge for country use.

He was more alert and springy in his motions than a countryman, and it was only by these tokens you could distinguish him from a native. He generally brought a friend with him, Jack Hildreth by name, who behaved in the same way. When business brought them to the village they tried to slip about incognito to escape the judge and the parson, and the inevitable invitations to dinner and tea. Their mail was carried to and fro by an old man who, with his wife, kept the Lodge in perpetuity, on the tacit understanding that they had secured a life berth. An old horse and wagon belonging to the establishment was used by the gentlemen to carry them to distant parts of their preserve. They spent the day wading up brooks in great india-rubber boots like trunk-hose, often in the drenching rain. The old horse was always there at the rendezvous, by a pair of bars with his head down—too low-spirited even to eat post-meat—when they wished to be taken home, where they entered like the blustering west wind, hearty, hungry, and happy, to find a roaring fire of light wood in the living-room, which Mrs. Burns had kindled. Soon the appetizing odors of broiling fish began to diffuse themselves all over the house. There is nothing a sportsman enjoys more than eating his own "catch" brown, and cooked to a turn, with the appropriate sauces. And Mrs. Burns was very good at sauces, which Mr. Legality had taught her to make after recipes secured at his New York club.

The interior of the Lodge was a little bare. A pair of

large hunting dogs went all over it at will, and made themselves perfectly at home at all hours. The living-room was mainly furnished with guns and fishing-tackle, artificial flies, and cartridges, and various trophies of the chase. A pair of immense hawks' wings were nailed against the wall, and the brush of a red fox. What is the use of curtains or shutters when you have no neighbors but the rabbits and squirrels and wild birds, and are very fond of sunshine flooding your rooms? Mr. Legality had purchased a few rocking-chairs, which struck his fancy, from the old women among the mountains, and these, with half-a-dozen braided hand-made rugs, picked up in the same way, were the main furnishings of the sitting-room. On the walls were photographs of one or two of the extra large trout he had caught. A few books lay about on the table or were crowded upon a little shelf over the chimney-piece. There was a file of a sporting magazine, an old copy of Isaak Walton, an odd volume of Horace, a few French novels, and one or two works on the best mode of making artificial flies. On the chimney-piece was ranged an assortment of pipes, cigar-boxes, and bottles. The corners of the room were taken up with old boots and miscellaneous "traps."

This was the bachelor's castle, the complete epitome of his idea of rest and recreation, free from bother and nonsense. Mrs. Burns could cook a capital fish or game supper, and he had the pleasure of furnishing the elements of his simple *cuisine*. The air was delicious, the scenery beautiful; with no one to trouble or annoy, no near neighbors, no social duties, none of the flummery of fashion. For a few weeks each year he was a free man. Every one about the establishment, both human and canine, did exactly as he or she pleased. Jack Hildreth, when he was staying at the Lodge, went regularly to sleep after supper, and slept the entire evening. Mr. Legality loved him more than a more brilliant companion, for he exacted nothing, fell readily into his old friend's ways, and took life on the easiest terms.

But of course when Mr. Legality emerged from his country shell and returned to town he was another being. The eager, sharp-witted, cultivated town man forgot the smell of spruce, pine, and hemlock, and rushed into the arena of the world clad in the habiliments of the most advanced civilization. If he had consulted his country self when he found such unalloyed enjoyment with his pipe, and his old boots, and his faithful and rather stupid friend, he never would have married. Mrs. Burns, smoothing her apron and squinting both ways for Sunday with her crossed eyes, would always have remained his ideal of domestic felicity. But it was while masquerading as his city self, enacting the fine gentleman in the intervals of absorbing "cases," that he fell in with a charming woman, who, if not in the first bloom of youth, was sufficiently beautiful, and possessed of a fine fortune and an enviable literary reputation. She shared all the lawyer's tastes and fancies. While sitting on a satin sofa in a handsome drawing-room she adored the woods. She had never angled for any thing in a mountain lake, but she was certain she should like it. She wrote an exquisite sonnet from Mr. Legality's description of the Lodge and the wild birds singing around the windows, and it was published in the *Pacific Monthly*. This was only a few weeks before Miss Musa became Mrs. Legality. A very pretty wedding it was, with a half-column notice in the daily papers, and a mention of all the distinguished people present.

It was arranged that after a few weeks of travel they were to spend the summer at the Lodge. The solitude would be so sweet to a happy pair newly wedded, exempt from prying neighbors, city visitors, and fuss and feathers. It was the cream of rural simplicity, a return to nature. Mr. Legality had always been so happy at the Lodge that in his fancy it was surrounded by a halo of light. He thought of his old boots and his fishing-tackle with sentimental fondness. All his days had been good there, and all his nights serene. The flavor of Mrs. Burns's coffee and broiled fish was sweet in his thoughts. How many delicious meals he and old Jack Hildreth had enjoyed under the rafters? How many blessed hours had been given to smoke and reverie, and the healthy rest that comes after vigorous exercise in the open air. His wife, with her poetic temperament, would be sure to appreciate the Lodge at its true value.

It was raining when they reached the village station, and old Burns met them with the ancient horse and wagon. Mrs. Legality had declared with enthusiasm that she loved to rough it, but her face fell when she beheld this rustic establishment, and her husband felt the little chill which ran down to the tips of her fingers as he helped her into the vehicle. All the woods and ways were damp and sweet with summer rain. The boughs dripped, and a mild incense came up from the earth, and mingled with the breath of verdure and wild-flowers. The mountain roads were crossed by brawling brooks, and the low-hung clouds opened to show the distant hills. Mrs. Legality said it was perfectly lovely, but a kind of homesickness crept over her as they went deeper into the forest, and her husband thought she was tired with the journey. Man-like, he had given her no particular description of the Lodge. He had told her it was plain and unpretending, but perfectly comfortable, and she had imagined something of quite Arcadian prettiness set down in the woods.

Her habits were very nice. She had always been petted, admired, and praised. The little house when she entered it, with Mrs. Burns ducking and courtesying at the door, gave her quite a new idea of savage rudeness. There were neither curtains at the windows nor carpets on the floors—nothing but scenery and bare walls. And she, a bride of only a few weeks' duration, not so young as she had once been, to be sure, but still with a high sense of personal distinction and value, had been brought to this place to pass the summer! Her husband tried to whistle as he always did when he put off the old man at the Lodge. He divested himself of his nice clothes, and got into that easy rig, the old coat and shocking bad hat. His wife did not like him in it. She secretly felt that if she had first seen him in this guise, she never would have married him. Although it had been tacitly agreed that Legality was to have it all his own way at the Lodge, and go on with his old life there, while Mrs. Legality ruled supreme in the city house, she could not help saying as she lifted her dainty skirts to keep them off the bare floor:

"Don't you think, my dear, it would be well to clean?"

"Oh, I let old Burns and his wife manage all that. They sweep and scrub the house out now and then, I suppose. Why, my dear, do you find any thing amiss?"

"Oh, no," she responded at once. "The situation is perfectly charming."

Mrs. Burns cooked as nice a supper as she could for the bride, but the table-service was not very elegant, and Mrs. Legality, whose tastes were fastidious in such matters, could not at once find an appetite. Her husband had always been in the habit of pouring out his own tea and coffee, and now, when his wife took her place at the tray, he had an odd sense of not being at home. Their first meal was certainly not a success, although each tried to hide from the other how little it was enjoyed. In the evening the dogs came in shaking the wet from their thick coats. They lay down before the fire and soon the room was filled with damp steam. Strange to say, Mr. Legality did not seem to mind it. He spent the time in cleaning his old guns and putting his fishing-tackle in order. Mrs. Legality tried to interest herself in what seemed of such absorbing interest to him, but she discovered with some dismay that she had no taste for such things, and an incipient sentiment of jealousy arose within her toward this love of sport which had pushed her, for the time being, from the first place in her husband's affections. She could not endure the smell of the dogs; and the odor of old Burns's pipe came in from the kitchen, where he was smoking very vile tobacco.

She excused herself early on the plea of being tired, and went to bed. The silence of the forest around the Lodge was portentous. A whippoorwill came close to the windows and gave forth his mournful cadence. The tree-toads added to the Dantean chorus. Though not so very young, poor Mrs. Legality went to sleep sobbing into her embroidered handkerchief. What a bower for a bride! She had already come to the conclusion that she hated a lodge in a vast wilderness, although she had sentimentalized so much in her writings over this life with nature, this happy seclusion far from the madding crowd.

The next morning was warm and sunny; the forest glowed resplendent from the rain. A merry breeze blew the rain-drops like diamond spray from the leaves. Mr. Legality was up early to enjoy the birds and to wash some of the city dust, as he said, out of his mind. He invited his wife to go fishing, and they packed themselves into the wagon merrily enough with old Burns to drive. The old man was in his shirt-sleeves smoking a pipe of that same vile tobacco. The wind blew the smoke back into the lady's eyes, and almost spoiled the pleasure of locomotion over rough but lovely roads. The day was too bright for good sport. Mrs. Legality caught nothing, and she looked upon the patience with which her husband waited for a rise as quite phenomenal. The hours seemed long and dull. The black flies and midges troubled her not a little, and she saw a large black-snake near the lake-side, which made her feel that she could never go back to that place with any comfort.

After that day she excused herself from fishing, and remained at home with Mrs. Burns, who showed her the chickens she had reared that the master might have a new-laid egg for his breakfast; and a litter of young puppies in which he took delight. But these things' had their limits in the way of diversion. She had often felt lonely even when the center of a brilliant circle, and she had found relief in breathing out her longings in verse: but she had never felt as lonely as now that she was united to the man of her choice, and trying vainly to enter into the joys of his life. Yet it would be ridiculous to publish her heart-pangs to the world. Her husband came home too tired from his day's sport to engage in literary conversation. Her writing gift seemed to have left her. She had no neighbors or friends—no one but Mrs. Miggs, who brought them milk and butter. Her fine clothes were of no avail. When she dressed for dinner, her husband did not seem to know it, so she took to wearing a flannel gown all day, and she wept as she awoke to the reality of things. She hated roughing it in the woods. She was sophisticated and conventional to a degree, and, worse than all, she was worldly. She could not blame Mr. Legality, but she discovered that she had been shamming and posing about something of which she was ignorant.

Mr. Legality, finding that his wife, though a charming woman, had no taste for sport, and could not sympathize with him about flies, and bait, and fish-hooks, and did not even treasure up in her memory the exact weight of the big trout he caught on Thursday, turned with affectionate longing toward the thought of Jack Hildreth, who for so many years had been his faithful comrade. But when he proposed that Jack Hildreth be invited for a six-weeks' visit to the Lodge he found his wife adverse to the plan. She disliked Jack Hildreth, that big, burly, red-faced man, with no conversation, who cared for nothing but eating and drinking hot toddy, and went regularly to sleep in his chair of an evening and snored in all the notes of the gamut. Mr. Legality, with a good deal of inward resistance, gave up the idea of inviting his old friend Jack.

But it happened just at this time that he was called to a distant city to attend to a law case involving a great sum of money. As his absence might extend to two or three weeks, he suggested that his wife invite her friend Miss Leeds to pay her a visit. Mary Leeds had a pet mania for architecture and house decoration. And almost the first word she said after entering the Lodge was: " How can you live in this barrack ? Not a carpet, nor a rug, nor curtain to the window. But it has possibilities, my dear," she continued, half closing her eyes and taking it all in. Her fingers itched to get hold of the little bare place and transform it into something habitable and inviting. In two days she had persuaded her friend to do over the Lodge on her plan, which was simple and practicable, and to give Mr. Legality a charming surprise on his return. It was with some fear of judgment to come that Mrs. Legality took the house in hand. But once in the thick of carpenters and decorators, she forgot all about the consequences. Her own artistic furniture was sent up from the city, and she and Mary Leeds worked like nailers to get every thing in order. New servants were hired and drilled, and poor old Mrs. Burns, in a tearful state, was degraded to the position of head scullion or general kitchen assistant.

" Master won't like the doin's—I know he won't," she said, as she saw all the guns and fishing-tackle translated to an upper room. " He'll be like a cat in a strange garret."

The Lodge certainly came out a thing of beauty under

the skillful hands of the ladies, and there was much heart-trembling to see how Mr. Legality would take it when a telegram arrived announcing his speedy return. He took it, all things considered, better than could have been expected, although he seemed a little dazed at first, and could hardly put two words together. Mrs. Burns dethroned, the guns and traps all put away, the dogs kept out of the house! Where was he? He rubbed his eyes. The old happy bachelor days had vanished forever. But how could any one, even his own wife, know what this place had been to him in the past? Mrs. Legality watched him closely. There were no outbursts, no reproaches, only compliments, a little satirical, for her and her friend.

In the evening he took a walk in the woods, and sat for some time smoking and musing on a log, and when he came into his transformed cottage he sat down at the new Chippendale desk, and wrote several letters. His cheerfulness and serenity had entirely returned. In two or three days he announced to Mrs. Legality that he had purchased her a house at Newport—"Tom Bly's, you know, my dear. I bought it at a great bargain. It is beautifully situated, and I think you will enjoy it."

Mrs. Legality has spent several summers in her Newport cottage, and Mr. Legality is occasionally seen there, but part of every season he spends at the Lodge with old Jack Hildreth. The place has lapsed into its former aspect, as the artistic furniture has all been removed to the Newport house. Mrs. Burns again reigns supreme in the kitchen. The mistake Legality made was in marrying the town man and neglecting to marry his country self. The mistake that charming woman, Mrs. Legality, made was in supposing she could live up to her own poems. Mr. Legality most unreasonably hates Mary Leeds. When we have made a mistake it is natural to hate some one else in order to draw the lightning away from home.

CHAPTER XXVII.

THE "DIGS" BOARDING-HOUSE.

THE arid heat which changed all things to a lifeless semblance has moved off, who can tell where? Now the fresh southwest is blowing, and the baked foliage opens and expands its leaves like lungs. The sky fills up with loose white clouds that drift idly or pile themselves up into thunder-heads, with pale-fire gleams and Vulcan forges glowing in their breasts. The light breezes skip about like young nymphs sipping honeydew, and inhaling the best of the perfumes. These are hammock days, when the sky with the tree-tops resting against it is sufficient for happiness. The birds seem like music-boxes as their notes steal out of the shade, and the fullness of nature's life is so perfectly content with itself, you fall into the same mood; you lose the sense of responsibility for the miseries of the human race, and the eating edge of your own cares is turned aside.

The large walnut and butternut trees stand quiet in the home fields in their dark branchiness, and cast down rings of shade upon the sun-splashed grass. The cows huddle about them, or wade into the shallow streams and cool their legs as they idly switch off flies with their long tails. To lie in the hammock while the scent of mignonette and sweet peas steals upon you from the garden, to rest in the shade against a hay-cock while other mistaken and ambitious people do the work of spreading, cocking, pitching, and loading, is to make a good use of life.

The country invades every village nook, steals in on every breath of air because it is haying-time. The gardens are at the height of their beauty, but without this sense of union with woods and field they would not be half so charming. Every body looks rustic, and carries an out-of-door atmosphere. The doctor has put on an old straw hat, and looks like a respectable farmer. The judge, even, is caught raking in his shirt sleeves, and says it makes him sleep well. Women when they drive out with their slow, gentle nags, come home with the buggy full of swamp flowers. The children string berries on straws and dangle them along, while hands and faces gather a purple stain. Young lovers walk in the fields to taste the sweetness of the haying. Merry boys and girls romp in the barn, and chase each other up and down, while the old folks remember how they did just the same when they were young. They talk of the many years their aged trees have borne good fruit, and how they hold out yet—old trees, old men and women—in the kind care of heaven.

Most of our young collegians are at home now for the vacation. Several of them keep boats on the river, and there are improvised races between them and the town-boys, in which the girls take a lively interest. Some of the students work a little in the haying field, or ride their fathers' old hacks, or drive the women folk about on social errands. Others, clad in the picturesque knee-breeches of the period, with canvas-topped shoes and rakish little caps, devote themselves to lawn-tennis and base-ball. A few reading-men come here to work for honors and shut themselves away from temptation in the form of fascinating sports and beguiling young women. They take their exercise early in the morning or late in the evening, and devote all the day to study. They are known as "digs," and are greatly despised by the active young fellows, who think that colleges were mainly devised to foster noble sports and "bleed governors." For several years past nearly all the "digs" have boarded during the summer vacation with a peculiar old couple known in the village as Wormwood and Gall. This old man and wife own a gloomy, stuffy old house much shut in by dense foliage trees. They live entirely in the kitchen part, and the front of the house has a funereal look except when reckless boarders insist on throwing wide the shutters and letting in the sun and flies. The two old people do all their own work. It would be impossible for them to get on with "help" of any description. They are not on speaking terms with many of their neighbors, owing to their violent tempers and the great ease with which they take offense. They are not often on speaking terms with each other, and have been known by ingenious devices to pass three months together without exchanging a word. Their power of "getting mad and staying mad" is considered quiet phenomenal even in a community where oddities abound.

It was owing to the absolute silence which so often reigns in that house, due to the fact that the old folks can't or won't speak to each other, that it was chosen as a vacation boarding-place by a mathematical "dig" of high standing in his college. As one "dig" attracts another, Wormwood and Gall have filled up pretty regularly ever since—with this class of boarders, and are now doing well with their rooms. When the old couple, through pride or obduracy, are unable to speak, they write to each other on a slate which hangs conveniently against the kitchen wall, somewhat in this style :

She—" I want you to get in some wood, to pick a mess of peas, and to go to Peckham's and get ten pound of granulated sugar, a bar of soap, and a codfish."

He—" I want you to sew a buckle on my galluses ; to look after them currants you are going to make into jel, and to give Hinckley's boy that shovel I borrered if he comes when I am out."

Sometimes, when a neighbor calls on business, they

break through their self-imposed silence and begin to talk at each other through him, and then, forgetting themselves, get accidentally on speaking terms. The boarders are always glad when these conversational episodes come to a close and silence again reigns in the kitchen.

This year, by an unlooked-for innovation, not at all popular at first with the "digs," one of the chambers of the house was let to two young girls from the city, daughters of a small jeweler on an unfashionable avenue. These girls had lived all their days in the noisy street over their father's shop, and had never enjoyed at one time more than a week or fortnight of seaside or country life. They would not now have come to the village for an entire season but for the fact that the younger girl, Amy, had developed a certain weakness of the chest. The doctor prescribed mountain air, a whole summer of the purest and best, and so they came to the village, and took the cheapest room they could find for two, which happened to be at Wormwood and Gall's with the "digs."

These unsocial young men almost refused at first to speak to them, even to look at them at meal-time, but at length, as Amy was very pretty and Hannah was hardly less interesting in her way, the ice was broken, and there came to be a little subdued talk, even laughter about the board. Their influence was felt in the kitchen, and old Wormwood and Gall had not been so amiable in years ; they were almost as good to each other as when suffering from an influenza or sore throat, for in sickness they are *good ;* like so many quarrelsome people, they are necessary to each other's comfort. Hannah and Amy were not like the over-dressed, underbred young women one so often sees coming out of the tenements on city avenues. The mother died when they were both young, and after Hannah was graduated from the public school her whole life was absorbed in taking care of her father and sister.

She only regretted now that she could not cut herself in two, the one half to remain in town with her father, while the other half took care of Amy in the country. Her letters to her father were mainly filled with items like these:

"The weather up here has grown much cooler, and if the change has reached the city, I do hope you will put on your medium flannels—the soft red ones in the right-hand corner of the upper bureau drawer."

On coming to the country she had brought a bag of all the possible remedies and medicaments Amy might need, each bottle neatly tied up and labeled. The collection also contained a flask of liquid blacking with which she polished up Amy's rather shabby old shoes and her own. Pretty Amy, lying on the bed at night, would see Hannah working away at the shoes as she placed them along the wall in a row standing upright upon their heels.

"They look as if they were praying," said Amy languidly—"like black priests, you know."

"So they are," responded Hannah—"praying for new soles."

There wasn't a thing any body wanted, from a shirt-button to a clothes-brush, that Hannah did not seem to have it about her. Her work-basket was the very epitome of herself, stocked with a dainty needle case, the needles all stuck in one way in precise rows, with neat parti-colored balls for darning Amy's stockings, and varied spools of silk and cotton for mending Amy's gowns. Her own never seemed to need any repairs. Nothing was ever amiss with her small trim figure, and the old boots she said were praying for new soles looked better than new ones on any body else. But Amy was naturally careless and scatter-brained, and now in her languid, semi-invalid state she was sometimes a little perverse about taking the remedies or attending to the precautions her slave of a sister urged upon her.

Though Hannah was a slave to Amy, she found time to make friends with all the cats, and dogs, and birds, and babies in the village. She knew the Alderney calf down in the judge's back lot, and petted the long-legged, mouse-colored colt in the deacon's paddock. The country babies were so much cleaner and sweeter than any she had known in the city avenue, they were quite irresistible to Hannah; and yet she had often taken in those poor grimy city toddlers, bathed them, fed them, given them a nap and taken them home to their mammas, like tarnished little coins, rubbed bright, and showing a pretty image and superscription. So Hannah and Amy, who also was very fond of the little ones, gathered the babies and children all up and down the street. They came rushing into the front-door yard; they invaded the stoop of Wormwood and Gall, a most unheard-of liberty, for the village children had never dared to enter the premises, even when ripe plums and cherries hung temptingly within the garden fence. But now Hannah and Amy had the children about them under the trees. They dressed their dolls, and mended their toys, and taught them fascinating new games. They even induced old Wormwood to bake cookies for them, to the wonder of the neighborhood.

Amy could not sit up the entire day when she first came to the village, and the doctor soon discovered her, as he discovers every stranger within the gates. He walked up on to the piazza one day, and took Amy's hand, and perhaps he felt of her pulse. But he did not prescribe any thing. That afternoon he came round with his granddaughter in the old wagon. A pillow had been placed on the back seat, and he lifted Amy in there, almost without saying by your leave, and then they all trundled off on a round of visits to country patients. The doctor allowed Amy to go to sleep while they trotted along, but he never allowed her to talk much. They stopped sometimes at farm-houses and obtained a drink of buttermilk, and chatted with the old farmers about the crops. Every two or three days this country drive was repeated, and Amy grew so much better that when the father came out to pay his first visit to his girls, he went to the doctor and asked for his bill, and was as effusive in his gratitude as such a dry, undemonstrative man could be. But the doctor took offense. He hated gratitude put into words, and he had no bill.

The city jeweler was the dearest of all objects to his two girls. Amy hung upon him with affection, and Hannah watched over his comforts and sought to provide every thing unasked. It was a source of mortification to Hannah when her father was forced to suggest any thing he wished to have done. He was one of those neutral-colored men, who, though sturdy in constitution and physically strong, seem to have been stunted by shop life. He always walked and spoke and coughed in a certain way. Spontaneity seemed totally lacking to his nature. He soaked up all the care and affection of his daughters like a sponge, and made no sign. And yet he was an excellent father. When the girls led him to the woods and fields and showed him birds and flowers, all the things young creatures love, he took it like a dose of something he had bought for five cents at the apothecary's, which might possibly do good to his interior.

Of course all these things could not go on at Wormwood and Gall's without affecting the boarding "digs" more or less. Life had certainly changed there, and was far less tomb-like and silent. There may have been some open grumbling and more suppressed wrath. But when the father came, that great mathematical "dig," who had always lived the existence of an owl, working daytimes and going out for exercise at night, astonished every body by inviting him and his girls to a boating excursion on the river in pursuit of water-lilies. The afternoon was delightfully cool, and the river reaches smoothed themselves like polished silver, sensitive to the reflection of every leaf, and bough, of every spear of grass and gleam of daisy and cardinal-flower on the bank, until the under world grew into a magic scene, and the boat often seemed to slip through air above a garden of the gods, paved with clouds and spaces of the sky more beautiful than the real heavens. So they passed into little bights and coves where the water-lilies lay in tranquil fleets, and the happy girls pulled up the buds by their long, flexible stems, in anticipation of their opening in the morning.

Papa, though he never changed his expression, seemed to show a glimmer of enjoyment, as he sat in the end of the boat and talked with "Mathematics," as he was called, about the new standard time. The latter, as he hurled the boat along with the university stroke, sitting firmly braced, was trying to calculate the exact depth of a dimple in Hannah's cheek, a dimple which showed itself only when she was perfectly happy. Considering the very retired, solitary, owlish nature of Mathematics, that problem about the dimple seemed an exceedingly difficult one, and the other "digs," who had made less of a merit of their devotion to work, began mildly to chaff him. Even after the jeweler went back to town, Mathematics asked Hannah a few times to go out with him in the boat, in those long magical twilights of July, when the river blushes in sympathy with the sunset rose, which you must explore with sharp eyes to find a thread of crescent moon swimming in the pink vapors. Then the trees plunge darkly down into the depths and the vague purple lights of the zenith bring the first stars, with cool, delicious winds, and odors of new-mown hay from the low meadows skirting the banks. It is an hour made for the young, whether they be "digs" or pleasure-loving spendthrifts of time.

It is generally too late for Amy to go out in the boat, owing to the damp, and a classical "dig" has taken to sacrificing himself somewhat to her amusement. Were she entirely well and strong, he probably would ignore her. But he knows that a benevolent mind should be willing to divert a semi-invalid, let it cost what it may. So he sings her college songs, shows her some curious tricks at cards, and plays a good many games of backgammon with her. "Double-sixes, by Jove! I shall beat this time." Whoever beats, little Amy is likely to come out ahead.

Of course these things are observed. Old Wormwood and Gall have even been forced to talk about them a little with each other—mainly by grunts and exclamations. Wormwood has such a bad opinion of husbands, she may solemnly warn the girls against them before they go home. I can not affirm that Mathemtaics will ever marry Hannah. But it is certain that abstracted minds need just such motherly, care-taking wives as she, and if they do wed, the match, every body will say, was made in heaven.

CHAPTER XXVIII.

THE OLD SWEETHEART.

ON Railroad Street stands a row of small tenements that, like a number of breakfast-rolls in a pan, seem to have run together and combined their shabby ugliness without aim, for there is land enough and to spare for detached dwellings with yards and gardens. Most of these houses are occupied by laborers' families, but at the north end of the row live the Widow Bowen and her daughter, Susan. You will know the place, because it is free from old hats stuck into broken window panes, and the scrap of yard in front is neatly swept. "The Widow Bowen, she that was Jane Hinman." It is thus the neighbors always speak of her. In old times the Hinmans were of the village elect, and held their heads as high as any body. Jane was a handsome girl and had many good offers, but she chose in the end to marry Bowen, who was of no particular account, and finally faded out of life leaving his wife poor, with one little girl. She had buried four children on the hill, and had known troublous times all through her married life, and struggle and poverty and hard work had attended the widow's steps ever since. The fortunes of the Hinmans had run to seed. They had died out or left the place, and a generation arose which knew them not. Only the Widow Bowen and her daughter Susan remained in that poor corner tenement, where they toiled from morning till night at sewing-machine work, finishing off coats and trowsers at so much the dozen for a ready-made clothing house in a neighboring town.

Huge parcels came for them by the train, and were left in the care of the baggage-master and carried to the widow's door by Sambo Brown. Year in and year out the mother and daughter labored at this work, Mrs. Bowen doing the lighter portions, while Susan, who was vigorous, bore the brunt of toil. They often worked fourteen hours a day, beginning in summer at five o'clock. The hum of their machine was heard by the Irish laborers as, dinner-pail in hand, they trudged past the window at six. Sometimes a female neighbor with a gentle horse she could drive herself came and took Mrs. Bowen for an hour's airing in her buggy. But these were rare occasions. The widow could not spare the time on week days, and Sunday driving is not fashionable in the village. But Sunday being the only leisure time they had, Susan and her mother in fine weather often locked the house and went to the woods for the entire day, carrying their dinner with them. They seldom attended church. Some of the neighbors talked, as they will in a small place, and the sympathies of a certain strict class of villagers were alienated. But the young clergyman always remained friendly; and he often brought them the latest magazines and reviews, which Susan read to her mother in their Sunday outings. Being a modest man, he thought the new literature would do them as much good as his sermons; and he liked to talk over with Susan what she had read.

Susan Bowen was very plain. People said she did not "feature" the Hinmans, and as for the Bowens, they were of too little importance for any one to remember their characteristics. Susan's upper teeth projected, and she could not easily close her lips over them. Her hair was rather harsh and wiry, and her complexion dark and without bloom. But she was wonderfully strong in body and had never known a day's illness in her life. She wore large calf-skin shoes, a short gown of some cheap stuff, cotton gloves, and a little round hat which kept its place on her head season after season, regardless of the changes of fashion. Susan spoke out what she had in her mind without fear or favor. At sixteen she had said openly that she would never marry, because no one would think of marrying her whom she could accept. She talked of her plainness, her large hands and feet, and even made a joke of them. She never disguised her poverty or made the least pretense of hiding the family misfortunes, but on the contrary she made no appeal for sympathy. She was an unusually large, strong, vigorous girl at an early age, and it behooved her to maintain constant cheerfulness of demeanor, and to sustain her mother, who certainly was the weaker vessel. Genuine folk are recognized sooner or later even in spiteful little communities. People would bear a great deal of truth-telling from Susan just because she was Susan. Her word was as good as a bond; and she had the kind of manly honor that never breaks a contract or disregards a promise. Milly Grant, the village milliner, with whom she maintained the closest intimacy, had a great admiration for her because she felt that no one but herself had ever sounded the height and depth and fullness of Susan's genuine excellence. She regretted that Susan was not a man, so that she might marry her.

But Susan, with all her mannish virtues, was very womanly. She was strong to sustain, and she was tender to comfort and help. Her heart was capacious, and balanced her excellent head. The position of mother and daughter had been changed. Susan was the wheel-horse, as she said, and she felt a protecting fondness for her mother's foibles that made up to that poor woman for a great deal she had suffered. They drew together into a united life. Susan knew she could never have a romance, and her mother's young career was of the greatest interest to her. They lived it all over again in their leisure hours, retouching the faded colors, that Susan might realize what it is to be young, to win admiration, and to have lovers—she who had known no youth and could never enter personally into that magic realm. Mrs. Bowen possessed certain remnants of her old vanity, although so much had been beaten out of her by a hard fate. She was a little weak about dress, as so many bygone beauties are, and she liked to adorn herself, with the vague feeling that somebody might still come to admire her, although, in fact, nobody ever did come, at least not for a long time. Nearly all the small sums that could be spent on clothes were laid out for her benefit, Susan contenting herself with a style of costume in which she always looked the same winter and summer, spring and fall. But she dressed her mother's still unfaded hair, and put on the becoming ribbons and bits of lace much as a fond mamma adorns her little girl. She admired her mother more than any one, and wished to keep her young and pretty a long time.

The widow still possessed a few small trinkets which had not yet been parted with to pay the rent or to furnish necessaries. By far the most interesting of these, as a memento of her girlhood, was a gold locket containing two strands of hair, one auburn and the other brown, intwined together, with a curious cipher beneath them engraved on the gold. The auburn lock had belonged to Jane Hinman when she was a girl of eighteen. The brown lock had never grown on Bowen's head. It dated back to an earlier romance in Jane Hinman's life, the episode which now most deeply engrossed both Susan and her mother, the period they most frequently talked over in confidential moments. In Mrs. Bowen's worktable drawer there was a packet of yellow letters, connected with the locket and braided strands of hair, and a little story of broken vows and disappointed hopes. Jane Hinman had been engaged before she met Bowen.

There had been a misunderstanding, a quarrel, perhaps, and the ring was given back, and that was all. But it was a great deal to Susan, indeed the central point of interest in her mother's unfortunate life. Holding the letters loose in her lap, and with that locket open before her, she would try to realize the whole situation.

"And to think, Jane" (she called her mother Jane in her playful or sentimental moods)—"to think that Ben Fielding is now a United States Senator, a great man in his own State, likely to be governor soon, and possibly president. Just try to imagine how it would be with you if you had married him. Who would ever suspect that the possible Mrs. Senator Fielding has been finishing off slop-shop coats and trowsers all these years at starvation prices? Oh, Jane, that was a sad day for you when you quarreled with the future senator. But where would I have been had you married Ben Fielding? I could never have been born a senator's daughter. I presume I should not have come into existence at all. And I am so large and strong, such a positive character—there is so much of me—it is impossible to think calmly of the narrow escape I made of not getting born."

Mrs. Bowen had no great amount of humor. She generally let Susan's nonsense go by her like the wind, but it was a very serious matter to her that she had just missed being Mrs. Senator Fielding. It invested her with an amount of romantic interest in her own eyes which enabled her to despise the benighted people who knew not the Hinmans. It helped to keep her young and good-looking, with a certain elegance of manner that Susan admired because she had never been able to attain to manners. She was irrevocably barred out from that mysterious and fascinating region. Mrs. Bowen would sigh an answer to Susan's remark as she turned a seam or sewed on a button.

"He was very high-tempered and overbearing, Susan,

and always would get his own way. He made mountains out of molehills, and took his religion very hard (as if it had been some sort of contagious disease). He inclined to the Methodists, and dancing and light amusements were abominations in his eyes. He tried to make me promise I would not go to balls. But the Hinmans had always belonged to the Church. My grandfather built the little chapel at the Hollow mainly for his own family, and used to read prayers himself. He put up a cross in front, and some of the folks blamed him for it and said it was papistical. But being of the Church, we were always allowed to dance and amuse ourselves innocently, and when Ben tried to make me promise, there was trouble."

Susan, although she secretly hated the domineering person her mother drew, always took his part. "He had character anyway," snipping her thread. "There was something to him. If I had been there, Jane, I suspect I should have been on his side. I couldn't dance if I tried, any more than a cow; and folks are very apt to condemn the follies they can't indulge in. But I guess the senator has changed a good deal. I presume now he is as worldly as a Hinman. They say Washington is a pretty hard place."

"*He* never would go wrong, Susan. You ought not to suspect such a thing. His principles were just like iron. If he had been a little more yielding, or I had been a little less pleasure-loving, things might have come out different. Pass me that spool of black twist, Susan."

"I am sorry he took the wrong side on the pig-iron and whisky question," remarked Susan. "If he hadn't, I should have respected him more." Susan was a fervent politician, and watched the senator's course in Congress with a lynx eye. Once or twice she had thought of writing to him vigorously to protest against some of his measures which she did not approve. But she contented herself composing letters to him in her head, and putting in just as many forcible words as she could, while she shunned all fine phrases.

So these two poor women toiled on for their daily bread down there on Railroad Street, while they cherished an interest in the large affairs of the nation their neighbors knew not of. Senator Ben Fielding and his growing fame certainly did enlarge their horizon.

One Saturday night Susan had gone to call upon Milly on Main Street, and on her return she burst into the room and found her mother half asleep dozing in her chair in the soft brown twilight of a midsummer evening. Mrs. Bowen rubbed her eyes, with the dim consciousness that Susan was excited. "What is the matter?" said she drowsily, sitting up straight in her chair. "Matter! why, mother, he is here, visiting Judge Magnus. *He* came last night." Susan uttered the words as if she had been a Delphic priestess giving forth the oracle.

"*He*, Susan; whom do you mean?"

"He, of course; Senator Ben Fielding."

"You don't say Ben Fielding has come back to the village! Well, I dare presume he has forgotten me. He must think I am dead."

"You know that is a piece of affectation, mother. It is probable he has made particular inquiries after Jane Hinman."

"Jane Hinman is dead anyhow. He knows nothing about the Widow Bowen; and I don't see that his visit concerns us. Susan, won't you light the lamp?"

While Susan was lighting the lamp, and the darkness still lingered, she brought out her last great piece of news: "Mother, he is a widower; has been one two years."

"I dare presume, Susan. His wife, I heard, was a sickly woman. They had three children."

"One dead," put in Susan laconically, as she turned

up the wick, "and the other two grown, and doing for themselves."

"I don't see how it concerns us, Susan. I am a faded old woman." But her eyes looked singularly bright, and her voice quavered with a new emotion. Susan would not give in to her mother's artifices. She knew that somehow it did concern them that Senator Ben Fielding was in town. They did not talk much together, and though both pretended to rest well, there was but little sleep for them that night. The next morning they debated as to whether they should go to church, and finally decided in the negative. It would look too marked just to go to see him, though they did not say so. Neither did they speak of going to the woods or down by the river on their usual Sunday ramble. They sat at home all the morning, the sewing all put by.

Susan dressed her mother with great care. She even put an extra touch to her own appearance, she could hardly have told why. She was glad of the housework, which kept her busy. But the widow sat silent with her hands clasped and that bright expectancy in her eyes. Judge Magnus was to give the senator a grand dinner on Monday. How would he find time to think of poor Jane Hinman and her broken fortunes? But he did find time to think of her. It was just four o'clock when a stranger clicked the little gate. He was tall and rather imposing, with a square forehead, a square chin, and a powerful jaw. He wore square-toed boots, and even his watch chain was composed of little cubes of gold. The iron-gray sidewhiskers gave him an air of distinction he had not possessed in his younger years, but his eyes were of a steely benevolence, without humor. Humor was the one thing Ben Fielding had always lacked.

Susan hastily kissed her mother when she saw what was impending, and then dashed out the back way.

She slipped through a broken picket in the dooryard fence, and crossed Mrs. Hodge's garden, and by winding ways reached a back street and made for a shady spot by the river. She sat down on the ground among the ferns and let her hat fall back, and with her hands clasped about her knees lost sight of every thing before her eyes in her intense sympathy for her mother. He had come to make a friendly call, of course, but Susan did not believe it. She knew that widowers, when their hearts have healed by the first intention, always have intentions. They are the least ingenuous members of the human race. See was thinking of Jane Hinman and the Widow Bowen, and the dark ways they had traveled as mother and daughter, when she had borne the laboring oar; and a tide of pity and love seemed to sweep her away, mingled with the excitement of this strange romance which was touching her mother again in the afternoon of her days.

Susan never knew how long she sat there on the riverbank among the ferns. She found it growing dark when she took her way home. Her mother met her at the door with her eyes half full of tears, and quivering with suppressed emotion. She put her arms round her daughter, and like Ruth and Naomi they clung together in silence for a time.

"Oh, you can't think what he said. It's all the same as if I hadn't grown old. He wants me to be his wife. He came here on purpose, Susan, to ask me. He says he has money enough, and every thing, and he don't care if I am ever so poor and don't know how to appear," she went on a little incoherently.

Susan put her mother down in the rocker and smoothed her hair. "You must quiet yourself, or you will have one of your bad headaches. But just tell me if you have promised to be Mrs. Senator Fielding."

"How could I promise," she returned reproachfully,

"without talking with you? It all depends on you, Susan, and the very thought of it makes me dizzy."

"I shan't stand in the way, mother; I shall never trouble him."

"Susan Bowen, what do you mean?"

"He can't be expected to marry the whole family. He has come for his old sweetheart, Jane Hinman, and not for Susan Bowen, clumsy old Susan."

"You want to make me sick," breaking out into sobs; "that is just what you want to do."

"No, I don't, mother; but I can't deceive you. We have always been one, you and I, but it can be so no longer. Jane Hinman was born for another fate. And now she is coming into her kingdom. But Susan Bowen was made to endure hardness, to live alone, and eat the bread of labor. *He* would not like my influence over you. He must rule alone; I can see it in the square set of his jaw."

"That's just it, Susan; he ain't changed a bit. Such men never do change. I can feel the iron Ben Fielding under all this new velvet. He didn't have his way with me when he was young, and he wants to get it now he is old. He let it drop that his God must be my God; and it was so like old times it made me shiver."

"I guess his God is made in the likeness of the senator," said Susan bitterly, but this was all she would say to influence her mother, who kept insisting that he was generous and kind, and wondrous condescending to the poor Widow Bowen. She felt it a grievance that Susan would not join in these eulogiums, but maintained a dogged silence. Her sturdy strong soul felt a sorrow tugging at her heart-strings, such as she had not known in all her years of toil and privation. The splendid prospect opened by the visit of the great man, though it dazzled the widow's eyes, brought no real joy to that poor house. Before going to bed Susan told her mother she would depart early the next morning by the train to take home the finished bundle of work, and leave the coast clear. The senator was to receive his answer that day. She did not sleep until near morning, and then it seemed that she had just fallen into her first uneasy nap when a nervous grasp was laid on her shoulder.

"I can't, I can't," sobbed poor Mrs. Bowen brokenly. "I've made up my mind I won't have Ben Fielding if he is to separate us. What do I care for his money, and his position, and his honors, compared with my child? And just as like as not he would despise me if I didn't bow down to him. I won't see him again. You must stay and tell him the whole truth. There never was such a one to speak the truth as you are. And I will go to town with the bundle of work."

Susan felt that her mother had risen to the height of the moral sublime. She took her in her arms and gave her a tremendous hugging as she laughed and cried. Mrs. Bowen did go to town, and Susan saw the senator, and they had rather a bad half-hour. Fielding lost his temper, and accused Susan of influencing her mother against him to her great injury. And Susan lost her temper and maintained her right to her mother with pertinacity. And when the senator went away he congratulated himself on having escaped such a dragon of a daughter-in-law. And Susan for her part hated the overbearing man worse than any one she had ever seen.

Many can rise once in a lifetime to the height of the moral sublime, but few can maintain themselves long at such a level. When the two poor women took up life again in that shabby tenement, things were changed. Perhaps Mrs. Bowen, as is the way with dependent, impulsive minds, secretly regretted at moments all she had given up for Susan, while Susan for her part saw these feelings at work in her mother and was wretched. But one day there came to Susan Bowen (it was while the spoils system still reigned triumphant in Washington) an official document which announced her appointment to a twelve hundred dollar clerkship in the treasury. Though she hated Fielding, he had done her this great good turn because that generous streak in his nature was marked.

When Susan and her mother went away happy and triumphant, Milly declared that strange old fairy, Truth, had left the village bag and baggage.

CHAPTER XXIX.

THE STORY OF JOB BIRD.

THE chestnut trees are in blossom. The hillsides show a rich tawny shade amid the darker and lighter verdure. It is a happy time, for one thinks instinctively of the bucolics and pastorals of the early poets, of the shepherds and Arcadians of Claude Lorraine, and the mountain slopes of Spain and Italy. It is the harvest time, when the tanned hay and the golden grain go down before the reaper. Earth takes a richer tone, like some rare porcelain in the potter's oven. It is colored all through with the life and energy of the sun. The thick trees seem to hold something of night in their branches all day long.

There is one farm on a lonely by-road under the mountain that seems always to wear a melancholy look of decay, even in early spring. The place is damp, and the neglected fruit trees are covered with a kind of mold. The red farm-house looks weary of standing so long on its foundations, and a row of gloomy poplars of the Lombardy variety, once very common in this vicinity, leads down to an unused gate, sagging away from its hinges. A fine view of the valley and opposite hills is entirely shut off by the barn, and the barn itself is now hidden by a rank growth of melancholy verdure. This is Poplar or "Popple" Farm. The house for several years has been unoccupied, and is said by the credulous to be haunted by the ghost of Job Bird, who was killed in a rather mysterious way in the hill pasture about a mile distant. There were no very near neighbors in Job Bird's time, and are not now; and a sinister look of desertion and neglect has taken complete possession of the place. A few hardy flowers which Mrs. Bird planted in her dooryard have crept out to the side of the road, as if they would rather be crushed by wagon-wheels or browsed by cattle than remain in that desolate place. The currants redden unplucked on the bushes, the cherries and apples are left to wayfarers or wild birds. Some spell seems to hover around the old house, though its ghosts are only the swallows in the chimney, which cause the belated teamster to hurry past at night with a loud clatter of wheels to keep up his courage, and send the urchin round on a side-road rather than pass the door.

And yet there was no stain of crime on Job Bird; nothing worse than slight aberration of intellect and settled melancholy, which he seems to have left as a legacy to his farm. He had rather a fair start in life for the country. When young he was considered a fortunate man. He inherited Popple farm free and clear of debt with all the improvements. There seemed nothing for him to do but go on in the tracks of his father and grandfather. It was not a first-class farm. There was a piece of swamp in the valley, with a tract of scrub-oak and pine covering a rocky ridge which ran through the center of the land. The strip of arable and meadow along the river was narrow, but with self-denial and labor it was possible to work the farm and keep out of debt. His father, Stephen Bird, was a terrible, relentless worker, who had crooked his back while still young, kneaded his muscles into whip-cord, and tanned his skin the color of mahogany. When he died the farm was free from mortgage or lien, and the Bird credit was good at all the village "stores."

But Job was a different sort of man. He was imaginative, dreamy, notional, given to visions and prophetic moods, and with a fatal weakness of the will. There was little of the stern stuff in his blood and bones which wrests a competence from the sand and granite of a poor farm. He dropped behind a little each year, and before many seasons had passed there was a mortgage on the land, and no neighbor would sell him any thing except for cash. He could not co-ordinate his headwork and handwork. He knew not when to loiter and when to hurry, when to rest and when to take up the hoe and spade. He had no method in his work, a common and fatal defect among poor farmers. His tools and farm implements were scattered, and the needed thing was seldom at hand. He was a natural procrastinator, and could not catch up with the seasons. His plowing, sowing, and planting were generally behindhand, and the snow sometimes flew before he had dug his potatoes or harvested his apples. He knew, perhaps, as well as the most successful of his neighbors, all the theories of agriculture. He was a reading man, and somewhat more intelligent than the average, but he could not apply his wisdom, nor make good maxims tell upon life. Bird bewailed fate, and felt himself marked out for misfortune. The hail fell on his fields of young grain, the lightning struck his barn, the drought burned up his crops, the weavil got into his wheat, the potato-bugs did not spare him when other people managed to escape without serious damage. His name Job was considered too singularly appropriate to be due to accident.

On the other hand, Job Bird had been blessed with chances which if they had come to any other man would have made him an object of envy. He had not only inherited a fairly good farm free from debt, but he had married a worthy woman with a little property of her own. Every body knew that Prissy Stowe came to Job Bird with money in the bank. A cool, sequestered, reserved woman was Mrs. Bird, much addicted to keeping her troubles to herself. Her long, pale face, with the faded blue eyes, was crowned by a high polished forehead and thin hair of colorless blonde brushed neatly behind the ears and twisted in a close knot at the back of the head. Her person was large and clean and bony, and the large hands showed signs either of excessive labor or of rheumatism at the enlarged joints. She managed well in the house and with that "faculty" always admired in country housekeeping. The wheels of her domestic machine were well oiled and moved without jar or noise. She used correct, rather elegant language, choosing by preference well sounding words. She was careful of appearances, taking pains to keep the best side out, and not to show the seamy surface of life. That decent pride with which she strove to hide the heartache in her breast was of course misunderstood. Some people said, "Miss Bird was stuck up," about the worst accusation that can be brought against such a woman in the rural districts. Still it was set down to her credit that she taught her children to respect Job Bird, and even treat his defects with a kind of tender reverence.

She always spoke of Job as Mr. Bird, although the neighbors had begun to speak of him as "old Bird" while he was still young. She scarcely ever made from choice a visit to any acquaintance, for she was a very retiring, home-keeping woman ; but the secret desire to excuse her husband's shortcoming and set him right in the eyes of the world sometimes drove her abroad. He was suffering from lumbago, and the work had got behind ; he had failed to secure help, and that long rainy spell had nearly spoiled the hay. In her low, precise voice, every word grammatically correct, she generally wound up by saying she was so glad Mr. Bird was a steady man, a home-keeper, with no bad habits. If Mr. Bird were a drinking man, like some she knew, she would consider herself a most unhappy woman. And then she would take her way home with the hope in her heart that she had made folks believe Job was not to blame for his bad management, but a victim of the conspiracy of nature. But the country people have very sharp eyes for the Job Bird class of men, and their judgments are often hard and pitiless. They wondered if "Miss" Bird was making believe, pretending that she did not know all about the man she had married, and thought she could pull the wool over their eyes.

If she knew, she also loved and pitied, and the deceits of such a heart are indeed pious frauds. She strove to keep Job tidy and respectable in appearance, with his clothes well mended and brushed. But he was a slouch about his person as he was about his land. There is an old adage which says you must not grind your seed-corn. Job Bird was always grinding away at his seed-corn. He worked prodigiously at the wrong time, and then idled away important days in the woods. He had always been a great dreamer, and sometimes he endeavored to foretell future events from dreams or from other signs; but his predictions never came out right, and even his wife refused to treat them seriously. He had thoughts of setting up for a weather prophet and making an almanac with startling weather predictions, but all it ever came to was the construction of a queer, meaningless diagram on a piece of board, which for many years went knocking about the barn. About harvest-time he was always troubled with a vision of the Apocalyptic beast, which he tried to draw with a bit of chalk on the rocks and fences. This diagram, composed mainly of tail and nippers, was called by the boys of the neighborhood the Apoplexy beast, and a superstitious feeling grew up about it. The boys did not dare rub it out, and in their fancy it soon took on the horns, hoofs and tail of Burns's "Auld Nickieben."

It was about the time the "Apoplexy beast" first appeared that folks, going back in memory, called to mind that Job's great-aunt, Hepsy Fairbairn, had been insane and died in a hospital. They predicted that he would go the same way. He was often under the influence of hallucinations and imagined the whole of nature in an attitude of unfriendliness. The trees mocked him, the clouds made faces, things stole out of the woods after him at night, and mewed and barked like cats and dogs. The whole farm seemed haunted, and an emanation of this feeling spread to the neighbors. He might be seen swinging his arms as he walked over the land and talked to himself. His only reading now was the Book of Daniel, which he carried with him in his pocket. His mind was always at work on the problem of the end of the world, and it was rumored he had made his own ascension robe out of unbleached cotton, and hidden it in the shed-loft in readiness for the great and awful day, quite indifferent as to the ascension robes of other people. It was even said that Job believed he was the only one to be caught up to heaven in that vicinity when Gabriel's trump should blow, wherefore the great significance of the unbleached cotton robe. In those first years, when the Second-Advent mania had taken possession of Job, the end of the world seemed so near it was manifestly useless to do much planting or sowing, plowing or hoeing on the farm, and gradually he gave up work of every kind, and left the management of the land to his wife and a hired man.

There was a shadow over the old house, naturally gloomy enough, and as the children grew up they escaped at an early age to where they could have a little more sunlight, and freer expression for their young lives. The boys sought their fortunes in the West. The girls married or taught school at a distance. Job Bird and his wife were growing old before their time. He was a harmless monomaniac, having gone, just as people predicted he would, the way of his Great-aunt Hepsy.

Still Mrs. Bird insisted on keeping him at home and letting him roam about the farm at his own will Thin and bloodless, with his clothes hanging loosely upon his shrunken limbs, he slipped through the daylight like a shadow. She, though erect still and keeping her correct forms of speech, was very pale, with hair like the snow. She did not now go about among the neighbors to excuse Mr. Bird's shortcomings.

But the old man grew dearer to her in proportion as he grew more dependent and helpless. His insanity was of so mild a form she was never afraid he would harm any human creature or even a bird. Her little money in the bank had long been exhausted, and now she let part of the land on shares, and part she worked with the aid of hired help, and her children supplied means by which the old place was kept in the family. Job roamed and roamed all over the farm, with that tyrannous restlessness symptomatic of the diseased brain. He watched the birds and small creatures for hours, and talked to them in a kind of gibberish which he thought they could understand.

About two years before his death he read in Revelations of a clear, white, mystic stone, and a thought came to him that perhaps by diligent search a piece of this stone might be found on the old farm to reveal to him those things he had vainly sought in dreams, in the shapes of clouds, and all manner of foolish auguries. This notion coming to his poor confused brain seemed to give him a new purpose in life. He confided it to his wife in great secrecy, and seemed to ask her sympathy and her faith with dumb signs, mainly through the eager, pathetic look of the eyes. This return to something like the old affection and trust of their youth was to her like the opening of a well of sweet water. Her children were all out in the world struggling as they best might, and she, a reserved woman by nature and much tried, was very lonely. But now her weak-minded husband, after stumbling on dark mountains for a long time, had come back to lean upon her in a trustful second childhood. She would often watch him from the door or window, going over the fields, his head bent, feeling neither rain nor sun, wind nor cold, nor burning heat, in quest of that stone which was to let him into the secret of life. The delusion, crazy as it might be, was appealing and pathetic, and sometimes she almost believed there might be something in his fancies. With the craft of the insane, he watched her narrowly, to detect the first glimmer of doubt in her mind. He gathered a great number of little stones, of all sizes and shapes and colors, which he sorted and laid away on the shelf in the barn. Some of these he tried to polish with rags and bits of newspaper, but they always disappointed him in the end. None were of the perfect form, or of that crystalline clearness through which Job imagined his eye could pierce the future.

His wife humored him; she let him think she believed in the possibility of finding the stone, that he might confide in her more and more. When tired out with his quest, he would occasionally come into the sitting-room and rest on the lounge near where she sat at work in the long summer afternoons. Thus lying on his back, with the tips of the fingers of the two hands put lightly together over his breast, his eyes fixed on vacancy, his lips moved inaudibly, while his forehead was corrugated under his white hair with the intensity of his thought. "He is always studying," said the old wife to herself; and she wondered what he had in his mind. She recalled stories she had read of the philosopher's stone, which turns every thing it touches to gold, of strange talismanic stones that reveal the true nature of all things, and of those mystic stones, urim and thummim, the Jewish high priest wore on his garment.

"What good will the stone do you, father, if you

should happen to find it?" she would ask. "It will reveal what is hidden," was his invariable answer. Whether this hidden thing were the secret of happiness or knowledge of future events, he would never say; but he was positive that the stone existed somewhere on the old farm, and might probably be found with diligent search. He never strayed out of the bounds, or gave trouble to any one, but thus wandered and sought and picked up stones and talked endlessly to himself. Near the center of the farm a ridge of granite rock crops out in a low hill crowned with a few young firs and birches thinly scattered along its top. A huge bowlder, one of those great traveled masses which had come down in the glacial period, lay bedded in soil on the western slope of this ridge. In its crannies had gathered a crop of evergreen ferns, mosses, and lichens, and a stalwart young ash had rooted itself in one of the deeper clefts. Old Job Bird had gone over the stony ground all about the bowlder again and again, when it occurred to him to try and move the half-detached mass of rock through which the roots of the ash tree had worked their way. He did not let Prissy know what he was about. His cunning told him she would not approve this herculean labor. So he dug and dug about that side of the bowlder where it was weakest, trusting that some heavy rain-storm would give him the help he required to set it in motion down the hill. For two or three weeks he worked faithfully at dislodging the bowlder in that distant pasture, where the silence was only broken by birds, and by the gambols of young heifers that looked at him with shy, wild eyes.

One warm July day Job did not come home to the mid-day meal. His wife thought little of it at the time, for the old man's habits were always irregular. But when a severe storm came up in the course of the afternoon, and the lightning flashed, and the thunder cracked bodefully among the hills, Mrs. Bird fell a prey to intense anxiety. She could hardly tell why, for Job did not mind cold or wet, and often was abroad in snow and rain with seeming enjoyment in the wildest weather. But this was an exceptional storm and almost tropical in the volume of its rainfall. Great sheets of water poured down from the clouds for two hours, and built a solid wall between the lonely woman and the outer world. When it cleared away with sudden relenting, the low sun looked out from diffused gold under a heavy eyebrow of blue-black cloud, and the roads and paths ran with gurgling brown brooks; the trees and bushes glittered with untold splendor, and the corn was lodged and some of the fences blown down, and the river in places had overrun its banks and washed the cocked hay of low meadows down stream.

Mrs. Bird took her way through the bars of the cattle-yard and across the wet fields, unmindful of the destruction of her crops. She was worried about her husband, and when she got beyond the home acre and reached the mowing lot she stopped and called, but only the cawing of a crow that flapped its wings lazily in the strange yellow light over the west wood answered her cry. On she went, striking into the rocky pasture, where the soil was poor and in spots red with sorrel. She cast her eyes on the great bowlder half-way down the slope; something had happened to it; had the storm broken off a large fragment and carried it down in a sudden flood from the hills? Her heart grew sick, and suddenly she felt her limbs giving way, and she fell with a moan, and then got upon her knees and crept forward. The cleft bowlder had rolled from its foundation, and in some mysterious way had fallen upon Job Bird and carried him partly down the slope, where it left him crushed and quite dead. They never knew just how the bowlder fell upon the old man, who possibly had taken shelter under it from the storm. But when they gathered him up a little smooth white pebble, round and shining, such as David chose from the brook wherewith to smite Goliath, was closely clasped in his hand. Perhaps at the very moment the bowlder fell upon him he believed he had found the mystic talisman. And, strangely enough, at that moment death came, and hidden things were revealed to the old man's eyes. That infinite of being which we call death opened before him, and perhaps perfect sanity and sweet reason came to wash away the confusion of the distracted brain.

People wondered that "Miss" Bird seemed to mourn for a crazy man—a man who, when in his right mind had been of so little use to the world. But who can measure the height and depth of such a woman's nature, that loves the more the more the object of her love is poor, despised, helpless, and dependent?

CHAPTER XXX.

THE OLD TAVERN-STAND.

THE crickets are singing in the stubble and the grasshoppers leaping in the hot noon. It is the time when scarlet and white poppies blow in the village gardens, those mystic oriental flowers with satin petals, moved by the slightest breeze. The August noons seem poppy-drugged, so silent are all the dusty roadsides.

At this season the little finch of the common yellow variety flutters about the edges of fields and along the road to pick up the seeds that fall from fruits and flowers. They have their romances—those pretty creatures, their little coquetries and flirtations. Their flight is a bird play set to music, and I have often thought the motion of their wings inscribed on the air the stanzas of a poem.

The shorn fields, with their grouped elms, look very peaceful lying about the old tavern-stand close to the road on the south side of the town, some mile or more from the center of the village. It is still called the old tavern, though there has not been a tavern kept there for half a century.

This silvery pile of ancient building constitutes a composite dwelling, with shed, milk-house, and carriage-house under the roof. Fifty or sixty years ago it was the most celebrated house of call on the turnpike. It stands at a fork of the road—that place where man and beast are supposed invariably to need refreshment and a genial innkeeper's hearty welcome. Two gigantic elms rise in front of the door, and throw a broad shade over the porch where teamsters, peddlers, commercial travelers, and tourists journeying in their own conveyances from town to town, formerly sat to rest and gossip, and sip a glass of something strengthening from the neighboring bar. The shade of those great towering elms, and the good cheer for which the house was long famous, were lures to the weary traveler along the turnpike. The tavern-keeper was both host and farmer, and made as much from his broad acres as from the profits of his house.

But there came a time when the last tavern-keeper died childless, and the farm was sold to a new-comer, who pulled down the creaking old sign fastened to a limb of one of the elm trees, and began a whole series of innovations, both within and without. The low-studded main part was raised. The tap-room was turned into a parlor. The old ball-room, with its "spring floor," was cut up into a range of bedrooms. Part of the horse-sheds were torn down, and other changes ensued, until the whole was fitted for an extensive dairy farm. For two or three years, it was said, all the peddlers' carts, teamsters', and itinerants' horses and dogs turned of themselves up to the old stand, and with difficulty could be convinced that it was no longer a house of entertainment. Old guests of the place, who had not been that way for years, would halt at the door in expectation of welcome, and seeing no smiling publican, and no sign hung under the elm boughs, would depart sadly, shaking their heads over changed times and the decay of good old customs. But in my time, when I first remember the place, only the tradition of the tavern remained.

The place was then owned by Josiah Belknap, and there was no Mrs. Josiah. To the children he seemed even then an old man, for he had grown gray very young. But Josiah was serene and smiling, always lifted up in an atmosphere of calm above the chatter of the women. It was a saying of Josiah's that he never minded the talk of women. Geese must cackle, and women must talk. They would die if they were deprived of this vent for the nerves, but it is the duty of the wise man to go his way and leave them to settle all questions among themselves ; but it was said in such a gentle, placid voice, and with such a benevolent countenance, no one ever thought of taking offense. Although Josiah had never married, protesting he had no genius for matrimony, he had a great deal to do with women all his life, and must have been deeply versed in feminine lore. His mother and grandmother on the father's side lived with him until they both died of extreme old age. These were Granny Barnes, as she was always called, and Mother Belknap. Granny Barnes was also known among the sect of Quakers to which she belonged as plain Betsey Barnes. And Granny would not condescend to put a handle to any body's name, not even to the president's ; she would have called the Father of his Country George, with a dignity all her own. She used the plain language, which is so sweet and winsome on the lips of the old. In spite of the quietistic doctrines which absorbed into the nature make a heavenly serenity around many Friends, Betsey Barnes still showed, even in her extreme old age, the rigid, severe, and rather unyielding temper which had been her inheritance. Grace had worked upon the craggy outlines, producing the effect of strength, dignity, and calm self-poise. She was very tall and spare, with a joint somewhere about the middle of her person, which gave way when she sat down, and left her as rigid and erect as before. She had been a preacher in her sect, and a person of authority, and she always carried the preacher about with her.

Her muslin and dove-color were of the neatest and most particular shade and fiber. Her thin, gaunt head was covered with a close semi-transparent cap that showed the scant gray hair. She sat a great deal in her old age in a high-backed chair with her hands folded over her drab gown, saying she was waiting for the summons. Still, though Granny Barnes thought she had got mainly through with life, she did take a keen interest in temporal affairs, especially in the affairs of her grandson, Josiah, whom she hoped to save from falling too much under the influence of Celindy Belknap. We are all of us at times in danger of mistaking the voice of our own prejudices for that still small voice which the prophet celebrates, and which the good Friends claim to hear sounding in the depths of the soul. Granny Barnes had a passionate, intense nature, and though she strove to subdue it to the pattern of her sect, the imperious will sometimes spoke out.

Mother Belknap, on the other hand, though she held firmly to those "blessed" doctrines of election and total depravity, was a trim, blithe little person, not decayed so much as well dried, with a stereotyped bloom on her cheek, and a quick, light step. Each of the old women occupied one of those large apartments which had been made out of the ancient ball-room. A middle apartment lay between them, their common sitting-room, where they daily met to make polite inquiries after each other's health, and how each had passed the night. Here, too, they sometimes engaged in religious discussion on controverted points, and the debatable land witnessed many a little word-battle when they cast Bible texts at each other's heads, and each withdrew to her own room with ruffled feathers, but the triumphant sense of victory.

Granny Barnes's room was the outward expression of her faith—calm, shady, spotlessly neat, with polished bits of ancient furniture, a few drab-looking books piled up in solemn iciness, strips of carpet before the bed and bureau, immaculate dimity window curtains, and bed curtains of the same, edged with knotted fringe; but no picture, no flower-pot, nothing but prim' starched neatness and quietude. Children seldom strayed into Granny Barnes's room, although they sometimes peeped slyly in at the door. But Mother Belknap, though she held such portentous doctrines as to the ultimate fate of the human race, loved children, especially babies, knew all about their ailments, and was perfectly instructed in baby talk, in how to trot, and dandle, and croon nursery-songs, so that young mothers instinctively brought their little ones to her, to lie on her great bed and be cradled in her maternal arms.

Mother Belknap loved brightness, and cheeriness, and bustle. Her room, I well remember, was done up with much high-colored chintz representing wreaths of red roses and yellow and blue birds. A string of gold beads encircled her neck, and she snuffed judiciously out of a pretty tortoise-shell box. It was the fashion in her time to wear a large bow on the front of the mob cap called a windmill. Mother Belknap's windmill was always made of bright colors, and her gowns and aprons partook of the same cheery glow. Long after Granny Barnes had taken to walking with a cane, Mother Belknap was quite active, and she thanked God that she preserved her sight and hearing, as any one who believed so implicitly in the doctrine of election should. She could thread a cambric needle without "specs" long after Granny Barnes had ceased to sew or even knit. But it was a secret scandal to Granny Barnes, this unmannerly display of cheerful worldliness on the part of Celinda Belknap, who held with such stubbornness to the doom of the greater part of mankind, and seemed to enjoy the idea. Celinda Belknap had added the enormity of saying, in so many words, that she did not believe in drab angels and saints, and very much doubted whether they spoke the plain language in heaven.

It was for the soul of Josiah, the son and grandson, that these two ancient dames contended. Josiah, though he had passed through a religious experience at a certain period of his life, strange to say, had never joined a church. He owned to his conversion with a kind of childlike simplicity, but he would never state his exact theological views, or make any explicit confession on doctrinal points, especially that one so dear to his mother's heart, foreordination and election. Still, Josiah never blinked the fact that he was a religious man, deeply interested in spiritual concerns. The music of the parish received great help from Josiah, who had a natural gift in that direction, and could play quite sweetly on several instruments by ear, never having taken a lesson in his life. He confessed that his best seasons of prayer and meditation were in the morning alone in the fields, when the catbird and song sparrow made the air tremble with melody, and the dew lay white on the grass. Then things unutterable stole into Josiah's heart, and since, like Burns, he could not go into the little square chamber with the wooden table and pour his feelings all out in immortal verse, he would sometimes drop his hoe and come directly in from the fields, and seat himself at an old reed organ in his own vast chamber, and pour out an improvisation which seemed to express every thing. I can see him now, the beautiful old bachelor, so unworldly and gentle, so oblivious to his own good deeds, his self-sacrificing life, and untiring patience with those old dependent people, and all about him, as he sat at the organ, his healthful, calm face with a slight bloom upon it, delicate as a woman's in feature, with the long silvery hair almost touching his shoulder.

Granny Barnes had been partially deaf for many years, but Mother Belknap prided herself on her good hearing, a fact which Granny Barnes always ignored in speaking to her. "You needn't scream so," Mother Belknap would say, with as much asperity as is conformable with perfect politeness. "I have my hearing, thank heaven, good as ever. Folks as haven't their hearing think every body else deef as posts. I am sorry to see you don't hear nigh as quick as you did last year."

Granny Barnes generally shut her eyes and remained rigid under this infliction, and as it is very difficult to talk to a person who insists on keeping her eyes closed, and who is as you know deaf as a stone-wall when she does not choose to hear, Mother Belknap generally gave up, tacitly defeated. In a day or two Granny Barnes would hold a secret interview with Josiah : " I think I ought to tell thee, Josiah, that thy mother is failing. It is borne in on my mind that she is growing childish. Thee may have noticed that she wears a pink lutestring windmill on her cap. I must bear my testimony against such worldliness. I tell thee I am forced to shut my eyes when I see those pink lutestrings."

" Mother always was fond of bright colors," Josiah would answer, " and that kind of weakness grows on folks as they get old ; but it is more harmless, ain't it, granny, than harsh judgments and uncharitableness ? "

" Thee is right, Josiah, and I am rebuked."

" No, granny ; but we must bear and forbear with one another, having patience, and long-suffering, and brotherly love." Thus he poured oil on the troubled waters, only to be waylaid by his mother. " Have you noticed, Josiah, how granny is breaking up ? She's harder of hearing than she was, and she don't seem to sense things quick, but still she is pretty techy. The old lady is all going to pieces. I thought you ought to know it, Josiah, so it shouldn't come upon you unbeknownst. But it is strange how obstinate she is. She holds to free grace in the face of all reason and of Scriptur'. I hate to see her so sot in her own delusion."

" Don't worry about that, mother. There may be more ways than one."

" There ain't but one way, Josiah. It's an awful and

solemn fact. You can't climb up the sheepfold on the wrong side. Straight is the road and narrer is the way, and few there be that find it. Many are called, but few are chosen, Josiah," laying the fore-finger of one hand in the palm of the other.

"Well, if it gives you any comfort to think so, mother, I am glad, but I don't quite see how you can be so cheerful under the circumstances. As for granny, you couldn't get along without her, mother, she makes you feel so safe and comfortable."

The old lady looked at him half-puzzled, half-resentful. "Josiah," she would say, warningly, "I do hope you are not going to let *her* get the upper hand. You have been converted, and you know you have got grace in your soul."

"Yes, I think I have, mother, at least sometimes, though it is a conceited thing to say."

Mother Belknap had her favorite spiritual shepherd, a rank Calvinist, whom she always entertained in her own room, coddling him with seed-cakes and a favorite drink of her decoction called metheglin. Granny Barnes was excluded from these conferences and seasons of soul-refreshing as being heretical. On one of these visits Josiah was at work binding grain behind the barn. The parson thought it might be a fit moment to try and get a doctrinal statement from him, and Mother Belknap trotted out into the field to hold a religious talk with her son. "Josiah," she began, as if speaking of the state of the crops, "when was you converted? Brother Brewster here would like to know."

Josiah was always respectful to his mother and very patient. He was one who honored the ministry and was much given to entertaining the saints. But now the spirit of a man rebelled within him against this effort to pry into the most sacred part of his experience.

"Go and ask God, Brother Brewster," said Josiah,

without stopping his work. "He knows all about it—and you are very intimate with Him, judging from the way you preach and pray. Go and ask Him."

The parson went home much offended, and might never have taken Josiah back into his good graces but for the comfortable beds and excellent cheer at the old tavern house. Granny Barnes, of course, heard of the rebuke Josiah had administered to the parson—"the hireling priest, who preached in a steeple-house"—for it was a peculiarity of her deafness that she always heard every thing she wished to hear.

"Thee sees," she said calmly to his discomfited mother, "Josiah after all belongs to my side of the family. His father strayed off and married out of the meeting, much to the grief of all who had his good at heart; but Josiah is one of us. Thee can see it in his life. He is a natural peacemaker, but he won't be imposed on. His music is all peace. It is nearer quietness than any sound I ever heard. Thee knows we bear testimony against worldly music, and all that goes with it, but I call Josiah's music heavenly."

Such praise of Josiah could not placate Mother Belknap. "You mean that Josiah belongs to his father's side, and that I haven't any part in my own son."

"I wouldn't say that, Celinda Belknap, for thee knows that though Josiah is such a peaceable man, with such quietness of nature, he is an obstinate man. And thee can tell where his obstinacy comes from."

Josiah's sister, Mrs. Phœbe Elderkin, had been widowed young, and had come to live with him, bringing her three children. Josiah never complained of the added burden of this family. He brought up the Elderkin children, and saw them well started in life. It was just at this point, when his mother became too infirm to attend to the house, and both the old people needed much waiting upon, that a near neighbor, who had lost his wife the previous year, began to come frequently to the house. Sometimes an inquiry after hoop-poles, at other times after sap-buckets, and once or twice for a stone-boat brought him there. It turned out in the end that the hoop-holes, sap-buckets, and stone-boat all meant Phœbe Elderkin. One day Phœbe went out in the great mowing lot, a noble meadow on the intervale, to tell Josiah that she was going to marry Simon Strong. Josiah was utterly amazed. Such a thought had never entered his mind.

"Sakes alive, Phœbe," he exclaimed, "what luck you do have marrying! I could never get one wife, and you are going to take a second husband. And there is Deacon Spender's wife living with her fourth. It beats all, it beats all!"

This was all he ever said—not a word of reproach to Phœbe for leaving him at a critical time after he had tided her over the difficult years of her life. But at that time Josiah began to play rather gloomy psalm-tunes on the old reed organ, and he was a little depressed and discomfited until he had secured a distant cousin, Miss Jane Farrar, to keep house for him. Jane when she came was rather a spiteful, snappish old spinster, with a mania for neatness sufficient to drive a less placid man than Josiah out of his mind. There seemed to be no chair he could sit down on in his own house, no object he could handle. One day Jane was sweeping the room with that peculiar snap of the petticoats which marks the overzeal of such a nature. Josiah kept moving his chair so as to get directly in the path of her broom. At last, out of all patience, she exclaimed, "Josiah Belknap, what do you mean?"

"Why, Jane," he answered mildly, "I thought I'd see if you wouldn't sweep me right out-of-doors, and never know I was any thing better than floor litter. I expect you think it's an awful trial to have men folks tracking around and making dirt, and if you should sweep me out you would get rid of me in an easy way."

Jane never forgot the lesson. She could not quite change her nature, but she came to reverence Josiah as every one did who knew him. She took the best of care of the old people, who both became bedridden before they died, and in the last years, when Josiah was an old man, she would listen at the door to hear him playing on the organ. She always knew by the tones whether he was sad or cheerful, and sometimes she felt that he had escaped to regions where she could not follow.

CHAPTER XXXI.

ZIP COON, A DOG STORY.

THESE days, so persistently breathed upon by the moist, languid South, have a supplement, or hour of cooling on the river. A vague mystic light reflects from its mirror long after the sun has set. The placid waters dissolve the real world and recreate it in wonderful form. Another sweep of the oar, and you may break into strange silent seas, a million miles from any thing you have ever known. Late haycocks dot the low banks and send forth pungent sweetness. Dim gleams from the sunset, which has left a glowing red crater like a coal in a heap of ashes, plunge far down to where the water-nixies live. The banks, and houses, and distant hills, and clumps of trees have melted like dissolved diamonds into the sky, or have taken on a velvet brown as soft as the plumage of a raven. The shadows plunge down into the crystal, like ebony columns, and the spaces in between seem too pure for water. We imagine our boat has glided upon air, or even floated forth to interstellar ether.

There is a young moon to-night, a mere silver sickle, but it begins to make its waxing tell. Its tricksy beams glide deftly in among the boughs of the black trees as if in search of elves and fays. All plants breathe out the best they have. No noxious thing grows here ; henbane, nightshade, poisonous ivy, the nymphs will have none of you. They choose cool sedge, and whispering reeds, and fresh-smelling grasses, sweet clover from the water-meadows, and mint from where the brooks come down. Far off in the east a cloud hovers invisible, except when it sends out broad sheets or twisted serpents of pale red heat-lightning. Then you see the cloud is composite, an air palace, having walls, and pinnacles, and towers, and domes, with strange gleams as of Oriental cities flashing out from an unknown strand.

This goes on in the sky while the shadows creep and broaden. A light mist begins to rise from the river banks, and a great frog has had the temerity to sound his bass note in a silence the breezes respect as they go whispering, feat-footed, amid the boughs and over the meadow grass.

The village gardens are lovely at twilight; dim lights gleam through the shrubberies when the star of love rises, and ladies in white gowns go flitting about among the flowers, young girls fly across the street bareheaded, children romp in and out. There is a little reception in nearly every garden, where people have come to glean the odors of the sweet pea and the verbena, the mignonette, and carnation. Old-fashioned blossoms, common flowers as they are called, are much cultivated in the village. They grow in accord with their own fancy, springing up beside grassy paths in bright knots and clusters without the stiff order of beds.

The doctor's garden is a perfect specimen of what such a lawless village garden should be. One side of it is shaded by tall plum and cherry trees, and there are other places devoted to great branchy trees bearing delicious bough apples. In the center is a little rustic arbor, covered with a mass of blooming clematis and madeira vine. The arbor is sheltered by the boughs of a large catalpa, one of the few catalpa trees in this part of the country, with a circular bench running about it. Growing in among the tall corn and the other vegetables are immense sunflowers, while the hardiest common blooms edge every path. There is one nook by the wicket gate made by a great mass of sunflower, scarlet and white climbing beans, and hollyhocks of all shades. It is such a bower as Arachne must have lived in when she excited the fury of Minerva by her exquisite embroidery and the envious goddess turned her into a spider. The doctor has great pleasure in watching the humming-birds when they visit this huge bouquet, and dive their bills into the cups of the flowers.

One evening the doctor and his wife and grandchild were all out under the shade of the catalpa tree just at that witching time when the brown night-moth goes droning on his heavy wing. The doctor's wife looked almost young in her light gown, with soft lace at the throat. The young girl was frolicking with a string and a white kitten. They could hear Hugh playing tennis with the Spencer girls behind the hedge next door and giving forth his Homeric laugh. The village is a whispering gallery on a warm evening when the windows are all open. It is even said that when Mr. Johns proposed to rich old Miss Merkland, who is deaf, he was heard quite a way down the street.

As the doctor and his family sat thus in peace, enjoying the coolness of the summer evening, a light tap, tap was heard on the gravel walk, and a yellow dog appeared before them, a gaunt, hungry, mangy creature, with tail tucked between his legs in protest, as if he expected to go yelping away the next moment from the kick of a sturdy foot. One ragged ear hung down dejectedly, while the other perked itself up in the air with a ludicrous attempt at smartness. The dog had been around to nearly every house in the village, running through the gate and in at the door if it happened to be open. Some had given it hard words, some had kicked it, or shoved it out with a broom, and others had thrown stones at it. A company of bad boys had even tied a tin kettle to its tail and sent it crying with pain and fright down a cow-lane toward the river.

Not one human being had given it a kind word or a crumb of any thing to eat. The poor creature rid itself as best it could of the tin kettle and crept back into the village, slinking along to avoid observation and blows as much as possible. It was unmistakably hungry, and the pathos of its eyes said so. It continned its doggish quest until it came into the doctor's garden and to where the good man sat in the arbor. It came close to his feet and whined and wagged its ragged tail, and looked up appealingly into his face, with an assurance of comfort that it had found a friend. The doctor ordered the girl in the kitchen to feed the dog, although Mrs. Rivington protested. She was a charitable woman, but she felt that the line must be drawn somewhere, and vagrant dogs, especially of that common yellow breed, had always been her aversion.

The doctor's household went to bed, the whole village went to bed. The stars looked down through the elms, and stray moonbeams from the setting orb winked here and there upon the projection of a roof or threw their light along the dewy grass. Every body had forgotten the vagrant dog. In the morning, however, when the doctor awoke and went out to the stable to order his horse for a round of country visits, there lay that yellow, mangy, lop-eared, ill-conditioned cur directly in his path. The poor creature showed all his ribs, as the doctor could see in the morning light, and there were upon him the scars and sores of many a battle with stronger and better-fed dogs. The doctor's professional eye saw that he had a gaping wound on one of his hind legs, where the flesh had been laid open to the bone, and was raw and bleeding. The human heart in him could not leave the leg of a stray dog in that condition. He hurried again into his office and brought out a flask of ointment. He cleaned the wound and applied the ointment, and the dog's eyes looked as if they were filled with grateful tears, while he fairly whimpered with gratitude. He had slunk away, expecting a kick from the doctor's heavy boot, but the doctor never kicked any thing weaker than himself. It was only meanness and selfishness and utter ingratitude the old man felt the impulse to chastise. Now, as he again looked at the dog, a gleam of recognition came into his mind. Surely he had seen those eyes, that one lop- and one prick-ear, but his memory failed him; he could not place the dog. But he had him fed again at the kitchen door, and then he drove him out of the yard and told him to go home. But he was no sooner seated in his wagon and trotting along the road than he was conscious of the fact that that common "yaller" dog was trotting along by his side, accurately adapting his steps to the pace of the old mare.

The doctor spoke crossly to him and again told him to go home. But the ill-conditioned creature only looked around under his lop-ear, as much as to say: "I'm going home and you are going with me." Finally the dog edged along and took the lead, first on one side of the road and then on the other, keeping a certain distance from the mare's heels, and occasionally looking round at the doctor to see if he was observing his motions. The doctor, who was a close observer of the habits of animals, could hardly help becoming interested in this creature's maneuvers. He had expected him to dart away at every lane and turning, but the persistent dog-trot he kept up in front of the wagon finally produced the impression that the dog must have some set purpose in his mind.

When they came to a fork of the road branching off to Windham one way, the doctor took the left hand turning to go on a visit to Felix Brown, who had been dying of lung consumption for fifteen years, and would yet perhaps outlive some healthy folk. But the dog wished him to take the Windham road for reasons known only to himself. He squatted down in the dust, lying flat on his stomach, and whined, and howled, and scratched with every sign of distress. The doctor, who was slightly superstitious perhaps, as we all are, watched the dog's behavior with surprise and interest, and after debating a time with himself, half ashamed at his own weakness, he decided to let the creature have his way, and turned his mare's head down the Windham road. Fortunately there were no very pressing cases on his calendar that morning.

When the dog saw that the doctor had yielded to him, he went quite wild with delight, barking, and yapping, and nearly leaping into the wagon in the delirium of his joy. The doctor was a firm believer in the instincts of the lower orders of creation. He had a theory of his own as to the dim border-land between the limits of instinct and the domain of human intelligence, and it was this which led him to try and discover what the dog meant by his strange actions.

A long way the dog led the bewildered doctor, keeping on and on with a persistent trot in spite of his lame leg. He did not wish to go to Windham, that was clear, but struck off on a stony by-road leading quite away from the hills and the river valley, until they came to a miserably poor country, and into the edge of an extensive piece of pine timber. This the doctor at once knew was the pine barrens, a region he had not visited for several years. All cultivation soon ceased, and every sign of life disappeared except such as clustered here and there about the slab shanty of a turpentine-maker. In a cluster of these —three or four standing together—the doctor caught sight of the vagabond Jabez sitting sunning himself in the door of one of the slab shanties, with his knees drawn up until they nearly touched his chin. The unkempt hair was hanging in tangled wisps on his shoulders, and he looked sickly and haggard. His feet were bare, and his lean person was scarcely covered by rags. He nodded to the doctor as if not in the least surprised to see him there, and now the doctor at once knew where he had seen the dog, for the animal had attached itself to the wandering fortunes of the child called "Chippie" even while Jabez and his miserable family lived in the doorless house in the woods. It was several months since Jabez had been moved by Farmer White down to the barrens. The doctor looked at Jabez, who did not rise or change his position. He leaned forward in the wagon and grasped his whip firmly. "What's wrong here?" he said sternly. "Purty considerable," drawled Jabez, lifting his lack-luster, leaden eyes. "She (referring to his wife) and that there boy baby she called John Rivington both died of dipthery nigh goin' on two week ago. And the folks here at work in the turpentine made their graves down yender in the sand. They was took and died sudden like before we could call a doctor; and I was took the next week. And I hain't got around any to speak of yet. And the gal she's laying sick there inside."

He jerked his thumb back over his shoulder, but had not the energy to turn his head. The doctor sprang out of the wagon with something that sounded like an imprecation, and stumbled over Jabez into the hut. The dog was already there beside Chippie. Her poor little wasted hand lay on the ragged coverlet, and the creature was licking it all over and extending his caresses to the sick child's face. She lay on a truckle-bed with an old straw tick under her, and had no covering but the ragged quilt. A woman's cotton skirt, one of the dead mother's, was bundled up to serve as a pillow. One of the pitch-boilers in the barrens, a kind hearted, rough young fellow, whose every other word was an oath, had brought the sick child part of his breakfast. It stood untouched on a broken chair—salt pork, leathery flap-jacks, and thick muddy coffee. The child was very feverish. Her lips were baked and dry, and the great eyes seemed to have burned their way into the sallow, pinched face, making circles of darkness. The cabin was such a picture of poverty, wretchedness, and filth as the doctor had never beheld. He felt a great rising in his throat, and could not speak to the child for some moments, though she was perfectly conscious, and had her wistful eyes fixed on his face.

Her mother and the baby were gone, that baby she had tended nights, and toiled for days, and loved so dearly ; that poor, nerveless, sick, discouraged mother she had taken care of as if nature had changed their relations and made her the parent. But deliverance had come to her. The good man who looked to her so like a savior laid his fatherly, kind hand on her hot forehead and touched her so gently poor little Chippie thought there was healing in his touch. He gave her a dose of something from his medicine case, which he mixed with a little water in a tea-cup, and she dropped asleep and slept and slept whole days and weeks and months, it seemed.

When she partly awoke, Chippie fancied she was slowly moving out in the fresh air she loved. She heard the birds singing and her dog Zip Coon barking and yapping joyfully ; but she could not tell where she was, so she fell asleep again, and when she awoke she found herself in a clean chamber with windows opening to the east, in a white bed, dressed in a little fresh-ironed gown, and lying so sweetly at rest, with a sense of new life and strength coming slowly into her limbs, she thought at first she was dead. She looked at her wasted hands and lean arms and wondered if she had gone to the same place where her mother and the baby were. She tried to stick her foot out from under the sheet, to see if it were really hers, and finally she gave it up, as costing too much effort. She might be somebody else, but she was very happy.

She was lying in a chamber in the doctor's house. He had brought her home under the influence of an anodyne, and had her warm-bathed, and dressed clean in one of his granddaughter's gowns which she had outgrown, and put to bed. The neighbors all remembered Chippie kindly, and they came to see her and coddle her in her convalescence with fruits and flowers, and jellies and custards, and dozens of dainties the poor child had never tasted before in her life. Every body talked over the remarkable sagacity and affection manifested by the dog. Some even went the length of saying they believed dogs have souls. They were the very people who had flung stones and broken crockery and brickbats after Zip Coon when he made his tour of the village as an itinerant cur. The doctor has never explained the dog's behavior quite satisfactorily to himself; he is inclined to think that some dogs may have long memories, and may even go through a mental process which is akin to the association of ideas. The young girls of the village, headed by the doctor's granddaughter, formed themselves into a society to provide Chippie a wardrobe ; and with the zeal of young girls every thing must be tucked, and frilled, and prettily trimmed.

The neighbors were fully impressed by the tragic end of Mrs. Jabez and the infant John Rivington, but they could not help laughing at the fate which had brought Jabez back upon the doctor's hands. What to do with Jabez had again become a burning question. He had agreed to give up control of Chippie if some provision were made for him. When asked what he thought he could do, Jabez scratched his head and after meditating said he would like some place under government. He guessed there were some as " poor cusses" as he was who got pretty good fat offices if they only had "inflooence." The doctor keenly appreciated this satire on office-holders, but as it was not feasible to try and gratify the ambition of Jabez for political preferment, he thought of trying to get him a place as flagman on the railroad. This raised such an outcry in the town among people who declared they would never trust their necks on the road if he were flagman, because they were sure he would always be asleep in his little house when the trains came along, that the idea had to be abandoned.

At last Jabez reverted to his one idea of " pop." He felt sure he could make a " pop," if he had the small capital to start on, that would seduce the very elect. The doctor furnished the capital, and having dressed Jabez in a suit of his old clothes several sizes too large for him, sent him to Windham to set up the " pop " business, where he bottles a kind of stuff which he calls ginger-ale, and sells to the turpentine and pitch-workers. The doctor would have taken Zip Coon, the faithful yellow cur, for his own watchdog, but Zip never would live apart from Chippie. If he were tied up in a strange place for days, as soon as he found himself free he would make his way back to the child, lying by the path where she had walked, or scratching at the door she had entered. Chippie has been partially adopted by an eccentric old lady who quarreled with all her relations, and lived alone, but still needed a young girl to run errands and do light work about the house. The old lady has been obliged to adopt Zip Coon also, and now he is fatter in the ribs than he was. You would never know Chippie in her new clothes—dear, patient, unwearied little Chippie, so willing to run her feet off to please her mistress, so eager to learn in the village school. Who can help loving Chippie, whose life's dawn was so sad and clouded when she lived like a bird in the hedge? Dear to God is such a wild blossom, and He will guard her. The doctor has had the mother and baby brought from their sandy graves in the pine barrens and buried on the hill, where Chippie can go sometimes to sit beside them. And then her face seems older and more thoughtful than it should seem for one so young.

CHAPTER XXXII.

A DOMESTIC TYRANT.

THERE is a drive called the Roundabout Road, which makes a circuit of exactly seven miles, and takes in some of the pleasantest bits of scenery in this region. The hills are nowhere very steep, and there are many old horses in the village that know the Roundabout Road as well as their own stalls. It crosses several brawling trout streams and rustic bridges, and passes the prettiest watering-troughs, where the gushing mountain springs, bright and mobile as quicksilver, run through channels made in mossy logs. Near one of these grows a bed of the wild forget-me-not with its eyes of heavenly blue. The arethusa is now to be found on the river meadows. It is of a purple such as is only seen in evening and morning clouds. Before many weeks have passed the fringed gentian will open along the drive, in such places as it has chosen for its habitat.

At Dexter's chair factory the Roundabout enters a little glen fringed to the very top of its walls with the light foliage of young birches, beeches, chestnuts, and ash trees. Late in the season this place wears the aspect of early spring; and in the cool crevices of its rocks ice is found until July. The hermit thrush builds and sings here, and may be heard at some moment of rare good fortune. Autumn comes first to this spot and runs like fire in the low undergrowth. The sumac bushes turn the most brilliant dyes. The young maple-shoots are red like blood. The ash shrubs seem to drip with gold.

Many people drive over the Roundabout Road every fair day. It is a road that never wearies, for the hills are continually changing under the varying influences of light and shade, heat and cold, wind and fair weather. Several retired clergymen and college professors live in the village, having come here to pass their last years. Nearly all of them keep slow, ambling, sure-footed nags, who possess all the equine virtues except speed and the power to raise their noses more than three or four inches above the dust. They amble along, never varying their gait except to stop stock still. In the retired clerical set it is considered a sin to use a check-rein or a whip. They are mostly mild, quiet, old ladies and gentlemen who belong to the past, but have lingered along into the present with the understanding that they are practically laid upon the shelf. Though they have once doubtless been important and celebrated, it is conceded that their day is over, and they are just biding their time and trying to make themselves as comfortable as circumstances and small incomes may permit.

Chief among the superannuated clericals is the Rev. Elkanah Stackpole. He occasionally preaches in the village church, when most of the congregation scatters, some to visit their friends in the country, others to go blueberrying or nutting on the sly. The few who do attend church from conscientious motives generally fall asleep in the pews. It is thought that if Mr. Stackpole were to preach three consecutive Sundays, every soul would desert the church except old Amen Anderson, who is as deaf as a post and who says he always goes to meeting, whoever preaches, for "innerd edification." You will know Amen by his standing up in his corner and singing the hymns on a plan of his own. He pays no heed to any body or any thing except long and short meter.

The Rev. Mr. Stackpole halts in his walk from chronic rheumatism, and Mrs. Stackpole is a nervous invalid. They live in an old-fashioned gambrel-roofed house, where perpetual quietude and twilight formerly reigned, a green twilight thrown from the thick trees growing close to the windows, and from the prevailing tone of the furnishing. Every body in the village knew the Stackpole's maid, Araminta Sophronia, called Minty for short, and the Stackpole's horse, Spicer. Spicer used to trot over Roundabout Road every fine day in summer. He came to the door about nine in the morning from the stable where he was kept. Minty bustled out with two air-cushions for the excellent couple to sit on. She was also provided with an armful of wraps and umbrellas and a hassock for Mrs. Stackpole's feet. The operation of loading the Stackpoles into the chaise was a difficult one, but Minty was always equal to it. When she had once tucked them in under the lap-blanket, and the Rev. Elkanah had feebly grasped the reins, she then turned her attention to Spicer.

If Spicer was in the mood, he would start off promptly, and keep up a slow trot for a certain length of time. If Spicer was not in the mood, he would lay back his ears, and shake his head positively. Then began a coaxing process on the part of Minty. She patted him, whispered in his ear, and generally administered one or two lumps of white sugar, when Spicer, being placated, would dart off so suddenly as to throw Mr. and Mrs. Stackpole against the back of the chaise. But Minty knew that if she once succeeded in starting Spicer, he might be trusted to bring the old couple home in perfect safety. There were places on the road where he persisted in walking, and he had even been known to stop in shady spots, spite of all the Rev. Elkanah could do, to crop a little tender herbage. When he had swung partly round the circle, he began to smell the stable, and generally came home in fine style.

Minty ruled for many years in the Stackpole house. She was an admirable housekeeper, but having usurped supreme power, the vice of power, a tyrannical and overbearing spirit, grew upon her. Few great minds can resist the temptation of power, and Minty was not a great mind. The old people came to feel that Minty was indispensable to their comfort and well-being, and the ability to govern themselves gradually slipped through their fingers. No one in that house attempted to oppose Minty except Fielding Stackpole, the only son, who was a civil engineer, living in another state. When Fielding came home on a visit, as he did several times a year, he brushed aside all Minty's rules and regulations. He smoked where he pleased, carried the parlor chairs out on the lawn and left them there, tumbled the book-cases, came down late to breakfast and ordered fresh coffee and hot buttered toast, exactly as if he were the master in his father's house and not at all subject to the rule of Queen Araminta Sophronia.

The conflict of wills between Fielding and the maid put a very sharp edge on Minty's temper, while Fielding always came up more and more bland and smiling, with the conviction that he should win in the end. Minty had carried it so far as once or twice to refuse Fielding admission to his father's house when he arrived unexpectedly late at night, on the ground that she was house-cleaning and the rooms were all in disorder. But Fielding calmly climbed in at a pantry window and established himself without ceremony in his own room. After Fielding's visits the old people were always more insubordinate, and it gave her a little trouble to break them in again to rules and regulations.

Minty, in spite of her name, did not come from Burnt Pigeon, but from a place down the river, called Salt Lick. She was always talking about the Lick in a most misleading way, as if it were something to eat. The Lick hung like the sword of Damocles over the head of poor Mrs. Stackpole, especially after the old people came to feel that in their helpless state they could live neither with nor without their domestic tyrant, for Minty often threatened to leave her at a moment's notice, and return to the home of her infancy.

It was understood that Minty had married a Salt Lick man in her girlhood who had not proved a brilliant ornament to society. She soon rid herself of the encumbrance. She never mentioned this part of her experience, but the asperity with which she spoke of mankind in general, and of Fielding Stackpole in particular, was supposed to have sprung from a thorough acquaintance with the sex. She was of a thin, wiry type, not very large, but with muscles of steel. Her face came to a sharp, hatchet edge, and her gray eyes, mottled with yellow, saw every thing. She was confessedly the smartest servant in the village, and she had a standing of her own.

Her neatness, of the inflexible, cast-iron kind, was a terror to the neighborhood. Even particular housekeepers trembled under her dreadful cat's eyes. Her house-cleaning was thought to be as bad as the concentrated three movings which equal a fire. But the excellences of Minty were as pronounced as her foibles. A tea invitation to the Stackpoles was something to date from. The ladies seldom took much dinner on those days, in order to save their appetites for Minty's dainties. If the invaluable servant did not sit down in the parlor with the guests, or preside at the tea-table, she still carried off the honors of the occasion. Every body praised her cookery to the skies, and it was a great point to ask for Minty's receipts, which she gave or not, just as the whim seized her.

Her tea-table was a work of art, and she adorned it with a tasteful arrangement of flowers from the garden. The old-fashioned Stackpole china, glass, and silver, were burnished to exquisite brightness. The napery was ironed only as Minty knew how to iron. Her tea-biscuits melted in the mouth. Her cake was always something new and original. She knew all about potted tongue, veal loaf, boned turkey, and brandied peaches. Such coffee, whipped cream and sherbet as she made was never found elsewhere. So it was in every department of housekeeping. A favorite subject of debate among the village ladies was whether it would be possible to endure Minty's tyranny for the sake of her culinary virtues. The shameful subjection of the old clergyman and his wife to this strong-willed domestic was a standing topic of discussion among the village gossips. Every fresh usurpation on the part of Minty was commented on with exclamation points. She knew she was talked about, and it made her proud. She fully expected to be buried in the Stackpole family lot, and to have a coffin-plate equal to her master and mistress. It was reported that poor Mrs. Stackpole said one day to Minty: "I have asked my sister Jane and her daughter to come and pass the day with me on Thursday next."

To which Minty immediately replied: "I can't think of having them on Thursday, ma'am. There's the sweet pickles to make, and I must clean out the cellar. I never can have company days when I am cleaning out the cellar. It's unreasonable to think of it." Minty always planned to clean out the cellar when the idea of company was obnoxious to her. Mrs. Stackpole was therefore obliged to telegraph to "Sister Jane" that she must not come. And she found herself more and more the bond-slave of her incomparable domestic.

The ex-professor had made a brave effort to secure some portion of his own house for his exclusive use and benefit, which should not be too ruthlessly invaded by the broom and duster. He wished to set apart a small closet where he might think his own thoughts, and doubtless pray, where he might occasionally indite a sermon or a report of the missionary society for carrying the Gospel to the Zulus, of which he was secretary. But all in vain. Araminta Sophronia did not believe the best of men could think holy thoughts in any place from which her cleaning hand was excluded. If she could have taken out the conscience of poor old Stackpole from his bosom, she would doubtless have washed and scoured it. For years he was forced to see his desk, his pens, his papers arranged in an order foreign to his soul. But no one had ever done up his fine shirts and white neck-cloths like Minty; and when he was ill her broths and gruels were delicious. Minty always attended family prayers and sometimes read devotional books, not because she had a taste for them, but for the reason that she lived in a minister's family, and was bound to keep up the character of the household. It looked well to have a volume of dry sermons on the kitchen shelf and illuminated Bible texts hung about on the wall.

When Minty first went to live with the Stackpoles, she made up her mind that she would not allow them to harbor poor ministers, religious book-peddlers, or itinerant missionaries. They were accordingly sent on to Deacon Hildreth's, to the old Tavern House, or to the doctor's. And the old couple, as they could not help themselves, were rather grateful for the protection they enjoyed. Occasionally guests from a distance came to stay at the house unannounced and before Minty's fiat could reach them. As there was no hotel in the village at that time, Minty could not turn them out of doors. But she always discriminated against city visitors. She forced them to unpack their trunks in the barn. She thought country folk much the cleaner. Minty knew how to make herself very disagreeable to guests without letting the old people know any thing about it. She had been sometimes approached with "tips" in the hope of placating her dragonship, but she repelled all attempts at bribery and corruption with scorn. No one except Fielding Stackpole ever staid more than five days in the old minister's house. The neighbors kept close watch to see if the rule were infringed.

There comes a day of reckoning for all tyrants. The standing quarrel between Minty and Fielding had never been healed. The best they could do was to proclaim a truce. Though the warfare often broke out afresh, still they could manage to exist together under the same roof a few weeks each year. It was a terrible blow to Minty, therefore, when the marriage of Fielding Stackpole was announced, and of all things to one of those " hity-tity, good-for-nothing city jades." Another great blow was the fact that Fielding and his bride were coming home to pass the summer. Old Mrs. Stackpole did not even ask Minty's permission to have them come. Re-enforced by a strong letter from Fielding, she simply said it would be a great pity if her children could not come to their father's house whenever it suited their convenience. This sounded like the tocsin of open rebellion, and Minty's soul was troubled within her. She saw that the old lady had already taken the bride into her heart. But that night Mrs. Stackpole had a nervous attack, and Minty rubbed her and worked over her for several hours. She was always good in illness; and the old woman tacitly asked her pardon. Things were in this unsatisfactory state when Mr. and Mrs. Fielding Stackpole arrived. As a first act of resistance, Fielding refused to have his wife's trousseau inspected and fumigated in the barn by the domestic customs officer. Minty, though she had to yield this point, felt strong in her intrenched position, for she was certain the Stackpoles could not live without her. Fielding felt strong in his position of son, especially when supported by a young, bright-eyed woman who looked upon him as a great moral hero, although he had never done any thing to merit hero-worship. He, however, felt it would be a noteworthy thing to deliver his aged parents from domestic servitude. The bride was now the great center of attraction. The old people petted her and received her pettings in a way Minty thought perfectly silly. Every body admired her pretty costumes, her piano-playing, and the fact that she spoke French like a native. The neighbors were running in at all hours. Meals were irregular. The lights were no longer put out in the house exactly at half-past nine. The window screens were left out, and flies buzzed through the rooms.

Minty endured it as long as she could, until, like Spicer, she felt that her time had come to balk. Mrs. Fielding Stackpole's star was in the ascendant ; hers was on the wane. Her main hope lay in the old lady's nervous attacks, which no one could allay but herself. The time had come to try her strength with Fielding. It was at a moment when the minister was absent from home, and Mrs. Stackpole was in her own room with her daughter-in-law. There was a terrible scene, but in the end Minty packed her trunk, took an angry leave of the household, and departed for Salt Lick—departed expecting perfect submission on the part of the old people as soon as the loss was felt, and to return in triumph at the end of a few days, to the total routing of Fielding and his wife.

She found herself ill at ease at Salt Lick. She was a person of not the least moment to the Salt Lickers. Day by day she expected her recall to the Stackpole kitchen, and when a week, a fortnight, a month passed without the summons, she could restrain her anxious curiosity no longer. Old Mrs. Stackpole might have died, any thing might have happened in the absence of the grand vizier. She therefore took the train one morning and unsummoned returned to the village. The old people were going out for a drive on the Roundabout. Spicer stood at the door. Presently they came forth, attended by the daughter-in-law in a charming white morning costume. They mounted the chaise without assistance, and Minty remarked that they seemed unusually young and spry. Even Spicer moved off briskly with nothing more than a pat from Mrs. Fielding's fair hand. Minty reconnoitred the house in a state of mental collapse. All looked calm and peaceful. No domestic earthquake had shaken the foundations because of her absence. She stole round to the kitchen. Phemy Jones, a young thing she knew quite well, was standing in the door. Phemy Jones to come after her! The thought of the course of bad cooking the Stackpoles had gone through gave Araminta Sophronia a feeling of exultation. Phemy met her with no outward sign of deference, and she walked into the kitchen and looked about with lynx eyes.

"And do you do the cooking for the family, Phemy Jones?" she asked *sotto voce*. "I'm a learner," responded Phemy, evasively. "And pray, who is teaching you, Phemy Jones?" "Young Mrs. Stackpole. She is a splendid cook, and the old people are just in love with her. Everybody says they are growing young again." Minty arose in a dazed way, shook her skirts, and went out of the door. The first person she encountered on the garden path was Fielding Stackpole with a satirical smile on his face, as he looked into the eyes of his old enemy.

"I hope you are satisfied now," she blurted out, with a feeling of hot tears in her eyes.

"Oh, yes," returned Fielding, "perfectly satisfied, Minty. I married the head scholar in the Boston Cooking School; and I knew I was safe."

Minty has taken another situation in the village, but her glory has departed. She no longer hopes to be buried in the Stackpole lot and to have a coffin-plate equal to that of her old master.

CHAPTER XXXIII.

THE HOLWORTHY GIRLS.

THE sound of the wind in the thick-leaved trees is a perpetual inspiration this month, when most of the birds are silent, and only shrill-voiced insects—cicada, grasshopper, and cricket—make a strident chorus. The wind symphony lasts sometimes a whole day and part of a night, and comes between those great calm pauses of silent weather when the sunlight falls unclouded for hours, and the hills steep in richness of color. Then the sun departs like ruddy metal dropped suddenly behind the hills, and the still moon steps in and fills the dew-dripping night full of mysterious light and black shadows.

But in these dry wind-storms there is a great swaying of trees and skurrying of clouds. The bustle among the airy-tongued leaves is contagious. You lie on your bed at night and seem to rock in the branches. Your spirit goes forth to partake of the excitement, the wild glee, the sad wailing of nature. The moon looks out at intervals through the rack like some lone goddess—a Psyche who has lost her love. You feel that a great change must have come over the world with all this business progressing through the night, but when you rise there are the splendid blue hills firm on their foundations, with the clouds dazzling in glory, as the sun peeps from behind them, and the shadows flee across the slopes.

The earth must soon feel those first twinges of rheumatic pains that come after the long summer of bliss. She will ripen now like an apple or a plum. She will have a dressy autumn and a calm golden old age before the snow flies. The first tree in our region to turn from crown to base is the tall rock-maple that stands on a high plateau to the north of the village. As soon as the Holworthy maple has reddened like a dome of fire the other trees seem to light their torches by its flame, and one can day by day watch the tides of color rising and advancing, catching and flickering, and sparkling all through the valley and on the hillsides. For this reason it has become an autumn beacon to the country. That red-and-yellow signal means apple-gathering and cider-making, nutting, and potato-digging and corn-husking in the fields, and the dragging of cord-wood, much of which is used in our primitive kitchens, and the lighting of fall fires.

The old Holworthy place is surrounded by an excellent stone wall, but the land is rather poor. It lies spread out on the hillside like an old-fashioned bed-quilt, the fields accurately marked off by light and dark grain and differing shades of brown and yellow, indicative of plowed ground, fallow, and stubble. In the south-west corner just now there is a lovely patch, of the blossomed buckwheat, snow-white, like a bleaching napkin. The pasture is all up the mountain, where you hear the cowbell tinkling in the sweet fern; and there are but one or two river meadows where the hay is gathered late. Old Amos Holworthy's grandfather cleared that mountain farm, and old Amos thought it the best place in the world. He was always bragging about the good air and the excellent mountain spring that supplied the kitchen pump, as other people boast of their riches and grandeur. The view from the place, far down the valley with the flanking hills, and vista upon vista of blue air, until the Wilton Mountains close the distance like cloudy gates to some grand city, is one of the most perfect in this region. It seems to satisfy that craving for a vast horizon, an outlook toward the unknown, of which Mr. Ruskin speaks, and is perhaps one of the secrets of the strong attachment which all the Holworthys have ever felt for their mountain farm.

The three Holworthy girls loved it as the Brontë sisters loved their lonely house on the moor. Their love differed from that of the old man, their father, for with the educated consciousness they entered into all the beauty and charm of the place, while he loved the soil, the stones, the scrub-pines, the water and air, but never descanted on the view, except to say it was a sightly place, and that "his gals were mighty took up with sketchin' the scenery and botanizing, and the Lordy knew what." Next to his rugged bit of a farm old Holworthy was proud of his "gals," although with great simplicity he confessed he did not understand them. He had never crossed them in his life, neither he nor his old woman, and according to his account the "gals" always had their noses buried in books even from their tenderest years. Old Holworthy had not much knowledge, neither had his wife, but they both reverenced the love of it in their three daughters, Faith, Hope and Charity, as they were called, after the three Christian graces.

As the girls desired "schoolin'," the old folks worked hard to give it them, and after they had got it it was a pain to the excellent Holworthys that they could not always keep their "gals to hum." No, they would go off West and South instructing the freedmen and teaching in academies, and only once or twice a year did they then gather under the Holworthy roof-tree. They always came at Thanksgiving, these girls who were such paragons of learning in the eyes of the old folks. The mother was what is called in the country a "driving woman." She dressed in a short skirt and sacque, and wore a broad-brimmed hat. It was said that she sometimes smoked a short black pipe up the chimney. Her face was broad, kindly, and brown as a berry, with keen dark eyes set deep in her head. She made the garden, attended to the farm animals and the poultry, milked the cows, harnessed the horses, and often drove a pair to the village to do her "trading," or to the mill to get a bag of flour. She had a strong frame and corresponding strength of sense. The old man looked up to her for her practical wisdom, while he revered that remote ideal bookish realm where dwelt his family of remarkable girls. Though the three theological virtues, as they were called in the village, had read and studied a good deal in certain directions, they retained the simplicity and unworldliness of children of nature. Two of them were plain and red-haired, but the youngest, Charity, or Love, as her friends often called her, was a beautiful woman, even in her maturity.

The sisters had taken possession of the roomy garret and transformed it into a general study, which they partitioned off by cheap curtains for use when they wished to be alone. The views from all the garret windows were of perfect beauty. Visitors were always taken up there to be entertained, and then the three sections were thrown into one. Charity botanized and had arranged her herbarium and dried plants in her own part of the garret. When she was at home this section was adorned with an exquisite arrangement of wild grasses, bright berries, ferns, lichens, toad-stools, and rare wild-flowers she had gathered in her favorite haunts in the woods. Hope sketched somewhat. The window of her rustic *atelier* looked far down the valley. She pinned her sketches against the rafters and backed them with bright bits of stuff, giving the artist touch to all she did. Along the chimney and side walls she had painted a vine which seemed to come through the scuttle and meander with splashes of sunlight.

Faith was always writing a little book of reflections

and meditations (not for publication), but resembling the French *pensées*, and her little study end of the garret was the book-room, fitted up with braided rugs, patchwork cushions, comfortable seats, and bits of old furniture which had been put away as too antiquated and rickety for the lower rooms. All the girls were handy with tools. By their united wit they had contrived to transform an old bedstead into a lounge, and with hammer, saw, and nails had devised a handy set of shelves for their little library. Here were all their small treasures, the few choice editions of the classics they had skimped on their plain dress to buy, the gift-books of their scholars, and those well-thumbed favorites among the older poets, especially Spenser and George Herbert, they almost knew by heart. They brought all their united treasures to make Faith's den particularly attractive. For Faith was supposed to be weakly; at least, there was some constitutional trouble which showed itself at times. At home Faith was always well. It was only when absent from her native air that she drooped and seemed of a fragile nature.

Though in no way very remarkable, the Holworthy girls had their individual modes and manners, which rendered them interesting. When they sent invitations to their friends in the village to come up to the farm to tea, they generally fastened the note with a chicken feather. Charity, the naturalist, had a signature of her own, a zigzag blurred line, supposed to resemble the track made by the foot of an ant in wet sand. The billets were generally in rhyme, and were often addressed in some peculiar and fantastic manner. The old man, who delivered his daughter's missives, though he was immensely proud of them, sometimes felt it necessary to apologize for their queerness.

"Lordy, now," he would say, with his old face screwed into a puzzled look, "I don't know what them gals are up to. They have so many notions in their heads, I don't pretend to keep track of 'em."

But there was really no rupture between the daughters and the old people such as is so often seen between educated children and their hard-working, rough-handed old parents. Though Amos Holworthy was always asserting that he did not understand his "gals," that they were miracles of learning way out of sight of him and the old woman, there was a perfect understanding, a devoted bond of amity binding the whole family together. The girls had never lost their taste for a simple, primitive mode of life or their passion for nature. They loved the old home so well it was hard to induce them to come down the mountain to "visit" in the village. Their friends must come to them. They hung out signals from their station on the hill as soon as they arrived. Red and blue, yellow and white signals, all had their special meaning to various friends below. An excursion to the farm, with a moonlight drive homeward in the evening, was always a much enjoyed event. The old people were so hearty and kindly, the girls were so original and interesting ; such a visit offered a new experience.

The Holworthys had ways of their own for doing every thing. Their hospitality was boundless, but of the simplest kind. The girls from a very early age had set their faces like flint against the diseased New England appetite for pie and sweet-cake. They never offered either to their guests. In the village not to have pie of every variety at Thanksgiving, and not to offer cake on the company tea-table, was as unorthodox and perhaps as wicked as to deny the doctrine of original sin. At the Holworthys there was always an abundance of nice bread, fruit, custards, and cheese, milk, cream, eggs, and honey. They set the fashion of putting fresh fruit on the table at a time when people thought uncooked fruit unwholesome, fit only to be canned or preserved with pound for pound of sugar. The girls had brought old Mrs. Holworthy over to their notions, and she allowed it did save a "sight of trouble." Their revolt against pie and cake was set down as one of their least excusable eccentricities. But a day at the Holworthy farm, when the girls were at home, was a happy event. They had a small microscope to show the structure of plants and the wonders of insect life. They displayed new and beautiful flowers that had always grown in your home fields, but which you never had observed. They talked over their favorite books with the enthusiasm of students, and with the keen appreciation of nature which only born lovers can feel, they led you to the different beautiful points of view—the lookout, sunset rock, the little ice glen, and through the wood-path to their fernery.

These simple girls in their loose comfortable gowns of plain stuff lived literally on the heights. When they came home it was always tacitly understood among them that they were to relieve mother with the housework, and give her a chance to go away and visit Aunt Gill, who lived about fifty miles distant on the railroad. The old lady had never been in a rail-car. The wonders of the steam-engine had been explained to her by the girls. She had often gazed upon the engine and the train at a safe distance from the village station, when she had driven her team into the town. Her going to see Sister Gill on the railroad was really a fiction, a dream, something she cherished in her fancy without ever attempting to carry it out. So the strong brown-faced old woman continued to work hard until she died quite suddenly and was buried in the little family burying-ground on the mountain.

It was a hard blow to the old man. He could not understand his "gals," that he admitted; but he knew every fold and involution of his wife's mind, and he missed her sadly. His "gals" were the pride of his soul, but the industrious, strong old wife was a necessity, like the air and water of the mountain. Just at this time Abel Holworthy, his rich brother in California, died and left him five thousand dollars. At once the whole aspect of his life was changed. He was a rich man for the mountain, and he summoned his girls to come and live at home permanently. It cost Faith a pang to give up her colored school in North Carolina, but, like her sisters, she obeyed the mandate to come home—no more to roam abroad—to live with the solitary old man, and to make him forget his loss if possible.

The only thing he ever said about his wealth was, "I wish mother could have lived to see it. I wish she had taken that there journey to Sister Gill's. That's a thing that hangs round my neck and hectors me. She never rode on them cars, and I kind of think if I had insisted she would have trusted herself to steam navigation. My gals don't think as I do about steam navigation, that it's one of the wonders of the airth. I've heard them say for their part they'd jest as soon there wasn't any. But I guess they were joking." "Steam navigation" and the thermometer were the two great scientific delights of old Amos. He kept a thermometer on the back porch, consulted it several times a day, and tried faithfully to regulate his sensations by it.

Every Sunday the old man harnessed his team and brought his family down to the village church, where he fastened his horses under the long shed attached to the sanctuary. Invariably he fell asleep in a corner of the pew, and emitted so much nasal melody it took something more than a strong nudge to bring him to the consciousness that he was, as one of the neighbors expressed it, "running an opposition to the minister." His constant labors in the open air on the mountain top, so much more invigorating than in our own valley, produced somnolence at once when he came in-doors. On a certain Sunday, only two or three years before he died, a somewhat celebrated clergyman of a metaphysical cast of mind exchanged with the village parson. Good old Father Holworthy slept the sleep of the just throughout the sermon, which certainly was somewhat abstruse for a plain country congregation. On coming out of meeting one of his friends tapped him on the shoulder and inquired how he liked the sermon. "It was a splendid discourse," said the old man enthusiastically, "but, Lordy, I didn't understand a word on't; my gals did though. They took it all in, and we shall have it laid up in the family."

Now that the Holworthy girls were at home, with the design of spending the remainder of their lives on the mountain farm, and with a small increase of fortune, they gradually re-arranged the house to suit their tastes. The rag carpets were not banished, nor any of the quaint old furniture, but the florid, high-colored Scripture prints their mother had delighted in were removed, and some engravings of a higher order substituted. Hope indulged her fancy in painting the quaint old wooden chimney-pieces with the vines and berries and wild flowers her sister brought from the woods. Books spread all over the lower part of the house, and the old man was seen to be a little better clad and brushed than of old.

The daughters led a simple life of enjoyment of nature, contemplation, and study combined with homely household duties—such a combination as is scarcely to be found out of New England. Charity, the beautiful sister, with her dark eyes, abundant curling brown hair, and lithe figure, certainly had "offers." Two at least were known to the villagers, but the banner of matrimony was never flung from the farm-house along with the red, blue, white and yellow signals with which they telegraphed to their friends below. The prosperous merchant widower, or well-to-do farmer who came up the mountain in the hope of winning Charity found that Charity was bent on remaining at home, and the journey had been made in vain. It was wise for those maidens to refuse to be transplanted. They never could anywhere have been so happy or so charming as on their native soil. They were rooted in the mountain earth like those delicate growths, the arbutus, the harebell, the gentian, and the fragile, lovely ferns.

The old man died peacefully one day on the place where he had lived, convinced to his last hour there was no such air and water anywhere as could be found on the mountain, except, perhaps, in the New Jerusalem. They had a simple funeral on a beautiful June morning, and for a long time the girls kept the old man's grave in the family plot covered with blooming laurel and other wild flowers. Hope, the middle sister, also has passed on by some mild and painless disease. She died sitting in her chair, making some little gift for Charity, and her needle remains sticking in her work, just as she left it when death knocked at the door. Her Testament was turned down at the passage, " To die is gain."

Now there are but two Holworthys left, white-haired women living in their sheltered nook, cheerful and happy. I have had the privilege of looking into Faith's unpublished book of meditations, and I recall one passage : " If the flower is perfect the fruit will be sound and good. If the fruit mature it will produce a healthy seed. Each succeeding period of life is one of progress. Death belongs to the series, but we must take a step in the dark to behold the new blossom. Death is the mold in which the ripe seed is buried. Let us await joyfully the springing of that immortal germ."

CHAPTER XXXIV.

THE MOST POPULAR GIRL IN THE VILLAGE.

LIKE all other properly constituted communities we have our great men, who, living or dead, we cherish with commendable pride.

We have produced a showman, a great patent-medicine man, the editor of a daily paper, the inventor of a pump, a story-writer of the school of Sylvanus Cobb, Jr., a funny man who is thought to have gone ahead of all others in the art of distorted spelling, and a sensational preacher. Our slow, bovine virtues are far less exciting to the mind of youth than the merits of the patent-medicine man, for instance, who is supposed to have made from a common weed and some poor spirits a nostrum warranted to cure consumption and cancer. This man has amassed an enormous fortune. He does not live in an ordinary plutocrat's mansion, but in a palace where he draws his hot and cold water from solid silver faucets. The story of his great riches and the luxury of his bathroom is almost as alluring to the young mind of our village as the tale of the great defaulter who managed to escape to Canada with nearly a million of dollars.

Besides those among us who have already achieved greatness and come to happy fame and the immortality of the newspaper, are those rising people who we expect may yet achieve something considerable—the promising young men, the ambitious maidens of native growth who are yet to illustrate our annals and add luster to the village name. Among these is a young professional man, the son of an old resident, who was graduated with some *éclat* at his college, and is now connected with an excellent law firm in one of our larger cities. Why great hopes have been placed on the future of Ned Buckner it is not easy to discover.. He is good looking, has easy manners, is tonguey, with great readiness in displaying all he knows. He has corresponded for a newspaper, and even written leading articles ; and the old people say he can lie in print like a lightning-rod man or a book-agent. All Ned Buckner possesses is readily made available ; and it is firmly believed in the village that he is endowed with the great American virtue of getting on. When in college he never had the slightest modesty in approaching the wisest and most venerated men of the day with familiar ease. As a stripling he could ruffle it with the best, and now he talks of celebrities as if he were hand in glove with them.

Ned Buckner was always very successful with the fair sex—the girls of his village. Though for several years he was considered as good as engaged to Sylvia Macy, still he was a prize the other maidens were not willing to abandon without a struggle. In a community where every other place is owned and occupied by an unmarried woman or a widow tax-payer, a man like Ned Buckner is sure to stumble into pit-falls unless he is extremely wary. Ned has never been wary. He has given all the prettiest girls in the village—those with whom he was brought up and whom he called by their Christian names—reason to think he was fond of them. And I have no doubt he was. Seven or eight of them wore his college colors, and were intensely excited over the boat races and other contests in which he took part. How it came at length to be understood that he was engaged to Sylvia I hardly know. She was one of the most modest, quiet girls in the village ; still of tongue and unobtrusive in every way. Ned had played with her when they were children together ; had dragged her to school on his sled ; had given her bites out of his apple behind the desk, and had done her sums for her on the sly. For Sylvia was singularly unmathematical. I am not sure that she ever fully mastered the multiplication table. But she grew into a young woman whom every one loved and trusted.

Some time after the engagement of Ned Buckner and Sylvia was tacitly accepted in the village, most of the wearers of Ned's colors gave up hope. Some married and others settled into the calm of single blessedness, devoting themselves to the Bible-class and the Sunday-school, or to foreign missions. Nearly all discontentedly relinquished the rising young man to a girl whom they unanimously considered plain. There was one exception. Fredonia Haven was ironically called the most popular girl in the village—popular among the men, while the women, with their usual maliciousness, could see nothing attractive in her. Miss Freddie was considered in the village just a little fast. Cautious matrons said she actually made eyes at their husbands; but I don't believe it. Her iniquity chiefly consisted in having smoked cigarettes with one of her admirers, which made her rather ill. She liked fast horses and rather showy costumes. She was skillful at all kinds of games, and had won various prizes in archery and tennis. Her clothes always fitted her to perfection, for she had great skill in dressmaking, and it was her habit to spring something entirely new and original upon the neighbors which could not readily be copied. The most severe charge brought against Freddie Haven was that she did not care for women, a woman's love for her own sex being the touchstone always applied to aspirants for female favor. Freddie frankly declared that she liked men better. And they liked her, old and young, grandfathers, fathers of families, the middle-aged, and boys in their salad days. At one time she had had great success with the clergy. Freddie had spent part of her girlhood in a college town, where large numbers of the youth of the land were victims of her bow and spear. Such a collection of boy trophies as Freddie possessed was not held by any other girl in the village.

But these were only tokens of her pastime. The serious affairs of Miss Freddie's varied life had been enacted with Ned Buckner and a few others. Her boy friends were wont to complain that first she used them, then amused them, and at last abused them. So many boys had offered her undying affection, it was one of her diversions to read over their love-letters with her maturer lovers. No pent-up Utica like one small village could afford a fitting sphere for a person of Freddie's genius. She carried her conquests into neighboring towns and cities, and often spent whole months in the place where Ned Buckner was practicing his profession. Then every body pitied Sylvia Macy, though the village breathed freer when she was out of it. On her return the matrons ruffled their feathers, or looked sharply after their lords. The marriage of Freddie Haven, it was conceded, would be a public benefaction; but while she was still free and able to roam at large, there was no telling where the lightning might strike. No one in Freddie's family was able to control her. She lived with a married sister who was buried up in a large family of children; and her brother-in-law, it was thought, was a little too indulgent toward her. Freddie had independent means of her own, and could do as she pleased. No wonder she kept the village stirred up! Of course many things were said of her by malicious tongues that had no foundation in fact. It is to be taken for granted that a person of the Freddie type, in a small village, is never so black as she is painted.

Freddie's sister's house stood, as we say in the country, catacornering to the house where Sylvia Macy lived with her widowed mother in that calm, still air of refinement and respectability which surrounds the best people, the elect of the village. From the windows of one house it was easy to see whoever entered the door of the other. Freddie had tried to train a screen of vines over her porch on the Macy side, but it "winter killed" so often she finally abandoned the effort. Her deeds must stand uncovered before the eyes of the Macys, and she was not ashamed. There were many hours of triumph for Freddie, though she was not quite young now. Indeed, it was necessary to begin to study the art of "making up." But, although Ned Buckner was engaged to Sylvia, he always spent, when he came to town, considerable time with Freddie Haven. He never meant to spend any time with the most popular girl in the village, but when you have a certain intimacy with a girl of that kind how are you to help yourself?

If he passed Freddie's house early in the morning there she was, gathering flowers in the garden, or singing his favorite song at the piano in the parlor, or sitting on the shady porch in a perfect costume, engaged on a large rich piece of embroidery which represented a spider's web in a blackberry bush, with the spider at home, and a fly sending in his card. The whole thing was very quaint conceit, but it was wonderfully suggestive. Freddie beckoned him in the most natural way, and then he lost his will-power, and during his stay at home he boated, and walked, and dawdled a certain amount with Freddie, while Sylvia was supposed to be watching in jealous rage through the blinds of an upper window. But this was false. Sylvia would scorn to spy on any one. When Ned was in the village she and her polite, high-bred old mother never mentioned Freddie Haven's name. They shut their ears to all gossip, though of course they did keep up a constant thinking.

But things could not go on always in this fashion. Ned would have liked to let them slide. It was flattering to his vanity to be the center of talk, the person on whom all eyes turned, the object of intense interest to two such women as Sylvia and Freddie. But the crisis came one sunset hour, when the fields were brown, the roads dusty, the mountains hazy with amethystine mists. A great wing of dove-colored cloud rested over Saddleback, and beneath it the vivid beams darted forth like a sheaf of thunder-bolts held in Jove's strong hand. Then came a sudden sunburst, and the calm fields, the river, the woods, touched with the afterglow, turned to fire. The river ran crimson between black banks. The fields were ensanguined to their deepest clods. Every bush and stone and bit of crooked fence turned to ebony out of the light. The gleam strayed down the country road. It caught the under leaves, where the boughs were transparent, and they seemed to break into flame; then the glow faded, except in the west. Shadows climbed the sky. The river still ran crimson in the coal-black land, and in the very heart of the red stream glided a little boat.

Two people were in the boat. You could just see their outlines by the fading light. A young man and a maiden rowed on that glowing stream, while the evening breeze began to ruffle the trees up the bank, and brought the odors of the fields. The young man was tall, and he bent to the oar. The maiden sat like a statue in the stern of the boat. Not a word seemed to pass between them. They came to the landing-place on the little pebbly beach under the water willow. Silently the rower leaped to shore, drew in the boat, and handed the lady out. They walked up the bank in the soft, creeping shadows, just as lights began to twinkle in the village houses, and shone with a mysterious charm through the dusky elm trees. They had not spoken a word as they turned into Main Street, and he opened the gate of a pretty cottage; then *she* turned her face toward him, rather to look goodnight than with the intention of speech.

Freddie had crept down to the boat-landing by the bridge in the middle of the afternoon, when most of the village gossips were napping. There had been no definite appointment made with Ned Buckner, but she knew he would be there. She was dressed in a white flannel boating-gown, with a large bunch of brilliant red flowers in her bodice, and a hat of the most stylish trim. Ned was lounging about the river bank when she arrived in the most natural way, and they stepped into the boat and pushed off to a woody part of the river, where several aged hemlocks hung low over the stream. It was only in the black velvety and crimson gloaming that Freddie sprang her secret upon Ned. Before that hour she had been pensive at moments, at others rather wildly gay. But now she told him with solemn—almost tragic—earnestness that he must decide her fate. She had been importuned to marry a Polish count, who was then metaphorically on his knees before her. With a tremor in her voice and tears in her fine eyes she confessed she did not love the count; but if Ned advised her to marry him she would meekly sacrifice herself. She would go like a victim to the altar, and bestow her hand, though her heart was not in it. She did not wish Ned to give precipitate counsel. He was to come to her house the next afternoon, and they would talk the matter over calmly and dispassionately.

Ned Buckner felt dazed when he suddenly found himself in a trap. He had been sailing along gayly with these two girls both in love with him, and now there was to be a sharp game played upon him, from which it would require all his lawyer wit to extricate himself. This was the situation when he and Freddie walked in perfect silence up the bank to the village street, and parted without a word at the gate. Ned wandered about awhile in the dusk smoking a cigar. He felt sulky and injured in his most sacred affections. He could see no way out of his present scrape but to give up one of his girls. And this he particularly disliked to do, for at that moment he was almost equally fond of both. Suddenly he remembered that he had an engagement to take tea that very evening with his other girl, Sylvia Macy. He went home and dressed himself with great care in evening toilet.

The Macy house is one of the pleasantest in the village. Now the lamps were lighted and the tea-table was set out with a choice array of flowers. Such a refined tea-table is a mirror of the mind of the mistress. On that table there was never too much, nothing so exquisite as to detract from the pleasures of good conversation, yet the food had an aroma of its own. Ned was a little late, but Sylvia met him in the wide old-fashioned hall in the sweetest temper. She, too, was in white—a diaphanous robe with a few sprays of the fragrant honeysuckle at her belt. Ned had never seen her look so charming in her choice simplicity. The whole atmosphere of the house affected his impressionable nature like some delicate perfumed wine. The old lady, so dignified, benevolent, and wise, sitting at the head of the table, was all his æsthetic instinct desired. Ned felt himself to be almost as much in love with her as he had ever been with either Sylvia or Freddie. It was partly the desire to be son-in-law to old Madam Macy that had won him over to an engagement. In her presence he felt virtuous, noble, almost religious. The fact that she believed in him was like a back-stay to his character.

Sylvia had never looked so well as on this particular night. There was a slight flush on her cheek, her eyes were of a deep, still brightness, and her blonde hair shone golden. Ned was a captivating talker when he chose to be, and now he exerted himself to fascinate those two women. It was only when he found himself alone in the parlor with Sylvia that some consciousness of what he was swept over him. Old Mrs. Macy in saying good-night had put her hand affectionately on his shoulder. He knew she trusted him, and for a minute he was ashamed. He looked shyly at Sylvia. How natural, pure, and good she was in her easy gown, free and untortured. She wore no false locks; she knew nothing of cosmetics and " making up "; she was as natural and true as a mountain brook. Ned half suspected he was a scoundrel. Now Sylvia sang and played for him on the old piano without any of the foreign airs and graces of execution which Freddie possessed. They sat together and talked of indifferent things. But at last Ned, though he was half afraid of this simple girl to whom he had been engaged two years, drew a little nearer, seated himself on the sofa beside her, and ventured to take her hand. Sylvia blushed deeply. There was a constrained silence. Then she said, trying to steady her voice :

" Ned, dear, there has been something on my mind this good while I wished to say to you, and yet I hardly know how to say it. I have felt that—that possibly you might choose to take back your word and to be free again. Perhaps—that is—you may not quite have known your own mind when you asked me to marry you."

She was too delicate to mention Freddie Haven's name, but, of course, Ned knew that she knew all about Freddie. She slipped the engaged ring from her finger and held it out to him. What could a man with a spark of honor and decency do but refuse to take the ring and try to comfort and reassure the girl to whom he had plighted his troth? She gently put aside his caresses, though she did allow him to slip the ring back on her finger.

"Remember," she said, as they parted at the door, " you are to think it all over very seriously. Come to me to-morrow afternoon, and we will have a long talk. Tell me the exact truth. Tell me all there is in your heart."

As she stood there she looked into his eyes just one

moment, and he could hardly bear her gaze, and then she shut the door. Ned Buckner well knew what her words implied; he must give up Freddie Haven forever if he would retain Sylvia. When he found himself in the village street, he remembered his appointment with Freddie the next afternoon, to decide her fate. Sylvia had appointed the same hour to give him back his troth if he so wished. He had only to tell her that he loved Freddie Haven, loved her in spite of his better self, and the solution was easily reached. Sylvia was a calm, serene, placid being. She would not break her heart over one disappointment; but now he remembered he had at times noted a depth of constancy in her which had alarmed him. He recalled her every attitude of the evening—the white clinging gown, the faint odor of the honeysuckle, her pure, calm face and gentle tones. It was plain he would not give her up without a struggle, to live under the ban of the village and her mother's silent reproach. Then Freddie's splendid dark eyes came flashing toward him, claiming him for their own.

He took a long walk into the country and tried to think the thing out. But there was no use in thinking. It was hard to give up either girl. Both seemed necessary to different phases of his nature. At last he decided to leave the issue to chance. The moon had now risen, and bathed the dewy world in radiance. It was almost as light as day. He plucked two pieces of grass of differing lengths; one was Sylvia, the other Fredonia. He arranged them in his hand behind his back, trying not to juggle with—himself. Then he drew lots, and for a time dared not look at the result. When he did he found that Sylvia had won. He walked calmly home and went to bed. A paltry character, you will say. Yes, but how few of us seem otherwise than paltry when the inmost fiber of motive is dissected! How few of us are heroes and heroines to ourselves!

The next day Ned Buckner did not call on Freddie Haven. He decided to let her settle the question to marry or not to marry for herself. But he went early to visit Sylvia, and so effectually allayed all her doubts and fears that the wedding-day was appointed for the following month. Every one in the village where he was raised knows that Ned Buckner, though a brilliant young man, is not good enough for Sylvia. But how few husbands are good enough for their wives in the estimation of friends?

Freddie has not yet married the Polish count, and some people think he is a pure invention of her brain. There is talk of her going into the Romish Church. She still works on that great piece of embroidery representing the spider's web in the blackberry bush; but most decidedly it would not do for an altar-cloth.

CHAPTER XXXV.

THE MYSTERY OF STYLES GARTH.

THE civilized man who hides in the forest reverts to half-savage instincts. He takes on the silence, the stealthy step, the cunning of the Indian. He becomes mysterious to people who live in the clearing and see more daylight. A large tract of forest like that which stretches away from the north end of the village called Holman's Range is the natural link between civilization and the wilder life of the mountains. A portion of it is filled with winding paths made by cows, berry pickers, grouse shooters, and picnic parties. An old abandoned road runs through one part of it, which, though now unused by wheeled vehicles, is much favored by equestrians. It has grown up to the most beautiful form of wild garden. Many of the oaks and nut-trees, having room to spread their boughs, have attained to large size. The old roadbed is clothed with fine grass and golden moss, as soft as velvet to the foot-fall. The rarest spring-flowers are found along this path that coquets equally with sun and shade. It is spiced all through with the trailing arbutus in May, and later come the columbine, the laurel, the lady-slipper, and fox-glove, and in early autumn a splendid array of the golden-rod, and bright cornel berry, the mountain-ash, and brilliant colored leaves.

Many years ago this old road through Holman's Range had one inhabitant. To-day it has not one. The ruinous house of this solitary resident is still seen there thickly surrounded with bushes and the vigorous saplings of the elm, maple, and chestnut. The roof has fallen, and the wall of logs has partly broken down. The stone chimney still rises in the middle of the house, but it is like the altar of a forgotten god that has long ceased to smoke. A beautiful spring gushes up near the cabin and flows through a broken conduit. In what was once a scrap of door-yard, walled in with rude stones, two or three stunted apple trees struggle through the wilder growths and continue to blossom when May comes round, obedient to the law of their being.

Many years ago a lone man lived in the log-cabin. If you happened then to stray down the wood-road you would see his scant linen fluttering on the line which he had washed and hung out to dry, while the smoke from his rude stone chimney curled softly up among the boughs of a great white pine that shaded the roof of his dwelling. This man's story while he lived here, though quiet and entirely uneventful, had something pathetic, even tragic, in its implications. As absolutely nothing was known of his early history, he soon became a mythical character, and many of the myths created in his lifetime have gathered sharper outlines and more definite details since his death. His career, so far as we know, is but a leaf torn out of the book of his life—a tale without a beginning, a mystery never unraveled. It is now too late to hope it ever will be.

Once upon a time, as the children's story-books say, a stranger, well clad and with the air of an educated man— a gentleman who had lived much in the world and knew its ways—presented himself to an aged clergyman in the large town nearest the village. He had come in on the stage one dark night from Hillsford. He at once proceeded to the parsonage and requested a private interview with the clergyman. This was readily granted, and was held with locked doors. It happened to be a stormy, windy, blustering night, and the interview lasted so long that Miss Mercy, the clergyman's daughter, went and spoke to her father through the door. He simply replied by requesting her to go away. At midnight he let the stranger out of the front door and carefully closed the house. No one ever knew what passed between the two men in those long hours. It was always believed, however, that the stranger had confessed some hideous crime, committed perhaps in a foreign land from which he had fled, and had asked help and protection from the old minister. On this point it was useless to try and interrogate the clergyman. When the name of Styles Garth was mentioned he looked blank, and declared he knew no such man. But Garth, as he was called, did appear among us bearing a line to Mrs. Abby Hastings in our village. It was literally a line, for it only contained the name and address of Mrs. Hastings in the old clergyman's handwriting. Mrs. Hastings cherished that scrap of paper for years, but she could never make any thing more out of it than was patent on its face.

Mrs Hastings was an acquaintance of the clergyman, a widow with three small children and an aged mother, to maintain by her own efforts. She worked at dressmaking, fine shirt making, went out occasionally to nurse the sick, and took in boarders and lodgers when they offered, which was but seldom in those days. The stranger entered the village in an unassuming manner, with a little square trunk having a strong handle in the middle, and no other luggage. He carried the trunk himself and had walked all the way from the county town, bearing it in his hand. He presented the minister's line to Abby Hastings and asked for a lodging, and she promptly gave him the best room in her house, which, barring the noise of the children, was a goodly room, with an old-fashioned fire-place, and an alcoved bed divided off by chintz curtains. The stranger asked for meals in his own apartment, and promised to pay a small stipend in addition to the regular board for the privilege of taking them alone. Mrs. Hastings granted the request, not very willingly, to be sure, for from the moment of his arrival at her door, with the little square trunk in his hand, he excited her itching curiosity. Abby was the greatest talker in the village, and had the Yankee genius for asking questions in excess. She was not slow in plying her new boarder with queries as to where he came from, what was the object of his visit to the village, was he a married man or a bachelor, and how long did he intend to tarry.

But for once Mrs Abby had met her match. He made no pretense of being deaf, and he certainly was not dumb, but he parried all her attacks with stolid, imperturbable silence, even turning his back to her and drumming on the window-pane, until at last she refused to speak to him except when it was absolutely necessary, and a kind of sign language grew up between them which was but sparsely supplemented by uttered words. The stranger had a slight accent which might have been foreign or might have been acquired by an American by long residence in foreign parts. His voice was singularly mellifluous and agreeable to the ear. After he had assumed the garb of a poor countryman and allowed his beard to grow you would have known he was a cultivated man by that delightful voice, had it been your privilege to hear him speak. The stranger had given his name as Styles Garth, of nowhere in particular ; but the one letter he received during his twelve years' residence in and near the village, and which was forwarded by a New York banker, had the original superscription carefully scratched out, and Styles Garth, Esq., and the village address scrawled in the only unoccupied portion of the letter back, which was covered with foreign and American postmarks and confused scribblings. The postmaster and Mistress Hastings, who was his first cousin, spent a whole evening scrutinizing the letter before they delivered it to the owner. They held it up to the light, examined the seal, and picked a little at the same without venturing to break it. But nothing at all was gleaned from this letter. It only deepened the mystery which surrounded the so-called Styles Garth.

During all the years he lived in the country he ceased not to be the object of endless curiosity and gossip, and yet he was by no means a marked or peculiar man in his appearance, and his manners were not ungentle, save that at times he shunned all intercourse with his kind and spent whole days wandering about the wildest parts of Holman's Range. Then again he would return and mingle with the men of the village with a kind of avidity, as if afraid to lose the use and wont of human intercourse, and to forget the sound of his own voice. A singular charm distinguished these moments of converse. Styles Garth was evidently a man who had traveled far and thought deeply.

He was learned in men and affairs as well as in books. The farmer, the mechanic, even the drover and teamster on the road could learn something about his own trade and calling from this man's talk. He conversed only with men and children; with women he held absolutely no intercourse, never doing more than to nod to the old dame who sat knitting in the house porch. Soon after his arrival in the village he discarded his more fashionable clothes, having had himself fitted by a country tailor and shoemaker with the garments common to the region. He donned a plain hat, and with a thick, knotted stick in his hand went about looking like the most ordinary farmer. He also allowed his beard to grow.

But these changes were made gradually, and it could hardly be conjectured that he had made them for the sake of disguising himself. It was apparent he had put off the old man. His past was absolutely detached, cut sheer off from what he now was. Every tie was sundered, every association left behind. He had no lack of money, and sometimes paid out for the simple necessities of his life old gold coins which would have sold to collectors in the market as rarities. I hardly know how the floating conjectures about Garth's past came to crystallize into the singular story that Garth was a wealthy Englishman, and had committed a murder in his own country; in fact, had killed his wife in a fit of jealous rage, thrown her body into a well, and then, seizing such valuables as he had on hand, had fled from the land under a disguised name. The gratuitous assumption of the murdered wife and the body thrown into the well was really amusing, as there was not a particle of evidence whereon to build it. Still people felt justified in inventing the wildest legen rather than confess thay knew nothing at all of the past of Styles Garth.

They pointed to the strange conduct of the Rev. Peter Mifflin, that aged divine to whom Garth had first betaken himself on his arrival in the country, and to whom he owed his introduction to the village and to the house of Mrs. Abby Hastings. The Rev. Peter was a man much revered for sancity and purity of life and soundness of doctrine. All his family connections were known. His whole career was open to the daylight. He was noted for his gentleness and urbanity, and that persuasiveness by which he lured sinners from their ways, instead of thundering forth the terrors of the law.

Suddenly the old man drooped and sickened under some peculiar malady to which no name was given, and he was ordered away by his physician on a vacation journey of six weeks. It was remembered that the Rev. Peter's illness began on the very night when he had been closeted for several hours with the mysterious stranger. But change of air and scene soon restored the hale old man to perfect health. When any thing was said to him of Styles Garth he claimed never to have heard the name. When he drove occasionally to the village in his chaise to attend ministers' meeting, or exchange with the local clergyman, he sometimes met the stranger face to face, but no glance or sign of recognition ever passed between them.

If Garth ever heard the gossip about himself with which the village teemed, he was perfectly indifferent to it. At Mrs. Hastings' he lived intrenched. One knock on the wall of his room with his thick walking-stick indicated a desire for hot water to be left at his door; two sharp raps were a call for breakfast. His board money he left wrapped in paper on his table, where he expected the receipt for the same to be duly deposited. His soiled linen was placed in the eastern corner of the room, and returned mended and darned on a certain day in each week. As Mrs. Abby expressed it, she had never "mended, washed, and fed such another boarder."

This stranger had put a curb into the mouth of the most inveterate talker the town had ever produced. Only one peculiar fact was noted in regard to Styles Garth, and this was gleaned after long and careful observation. He was literally afraid of his own shadow. Of this there came not to be the slightest doubt. When the sun was east he would never walk west, so that his shadow was east before him. When it was in the west he never would turn his footsteps eastward. If he caught sight of his shadow by chance on the road he stood transfixed with an unspeakable dread. Superstitious people declared that the shadow itself was of a sinister and menacing form—elongated beyond all proper shadow limits, bickering, mocking, and mowing in pantomime, and taking on queer shapes to the developing of a demon's hoofs and tail.

But all this was the veriest nonsense. Garth's shadow was perfectly normal, fantastic to be sure, as all shadows are, but entirely without significance to an observer. Why his face blanched and his eyes changed to an expression of helpless terror when he caught sight of his own spindled legs and distorted figure moving before him gave rise to the wildest conjectures. Rivington was then a young medical man just settled in the village. With the sckpticism of his class, he pooh-poohed the absurd stories about Styles Garth's being haunted by his shadow. In his opinion he was a monomaniac on some one point, and otherwise quite rational. He had probably wandered away from home, said the doctor, under some mild form of mental aberration, and was in fact one of those mysterious disappearances of which we so often read. Two or three years after Garth came to the village the railroad was built through the valley. This new road seemed to terrify Garth, while it attracted his footsteps. He would walk along the track for miles and miles, with his head bent, tapping the rails with his stick and listening intently to their ring. He would pass from side to side in a long zigzag, as if trying to evade something invisible to all eyes but his own. But after the trains began running he never went near it again, except at night, when he would sometimes follow the line as far as Upton, fifteen miles away.

It was after this that Garth hired the log-cabin built in the woods, on the old abandoned road, and took his permanent leave of the lodging of Mrs. Hastings. It was reported that he had gone to live in the woods because his shadow troubled him less in a place where the sun shone but fitfully. Was it the memory of a crime, of disappointed ambition, of a cross in love, or was it some fearful vision of a diseased brain which this strange man was trying to elude? No one was ever afraid of Garth who came in contact with him. He did many helpful, kind acts about the country, saving the farmers' cattle from pound, curing their diseases, and prescribing skillfully for all the complaints of horses. He never would take a penny for any service. Once or twice he had carried a sick farm-hand into his cabin and nursed him through the typhus fever. He doctored these people on a principle of his own, giving no medicine, but attending strictly to cleanliness, bathing, ventilation, and a simple and abundant diet. This he did when stifling and starving was considered the proper treatment for fevers; when people were fed on blue pills for slight ailments, and when they took a course of strong medicine and emetics in the spring as regularly as they cleaned house.

When the village people came to spy out the land they found absolutely nothing to satisfy their morbid curiosity. His cabin door stood open day and night, and birds and squirrels entered freely. He kept a drinking vessel at the spring for those who wished to taste its pure, cool water, and a bench under the pine was free to all. It was known that such money as he possessed was deposited in the county bank. There was nothing worth stealing in his cabin. The wife of a poor man in the nearest clearing did his baking, and he lived mainly on milk and berries in summer.

One day a curly-pated lad of five or six ran away from his home in the village and got lost in the great wooded tract of Hinman's Range. The neighbors turned out in a large searching party. The poor mother wrung her hands and wept in extreme anguish of soul. She had buried four children, and this boy was the only one left to her. At that time it was believed that bears and catamounts roamed at large in the wilder parts of the woods. The little lad's footsteps were traced to a pond which lies deep hidden in the very heart of the range, and there they disappeared. He had stopped to build small play-houses with stones and bushes in the path, and by these he was tracked to the pond, and then the pathetic little tokens ceased, and the footprints last seen went wandering about the shore.

They were talking of dragging the pond for the child's body on the second day of the search, when Styles Garth suddenly appeared in the village bearing the little lost boy in his arms. He had found him in the wildest, most desolate part of the forest, at a place known as Rattlesnake Ledge, where the little fellow was plucking blackberries for his breakfast with the homesick tears dripping down his cheeks. He was scratched and torn, dirty and disheveled, but otherwise unharmed. He had slept in the rattlesnakes' den on a great bed of moss among the rocks, but nothing had hurt the boy. He was tired of his long wanderings and grieving much for home, and he confided himself to Garth's care with childlike faith. His shoes were all worn out and his feet had been cut on the sharp stones, and Garth soon took him in his arms and brought him, a heavy boy, nearly five miles to his home. The mother's heart overflowed with gratitude to this strange man for the rescue of her child. But he would not listen to any demonstrations. He deposited the boy in her arms and escaped as quickly as possible to the forest.

This incident made an era in the hermit's life. An unexplained tie of interest and affection bound him to the boy he had found in the woods. It was the first humanizing sentiment that had fallen on his heart since he appeared in the village. He sometimes came about to seek the boy, and as he grew older he spent whole days with Styles Garth in the woods, who gave him his first lessons in the knowledge of plants and animals, and the wonders of nature, and laid the foundations of a scientific curiosity in the boy's mind that ultimately shaped his career.

The mother, though she was afraid of Styles Garth, could not keep the child away from him wholly, and when she found that he taught the child nothing evil, but awoke and stimulated all the powers of his intellect, she allowed the intimacy to go on. Fanciful people invented the story that when Ben Hoadly was with Styles Garth he was not afraid of his shadow, the innocent nature of the boy acting as a shield against those dark and mysterious influences that at times seemed to haunt his life.

Ben was fifteen when Styles Garth died. He had taken a severe cold while on a visit to a sick laborer on a winter day. Our doctor attended him in his last hours, and Ben Hoadly was with him and held him in his arms when he died, carrying his secret down to the grave. When the small hand-trunk was examined which Garth had brought with him to the village it was found to contain only a few pieces of money, sufficient to defray the expenses of his simple funeral. The Rev. Peter Mifflin died a few months later, at the age of eighty-five, but he left no scrap of writing, nothing to indicate the nature of the secret which had been confided to him by Styles Garth. The curiosity-mongers were foiled all round, but they had so often told the story of the murdered wife, and the deposit of her body in the well, with full and minute particulars, that in the end they came firmly to believe it.

Years and years after the death of Styles Garth, Ben Hoadly, the only being who had ever loved him in the village, erected a plain stone at the head of his grave on Burying-Ground Hill, and inscribed it with the words, "To My Earliest Friend." The superstitions which attached themselves to Garth during his life have in some strange way been transferred to this stone. It is said that at times it casts queer shadows, quite abnormal and inexplicable, on any known principle attaching to facetious tombstones. But you may safely set this down among the number of village myths.

CHAPTER XXXVI.

JOHN DEAN AND ORIANA.

THE polite and refined ladies who belong to the best village set would be shocked to have it said that they are given to tattle. Their mode is only an extension of the circulatory and respiratory and nervous systems of the body by which each becomes a member of all, and news is communicated one knows not how—perhaps by touch or some other sense perception. The best village ladies have a wholesome horror of backbiting. It is not only scandalous, it is vulgar. It has been so much preached against and moralized over that the spinsters, whose special function gossip is supposed to be, are very careful how they "talk." It is only about twenty years ago that one of the most inveterate old-maid tattlers and gossips ever known here was publicly expelled from a benevolent society and reproved in the weekly prayer and experience meeting.

Such a thing could not happen now. If there is an occasional survival of the unfittest in the form of an old-fashioned tattler, who makes trouble by the too free use of her tongue, you may be sure she does not belong to the best set. In that circle there is intercommunion of thought and feeling, a subtle magnetism which puts every body *en rapport*. If the ladies get together and talk over neighborhood affairs in rather too free a spirit, with an occasional verging toward something which might by an uninitiated and blundering outsider be called tittle-tattle, some one is sure to remark that this class of talk comes under the head of social criticism. Of course, she says, persons who discriminate at all, must see things in their friends and neighbors—little peculiarities and foibles which it is not treasonable to mention in a kindly way. The people who praise every body indiscriminately, those unmitigated optimists who do not know that the kettle is black, but call it a fine shade of brown or gray, are insipid creatures with no niceness of perception, and therefore, owing to their universal benevolence and mushy good nature, not in the least interesting.

In the best set a wholesome equality is cultivated. It is not considered in good taste for some people to dress more expensively or wear finer jewels than others can afford. Mrs. Judge Magnus, who is a woman of great tact, always puts away her diamonds and her best gowns when she comes home from Washington. She wishes frankly to resume her place in the village sphere she so much enjoys, and to incur the least possible amount of social criticism. The judge himself always tries to come down a few pegs on his return, and to play the equality business with a wholly unconscious air; but the knowledge that he is the great man of the town—in other words, the biggest toad in the puddle—causes him in time unconsciously to ignore his forced humility and to put on his natural expression of owning the village, and, indeed, the county.

The judge is not gifted with penetration, but his wife has enough for two. She knows how to enter into all the angles and sinuosities and crooks of village life, and to make herself thoroughly popular. So that, although the judge imagines himself endowed with headship and swells around mightily in consequence, his wife never swells, never boasts, never assumes any thing or puts on airs, steps about in her neat, plain tailor suit, with her keen eye out, and when the moment is ripe seizes any advantage she covets.

"A fine woman," says Jake Small, spreading himself,

"and the best of the team by a long shot. If gumption and sense could get the gore out of me, she could, but it ain't to be did." At that very moment Mrs. Magnus was sending provisions and necessaries to Jake's wife, who had just added her eighth to the illustrious family of Small.

The judge's house was not the center of our best set. It would have been inconvenient, for she often entertained distinguished strangers from a distance, at which times the village intimacies would have clashed. She was an adept in knowing how to keep people in the right place, to placate them, cherish them in good-humor, and make them useful on occasion. The house where all the social telephone wires came together was John Dean's. Mrs. Dean's parlor was the great vibratory center, where was gathered and distributed the peculiar village life of which I have spoken. It was a very pretty parlor, for Mrs. Dean had brought a nice snug fortune to her husband, and if he had no other virtue he possessed fine taste in works of art. The charm of the house was not in upholstery, but in rare etchings and beautiful editions of old books, and in a case of replicas of some of the finest engraved gems in the world. Mrs. Dean had early set her face against Eastlake and all the tide of cheap art decoration that came in with him, therefore her house had a distinct character of its own.

It was known that Mrs. Dean had consented to become the center of the best set in order to find some little relief from John Dean—as her sister, Oriana Freeborn, said, "some outside life" was indispensable to poor Elspeth. John Dean was jealous of feminine influence in his home, but the women of the village despised his selfishness, and had conspired to give his wife the change she needed. Their influence was as pervasive as the wind, and in time John Dean ceased to resist it, and settled down in a state of armed neutrality. Mr. Dean was a cultivated man, with a perfect appreciation of the art treasures he had collected with his wife's money. He was too cultivated. A book-worm from his earliest years every thing he had ever learned in the line of his favorite study, the philosophy of history, stuck to him like beggars' lice in the field. He could not rub off a single fact or date, nor for the life of him get rid of any of that tremendous store of information that made his specific gravity so overpowering. It was not the philosophy of history alone that engrossed him. He had views and theories on all subjects, which he poured out in a continuous, slow, sluggish stream that resembled very thick treacle.

John Dean had tried to write, indeed, had written books; but the firm that published them broke down from their weight, and the very truck which conveyed them from place to place was hopelessly wrecked in the street. He obtained a professorship in a small college because of his vast learning, but one by one the boys slunk out of the lecture-room, and he was left slowly gesticulating to the empty benches. He had tried platform lecturing with the same result, and now he was reduced to the home audience.

No one of her friends could understand why Miss Freeborn, with all her advantages of fortune, good looks, and general agreeableness, had ever consented to marry John Dean. Her sister Oriana says it was because *she* was in Europe that year, and Elspeth was not very well, and was crushed by John Dean's elephantine advances and the statistics of the Roman Empire until she had no will of her own. Every body pities Mrs. Dean, but being a heroic little woman she never complains. The terrible fact of the business is that John Dean is always at home. There is no escape from him save in that community of feeling which pervades the best set; and therefore Mrs. Dean has given herself up more to the trivialities of village life than her taste inclined. The public having decamped from John Dean, and his books having fallen like lead into the bottomless sea of oblivion, there is nothing left to him but to tutor his wife. They have two boys, and Mrs. Dean is rejoiced to see that they both take after her family. The Freeborns are jocular, lively, sensitive people, with a certain amount of indirection and subtlety in their fun. John Dean has never in the whole course of his life been able to comprehend a joke, and his wife finds no relief in exercising upon him her natural weapons of irony and sarcasm. She is obliged to sit and receive the leaden shower of instruction, while with the rotary motion of his thick finger he seems to bore into her mind like a gimlet. John Dean goes upon the principle that a wife's mind is or ought to be entirely emptied of its contents, into which it is the duty of the husband to pour his accumulated facts. He assumes that she knows nothing, never has learned any thing, and that it is absolutely necessary to start with first principles.

Mrs. Dean's mind is by no means an exhausted receiver. She is a lively, independent personality. To be sure she has been much crushed by Dean's accumulations of knowledge, all of which he tries upon her with the heavy theories he has formulated before using it in other shape. But since she became the recognized center of the best set it is remarked that she is much livelier, poor thing, and more herself. In her parlor it has been decided that Mrs. Worldly Wiseman dresses too much even for a bride, and all the peculiarities of Drusilla and the Rev. Arthur Meeker have been discussed in the spirit of an enlightened social criticism.

Mrs. Dean looks with amused sympathy upon the Rev. Arthur, who is certainly growing a little stouter. Drusilla has ascertained that he now weighs five pounds and eleven ounces more than he did at the time of his marriage. But it can not be said that his manly spirit has yet reared its head in resistance to Drusilla's tyranny. A funny thing in connection with the Rev. Arthur is that St. Patty has furtively and cautiously taken his side, and tries in her own sly way to encourage him to eat things upon the interdicted list of edibles. But as yet he only looks frightened when she suggests such a thing. Mrs. Dean in certain moods feels that she and Arthur Meeker are in the same boat—victims of matrimonial oppression of a kind which ordinarily elicits but little sympathy. It may be that she will yet enter into a silent conspiracy with St. Patty to give him the needed help in plucking up courage to throw off the yoke. For herself she sees there is no hope, save through those little loopholes of cheery life which come to her from without. When she is permitted to be frivolous, she feels quite happy and almost young. She must bear her heavy fate as best she can and try to live for her boys, in whom she will do her best to instill a proper hatred for the philosophy of history and universal knowledge. She rather hopes they may take to athletics, and she intends to teach them early that a wife is not by nature to be purely passive and receptive, in other words, to go to school to her husband all the days of her life, without breaking down under the strain.

But Mrs. Dean is much subdued—infinitely more jaded and spiritless than nature intended her to be. Her sister Oriana, on the other hand, is entirely unsubdued. John Dean does not particularly care to have Oriana make them long visits, for, strengthened by Oriana's influence, his wife acquires modes of thought and expression and an out-door air of independence which considerably weaken his hold upon her intellect. He thinks that if Oriana had come early under his formative hand she might have amounted to something, and probably secured a husband for her own private instruction. But the fact is there was nothing Oriana long viewed with such horror as coming under the bondage of matrimony. The sole reason why she has not married long before is the sad fate of her sister Elspeth. John Dean being a perfectly reputable man with no redeeming vices, Oriana, the irreverent, thinks she would like him much better if he had done something rather bad. His moral scrupulosity is quite thrown away upon her, and confirms her in a saucy mode of free thinking and acting particularly obnoxious to her brother-in-law. There is nothing which gives her such exquisite delight as to shock John Dean.

Oriana has all the advantages of fortune which Elspeth possessed. She lives with an aged aunt in a distant city, and when she comes to the village she gives it distinction. Her form is very elegant and her face is piquant and sparkling. She has an abundance of golden-brown hair of the loose, fluffy, wavy kind, and however she tosses it up it looks only the more lovely. It is impossible to imitate her style of dressing or behaving, for she never looks or acts twice alike, so varied are her moods ; but all have a certain brilliance. Oriana may be thirty or thirty-five, but she is one of those women who never grow old. Age can not wither nor custom change her infinite variety.

When she is visiting in the village, she is in a constant state of inward irritation with John Dean, which, for Elspeth's sake, she tries to cover with bland complacency. When she is a member of his household, John feels it is his duty to tutor Oriana, and his efforts to improve her mind in his ponderous, slow, persistent way nearly set her wild. It is extremely trying to a person of Oriana's disposition to have it taken for granted that she has never read any thing, and is ignorant of the commonest facts of experience, while all the time that dreadful finger rotates quite near her face, and the oppressiveness of his large, stout person is more than she can bear.

Oriana gets so morbidly sensitive to John's presence she hates the creak of his chair, the way he twitches his light mustache and ruffles his leonine locks, the rustle of his newspaper, and the manner he clears his throat when he prepares to begin to instruct. The only relief she finds is in saying very saucy things to John Dean, things sufficiently caustic to bite into his thick consciousness; and when John is aroused he retorts with a heavy hand. Dean is a great purist about words, and is always taking Oriana up as to the meaning and derivation of the terms she uses.

One afternoon just before dark, John and Oriana had begun by fighting over some little insignificant word of four letters, which he claimed she did not use in its proper connection. They had begun in a light vein, as light as John was capable of, but soon ran into personalities, and began telling each other the plainest truths. John had deprecated the influence of the volatile, giddy Oriana on the mind of his wife, and Oriana had twitted him most unhandsomely with living on his wife's income and boring her to death. They had both been very outspoken, and poor Oriana was more vexed with herself even than she was with John, who provokingly kept his temper while he told her what a very improper person she was, and set forth her violence and irreverence for her betters in glaring colors.

Poor distressed Elspeth could do nothing to separate them. But at last Oriana seized her bonnet and rushed out into the street. She was too indignant to cry, but her face was flushed and mottled with the excitement of the battle. As soon as she was alone she fell into a state of abject self-abasement for the words she had used to John Dean, and she was so ashamed of herself that she sped rapidly along, with her head down, not caring to see any thing or be seen.

The sun was low, casting beautiful long beams the whole length of the leafy arcade of Main Street, and the tepid, soft wind of September brought down the pale colored autumn leaves, and heaped them in drifts along the walk, or scattered them over fences and into the ruts of the road, covering the grass with bright patches. The trees looked higher than usual, and a vague, sweet, sad sentiment of the passing away of summer seemed to linger in the air. Oriana saw nothing, for her head was down and her cheeks were burning; but she half ran along the walk in the hope of getting to some open place beyond the town, when at the junction of Main and Market Streets she came in sharp collision with some one who was just rounding the corner. She fell back a step or two from the shock, and for an instant could not distinguish the person with whom she had collided. But it happened to be the young man named Hugh, the village historian and briefless lawyer, who boarded with Aunt Dido. He had been carrying an old family Bible under his arm which Mother Vibard had lent him to copy some dates—an old book worth its weight in gold. But the shock of meeting Oriana had thrown it into the dust.

"Hullo," said he, picking up the book and looking at Oriana curiously. "Whither away so fast, Miss Freeborn, that the lives of innocent, unprotected young men are endangered at every street corner."

Oriana, brought to her senses, was covered with confusion. She knew Hugh very well, but with her quick tongue she could not find a word to say for herself, until at last she did manage to stammer out: "I believe I was running away."

"From whom, pray?"

"Oh, from myself."

"Don't," said Hugh in a whimsically gentle voice.

"If you will promise not to, I will give you one of the arrow-heads I picked up this afternoon on Hoddon Hill, where the old graves are." And he pulled out of his pocket a queer little black stone almost exactly in the shape of a worn heart. Oriana took it and stood looking at it in the path, as Hugh went on whistling softly to himself. That night at tea Hugh told the little incident to Aunt Dido, who was dressed up unusually for her, as she had been out calling, and now was pouring her boarder a second cup.

"Hugh," said she meditatively, through the steam of the teapot, after a moment's silence, "why don't you shine up to Orianny?"

CHAPTER XXXVII.

HUGH GETS A LADY IN HIS EYE.

HUGH went strolling about in the September weather, with his hands in his pockets, whistling softly to himself. He generally carried an old book or a review under his arm. The woods were at their finest, just beginning to flicker with autumn's fires, although the great body of shade was still green. Hugh did not seem to care much for companionship. He seldom invited the young minister to walk with him now, nor could he be found in his accustomed haunts in the village parlors, browsing among his neighbors' small libraries, or spending his spare time with his favorite old ladies, or devoting himself to the young ones, who knew him so well they were content to be his friends without ulterior views, or side-glances toward love-making.

People were at a loss to know where Hugh had hidden himself. His local history was now complete, and was selling well by subscription. His friends advised him to devote himself to some new and larger work which would furnish a respectable field for his talents and attainments. The parson had strongly urged that he should write a book on the history and poetry of the great world cathedrals, an undertaking which he felt would be peculiarly sympathetic to Hugh's genius; it would force him to shake himself together, pick up the loose ends of his careless life, and go abroad for study. He would thus get out of the deep ruts in which he had lived so long. But Hugh shrank from the idea. He evidently needed some new interest in his life, but he was like a cat in the tenacity of his close-clinging local affections. The woods and fields and cow-lanes and byways of the village had grown to be a part of himself, and only some fresh and overpowering influence could detach him from the trellis where he clung like an unpruned vine.

It was curious the number of people who believed in the possibilities of this young man, and busied themselves in trying to find the exact thing he was good for. And as the years glided away, they entirely forgot that he was ceasing to be so very young, that he had in fact entered upon his thirties. But the interest in him was perennial. It showed a certain vein of genius in the man that he could thus awaken expectancy and keep it fresh. Mrs. Deacon Hildreth and the little sisters, and several others thought he might make a fine preacher if he only turned his attention to serious things. But first it would be necessary to convert him, which, they imagined, would be somewhat like dyeing him of a new color. But he had shown no tendency toward this mystic and wonderful process. Mr. Worldly Wiseman had even proposed to him to become a village real-estate agent, but Aunt Dido still pinned all her hopes for Hugh on his marriage to the right woman. She had a theory of her own, which she could not put into words, that if he fell desperately in love, it would bring together the elements of his character until they combined into something organic and noble.

Hugh felt in his soul that the celestial fire had been but scantily dealt out to him. He had a profound sympathy with nature, and yet he was a poet only in feeling. He loved harmonies, and felt their deepest meanings, and yet he was not a musician. The past allured him with power in all its picturesque aspects, and yet he could not be a romancer. He was infected with the disease of the premature youth of the age—the belief that no form of effort is very much worth while in the world constituted as it now is. If he felt like a poet and a musician, he was still afraid to spoil the spring of his enjoyment by peddling it out in the market-place. Hugh had run into a great many imperfect relations, and had formed but a few which would bear any serious strain. His keen sense of humor let him into most of the shams of life, and yet withal there was a kind of unspoiled freshness about his nature, like the odor of birch bark and pine cones. He loved to observe, and he thought a village as good a field of observation as any. The very ease with which he met all classes of people, joked with them, and left them feeling brighter and cheerier, covered the closely guarded center of his own life.

Dr. Holmes says that a man must get sight of the woman he is to fall in love with through a pin-hole. She is just like other beings, but he must get a special peep at her in a moment of susceptibility, and then she fills his eye and changes his life. Hugh took this special peep at Oriana when she stood there in the low-glancing light of the sun, under the changing trees, agitated and flushed, with her eyes gleaming almost as if ready to shed tears. He had never so completely taken this peep at any other woman, however charming, that her weaknesses, and her foibles, or affectations had not spoiled the impression. But since he had given the little black arrow-head, shaped like a heart, to Oriana, it seemed to Hugh that he was in love with some idea of her, not with the woman herself. And it took a long time for him to find out where he stood. The light halo of her hair, which the sun shone through that afternoon, was always before him. The expression of her face, with the half-shadow of some trouble upon it, seemed divine. When he thought of meeting her again in the old, easy, familiar way he was covered with confusion. Where was his well-established impudence, his persiflage and raillery? Oriana Freeborn had suddenly become a mystery to him. He went about secretly hoping yet dreading to meet her. He was afraid she would read his soul and think him ridiculous.

Hugh emptied his mind of all its trash, every thing he had cared about, had thought or read, to give it entirely to this new guest. In a certain way he tried to purify that inner chamber, to make it meet for such company by humility and self-abasement. It was not Oriana, it was the idea of her, that was so entrancing; and of course it would never come to any thing. He knew he had entered on a new and beautiful experience, but for a long time he did not know that he was in love. He revisited all his old haunts on the mountains, in the woods, even the most retired places by Fisher Brook and up the Hilham Gorge, because the notion came to him that if he were to think these new thoughts about Oriana in his favorite places, they would all be changed and forever associated with her image.

One day he lay under some tall pines on a knoll in Holman's Range. It was a very retired part of the woods, and he seemed to be buried in layer upon layer of forest, with the hills rising over it in round heads, or in long wavy blue lines. The forest was parti-colored, melting into violet and azure haze, and tangling the autumn colors in soft bright gauzy webs and veils. As he sat there he could gaze over the great mosaic for miles and miles, and hear nothing but the rustle of a rabbit or squirrel in the fallen leaves, or the cawing of a distant crow, save the wind that swept with a long even swing over the forest like the swaying of a pendulum—that wind of autumn which brings with it such multitudes of thoughts and memories and emotions. As he sat there at the foot of a great pine, with the lights and shades flitting over him, wondering why this idea of Oriana had taken such complete possession of him, the true meaning of the experience flashed on his mind. He was in love. Hugh took his head between his hands, and such a rush of blissful feelings came over him I am not sure his eyes were not suffused with tears. He had felt so long he could never have this experience; now it had stolen upon him unawares, it seemed a miracle like prophecy or the gift of tongues. Some glory and sweetness out of the unknown had come to him who was unworthy of such a visitation. It humbled his pride, and made him feel like a new man. And yet in that part of his intellect not quite under the spell, Hugh, strange as it may appear, knew even at that moment that probably he was not in love with the real Oriana. She might be wayward, perverse, or ill-tempered, even. But it made no difference. She stood there in a gleam of sunlight on the pine needles, the one woman in the world for him.

Now that Hugh had found out what ailed him, and was very sure it was not malaria or liver complaint, as Aunt Dido, seeing his pensiveness, had suggested, he wondered what he would be expected to do next. The expectation was of course confined to the calmer and more rational part of his consciousness. *She* might never know of this experience, which in his state of exaltation seemed so regenerating and transforming. He might never dare to tell her. He had known her a year or two. Why had he not felt this toward her at first? It was all a mystery. Perhaps it was a species of intoxication, like opium-eating or dram-drinking, that would leave him with a headache and a bad taste in his mouth. Hugh felt that he must take some time to find out what was expected of him now that he was in love, and especially as the lady of his love was profoundly ignorant of the fact and would probably scorn his proposals if he ever ventured to make any. This new virtue of humility that had come to Hugh seemed to sit rather awkwardly upon him, like a suit of ill-fitting clothes. At all events he must try to see Oriana. As he disliked John Dean, he would not go to the house, but he must watch and wait for her like a dog for his master's footsteps.

Oriana had been staying on at John Dean's, doing penance for her sins. She was trying, for Elspeth's sake, to be very polite to her brother-in-law, and a glacial state of courtesy had grown up between them. She talked with Elspeth about the weather at table because Dean would not converse in her presence now (he never talked), and waited until he should emerge from the sulks. But he tried to show her how he could heap coals of fire on her head by invariably giving her the tenderloin portion of the beefsteak. Had it not been for the two boys and their boy-talk, the meals would have been unendurable. When she encouraged them to chatter too loudly, Elspeth, who was watching her husband's face, would softly press Oriana's foot with her own under the table. The house was uncomfortable, and Oriana kept as much on the outside of it as possible in those beautiful blue September days. Why she did not go home to her kind old aunt, who was constantly writing for her to come, was, she said to herself, because her penance had not been long or hard enough.

She knew well that Elspeth would be more comfortable when left to herself. Perhaps her imagination had been slightly infected by the trifling incident which threw her in Hugh's way. She had always liked Hugh. A magnetic touch of sympathy seemed to flash out from his laughing eyes, and even white teeth which he showed when he smiled. She fancied he understood her little caprices, her changeable moods and varied impulses which made her original and unlike any body else. She often looked at the little arrow head he had given her. It was an ugly little bit of flint, worn almost like a pebble, but she prized it and carried it about in her pocket. At night she had once or twice put it under her pillow to dream on. But the idea of being in love with Hugh was ridiculous. She gloried in the plan of spinsterhood and perfect independence she had formed, seeing that hardly one of her intimate friends had married, as she said, happily. But to be sure her ideas of marital bliss were rather exacting. She abhorred the squabbles and bickerings, the fallings-out, and makings-up attendant on matrimony as she had witnessed it in several families, and more than all the stupid, commonplace, material life into which married people settle when they have become thoroughly accustomed to each other and have no new discoveries to make in that realm. Oriana was so pessimistic about marriage, she had always said if she ever married she would have to be captured; but she did own to herself that this might happen.

Moreover, she had vowed never to marry a man without a settled business and some income of his own. Hugh had neither, and was therefore out of the question. Hugh had also vowed he would never live on a wife's means. He despised John Dean for looking so fat, and sleek, and well-fed on Elspeth's money. He loved independence like a wild bird in a bush. The thought had at times come to him that he would go into the woods and live alone a year or two, like Thoreau, to find out what kind of creature a man is without padding and appurtenances. But when you are in love, all is changed.

As the Dean house was not pleasant for Oriana, she spent most of her waking time out of doors. The air was crisp and delicious, and sent the blood tingling to the extremities. The village gardens were full of rich fall flowers—salvias, gladioli, dahlias, and scarlet geraniums. The air was perfumed with ripening fruit. The brown nuts began to shake down from the trees. Apples lay in heaps on the ground. Plums, and quinces, and grapes filled the air with a delicate honey sweetness when it blew in puffs from the south. The changing leaves added to the pervasive sense of the ripe year which is more an influence than an odor. Oriana breathed it as she glided lightly along toward the woods, bearing a little basket in her hand to hold hazelnuts, beech drops, the Indian pipe, colored leaves, and above all the blue fringed gentian, should she be fortunate enough to find it. She also carried a small black satin bag on her arm, which contained a sketch book and a tiny volume of Michael Angelo's sonnets.

But she never read, nor did she sketch. She went to the woods to dream away the warm noons, when the sun brought out the brilliancy of the changing year, and made it drip with crimson and gold dyes as the leaves slowly fluttered down in grassy spots still of a perfect solid green. One day Hugh was coming home from a tramp along the slopes of Saddleback, by way of Birch Brook, and was just striking through the Cutter place, on the Roundabout Road, when in a little open ferny covert, not far from the brook and about a hundred rods from the road, he came upon Oriana sitting in the shade of a wide-spreading chestnut tree. She was dressed in gray and had put some bright leaves in the bodice of her gown. He had been so absorbed in the thought of her he was hardly surprised to see her there before him. But he noticed that she was slightly pale, and her lips were contracted as if in pain.

"I have sprained my ankle," she said, as she turned her head at the sound of his footsteps, "just a little, you know, by stepping into a treacherous moss-covered hole. How lucky it is you have come. I fear I can not rise without help. If you can get me on my feet, I shall be able, perhaps, to hobble home."

Hugh looked at her timidly, with a shyness that was entirely new to him. He did not say he was sorry for her accident, for he was too much absorbed, and the consciousness of all he felt for her came up into his eyes, and she saw it.

He helped her to her feet and she tried to walk, holding his arm and limping badly at every step. He saw the pain was severe. She grew pale even to her lips.

"Would you mind," said he, with the same timid, conscious air, "if I were to put my arm around you and lift you over the worst places? I could easily carry you to the road."

"Why do you ask?" she said with some petulance. "You must treat me as if I were a bag of potatoes."

"I asked because——" Hugh was getting miserably confused, and could not find a way to shape his sentences; "because I thought it unfair, at least, without telling you how dearly I love you." He had blurted it out because he could not help it, and they stood looking at each other under the trees, Oriana's face reflecting all the confusion that was manifest in his.

"I will leave you here until I can get assistance, unless you say I can help you now."

"Don't you think this is taking a mean advantage?" and the tears welled up into her eyes.

"I did not intend to, but quite the contrary. You have only to choose. If it is disagreeable to you to have me help you, I will leave you now and go for a carriage. Here is a dry place where you can sit."

Oriana had entirely forgotten the pain in her foot. "If I let you help me," she answered illogically, flying away from the point, and now quite angry, "you will use the permission against me by and by."

"No; I shall use nothing against you, Miss Freeborn. I had to tell you because I thought it manly. It told itself. Shall I go for a carriage?"

"But you have sprung the whole thing upon me so suddenly without warning." She was almost sobbing now. "I want time to think it over. I want a great deal of time—perhaps a year."

"Take all the time you want," said Hugh, putting his

arm around her. He could not help letting a triumphant look peep out of his eyes.

"Well," said she, with a sigh, looking terribly perplexed, "you had better get me out of the woods. I don't want to be left here alone."

Hugh just tightened his hold about her waist a little, and lifted her lightly until her small pretty feet in their neat boots were free from the ground. When they reached the highway she insisted on being set down.

"Did you ever," she said whimsically, with her eyes still dewy—"did you ever know any thing so ridiculous as this? I had made a promise to myself that I would never, never—that I would show the world what a noble woman an old maid can be."

Hugh's face was suffused with happiness.

"And I too," he said, "had made a promise that I would never, never. But when we are very much in love every thing is changed."

I am not quite sure, but I think Oriana and Hugh will be married soon and will go to Italy to live for a few years. It is possible the book on the "Poetry and History of Cathedrals" may yet be written.

CHAPTER XXXVIII.

A SPIRITUAL EXPERIENCE.

ALTHOUGH opinions and ideas change but slowly in the country, it would now be impossible for Dr. Abijah Manners to preach the sermons he once thundered forth in the village meeting-house, while beating the dust from the pulpit cushion with his strong red fists. The articles of faith are still subscribed, but in life many of them are inoperative. The young minister, when he was ordained, passed his examination on eternal punishment and foreordination more by quickness of wit and subtle new interpretations than by general soundness of doctrine. If he were now to preach the wrath of God and the eternal burning, in the plain unvarnished style of old Dr. Abijah, the people would rise up in fear and trembling and depart from the church. Modern nerves and the new sensitiveness to all kinds of suffering, including the pains of the lower animals, can not stand the old style of preaching.

It will not do to take curse words out of the Old Testament and fling them broad-cast among refined modern people, as the old doctor did, thus cutting a swath through sin and iniquity as clean as his mighty row in the haying-field. Even the stanchest orthodox members, though they would not acknowledge it, demand a diluted theology. The young minister confines himself mainly to the New Testament. It would not matter so very much to him—if he could preserve the Book of Psalms, of Job and of Isaiah—save as a matter of history, if the remainder of that wonderful old book were stricken out of existence. But Dr. Abijah Manners drew from the Old Testament as from an arsenal those mighty arms with which he attacked the world, the flesh, and the devil. Now, there is a great deal of implied doubt as to the existence of a personal devil. Even the young parson has been heard to say that our popular Satan owes his creation mainly to Milton, and is not found in the Bible, and the influence of Milton on the Calvinistic theology of a former age is passing away. Such opinions, uttered in his own parish, in his own pulpit, as one may say, ought to make old Dr. Abijah turn in his coffin. But the people receive them calmly, and a few have gone in Biblical criticism much beyond any thing the young minister would dare to utter from the sacred desk.

It is remarked that if he preaches a very liberal sermon on one Sunday, he is apt to tone down the impression on the next, by giving a doctrinal discourse which seems partially to fill the gap between him and the old-fashioned believer. So regularly do these changes occur that a joke has gone forth in the village to the effect that the minister has an orthodox and a heterodox foot. When he is standing on his orthodox foot some people do not particularly care to hear him. The judge, the doctor, Mr. Worldly Wiseman, and men of that class, are generally on hand when there is any prospect of his launching out and saying something to shake the old dry bones. It has been feared at times that he might lose his balance and go entirely over to advanced liberalism. But he knows so well when to advance and when to retreat that there is little danger of such a catastrophe. It is not at all probable that he will ever lose the center of gravity by standing too long on his heterodox leg; by shifting skillfully from one side to the other he enlivens his discourses and keeps up the interest of the congregation.

He is deeply interested in the new interpretations of old doctrines which so much lessen their native force. He feels an ardent enthusiasm for building the new church just outside the old, using the ancient substructure and such of the aged timbers as are not too rotten and worm-eaten. One old farmer describes the parson's plan of preserving all that is valuable in the past as similar to the history of a boy's jack-knife: First he lost the blade, and had the old handle fitted to a new one. Then the old handle wore out and was replaced by another. Still it was the same old knife. Who can tell, when the old church is thoroughly revamped, whether it will retain any of the ancient material?

Some of his parishioners keep step with him in all his efforts. Others are still in doubt, as they wish to see more clearly than they now do the direction in which the new current is setting. They are mainly hard-working farmers from the hills, and old people who have been brought up on strong Gospel meat. The tillers of a poor soil have but little consolation in their daily round of toil save in religion. They want it undiluted and positive. No doctrine shading off at the edges into euphemisms and vague declarations of the love of God can sustain them. They want to know if there is any thing positive to lay hold of in the hour of need.

To be sure, a number of the mountain farmers have grown stolidly indifferent to religion. They never go to meeting, and confine their acts of outward worship on a Sunday to putting on a clean shirt and whittling a pine stick as they sit on the stone wall, dull and ruminative. They could give you a ready opinion about "beef critters" and sheep raising, but none at all as to their immaterial interests. They have lost the faith of their fathers, and they do not speculate. There is little of the blessing of the seventh day left to them but the physical sensation of rest and vacancy. The women and children of these people occasionally gather at a school-house meeting where a traveling exhorter gives them a shouting discourse, and they pray and sing lively psalm tunes. But most of the men have lost interest in this sort of thing. These, however, are people who live in the lonelier recesses of the hills. Religious farmers are still as a body the mainstay and support of the village church—the old First Church, as it has always been called. They come of a Sunday morning in their wagons and carriages with their families, dressed in their best broadcloth suits, which sit rather uneasily upon them—well brushed, clean, with tanned faces, and hands knotted and browned by toil.

They have a sense of the divine ordering of nature as they till their fields and endure the hard winters. They are sober, solid men, who find the Bible a wellspring of consolation and comfort. Even in this trashy-newspaper, cheap-book-making age they cling to it faithfully as the rock of their faith—a sober, serious type, believers still, who, though they have relaxed the stern family discipline of their Puritan fathers, and the awful severity with which the Sabbath was formerly kept, still live as in the light of the All-Seeing Eye, and acknowledge divine guidance and the terrors of the moral law. These farmers, survivors of an elder generation who laid the foundations of character in New England, are not so numerous as formerly, but they do exist.

The men tie their teams under the long shed near the First Church, and, in their Sunday boots, go creaking to their pews. No other country can show such a body of strong, earnest-thinking tillers of the soil, who talk over the sermon as they go homeward from meeting, and look up the authorities and ponder on the thoughts in the fields. They, too, perceive that the world is moving, that great tides of opinion and conviction are carrying them on, they know not whither. The light of a new day has slowly crept into their valleys, and modified all the ancient life and practice. The old vexed questions of the salvation of unbaptized infants and the redemption of good heathen people who have not known the light of Christ seem almost antiquated, now that such a strain has come on so many of the more vital issues. The young clergyman does not give this class of his hearers an opportunity to go to sleep in their pews. He stirs them up and keeps them alive to the questions of the day. Only a few deaf men and old women occasionally indulge in a comfortable nap during sermon time.

The young clergyman keeps his congregation well together, which in these lax and degenerate days is a great achievement. It is thought in a few years he may be called to a city pulpit, and then, his friends say, when the villagers are thrown back on some fossil of the ancient unprogressive school, they will know how to prize this live man. The young minister feels, as do the most intellectual people in small communities, the lack of sympathetic companionship. The most active-growing mind in a narrow sphere, finds no one to keep step with him. He feels like a lonely forester breaking paths for his own feet, with no comrade to cry well done or give him godspeed. He is hungry and thirsty for the communion of liberal souls. For this reason the young clergyman seizes with avidity upon any stranger who visits the village and has interests in his own line of thought and inquiry. Then he finds relief in unpacking his breast of all its burdens, and basks in the rest and refreshment that comes from an hospitable soul.

Last summer a theological student, a young man of great promise and considerable anticipatory fame, was staying among us. His mother, a widow, lives in the outskirts of the village and is distinguished as a mother in Israel, a pious, praying woman, who by her ceaseless petitions had done much to influence her son's course. This young man, although he had another year at the theological seminary, was considered so remarkable it was arranged that at his ordination he should at once take charge of an important church. He had already preached in various pulpits. His fame had gone abroad in the congregation, and a brilliant future seemed assured. When he came to the village on his last vacation the young clergyman found him among the elect, foreordained to be his friend and brother. Hugh was preoccupied and unsocial in those days, and the minister felt himself to be exceedingly fortunate in discovering a rich estate in the nature of this brilliant young man, to whom he could preach all his sermons before he delivered them in the pulpit.

Jerome, as I will call him, was a fine Greek and Hebrew scholar. It was thought if he were to go abroad and take a course in a German university he might fill a theological chair in one of our largest colleges. The pious old ladies beamed upon him. The young lady church members blushed as they thought how much he would need a wife to help him fill his exalted position. He was a child of many hopes ; a very Samuel, dedicated to the temple service from his earliest years. But, with all these shining prospects, our young minister noticed that Jerome was not happy. He suspected the cankerworm of modern doubt had begun thus early to burrow in his mind. But with his optimistic view of things it did not trouble him. Has not a great poet said an honest doubt is worth half the creeds ? It might be well for Jerome to pass through the ordeal. He would doubtless come out stronger and braver for the trial.

But Jerome's trouble was deeper than our young minister suspected. It was laying the axe at the very root of the tree. When he prayed he was often cold and without any true feeling of supplication or worship.

The thought that labor is prayer tormented him. He was committed to a life of exhortation and lip service, but the world requires just deeds that bear within them the power and potency of the love of God. The talking age is passing away, so he reasoned, as he thought of a possible new church filled with a pentecostal life, and of himself as a possible reformer, but, like the heavenly vision of the prophet, there was no modern temple therein. To preach to respectable, elegant, well-dressed, well-fed people about sin, righteousness, and judgment to come, while the great wretched, reckless, suffering world stormed by the church door, indifferent to parson and creed, loathing sermon, and prayer, and psalm, seemed to him a service he could not perform, not even for the ten thousand dollar salary it was thought that he would soon be able to command.

He went abroad alone at night revolving these things in his soul, wondering what the experience was through which he was passing, and whither it would lead him. If it proved to be the spirit of truth and life, he was determined to follow wherever it might beckon. This was reality. All else he had known compared with it, even his preaching and life in the divinity school, seemed like an illusion. He wandered about late, when the nights were cloudy and the air good for transmitting distant sounds. Sometimes by putting his ear close to the ground he could hear a train come into a station six miles off. He alone was awake; his ear was open to catch some message, some whisper of truth from afar. He lay on a hill-top when the midnight moon arose solemn and sad in its first glances at the earth. A slight breeze rustled the grass and leaves like the footstep of a timid wild creature. He felt alone in the universe with his problem, and the stars in strips of sky peering through the thinned boughs could give him no answer.

He looked down upon the dark, quiet roofs of the village, and wondered how people could live without moments of soul-stirring quest for new light—live, in a quiet vegetative way, winding their clock at the same moment every night and going to bed exactly on the stroke of ten. The young minister was so cock-sure he was in the right line that Jerome could get no consolation thinking of him.

One night Jerome had gone home late, had crept into the house and kindled his lamp without waking his mother. He chanced to take up a volume that lay on the table. It was not the Bible; it was a modern novel, and as he opened it his eye fell on the words, "He descended into hell," in the context of part of the discourse of one of the characters in the book. Suddenly a new meaning of those mystic words flashed into his mind. The descent into hell was here in this world. It meant work in the earthly hells, among the masses in prison-pens and noisome places, where the creeping pestilence of moral and physical corruption runs riot. How could a spiritual teacher and guide of men know any thing of life's realities without making this descent into hell, and striving, not for the salvation of the rich, the respectable, the virtuous, but of the hopelessly wretched and degraded, who rot, fester, and die for want of a Saviour? He bowed his head on his arms on the table before him and sat thus the whole night through, revolving all the past and all the future.

But when the dawn came, silvery, washed white, like a face bathed in tears, he arose a new man. All doubt had departed from his being, and the work before him lay clearly mapped out like a long forward road through a dense wilderness on which the sun is shining. His brilliant prospects, his old dreams of usefulness and honor faded away before his high calling to labor for humanity, and he was calm and joyous. It was long before he could make his mother understand what had happened.

"And do you mean, Jerome," she said, weeping, "that you intend to give up the ministry?"

"Yes, mother. I can not now belong to a separate order. I do not wish to wear any badge or have any handle to my name that distinguishes me from others. I must work as a man among men."

"I can't understand it," she moaned. "I don't know what it means."

"I know you don't," he answered gently; "but can you believe me, mother, when I tell you it is a new birth——"

"It ain't like any conversion I ever heard of," she went on sobbing, "and you a child of prayer. Your father prayed over you when you was little, and hoped you would be a minister. He longed to see the day, but died without the sight. And here am I, old and tottering on the edge of the grave; and when I thought you was safe in the kingdom you come and tell me you have got converted in some unheard-of way. How do you know it ain't of the devil leading to perdition?"

"I only follow the light I see, mother. I have never known Satan to advise men to abandon the self-seeking spirit, and take up a hard lot for the sake of others."

It was all he could say. The experience was as strange to him as to the villagers, who wondered over it, and would not believe its deep significance. The age of profound spiritual experience, leading to sacrifice, they thought, had passed by, like miracles and speaking with tongues. Any remarkable display of religious sincerity seemed as strange as it would to see a bush on the mountain side bursting out with the flame that Moses beheld, or an angel stirring the waters of a river pool, that the sick might be healed. Of course cranks, and spiritualists, and visionaries, like Job Bird, pretend to have great experiences in these days, but Jerome was none of these. He was a man abandoning a brilliant career, the highest worldly advantages, because he thought he heard the still small voice of the Lord, saying : " Follow me, and serve where I show you work to do."

The young minister felt deep sympathy for Jerome. He was touched in the depths of his soul when he saw the new light of happiness that shone in the young man's face, although he could not approve the course he had taken, in yielding to what might prove a passing enthusiasm, an impulse born in a moment of exaltation. He was yielding to what seemed to him a dangerous individualism in rejecting the church as an organized field of labor—the best perhaps that could be devised.

The day Jerome left the village to go and take up his new career the young minister walked with him several miles down the valley, and finally bade him farewell in a little wooded dell beside the placid river. He almost shed tears at parting with his friend, and as he saw Jerome set off down the road toward the next town, with the brilliant tints of autumn hung out on all the hillsides, and the blue distance beckoning, and heard his cheery voice calling back a last good-by, he thought verily he would have gone with that new apostle of human brotherhood and worked by his side had it not been for the wife and babies at home and those affections, knotted into the heart-strings, which so often make cowards and reactionaries of the world's would-be reformers and high priests of progress.

CHAPTER XXXIX.

HOW BILL FULLER WAS INDEMNIFIED.

THE village seems lapped in a golden reverie under a hazy sky, languorous and warm. The canopy of elm trees is bronzed with pale gleams, and the finely divided foliage shines against the sky and imparts the peacefulness of perfect repose. The flaming clumps of trees here and there through the valley seem dissolved like rich jewels in this Indian-summer haze, and melt into the general tone of restfulness as music melts into silence. The long placid reaches of the river do not ripple, so still is the air, but find joy in reflecting all of heaven and earth they can hold. Like satin sheen those smooth reaches stretch out, darkening under the willows and the white birches, reflecting the varied hues of the trees on the bank, the scarlet of the maple, the russet and crimson of the oak, the yellow of the ash and chestnut, the parti-colored dogwood, and the ground tints now so splendid from the colors of weeds, grasses, and late flowers.

The winter apples are now gathering in the orchards, and the cider-mills are at work sending puffs of odor out into the road. Great activity prevails around barns where the grain is threshed. They are digging potatoes in the fields, and the late corn comes to the harvester's hands with the full ear. Brown October, flecked with glorious colors and bearing such ample fruitage, brings these soft lights of memory and poetic feeling, as if once a year she would make all labor look beautiful, and transmute the troubles and sorrows of mankind into a psalm of praise. The old unpainted houses seem changed as they stand in the magic Indian-summer light, and the woodbine reddens on the gray wall. The silk of the milkweed floats in the air, and gleams like a feather dropped from the wing of some good angel. The air is full of pleasant odors from ripening leaves and late herbs, and the fallen foliage rustles crisp around one's feet, singing a soft little good-by song to summer, and saying, " As I have fallen so you shall fall, you who hang so bravely now on the tree of life." The village looks larger, more spacious, more hospitable than its wont. House doors stand open still, and children play in the yards and gardens at " tag " and " touch the goal." Old people come out to breathe the air, glad that there is as yet no necessity for hugging the winter fire to preserve a spark of life in their old bones.

The housewives are out potting their choice plants, taking up bulbs, and transferring the oleander, the lemon tree, and the large stocky geraniums to their sunny south windows. Who can reckon the courage this little rescue from summer's green things has given to lonely, sad women in cold dark days when faith and hope are ready to fade out of the human heart?

One day the doctor was driving his gray horse and old mud-bespattered chaise (for it had rained in the night) through the village street, when suddenly the sun came out as warm as June, and sent a shimmer of soft light down upon the earth, while the gray mists rolled up into fleecy clouds, and the bright trees smiled gently to each other, and all things looked very fair. The doctor was in a happy mood. He had put aside all thoughts of his patients and his uncollected bills, and had forgotten the regret that sometimes gnawed at his vitals because he had not lived in a larger sphere and exercised a wider influence among men. He knew himself to be a first-class man in a third-class village, spending his life among obscure people, with few to share his thoughts or understand his aims. If he had gone early to a city and struggled mightily for a few years, he might have taken his proper position among those high up in his own profession. But here he was rusting away year by year as he drove about in his shabby wagon—growing older and by no means richer, fretting his soul out over the wants and woes, the weaknesses and wickednesses of his neighbors. But this morning a delicate reconciling spirit seemed to shed balm on the air. The doctor was all tuned up musically, and he felt his heart glow with suppressed poetry. Many choice and well-beloved lines came to his lips as he drove along the country roads.

Just as he turned Peckham's corner into Main Street, in this good frame of mind, feeling that he could leave the care and the meaning of the universe to its Creator, while he did his own nearest duty, he saw a tall, thin woman, with no suggestion of *tournure*, in a faded calico dress and sun-bonnet, beckoning to him from the sidewalk. He drew up to the curb, half-provoked at being forced out of his happy, tranquil mood by that old maid, Melissa Tooler.

"I thought I would ask you," the woman began, in the spiritless tone common to her, "whether you think there ought to be a funeral?"

"The devil," returned the doctor impulsively, thrusting his head out of the hood of the chaise and turning very red in the face.

"Don't use profane language," the woman returned, in a mildly rebuking snuffle. "Death is a dretful solemn thing."

"Sometimes it is," returned the doctor rather brutally, "and sometimes it is a great relief. I should think your sister would feel glad to know he is out of the world."

"I don't know how Sist'r Ann feels about that," returned the other, inclining to be lachrymose, "but she is a decent woman and a Christian, and she wants to do every thing that's proper."

"Will it not be proper to have him buried where he is?"

"She's had to dig him up to indemnify him," returned the woman, putting her hand up to her eyes.

The doctor was suddenly half-choked with laughter at the thought of digging up Bill Fuller to "indemnify him," but he managed to say: "As soon as I had indemnified him I should put him right back in the same place, and cover him up with neatness and dispatch. Then if he has left any money I think I would hire a brass-band and give a party."

The woman looked at him, shocked and horrified. "Doctor," she said, with solemn slowness, "I'm afeared you ain't a Christian. It's always right to speak as kind as we can of the dead."

"If I am not a Christian, I am not a hypocrite," said the doctor, hotly, "and I should never shed any crocodile tears over a man like Bill Fuller."

Miss Tooler went slowly home, rustling the dead leaves with her large shoes. She felt that the doctor was hard, that life is hard, that every thing is hard for most folks, and especially for lone women. She could not have told why she should cry for her brother-in-law, Bill Fuller, who had been a very bad and worthless man, but there was a sense of the tragic in this sudden taking off of the objectionable Bill that made her sad. She thought it all over as she was walking home—how he had abused and maltreated "Sist'r Ann," and had hurt his only child, laming him for life, and then having committed a petty crime, had abandoned his penniless family, and had not been heard of for fourteen years. She recalled that day, so memorable to both of them, when word came through a newspaper advertisement that William Fuller had been found drowned in the East

River at New York, and that as soon as the coroner had given his verdict of accidental drowning he was consigned to Potter's Field. Furthermore, the said William, it was discovered, had left a small property, valued at about fifteen hundred dollars, and now awaiting the appearance of the said Fuller's heirs. Of course, "Sist'r Ann" and her lame boy were the only possible heirs of Bill Fuller if it should prove true " that he had gone and got drownded" in a state of intoxication. The only inconceivable part of it was that Fuller should have left a "hansel" of property. It made the cold creeps run over Miss Tooler for fear this might be thief's money, an unholy deposit which was coming into the hands of unsuspecting Sist'r Ann. But she said nothing of this to Mrs. Fuller, who was already very much bewildered by this strange news.

Judge Magnus assured Sist'r Ann, if she could bring proof of her marriage, and was able to identify the dead man as her scapegrace husband, there would be no difficulty in securing the money. Abundant proof of the marriage was of course forthcoming, and the doctor, with his usual forethought, advised her to start at once for New York, and promised to consign her to a legal friend in the metropolis who was to look after her interests. Mrs. Fuller felt very much as if she had been struck by an earthquake. She had taken but few journeys in her life, and the strange dramatic errand on which she was going and the excitement of the anticipated trip introduced confusion into all her ideas. On the station platform she clung to her son Spence and to Melissa, and they all cried as if Sist'r Ann had been going straight to the Cannibal islands, to be made into rather tough steaks or chops for the delectation of the king.

"I'm all turned round," sobbed the poor woman, "and I shan't never get straight and untangled again the longest day I live. I am positive, Melissy, the sun rises in the west."

But the train came along, and they "boosted" Sist'r Ann into the car in her collapsed state, and handed up her basket and bag, and in a moment she had disappeared down the track. So Melissy went home to do the housework, and to assist Spence, who was not very bright, in the truck garden. She had years ago joined forces with her sister, and they had set up a little business, principally for the raising of asparagus and tomatoes. They also canned fruit and vegetables for the market in the season, and both women worked a good deal out of doors. They were adepts in the art of New England economy, and had been able to live independent and above board.

Melissy could not help turning over in her mind this strange event, the like of which had never happened before in her family. They were all steady, poor folks, away back as far as Gran'ther Tooler's time. There had never been a murder, or suicide, or sudden death among them ; and, as far as she could recollect, money had never come into the family. Bill Fuller's fifteen hundred dollars would certainly come handy. It would pay off the mortgage on their little place, and make life a great deal easier. Melissy never thought of the years of hard self-sacrificing toil she had given to her sister's need. That tall, plain, thin woman did not know she had done any thing very heroic. She had no envy, hatred, or malice in her nature, and be sure she did not "begrudge" Sist'r Ann any thing. She wondered what her sister would do if she found out Bill's little pile was thief-money. The thought made her shudder, and for her part, in such case, she could wish to take it up gently with a pair of tongs and lay it on the fire. This poor, drab-colored woman had the old Puritan conscience.

Melissy's imagination worked so wildly about her sister, and there was so much excited talk among the visiting neighbors, she could not sleep, for the first time in her life, and was obliged to take a "night-cap" to get any kind of rest. This gave her a racking headache the next day, and she was fast breaking down in a fit of illness, when a telegram came to allay some of her anxiety about Sist'r Ann. It ran thus: "Am obliged to have *him* taken up. Shall bring *him* home. Ask doctor about funeral." It was after this that Melissy spoke to the doctor. She knew just how Sist'r Ann would feel about the funeral. All the villagers would turn out from natural curiosity, and a big rousing funeral would be a real comfort and consolation to the abused and forsaken wife. It would partly take the stigma off his disreputable character and rehabilitate him in public esteem, especially as he had left property—a god all villagers bow down to at times. This would be a great satisfaction to poor Sist'r Ann.

They had never had a very large or imposing funeral in the family, and she knew how much a certain class of country folk count on such occasions. She went over in her mind all the minutest details; how she must stop the clock, and pull down the shades, and get in chairs from the neighbors, and have a cold collation ready for the mourners and friends. She lived it all over and began baking for the occasion before she heard any thing further from her sister. On the evening of the sixth day that poor woman came into the house quite unexpectedly, looking terribly jaded, and with black rings round her eyes and great hollows in her sallow cheeks. Melissy ran to her and helped her into the rocking-chair, and untied her bonnet-strings and took away her bag. Sist'r Ann sank down and heaved a great sigh. This was so different from the home-coming she expected that Melissy was dumbfounded, but she did manage to say, "Sist'r Ann, where is it?"

"Where is what?" returned Sist'r Ann, snappishly, closing her eyes as if she never cared to open them again.

"The remains."

"There ain't no remains."

Melissy gasped, and fell back against the door. She thought her sister had gone daft, but Mrs. Fuller opened her eyes, and looked at her with calm but weary defiance. "I shan't tell you a word of any thing until I have some tea. I'm tired to death, and worrited and fretted half sick," and with that her bonnet fell off, her hair tumbled down, and she leaned back in the chair and began to sob.

Melissy bestirred herself to comfort her sister. She bathed her hands and face, put a pillow to her back, smoothed her untidy hair, and soon had a steaming cup of the fragrant herb in her hand.

"Oh, it's so good to get home," sighed the weary one. "Though it's ever so humble, there's no place like home. Set right down, Melissy, and you, Spence, and I will tell you all I have been through, and how I have traipsed and traipsed, and spent my money and my time, as you may say, for nothing. You see, that lawyer-friend of the doctor's, he met me at the cars, and was kind, and took me to a very good place to eat and sleep, and then he attended to having the body what they call exhumed. So the morning we went over to the cemetery to take a look I saw two women in deep black wandering around among the graves. And the undertaker, who was a likely, clever man, he gave me the wink. And, ses he to me : 'Them two are claimants. They both say they are wives of William Fuller. If I were you I wouldn't give myself away. I guess you have as good a claim as any of the rest of his wives.'

"'Lord a-mercy,' cried I, horrified and consternade. 'What bad women them must be. I am his only true and lawful wife, and Spence is his only true and lawful child. The impudent brazen huzzies! to come here and own to their own shame!'

"But the minute I cast my eyes on the remains, I seen it wasn't Bill Fuller, but a much younger and heavier man—a stocky, short person with thick black hair and beard, and a kind of a Roman nose. Before I could get a chance to speak, the tallest woman in black, she swept up to the place, and putting her hand on the breast of the remains, she said in a mighty high tone: 'I am the only true and lawful wife of this man, William Q. Fowler. I was married to him in 1881, and I have here my marriage certificate to prove the fact. That woman,' pointing to the other person in black, 'never was married to him, and she has no kind of claim to the property. As to that old imposter yonder,' pointing to me, 'you can see for yourself what she is. She's old enough to be his mother, and her claim is simply ridiculous.'

"'I'm no imposture, mum,' says I, firing up, 'and I'd have you to know it. I'd no sooner set my eyes on the remains than I knew it wasn't Bill Fuller, my husband that was, or is, the Lord only knows; and as to William Q. Fowler,' ses I, pointing to the high-strung one that had spoken, 'you're welcome to him, mum, and all his goods and gear. You can fight it out with t'other woman. I don't believe either of you is any thing better than you should be, but I'd have you to know that I am a professing Christian, and never had no blots on my fair name.' And with that I kind o' staggered away, hardly knowing what I was about. But the lawyer, he came right behind, and I could see he was just dying to laugh. And, ses I to him, 'I'll pay you your fee, and then I'll be off home by the next train.' And, ses I, in the bitterness of my spirit, 'if old Bill Fuller dies twenty times after this, I won't take a step to look at his remains. I'll let any body claim him as wants to.'

"But that lawyer was very nice-spoken, and he persuaded me to stay a day or two, and take a look at the city, so as I shouldn't lose my journey altogether. And he gave me a list of places I ought to see, and then I began my tramps. I traipsed and I traipsed till I was nearly dead. Sometimes I rode on the elevated, as they call it, a railroad set up in the air on stilts, sometimes in the horse-cars, but most times I traipsed. I went up to the top of Trinity Church steeple, three hundred and twenty-five steps, for I counted 'em, and I thought before I got there you would have your funeral after all, Melissy. I walked over the Brooklyn Bridge, and I went to Central Park to see that stone thing they call Cleopatry's Needle. I went to see pictures that didn't look like any thing I was ever acquainted with and statues as naked as the day they was born, Melissy, and finally at last I traipsed up to Grant's tomb. I kept it for the last, as I was in a funereal state of mind, and I thought it would be kind of soothing. On my way to the tomb, I noticed a man following me, a crook-backed, old-codger kind of a man, and when I stopped he stopped, and when I went on he went on. He was done up atwixt two boards, a kind of advertisement called a sandwich. On the front of him was a girl in a party dress washing clothes, and on his back a baby in a wash-bowl blowing soap bubbles.

"While I was gazing on the tomb he stepped quite in front and gazed at me most impudent, and finally he took a step nearer, and ses he, 'The Lord help me, if this ain't Ann.' And I just give a screech, and ses I, 'For all the world, is this you, Bill Fuller?' I was so overcome! It was a great deal worse than not finding him in the coffin, to see him looking like a regular old sot in a bad hat, done up in boards like a living automedon.

"Well, he grinned, and, ses he, 'Ann, I saw that notice in the papers about my getting drownded and leaving a pot of money, and I knew it would fetch you down to the city. I have been on the outlook for you, and all day yesterday I watched you talking to policemen on street corners, and I knew where you stopped. It was an awful disappointment, now wasn't it, not to find me dead and buried?'

"I was so flustered I didn't know what to do or say, and, ses I: 'Bill, this is the worst turn you ever served me.'

"'Sorry I couldn't oblige you by dying, Ann. But how are all the folks at home, and what are you doing?'

"'You'd better ask about your boy as you lamed for life,' ses I, 'and who would have starved if it hadn't been for me and Melissy Tooler going into the sparrow-grass business.'

"'I'm awful sorry about the boy,' ses Bill, 'but I was in liquor when I did it, and now I don't drink a drop.' (I could smell his breath strong as anything that minute.) 'If you'll take me home with you, I'll try to do better.'

"'Take you home! Furyation!' says I. 'I am quit and clear of you long ago for abandonment, and if you come near I'll have you arrested on that old thieving business.'

"Well, then he begged and whined for a little money."

"You weren't so simple as that," exclaimed Melissy Tooler.

"Yes, I was. I couldn't bear to see him walking round in them boards, and I gave him all the money I had, over and above enough to pay my way back, and made him take them right off. Yes," she sighed, "I had hoped I could respect him a little the rest of my life. If we had had a nice funeral, and he was lying up there on the hill with a tombstone at the head of the grave, it would be some consolation. And now that is took away from me."

CHAPTER XL.

TULLY CICERO OLDHAM FALLS INTO ERROR.

IF you live in a village, you must neighbor it or live outside the swim. If you have more tomatoes in your garden than you can use, and little sweet corn, and Frisbies' folks next door have much sweet corn and few tomatoes, why should you not exchange vegetables over the garden fence? And standing there while the bread is rising in the pan, you may as like as not fall into a little talk about the helps that are at hand to enable us to bear life's burdens, or the immortality of the soul, and gleams may be let in upon household cares that will keep you thinking half the day. Old Miss Fermenter always used to get to preaching when she ran into a neighbor's back door on an errand with an apron over her head. An errand in quest of a recipe for root beer, or the best way to dye an old red shawl, would send her right off to sanctification by faith and the inefficacy of works.

When the little sisters had a load of unexpected company come in upon them the other day, Mrs. Judge Magnus sent her dinner right over, all cooked and ready to serve, with a frozen-fruit pudding and a pot of delicious coffee with cream. The judge was obliged to dine on bread and milk and cold pie. This is the kind of neighboring that whole-souled woman believes in. The little sisters mainly live on what they call picked-up dinners, especially when there is no one with them, and the pickupedness of the meal is manifest to any chance comer. A real dinner of the other variety is a red-letter occasion for them, so you can imagine how they felt when Mrs. Magnus sent over that meal for Eben's folks, just as if it had come in the four-cornered sheet the apostle saw let down from heaven. Mrs. Magnus is rich, but she wishes to take part in all the hospitalities and liberalities of village life, to feel the human current running right through her house from garret to cellar, like a great motor nerve. To see her in Washington society you would never suspect it, but at home she is a different person.

The young married women are let into the sisterhood of good housekeepers, and made welcome to share in all its sifted and clarified experience. The young mother comes over with her first baby, the most remarkable child ever born, and puts it cuddled to sleep on the lounge, and then she and the initiated go into long talks: how to turn every thing to the best account; when you have done up your quince sauce how to make a delicious jelly out of the cores. This economy, which always gets the sweetness out of the core, has a certain beauty of its own. It is in the order of nature to let nothing go to waste, but by cunning chemistry to turn its refuse into flowers, its brackishness and soot into splendid colors and sweet perfumes. The housewife's contrivance to make the best use of every thing when she puts ashes on the cucumber bed, and saves the smallest scraps for the hens, is by no means an ignoble art. It is the very secret of material life, the saving and gathering of the fragments into the baskets of the parable, that nothing be lost.

There are great adepts in this art in the village, and there is another class even more interesting, for they mix something spiritual with all they do, not only with their savings, but with their "riz biscuits" and waffles, their cup-cake and whipped cream. They are ladylike housekeepers who transmute domestic drudgery into grace. Though they know all about the lower processes, they are never too busy for the higher. They come in cool and neat from some serene kitchen depth to see the caller, with hair unruffled and collar and cuffs quite speckless. They move around to some inward music, and every thing falls into line. There are always fresh flowers in the parlor vases, and their work-baskets look like fairy gifts. They read a great deal more than most city women, and have out all the newest books of poems and essays from the library. There are two women who get along without help, save for the washing and ironing and heavy scrubbing. Most people do keep help now, but these two live in such an exquisite little world of their own making, they would rather do for themselves than have an Irish girl messing about, irrupting into all the niceties like a bull in a china shop.

Miss Elmore and her niece Margaret are true artists in this flower-like housekeeping. They have a world of comfort together in all their doings, and seem to fit each other like the acorn cup and the acorn. Their life is a kind of harmony into which sewing, sweeping, dusting, garden-work, little house adornments, the care of flowers and birds are twisted and twined. They read their books aloud, taking turns, and enjoying the comfort and snugness of perfect sympathy. Margaret paints and plays the piano, alternating her idealities, as she says, with the actualities of bed-making and keeping rooms. Every one says, "What a fine girl Margaret Elmore is!" And the next word follows of itself: "She ought to get a good husband." There are so many fine girls in the world now who ought to get good husbands. Miss Elmore is in all things a lady, old-fashioned, delicate, a little shy and timid, but with the purest, sweetest instincts, and the finest feelings. Margaret is the stronger character of the two, and has come to be the natural protector of her aunt, a sort of head of the family in the form of a rosy-cheeked, dark-eyed girl of twenty-three, whose every eyelash speaks of truth, sincerity, and frankness. Both these women worship one object—Margaret's brother Joe, whom they are sending through college mainly by parings and savings from their own personal expenditure, making the old gown and hat do another season, having the old boots tapped and heeled rather than buy new, and denying themselves in a thousand ways for Joe's sake.

It was just when they were in this pinch of saving for Joe that having a spare room at their disposal, it was proposed to them to take a boarder for one season, a thing they had never thought of doing before, and would not now, perhaps, except for Miss Elmore's great respect for science, her high ideal of men who pursue such callings, and the desire to turn a genteel penny for the student Joe's sake. The person who engaged her spare chamber, with all its pretty little fripperies and lady-like adornments, was a man who had been favorably recommended ; to wit, Tully Cicero Oldham.

Mr. Oldham was very deaf, and used an ear-trumpet with a long flexible tube, which, when not in use, he carried curled about his left arm. He had been a college tutor until his increasing deafness made it impossible to "coach" and "cram" students, and then he turned scientific specialist and devoted most of his time to the study of cryptogamic botany, and the lowest forms of vegetable life, known as smut, rust, mold, and mildew. When he set up his microscope in Miss Elmore's best room and prepared his little slides and specimens, she felt her house to be greatly honored, and mentally bowed down, not to Tully Oldham, who was by no means imposing, but to the great kingdom of science. which he represented, and which looked so fascinating and beautiful to her gentle, womanly eyes.

Oldham was a small man who went buzzing about with a springy automatic fussiness. His nose and large ears had a frost-bitten expression even in summer-time, and his short, stubby beard made him look rather painfully hirsute. The look of frost-bite perhaps came from the fact that he had lived for years in bleak college rooms, and to save fuel in cold weather had often sat and shivered, working with his hat on, done up in two sets of underwear, three pairs of socks, and a top coat over all his other clothes. He wore his hat indoors to keep the bald part of his head warm, and tore little square bits out of his worn-out under linen for pocket-handkerchiefs. As he could not hear the sound of his own voice, his conversation was pitched in a very high key, and gave the effect of a stridulous grasshopper. Living shut within a world of his own, Tully Cicero made an excellent little mole-eyed specialist. But in all practical matters he was a mere baby. He was suspicious of the hearing world, as very deaf people often are, and apt to take wild notions into his head, which to him wore the sharp outlines of reality, although they might be as impossible and foundationless as a nightmare. Moreover, he was egregiously conceited, thinking himself a handsome, fascinating person, for whom the fair sex had a special weakness. He knew, in fact, very little about women, having had but infrequent opportunities for enjoying what the old-fashioned novelists used to call female society, but the less he knew the more he considered himself a potential, if not an actual, charmer.

Tully C. Oldham was a great authority on smut, mold rust, and mildew. Learned men corresponded with him, and any thing he took hold of, no matter how difficult, he bored into like a wood worm into heart of oak. Thus he came with a glamour around him in the eyes of good Miss Elmore. If he had been Huxley or Tyndall, or the great Darwin himself, he could not have been more gently entreated.

He was translated at once from the discomforts of college lodgings of the poorer sort, where he had often lived on crackers and tea with only an occasional meat dinner, into this soft, warm nest, dainty, delicate, full of the breath of flowers and the sweet influence of two refined women who had never taken boarders, and were ready to get down on their knees to serve him for seven dollars a week. Miss Elmore carried his hot water up to him in the morning with her own hands, and set it down outside his door as if it had been a bath for Buddha. Margaret prepared for him cream toast, dropped eggs, and delicious coffee. Miss Elmore in her soft voice conversed with him through the ear-trumpet about the dignity of science—how it expands the mind of the devotee, just as if smut, mold, etc., were a pursuit fit for the gods. Delicately, coyly, these two women discovered that Tully's wardrobe was sadly out of repair. It only raised him in Miss Elmore's estimation, for when a man's head is knocking about among the stars how can he think of dropped shirt buttons or holes in his stockings? Piously did Miss Elmore darn those said holes, of large size and numerous. Meekly did she sew on buttons and tapes. She even went to the length of putting a new braid on his black coat, and cleaning all the spots away from its worn, shiny surface, with camphene and a flannel rag, just as she would have done for her boy Joe.

Tully Cicero had fallen into a clover patch, and soon he began to get stout and to feel certain shooting pains of youthful impulse he had not felt for many years. He filled his soul with vain imaginings, peculiar to his own special kind of queerness. Instead of making him thankful and reverent, all this beneficence poured out upon him by two charming women only tended to puff him up and feed his self-conceit.

As he pondered on their unfailing care and kindness, their gentle unconscious petting, he came to the conclusion that Miss Elmore was dead in love with him, and that Margaret was pretty far gone on the same road. This notion was firmly fixed in his mind after much watching of the elder lady's gentle placid face out of the corner of his beady black eyes, as she helped him to the best of every thing at the table, and the patience with which she talked to him through the ear-trumpet on abstruse scientific subjects. She would sometimes slip a vase of flowers into his room when he was absent, thinking that a botanist must be fond of bloom and fragrance, if he did devote his days and nights to smut and mold. But Tully with this wild idea in his head read the language of flowers, and believed that he saw in these innocent little nosegays a declaration of her passion. He was immensely flattered and went out and bought a bottle of bears' grease and loaded his hair with it until it scented the whole house. He studied himself before the glass by the half hour, trying on all his most killing expressions, and getting more and more fascinated with his own bewitching charms. But Miss Elmore would not secure the prize—no pressed wallflower for him: and that she might find it out gradually without any sudden rending shock, he began ogling Margaret at the table, and smiling on her with a silliness that was irresistibly comical.

Margaret looked on astonished. She had come entirely out of the glamour of science which blinded her aunt, and regarded Tully, apart from all love-making, as rather an objectionable little person, but now, that he had begun to ogle and make eyes, she at first suspected he had gone mildly mad. Then she began to watch him with the frank eyes of a wide-awake girl. She noticed that now he always wore a white field Marguerite in the lapel of that coat her aunt Susan had new-bound and cleaned with camphene. When he thought margaret was observing him he would slyly raise his hand to the flower, as much as to say : " I am your adorer and bond-slave for life."

Miss Elmore, in her sweet calm and benignity, never

saw any of this telegraphing, and when Margaret, who was amused, though hotly indignant at the little man's impudence, broke out in revolt, she would not, for a time, believe one word of the tale she had to tell. One morning her niece refused to bake waffles for Tully when he came down late to breakfast, and made signals to her with his ear-trumpet to let the old lady go away while they remained. Miss Elmore was very much surprised at Margaret's behavior, but she went out into the kitchen and baked the waffles herself, and came in with her delicate cheek quite rosed from the heat of the fire, and served him with the utmost politeness.

"Oh, the horrid, odious little creature," cried Margaret about two hours later, rushing into the sitting-room where her aunt sat placidly sewing. "He is making love to me, auntie. He actually squeezed my hand there in the passage, and when I snatched it away he stuck out his ear-trumpet for me to say something. Oh, if it had been an elephant's trunk, how gladly I would have run a big pin into it."

Miss Elmore sat straight up in her chair, and looked as shocked and humiliated as if she had heard that the great Darwin had tried to kiss her niece in a dark corner. It seemed immodest to entertain such a notion concerning a man of science. "Margaret, you must be mistaken. You know he is so deaf he can not be expected to understand every thing. He is like a child in his devotion to science."

"If he *is* deaf he understands well enough how to squeeze hands. And as for his childlike character, he has been making eyes at me behind your back for two or three weeks. I was ashamed to say any thing about it. I thought perhaps it was a sudden turn like crick in the back, that might pass off. But I see we have innocently been too kind to him, and have put the wildest notions into his horrid little mind. I suspect he thinks we are both in love with him. We must get rid of him, auntie, or else I shall telegraph to Joe to come home."

It was a long time before Margaret could open her aunt's eyes to the fact that the little "scientific gent" had something smutty in his nature. But when she began to watch him, a thing her high-mindedness rendered very painful, she was convinced of the truth. She had borne all his disagreeable little habits with divine patience, and now she grieved to find that science does not always ennoble its devotees. She tried to devise measures for getting him quietly out of the house, but before these could be perfected he had proposed to Margaret in the garden where she was watering her plants. He had kneeled right down in a particularly damp place, regardless of his trowsers, and had seized hold of her dress and poured out a wild profession of love in his high-pitched voice, and then he had reached her the ear-trumpet. Oh, the horror of having to refuse a man through an ear-trumpet, who is kneeling before you in the garden, right in the face and eyes of all the world! "Get up," she cried, severely, "get right up off your knees this minute." The ridiculous man arose rather sheepishly. "Now go and pack your trunk right away, and leave this house within an hour. You are utterly and totally mistaken. You have got an entirely false impression. Now don't be foolish and absurd, but go away quietly."

"I am not going away," returned Tully, his small eyes glinting with defiance. "I have paid my board a week in advance, and I am going to stay. I have been encouraged here in this house in a way that gives me a legal hold. Your aunt has made as good as open proposals to me, and you have both tried to throw yourselves at my head."

"You shameless, abandoned man!" cried Margaret, seizing the tube. "You know you are telling lies. I shall go and pack your trunk myself, and put your board money in it, and then you must leave this house. We shall not give you another meal."

They were just in the midst of this excited colloquy, Margaret pouring her strong words into the end of the ear-trumpet, and Tully vociferating at the same time, when Miss Elmore, hearing voices raised, came out on the porch with a scared look.

"Auntie," cried her niece, half choked with wrath, " he is a dreadful, bad man. He says he won't leave the house. He says we both of us encouraged him to think that one or both of us would marry him, and he is going to sue for breach of promise. Oh, auntie, what shall we do ? "

Miss Elmore's face grew very white. " Margaret," she whispered, forgetting he could not hear, " I am afraid he's gone suddenly crazy. Let us try to slip into the house and lock him out."

They both rushed upon the doorway, and in an instant the key was grating in the lock. They flew all over the house bolting, and barring, and fastening windows. And when the angry Tully began to knock and shake the door for admission he found the lockout complete. The shades were all drawn down, and the house looked as if a death had occurred in the family. After prowling about the kitchen and back entrance for some time, Tully took up his position opposite, where a vacant lot was bounded by a stone wall. He seated himself on the wall prepared to watch the house over the way with a view to slipping in and barricading himself in his own room should an opportunity occur. He had by no means given up the fight, and if he could not win the day he could at least annoy and torment two unprotected females. Tully was as full of spite as an egg is of meat.

There he sat all the afternoon gazing at the closed house. Occasionally Margaret would peep out of some-crack in the blind to see if he were still visible, and there he was perched up like an ugly little idol on the wall.

"I can't stand it," cried Margaret, passionately; "it is worse than a boycott. We shall have to telegraph in some way for Joe."

They had carefully packed Tully's trunk and cautiously shoved it out on the porch, instantly locking the door again for fear of consequences. Miss Elmore carried the microscope down in its case and set it on the trunk cover, while Margaret stood guard behind her with a poker in her hand.

"We never can endure life," the girl cried, "with that man watching us. Stop, I have a happy thought." She ran to the writing-desk and scribbled a hasty note; then she beckoned to a neighbor's boy, who was flying his kite in the next yard, and threw it to him out of the back window. The lad took the note and disappeared on a run down the street. In about an hour Dr. John Rivington came striding down past the Elmore house with his thick stick in his hand. He came up to the place where Tully Cicero sat perched on the wall, and the little man of rust and mold began to quail. The doctor lifted him down from his roosting place not ungently. Then taking him by the coat-collar much as a big dog takes a little one by the "scruff" of his neck, he gave him a shake.

"You miserable little wretch," cried the doctor, "to insult and terrify ladies who have been kind to you. You are too small to kick or I would send you into the middle of next week. Go on there, march before, and get a man to come for your trunk yonder, and take yourself out of this town in less than two hours."

Tully heard not a word the doctor said, but he understood him well enough, and the next train took him and his belongings out of the village. He has written Miss

Elmore an abject, penitent letter, begging her forgiveness; and now she can laugh about it a little, though for a long time it looked to her very dreadful and compromising.

CHAPTER XLI.

STRANGE DISTURBANCES AT STILLWELL'S.

SNUG and cheery looks the home when the nights are growing darker and longer. The piazza-chairs are deserted, the hammock is put away in the attic. The hens will no longer roost in the trees, they take up winter quarters in the barn. The cat comes purring in around your feet as you sit in your favorite corner with lamp and book, and the house-dog is no longer content to lie on the outside mat. This is the time when human beings begin to draw closer together, when they tell old stories, and recall the past around the evening fire; when the young girl touches the piano in the twilight, and sings some snatch of ballad music that is running in her head. The very street looks as if there was little to expect now from gardens and trees, human interests having come uppermost.

The few small shops wear a more inviting air. People begin to drop in again to chat with the old shoemaker, who has just been reading Schopenhauer and the translation of another German work called "Kraft und Stoff." He shakes his head and says he don't think they make as good philosophical waxed-ends as Aristotle and some of those old fellows, who are still way out of sight of the moderns. The post-office and the grocery store have again become resorts, and the apothecary's shop looks very pleasant, with its colored glasses, bright lamps, and clean panes. It is a neat little place, shining with new paint, and a neat little man presides over it. There is a gloss on his linen, a minute attention to his clothes, a delicate perfume about him, like some highly scented expensive soap, that might lead you to think Andrew Stillwell a fussy, prim old bachelor. But in truth he is very much of a family man. He glides around the shop with unsqueaking shoes, and deals out hair-oil, toothbrushes, bathing sponges and patent medicines. He puts up his prescriptions, which are not very numerous unless there happens to be an epidemic of scarlet fever or diphtheria, with a neatness which would do credit to a city pharmacist.

Every thing was apparently very happy in his home at the time those strange disturbances first began to be talked of. The little druggist's ruling passion was admiration for his wife. He was so grateful to her for marrying him, the sense of her great condescension kept him humble-minded. He never concluded the smallest business transaction without saying "I must first consult my wife. She has an excellent head for business and has often given me points." As to the control of his family of five children, that was all left to Mrs. Stillwell. It was her part to do the governing aud correcting, the spanking and admonishing. He played with his children and indulged them in small ways, but he did not think himself equal to the real bringing up. That was left to the very superior woman who had stooped to marry him. Mrs. Stillwell was half a head taller than her mate. The eldest boy, Theo, was now taller than his father, whom the children looked on as about on their level, and loved as one of themselves, a person they could do with pretty much as they pleased, while the mother, an intellectual woman, was too clear-sighted to be deceived, and was therefore thoroughly respected and even feared.

There is a thorn in every body's pillow, and the thorn that pierced Andrew was the fact that Mrs. Andrew had loved another man before she condescended to marry the village druggist. She belonged to an excellent village family of some wealth, while Andrew had sprung from little tenant farmers of no consequence. Mary Spear's early love story was pathetic and even beautiful, and was laid up in lavender there in the village archives among those odds and ends of actual romance that are always stranger than fiction. She had been engaged, when a tall, handsome, resolute young girl, to Mrs. Macy's eldest son by her first husband, and soon after the war of the rebellion broke out he, Ralph Freeman, had joined the Union army and marched to the front. Just previous to his departure the lovers had quarreled, and both of them being proud and obstinate, no reconciliation had taken place when Ralph left the village with his regiment. He was soon ordered away to join the army of the Potomac.

It was more than two years later that Mary Spear joined a corps of nurses to go and do duty in the field hospitals after the battle of Antietam. She went under the charge of a member of the sanitary commission, who was placed at the head of the little expedition, and they carried with them medical stores and a great quantity of lint and bandages made by the village women, besides several hundred flannel shirts and socks which the First Church Sewing Society had contributed. For a year these women went wherever they were ordered in the field, to minister to the sick and dying; they were always, it seemed, in the immediate wake of battle, and Mary Spear saw scenes of anguish and blood in those days which have left an indelible mark on her life.

It was just before Gettysburg that a few men on stretchers were brought into the tent hospital, terribly wounded while on a reconnoissance, by a shell from a masked battery. Ralph Freeman was among the mortally hurt. A fragment of the shell had torn its way through his body, and he was bleeding to death. But he was still conscious. He knew Mary Spear. He could even speak a little in whispers, and at last he died in her arms. When Mary came home from that hospital campaign, she had grown into a woman, strong and serious, through a variety of terrible experiences. Why did she a few years later marry little Andrew Stillwell? Why do thousands of such women in narrow spheres marry men inferior to themselves? Dog-like devotion, the kind of worship such humble, good, self-abnegating souls give to noble women, often finds its recompense, and love makes all incongruity to drop away and disappear, especially if the devotion of the lesser one asks little for itself but kind tolerance.

Mary Spear brought home with her a few sacred keepsakes Ralph had given her at the last. She did not show them even to his mother, and her husband, though he knew she possessed such things, had never seen them. They were kept with Ralph's picture and his old letters. He knew Mary put flowers on Freeman's grave every Memorial Day. Each time he passed from his little shop to his own house his eye rested on the small and rather ugly monument the towns-people had put up to the memory of their dead soldiers. On the principal face of it was written: "Ralph Freeman, Colonel of the —— Regiment. Killed on the field of battle! Oh, sweet is it to die for one's country." People said that Mary refused Stillwell twelve times, but she became Mrs. Stillwell in the end, and the mother of a fine family of children. What will not lovers' assiduity accomplish? Sam Blake proposed to Tilly Jones over a score of times, and the story is told that after she had refused him repeatedly she saw him open the front door one day while she was at the top of the stairs, and she called out, "You needn't come in, Sam; I will not have you." But she did have him, finally, and is now Mrs. Sam Blake, just as Mary Spear is Mrs. Andrew Stillwell.

There was that skeleton in Stillwell's closet—the soldiers' monument, the grave on the hill, the love-letters and keepsakes his wife keeps locked away, reserving a compartment in her heart for the dead Ralph. To be sure he married her when she told him her heart was buried in the grave, but all these years he has had an aching and longing in his breast for the love of his wife, something more than duty love; and though he has tried to ennoble himself and to rise above jealousy of the dead, it is hard, nay, impossible of accomplishment. Mary Stillwell's story was well known in the village, but of course her children were entirely ignorant of it. The name of Ralph Freeman was never heard in that house, but the memory of him was always in the mother's heart, and it was like grit in the eyes of Andrew. The village gossips sometimes raked up her pathetic little story out of the ashes of the past and rubbed it bright again.

No one could say truthfully that Mary was not happy in her family of three boys and two girls, all going to school now. They are fine, noble-looking children. People said there was not much Stillwell about them; they featured the Spears. Good little scholars they were, eager and ambitious, and still with an insatiable appetite for fun and play.

You should have seen them of an evening gathered around the table in the dining-room, with the hanging-lamp casting down its light on the brown-golden heads: the oldest boy, a lad of sixteen, preparing for college; Mary, the mother—with her dark keen eyes and handsome face, the hair showing steely lines in the brown braids—helping him with his algebra and his Latin, studying beside him that she might help him more effectually; the younger boys with their grammars and phrase-books spread out to parse with mother; the two little girls, eight and ten, the youngest golden-haired, with great blue eyes, busy with their slates and pencils, to show writing and summing and spelling all to mother. She had called her eldest boy Theodore, gift of God, and perhaps there was an implied sense of joy and consolation in that name no one knew but herself. The frank-eyed lad, so honest and true-hearted and manly, was Mary's mainstay. If any thing should happen to Andrew before the children were fully grown, there was Theo to take a father's place.

The Stillwells were not very well off. Mary had brought a little money in her hand, which was spent in buying and furnishing the house. This house was of the basement-kitchen variety, built upon a gentle slope, with a terraced side-hill garden and a small yard in front for flowers. During the evening the kitchen part was generally deserted, as the maid of all work often went home to sleep. The entrance to the sitting-room was at the side, up a steep bit of path from the village street, bordered with rose-bushes and flowering shrubs. Next door to the Stillwells lived Stephen, the taxidermist. Only a low picket-fence separated his garden from theirs. Stephen had often thrown sticks and stones and brick-bats into their yard on pretense that the Stillwell children were trespassing on his ground.

Many months had passed since Mary had spoken to her surly neighbor or paid the least attention to his pranks. She had taken the side of Stephen's mother in the trouble between them, when the son was so unkind and cruel, after the loss of his money, and he and the Stillwells were now at daggers drawn. Stephen had killed two of the little girls' kittens, and thrown them over the fence. If one of the boys tossed a ball by accident on his ground, they did not dare to go and look for it for fear of a stoning. The children were remarkably good and obedient; their mother saw that they never interfered with the neighbors. But Stephen had a special grudge against the druggist. He had ordered from him a quantity of crude drugs and chemicals used in his craft, and then had refused to pay the price agreed upon. Stillwell had brought suit against him to recover the money, and the matter was as yet unsettled. Stephen was away from home when the disturbances began at the Stillwells', and his house was closed. His mother was living with her sister on sufferance because she dared not go to her own home, where her son burrowed like a brigand in a cave.

Something was certainly going wrong at the Stillwells' and though the family were very close-mouthed about it, and would not admit that it could not all be traced to natural causes, it created an undercurrent of excitement in the village. Rats in the cellar that had come up through the drain, was the first explanation, but the noises were not at all like those made by rats, and twice there had been an alarm raised late in the evening that the Stillwell house was on fire. A red glare had been seen to burst out of one of the lower windows after the family were in bed, but when the alarm was given and search was made nothing could be found. The noises were said to be like those made by hogsheads and fifty-pound weights rolled about in the cellar. Shots had also been fired, and occasionally the mournful sound of a muffled drum filled every part of the house. Most of these disturbances occurred in the middle of the night, but two or three times in the daylight a shower of broken glass and pebbles had fallen on the roof.

When the cause of these mysterious persecutions had eluded discovery for a few days, Stillwell put the case into the hands of the constable and other village authorities, but he repelled all neighborly peeping and prying. A great change had taken place in the neat, alert little man. His cheeks looked flabby and livid. He was haggard and his jaw dropped every time the trouble in his house was mentioned. He had grown careless about his dress. His linen cuffs were spotted with the medicines he compounded with shaking hands. But he politely requested the neighbors to keep cool and leave him to deal with the mysteries which he did not attempt to deny had broken out in his house. But the more silent and reserved and nervous the family became the more the people whispered together.

"What do you suppose *they* want at the Stillwells'?" said Mrs. John Dean in an awed voice to Mrs. Deacon Hildreth, as the two ladies happened to meet on First Church corner.

"It ain't no *they* at all," returned stout Mrs. Hildreth, puffing a little from exercise (she had never parsed Milton's "Paradise Lost" all through). "It's a *he*, Mrs. Dean—no other than Ralph Freeman, him Mary Stillwell was engaged to years and years ago, and who you know got killed in the war. They do say he knocks in the chimney and all over the house and cries, 'Mary, Mary,' waking her out of her sleep with a deep groan to see his name, 'Ralph,' in red, fiery letters on the wall. They think Stillwell will go crazy, for he always has been jealous of Ralph Freeman, though the poor fellow was put under ground so long ago. But Mary gets angry if any one pretends to say it really is Ralph. She says malice is at the bottom of it, either malice of this world or the other, and she presumes of this. It's an awful cruel trick if it is a trick, but you know the spiritualists in town are all up in arms. There's an old ice-house made in the side-hill, and attached to the cellar. It was built on by Aaron Holmes when he lived there, but the Stillwells never have used it. They say the worst of the noises come from that old house. And the other night when the two oldest Stillwell boys tried to get in there, the door was held against them, and green fire and a bad smell of brimstone broke out all around the cracks. Mary has sent the little girls and the youngest boy away to her sisters. She says she means to hold the fort.

She's right down plucky, but Stillwell is all broken up."

"Dear me, I should like to see it," said Mrs. Dean, in a delightful state of goose-flesh and shivers.

"They won't let nobody come to the house, and the constable has orders to arrest prowlers."

There was enough truth mixed up with the stories floating all over the village to make the Stillwell family miserable. The mother was more courageous than any of the others. She had a theory that if the noises were inexplicable they would soon die away of themselves; if not, the truth would sometime be discovered. Still her heart was torn with old memories, and the cruel ordeal seemed often too hard to bear. After the boys had been frightened by green fire and brimstone, the old ice-house, called in the family the Black Hole of Calcutta, was thoroughly ransacked. The door was found ajar, and the place was quite empty. Apparently there was no communication between the Black Hole and the cellar. A solid, rough stone-wall met the hand and the eye on all sides. The knocks were of a deep subterranean sound, and when tried by the alphabet invariably spelled out " Ralph Free "—and then stopped. One night Stillwell and his wife were alone together in the house, the boys having gone off to sleep with a young friend, Abner Smith, in order to get a little rest. Poor Stillwell had lost appetite and color, and his flesh was fast falling off. He had always deplored the influence of Ralph Freeman's memory on the mind of his wife, and this trouble seemed to have come as the realization of an ill-defined dread that had lain in his mind for years. To have Ralph haunting his house (for in his weakened state he had come over to a belief in the miraculous) he felt would kill him.

"Why do you think he comes back to torture us in this way, Mary?" he asked, taking his head in his hands.

"He does not come back thus," she answered indignantly, "if he comes at all. He was a good, generous, whole-hearted man. Do you suppose he wishes to spoil our lives? It is most unkind to think it. There is some devilish work going on here, but it does not proceed from Ralph Freeman."

Andrew groaned. He had often longed to talk to his wife about his jealousy of the dead, but he had never found courage to speak Ralph's name. Now he trembled as the daring words came to his lips. "Mary," said he faintly, "did you not once tell me that your heart was buried in his coffin?"

"Perhaps I did years ago, when the grief and sense of loss were fresh and keen, but to-day he is only a sad and tender memory, I am heart-bound to my husband and children. You have made my life so good and so sweet, Andrew, I have no time now for vain regrets. I love you just as a wife should love her faithful, devoted husband."

Andrew felt his wife's words fall like drops of dew on his fever-parched heart. The real specter had been all the time pent up in his breast, and he never had found the strength to exorcise it by speaking frankly to his wife. And here in a moment she had made all clear and shining like the noonday. They had it all out that night—the perfect explanation of every thing—the good talk, that makes the heart feel light. Andrew discovered that there is a soul of good in things evil. If Ralph Freeman was haunting his house to spite him for marrying Mary, he had made an egregious blunder. Andrew slept soundly for the first time in a week, and arose next morning a new man.

The constable and his deputy, our one policeman, had watched the house two or three nights without discovering the cause of the mysterious rappings and other noises. Suddenly they all ceased, the officers went away to their warm beds, the excitement in the village quieted down, and vigilance relaxed. The lad Abner Smith, friend of the Stillwell boys, had a natural talent for what is called in country phrase snooping. Abner had made up his mind to do a little bit of amateur detective work on his own account. About this time Stephen returned from his journey, and was seen busy about his garden. Abner took to haunting the old ice-house, and spent a long time in examining the apparently dead wall. At last to his joy and surprise he discovered two loosened stones in the foundation, which could easily be displaced and gave direct access to the Stillwell cellar. There was a great air of mystery about the house after this, although the noises and disturbances had entirely ceased. The boys were always consulting together after dark, and carried on some kind of work in the cellar which they concealed from the household.

It happened to be All Hallow Eve. Mary spoke of it to Andrew, and said laughingly that "the spooks would be sure to visit them again on that witch-haunted night." The boys had made their own plans, and with matches and a dark lantern they had determined to watch in the large coal-bin down cellar. It was the witching hour after midnight, when darkness and silence brooded over the whole village. A spectral white figure seemed to rise up from the ground and then to sink away suddenly beneath the earth. In a moment there came up out of the Black Hole of Calcutta, not a groan, but a prolonged ear-piercing yell. The boys put a match to the dark lantern, and ran to the hole in the wall, nearly falling over each other in their haste and eagerness. Then such a turmoil of shouts, such a babel of voices arose from the lower regions, that Stillwell awoke in fright, donned a hasty garment, and took a candle in his hand. Mary, quite pale, followed in her night-cap and wrapper. She had no belief in spooks or rapping spirits, but it was All Hallow E'en. They crept down the stairs, and soon recognized Theodore's voice shouting and vociferating.

"We've got him, mother. The spook is bagged." On the basement floor, where they had dragged him, lay a long limp object, done up in a white sheet. "He's trying to play 'possum, to make out he's a sleep-walker," remarked Ab Smith, with the coolness of an old hand; "the nip of that big steel-trap took him right through the foot."

Andrew Stillwell bent down and allowed the light of his candle to fall on the prostrate form. It was his neighbor Stephen, who had hidden day-times in his own house for a fortnight, and had spent his nights in the unhallowed work of making life unendurable to the Stillwells', out of pure spite. Stephen had got in by the Black Hole, had displaced the stones in the cellar wall, and played spook and spirit-rapper with phosphorus, colored fire, sulphur, and an old bass drum purchased from a member of a strolling band. He had also contrived a sort of catapult to throw small stones from the top of the hill. It was first proposed to dress Stephen in a suit of tar and feathers, but Mary Stillwell intervened and made him buy his safety by signing a paper promising to do justice to his mother. The old lady has come home, and Stephen is now away in the South for his health. Indirectly those mysterious disturbances at the Stillwells', which the village spiritualists so exaggerated, have resulted in good to several people.

CHAPTER XLII.

BROTHER GEORGE.

AMONG the most deeply-rooted of all rural ideas is the dislike of paying debts. Of course most country folk do pay their debts first or last, but many of them do it grudgingly. It almost requires a surgical operation to get the old pocket-book—pathetically lean—out of the long trowsers-pocket, and it seems an eternity before it opens and the little money the poor farmer has scraped up with hard toil is laid before the remorseless creditor.

All debts are divided into classes. They begrudge less the paying out of money for what are called necessaries—what they eat and drink. Then come the taxes, which must be paid, or the sacred soil will be seized and sold. It is harder to meet the demand for the payment of children's schooling, which to many seems hardly so needful as children's shoes. Even at this late day there are country folk who shrewdly suspect that, beyond the three R's, schooling is a device foisted upon them by the enemy, to make the boys and girls less willing to work in the old groove their fathers have worn; which gives them high notions and separates them from humble but worthy relatives who are not at all strong in grammar. School money, therefore, stands in a category by itself, and must from the very nature of the case come hard. But it is paid with alacrity compared with the doctor's bill, the pew rent, and the newspaper subscription. There is something more intangible about the benefit conferred by these than even about schooling. If the doctor, the pastor, and the editor could be paid by a cord of wood or a little "sass," it would come willingly. For cord-wood and "sass" are far less mysterious and sacred in the eyes of country folk than those counters of civilization, bank-notes and cart-wheel silver dollars. "Sass" and cord-wood are often given away with a kindness most good and gracious. But unfortunately the fashion of paying with the fruits of the earth has gone out of date. The parson, a notably long-suffering man, has refused to take any more barrels of apples and quarter-loads of pumpkins in return for the spiritual pabulum he deals out of a Sunday.

I must confess that I have a good deal of sympathy with the farmer's reluctance to pay for medical advice and old drugs which perhaps did no good to his inside, but positive harm ; for old sermons now quite cold in the memory, and which refuse to warm over ; and for old newspapers, which it is conceded by every body, are the stalest of all stale things. It is what one may call this post-meridian view of physic, theology, and news that makes the demand for payment look so preposterous in the farmer's eyes. But still I perceive that the doctor, the parson, and the editor have a certain value in a community, and ought not to be allowed to starve outright, though they often do, as we know, waste away in a slow absorption of their substance, as bears live through the winter, sucking their paws.

You know very well that a man who attends to every body's business generally neglects his own. This to a marked degree had been the case with Dr. John Rivington. Inwardly he groaned over the confusion of his affairs, but outwardly he slipped along as he had done for years, recording the amounts due him in his ledgers, but making few vigorous efforts to collect long outstanding debts. He could be kind to every body but himself. So long as he was in the prime of life it did not matter much ; he could always manage to scrape together enough to live on. But now, though still vigorous, he was beginning to feel in himself those subtle approaches of age he knew so well—slight touches of gout, nipping pains in the joints, a coldness of the stomach in the morning that needed warming up with a dose of bitters, a disinclination to do night-work, slower motions, as if the old machine were beginning to run down, and yet no visible improvement of temper, but rather a tendency to look upon the present condition of the world as very black and hopeless, while all in the past lay steeped in the aura of childish happiness, when he and his brother George were lads together—how long ago in the dim and faded past!

Much had come and gone to make the brothers forgetful and indifferent toward each other, but now pictures of the old days began to come back to the doctor like sun-flashes, bright and warm, and at times he almost yearned with a woman's tenderness to see George again, to live over the boyish times when they went to school together, with arms thrown carelessly about each other's shoulders. Those things came back with such vividness that he lived over the sports and fun of far-away times; he heard the sound of George's careless whistle, the very tones of his voice in the room even before he arose in the morning. He was living in fancy in his mother's house, and the present seemed to lose its grip and reality. Then the doctor suspected he was getting senile. For over thirty years he and George had not met—had only occasionally corresponded for part of the time to make formal inquiries about each other's health and fortunes. They wrote always in a stiff, old-fashioned way now quite out of date. They sent these duty-letters to each other once or twice a year, closing " Your well wisher and ob'd't servant." There was an ancient courtesy about this correspondence that made one think of foolscap sheets and old seals. But the brothers had really so little to say to each other that they often ran aground in the first dozen lines, and eked out a sheet with the condition of the crops and the state of the weather in their respective neighborhoods.

All the years of separation until now Dr. Jack had felt his heart burning with a sense of a brother's wrong. George was less warm-hearted, hot-headed, impetuous, and uncalculating than his brother. They had quarreled about a girl, of course, and she had married George, as the doctor believed, through an unfair advantage which his brother had taken. But possibly he was wrong in all this. The hard feeling and the inevitable separation came all the same. George had gone far away to the south-west and had become great in mining business, in farming, and railroads. He was a rich and powerful man, but scorned of his poor brother, the village doctor. Dead silence between them for over twenty years. Then she died, George's wife, and he wrote to Jack for the first time. It was a kind of smothered heart-cry from a desolate man, and the correspondence began with a touch of sympathy, but soon lapsed into that formal, polite old style that mocks the heart and feeds it with the east wind when we long for a warm seat beside a brother's hearth. She was gone, and the doctor could hardly remember how she had looked. All the life and fire had gone out of that old time when he had quivered with emotion and suffered such burning heats and chills for her sake. But kinship has a longer and tougher root. It comes up in green shoots, and puts forth little blossoms long after we think it is quite dead.

Dr. Jack cared nothing about the rich man; indeed, was rather scornful and hostile toward him. The old quarrel had left enough acerbity for purposes of family criticism. Yet, unaccountably, he longed for the brother he had lost so long ago. Oh, that he might get the lad back again, and dog on behind him as he used to do up the hilly lane, all aglow from swimming in the pond! He lived over their boyish scrapes in the barn and on fishing tours; how they played truant from school to dig out a muskrat; how the old horse Deacon ran away one Fourth of July when they were going to a "celebration" in the next town, and threw George out and stunned him and cut his head a little, so that the blood flowed down his temple, and how scared he (Jack) was.

He knew he was getting senile, because he continually lived over the old boyish life of fifty years ago when he was driving along country roads, and the autumnal scents and sunshine warm on the dying leaves touched some chord in his heart and made it vibrate. He would laugh aloud to himself over George's tricks and sharpness when a boy. He (Jack) always came out at the little end of the horn with his brother in a trade, a bargain, or a swap. George got all the best things in the end, and there was nothing belonging to old blunder-heels Jack, not even his sweetheart, which he coveted that he did not contrive to win away. But the doctor could think of it now with a kind of admiring indulgent tenderness for George, making him only the fonder of the lad.

Strange to say, in his letters to his brother he never hinted at these feelings, which he would have been ashamed to confess to any body. The rich railroad-man and land-owner in the south-west, an oldish man now, alone in the world, and somewhat broken by ill-health, was not George, that sharp, wide-awake, cunning little chap. But where was George? he asked whimsically. Somehow he had miserably perished out of the world. The boy was non-existent. He could never even hope to meet him in heaven, if there is such a place, and yet the old doctor longed so for him his heart at times felt actually sore; he had a dim notion that old blunder-heels Jack, who had allowed himself to be hoodwinked, and cheated, and ridden over rough-shod, was somehow intact in his own breast. Many and many a time he had backed little George up the lane to show his superior strength. Alas, he would never do it again. Soon they would carry him out by the feet; and there was no hope of finding in the other world the lost lad that he had loved.

So you see the doctor, with all his pathological insight into his own case, was an inveterate dreamer. His dream territory was much larger than his actual possessions. It took only a line of poetry, a strain of some old song his granddaughter sang at the piano, and which he caught of an evening as he opened the door, to set him tingling all over, every fiber quick with young feeling. But now his granddaughter was growing up a tall, handsome girl. She must be sent away to school. She must be portioned some time in marriage. The little fortune left her by her grand-aunt (greatly exaggerated by public rumor) had now it was discovered dwindled away to a mere nothing owing to its original investment in the stock of a wild-cat mining company. These thoughts came to him one day when he discovered Effie was no longer a child, but had put on long dresses and wore her hair "tucked up." Indeed, the top of her curly head now came higher than his shoulder. The doctor put his arm round her with the confused feeling that he was doing something improper in embracing a strange young lady.

That evening, with a great deal of inward groaning and many grimaces, he drew down from his office shelf his old dusty ledgers, some of which dated as far back as 1850. His wife had always been mildly urging him to collect his bills. Now he had two lamps brought in, and, locking the office door, he settled down to a long spell of work, the hardest job of his whole life. After long years of carelessness and neglect of his own interest, he was resolved now to have a settlement with his debtors, and to call in at least a portion of what was due him. It is safe to say that he would gladly have endured much physical torture rather than put his hand to this needful business. He had lain awake the previous night and planned to send the bills out through the post, thus screening himself as far as possible from the well-merited wrath of his neighbors. On looking the case over dispassionately, he found himself taking their side in advance. As he clapped the dust off the covers of those old ledgers he hated them with a deadly hatred. A thousand times he had been tempted to burn them, and he bitterly regretted that he had not acted on his impulse, for the futility of what he was about to do weighed him down. But he owed this sacrifice of personal feeling to the child. He would have given his heart's blood to her, and now his gray head went down over the hateful page. He squared his elbows, savagely dipped his pen in ink, and began to run his eye down long rows of entries—names, dates, figures. He muttered, and mumbled, and groaned to himself as he tried to make head or tail out of this dreadful piece of work. "M-m-m, M-m-Fisher, ten years' medicines and attendance. M-m-m-Forbes, eighty visits. Old man dead. M-m-m-m-m-Hicks, paralytic. Jones, debt outlawed."

For a week, girding at the horrid task, ejaculating and spluttering as if taking some of his own bitter stuff, the doctor kept on intermittently with what he had in hand. In spite of all the outlawed debts, the removals, and the large sums he had given outright to the poor, and crossed off finally, he was appalled by the amount justly due him in the country. He thought the matter over for a few days, and then decided to deduct twenty per cent. from all the bills, and to inclose each in a little explanatory note modestly setting forth his necessities. This he hoped would partly take the curse off the whole proceeding. He called in his granddaughter to copy all the bills, and write the letters in her school-girl hand from a form which he had prepared. Perhaps he secretly hoped that innocent chirography might make its appeal to the hearts of his neighbors.

The bills were sent out on a Thursday afternoon. Luckily it was a healthy time ; and for three days thereafter the doctor kept as much as possible within doors. He felt so ashamed and humiliated he knew not how to face any body, and yet, as he fumbled about in his mind, he could discover no just ground for the feeling, unless it was that he had so long neglected his duty to himself, his debtors might feel that they had a claim on his criminal carelessness which would offset all they owed him. He knew the pinch would come, like turning a door on a finger in the crack, and he felt for his neighbors quite impersonally by aid of the sympathetic imagination with which he was endowed.

For a few days the village was sullen and silent. Its astonishment knew no bounds. But at length the clamor broke forth. One old woman complained bitterly that all the members of her family he had doctored were dead. He could only answer that one was a cripple, and another a very old person, and he had prolonged their lives for years, often riding five miles on cold winter nights to minister to them. It is peculiar to human nature, let the disease be what it may, to believe that if a friend had been differently treated he or she would have recovered. Now all the old cases were raked up out of their graves, and to hear the talk in the village you would suppose that earthly immortality might have reigned there, and Burying-Ground Hill be now untenanted, but for the doctor's drugs. Can people be expected to pay the doctor for killing off their relatives, especially after the debts have mostly outlawed ? The idea is preposterous. A few friends, especially the little milliner and Mrs. Judge Magnus, were hotly indignant at all this ungrateful, hard-hearted talk, but their heat did little good. Some people refused to pay the old bills because they had lost all track of them, and did not believe they were owing any thing. Others demanded large reductions, which the doctor made with a sardonic smile on his face. He had worked for these people year in and year out, and yet they would stone him if they could, when he asked them to pay only a small part of what was his due. One day he came into his wife's sitting-room looking thoroughly disgusted and out of tune.

"Well, well," he grunted, "you made me do it. You got me into this scrape. You would keep at me about the bills" (the doctor could be terribly unjust in such moods), "and now I have turned all the folks against me, and all for nothing. I have only been able to collect less than a thousand dollars, when there are eight or ten thousand due me, at the lowest figure. When I die there will be nothing left for you and Effie except this house, unless I insure my life and put a ball and chain on my leg."

"No need of that," said Mrs. Rivington, in her low, sad voice. "I shall go first, and Effie will marry a better business man than you are, John, and she will keep you when you are old."

The doctor gave a scornful laugh and flung out of the room. When his wife wished to exasperate him she always began to talk about "going first." He went to his office and slammed and locked the door, and began to smoke like a steam-engine. He was angry with his wife, but he knew she was as innocent as a saint above. In a few days, when he had nearly smoked himself to death, he came out into peace of mind and sweet reasonableness, sweeter than clarified honey. He went one afternoon and picked some late artemisias in the old garden, and came and pinned them gallantly in his wife's kerchief. "Judith," said he, "let the old debts be d——.

I know I am a dragon to live with, and I wonder you have stood it so long."

She looked up with her lovely old eyes just slightly suffused. Ah me, if we could only be a little kinder to those we love!

It was just as this scene was taking place within doors that the best depot hack drove up to the door. That hack charged fifty cents apiece for passengers, while the second-best charged only twenty-five. When the best hack drove up to the door people always felt that somebody had been rather recklessly extravagant. "Who is it?" said the doctor, as he looked out of the window. "Are you expecting a visitor?" And then he motioned to his wife with his eyes. She shook her head, and went and looked over the doctor's shoulder. The man who alighted from the best hack was older in appearance than the doctor, and quite white about the brow. He walked a little lame, and leaned on a stick as he came slowly through the front yard. He entered the house without knocking, as if it had been his own. The doctor stood riveted to his place, with something of wonder, almost of fright, painted on his features. The stranger came in and took off his hat to Mrs. Rivington, with a gesture that would have been most urbane but for the tremor in his hands. He never knew what he said. He drew near to the doctor, and their hands felt for each other and clasped. They looked into each other's eyes, and the boy George must have come up some way into those faded, pale-blue orbs, for the doctor fell on his neck, half-choked and fairly sobbing, "My brother was lost, but is found."

George Rivington sat down gasping a little. It was evident his heart was not very strong. "I will get you a draught," said the doctor, alarmed.

"No, no, I want you," returned George, faintly, reaching out his hand. Like so many poor creatures, he was ill for that vivifying affection that brings new life.

It was enough to spoil our petted and pampered pessimism to see those two old brothers going about the village together. It seemed to bring back the feeling of a fount of sweet, pure goodness welling up in life—a principle divine and incalculable, in spite of our arid doubts or more arid beliefs. They lived their lives all over again. They even came to the most perfect understanding about the long estrangement and its cause. They laughed and slapped each other on the back as they talked over their old boyish scrapes. They smoked together, and sometimes sat hours in silence, feeling that the luxury of unspoken intercourse brought them nearer than words.

One morning the doctor came to seek his wife in her own room: "My dear," said he—he seldom called her "my dear"—"George is going to take charge of Effie's education, and if I go first"—this with a little malice—"he will see that you want for nothing. You know," he added, straightening himself a little proudly, "I can take it from a brother."

The good doctor knew how blessed it is to give; he now knows how blessed it is to receive for love's sake.

CHAPTER XLIII.

THE UNEARNED INCREMENT.

AFTER the people had treated the doctor about as badly as they could, and had flung their hard words at his head, they began to feel ashamed of themselves. It was rumored about town that the doctor had thought of selling out to a young practitioner and going West with his brother George. Then the village discovered that he was the chief jewel in its crown, and that it could not live without him. All the bitter, sarcastic remarks bearing on his physic and treatment of cases were forgotten, and the village felt desolate in advance by the mere suggestion of his departure. Have you ever remarked that singular trait in human nature—that people will try to make up by a needless spurt of generosity for some essential failure in justice? It is like the man who beat his wife and then tried to soothe her feelings by taking her to a circus. Now, the villagers thought to salve over the sore place in the doctor's mind by some such attempt. The whisper went round among the frightened people that it would be well to do something to show their gratitude to the doctor, to prove to him how dear and valuable he was to them, and to bind him to them by new and lasting ties.

Judge Magnus made it a point to see his friends, the richest and most influential men in the neighborhood, and to say, with beautiful expansiveness and manifold gesticulation, that something must be done. "I tell you, sir, we must celebrate his sixty-fifth birthday in Library Hall, and we must do it in fine style—handsomely, sir, handsomely. I think we ought to present him with a piece of plate—a pitcher or a salver. Yes, sir ; we must do the thing in fine shape, and show the doctor he is appreciated. A glorious old fellow, sir, if there ever was one. Mrs. Magnus is devoted to him, and so am I ; and if nobody helps buy the testimonial, I will do it all, sir, out of my own pocket. It is a shame the doctor has never received any token of regard from his townsmen. I shall be proud to head a subscription for this admirable purpose."

Milly, when she heard of it, remarked dryly that if the judge bought the testimonial and presided at the meeting and made the speech of the evening, he would forget all about the doctor and present the piece of plate to himself in a perfect sun-burst of self-admiration.

But the judge began to fuss about, looking more portly and imposing than ever, with a subscription paper in hand, which he had headed with the sum of one hundred dollars. The ladies consulted together and decided to trim the hall with flowers, greens, and autumn leaves, and to give the refreshments, which were to be of the choicest. By some means or other, the doctor got wind of the affair. *Donner und blitzen!* You ought to have seen the storm of scorn and rage raised in that good man's breast. Heavens ! had he come to the ignominy of a subscription paper ? " Go along with your testimonial," he growled, with other expressions I should be sorry to write down in cold blood. " I will have none of that nonsense. A piece of plate, indeed ! What do I want of plate, beyond a door-plate or a coffin-plate ? I tell you I will not give the thing house-room. Nor will I have any hypocritical fuss made over me. But I have learned a wrinkle or two from brother George, and I give you fair warning, every six months hereafter my bills will be sent out promptly, and if they are not paid, they will be placed in a lawyer's hands for collection."

Now the feeling in the village is that the doctor is of a

very bearish, uncertain temper ; that his peculiarities are growing upon him, and poor Mrs. Rivington is very much to be pitied ; and that this new rule about bills is a reason for keeping as well as possible and not calling in the doctor nearly as often as in the old easy-going days.

The young clergyman is apt to preach two or three startling sermons after he comes home, and the vacation supply of ex-college professors and clericals ceases. He knows his people deserve some compensation for sitting under a preacher like Stackpole and listening to his long-winded discourses about how Joshua blew down the city wall with a ram's horn, and how the sun stood still upon Gideon. Besides his orthodox and his heterodox foot the young man has a third means of support as yet unclassified. When standing on this he preaches practical sermons on the conduct of life, sermons which, we may say, relate to contemporaneous human interest, and often open long reaches of thought and are as innovating in certain ways as his free-thinking discourses. When he brings in discussions about egoism and altruism, the people feel not a little complimented. It is doing reverence to the village intellect to suppose it can understand such things.

About a year ago the young parson preached a remarkable discourse on sacrifice, in which he attempted to show that the commonly received opinion of sacrifice is wrong and immoral. We have no right, he said, to demand the abasement of a high, pure, beautiful nature to a low, selfish, bestial character. We have no right to crucify the best and noblest in us to pamper the evil passions and indulge the coarse vices of degraded beings. Such an immolation of the good, though it is often lauded by people calling themselves Christians, can not be acceptable to God. He illustrated his discourse by allusions to characters in two well known novels—a rather startling thing in itself—to show how virtue is often trampled under the hoofs of vice in obedience to a false standard of morality. Then he dwelt on the duty to the individual soul, the effort towards self-perfection as an aim of life, the good done by raising the level of character, and wound up with a long and thrilling poetical quotation.

The seeds of that sermon fell here and there—some doubtless on poor soil, some on stony ground, but a few were dropped and germinated in the most unlikely place. Sitting in one of the front pews with Salmon A. Poindexter's children and the governess who taught them French, German, and music, was Miss Christina Poindexter, sister to the said Salmon A. She was one of those round-faced, placid, mild-looking New England women who never crimp the front hair, or "bang" it, but brush it smooth against an unlined brow, and look out upon the world with thoughtful and intelligent eyes and no little sweetness and charm of expression, long after they have passed their first youth. The Poindexters are not exactly of the village. They live upon the fringes of it, two or three miles down the valley, on the slope of a green knoll, which has been adorned with beautiful lawns and shrubberies and a goodly number of rather poor statues, which are to Mr. Poindexter's taste, though his wife more than half objects to so many unclad composition nymphs shivering about in the wet and cold. The house is new and large, of staring red brick and terracotta, and it commands a lovely view of the valley and distant ranges of hills. When it was first erected, it was so very red, the joke went about the country that the scarlet fever had broken out on Poindexter's place.

Salmon A. Poindexter has been a very prosperous business man; moreover, he has had the good fortune to marry a rich wife, whose thousands he has increased to tens of thousands by shrewd investments, until now it is said that he is very solid, worth at least a million of dollars, and perhaps more. Poindexter comes flashing through the village with his high-stepping horses, his glittering equipage, and jingling sun-bright harness. He looks about him as if he owned every thing, and we, poor creatures, were only there on sufferance. His sense of ownership and moneyed superiority is not at all like that of Judge Magnus—a simple, old-fashioned, local pride, as transparent as window-glass. Salmon A.'s has an element of arrogance the people resent, while they love the judge and laugh at him with right good will. Poindexter's prosperity is new and shiny, and so full-blown it pervades every thing like a too rank vegetable odor. Poor devils who have not chanced to make a success in life, though they have tried with the best intentions, find themselves squeezed against the wall in his presence. Salmon A. naturally likes to associate with millionaires. If he condescends to men of low degree, there is something of offense in his manner, as much as to say, " I could buy and sell you twenty times over if I chose to put my hand in my pocket." There is hardly any one in the village with whom he feels he can associate except the judge, and the latter always likes to play first fiddle in his own district ; he does not, therefore, care much about mixing up with Poindexter.

Salmon A. respects his wife because she is his wife, and because her father had the good sense to accumulate a large fortune for him to handle, enlarge and enjoy. But it may be said that his sister Crissie, that plain, modest, unassuming old maid, was nearer to him for years than any body else. He thought he knew, about the time I am writing of, every fold and crease in Crissie's nature, for she was a part of himself, and had never had any other life than his life, or any other interests than his interests. Before he married, Crissie had kept house for her brother, and later, it may be said she still kept his house. Though Mrs. Poindexter was the head of the family, like many of the wealthy and pampered people of our time she was uneasy and restless in a beautiful home, and liked to flit about to the South, and to Europe, to the watering places in summer. She was perfectly well, but she still felt that the state of her health demanded frequent change.

But Crissie was always at home as care-taker and general manager. The children could be left with her at any time. Mrs. Poindexter was aware that Crissie knew more about their diseases and dispositions than she herself did. The middle girl, Beatrice, had slept with her aunt until she was five or six, and the children certainly minded Aunt Cris with as much alacrity as their mother, and perhaps loved her more. But Mrs. Poindexter was not jealous. Crissie was too great a godsend to her for that. She wondered and speculated about her sister-in-law a great deal. She tried to penetrate into her mind, and learn the secret of her placidity. Why did she go on with this life? Why did she not break violently away? Not for worlds would she have been Cris. She contrasted her own rich and rather flamboyant dress with Crissie's plain, demure style. How could Cris stand it? Always at the bottom of her mind lay the dread that Cris would some day discover she was not bound over hand and foot for life, and would assert her independence.

When Mrs. Poindexter was at home, she liked to have the house well filled with fashionable friends, and it sometimes happened, at an over-crowded moment, that Crissie's room was required by a visitor. Then she went quietly into the nursery and slept with one of the little girls. Moreover, if the pastry cook departed at a moment's notice, as pastry cooks are apt to do, Crissie could be depended upon to make delicious desserts, pastry, and ices, and cake, and cream, all in a dainty fashion of her own. And yet she was a highly cultivated woman, although Mrs. Poindexter's guests were not often of a sort to discover the fact. She had read much and enjoyed music, and pictures, and all refined, good things. She was interested in ideas, and had a great many of her own stowed away under her smooth brown hair and back of those clear gray eyes. She had not cultivated expression, for she feared to be put down by the heavy hand of Salmon A., who felt that he was quite able to do the thinking of the family. He would not openly tolerate ideas in his women kind, especially in Crissie. Mrs. Poindexter, having a large fortune in her own right, was entitled to some freedom of opinion, but Crissie, being his creature, was expected to catch the reflection of his mind and live according to what he deemed proper for a legal spinster.

Mrs. Poindexter, spite of the fear in the depths of her mind, and though she desired not to be untrue to herself, was in the habit of saying to her friends that Crissie was the most domestic creature in the world. No existence would suit her but the life she led in her brother's house. She loved the children so dearly it was impossible to separate her from them a single night. Nothing was so delightful to Crissie as to give up her own bed and go in and sleep with the little girls. Moreover, she enjoyed the care of the place, and was very fond of breaking in green, stupid servants. It was a pleasure for her to be alone with them part of the year in that great house, for no one cared so little for society as Cris.

This was Mrs. Poindexter's story, and she had repeated it over so often that at moments she almost believed it. She was a worldly woman, but not absolutely unfeeling. In one corner of her heart she loved Crissie and pitied her. She wondered at times to herself, as she dreamily slipped the diamond rings round on her finger, sitting in luxurious ease before the great open fire in the wide hall, how Cris could have lived all these years unwedded—a kind of foot-ball in her brother's house—and yet have kept her sweetness and her good looks; for she could not but confess that at times Crissie, with all her plainness, was very attractive. Through a refined selfishness, which it was impossible for her psychological analysis to separate from pure good feeling, she tried to take her sister-in-law's part with Salmon.

"You ought not to speak so to Cris," she would say in these moments of wifely discipline. "You know she is very sensitive. If you must bully somebody, bully me. Wives, I suppose, were made to be bullied."

"Bullied—sensitive; what do you mean, Angeline? Don't I know Crissie just like a book? She is my own kin, and it's a pity if I don't understand her better than any body else. Do you suppose she minds what I say to her when I am vexed? Poh! Why, she expects I will be a little rough sometimes. Father was before me, and she knows where it comes from. Don't try to teach me, Angeline, how I am to treat my own sister. Leave Crissie alone; she is a level-headed woman if ever there was one."

"Well, I know I should resent your roughness if I were your sister," laughed his wife. "I often wonder how Crissie can stand it."

"I am very glad you are not my sister. We should always be fighting like cat and dog, but as my wife, with all your whims indulged, we get along comfortably enough."

"It don't cost you any thing to indulge my whims," returned Angeline, with the asperity a rich wife knows how to throw into a cutting little speech.

Crissie had thousands of thoughts she never told to any body, and consequently she led a suppressed life. She was one of the "shut-ins." In her own room at night, while the others were entertaining company down stairs, and the children were in bed, asleep, she read and reflected. Somewhere in a work on political economy she came upon the theory of the unearned increment of rent which should be taxed for the general good, and the idea struck her in quite a new and original light. There, she said to herself, that is just what I am, an unearned increment, something that belongs to the proletariat, a kind of common, to be beaten down and cropped by all the herds—a thing without individual life, a convenience, a poor undivided remainder, left over for all the members of a large family to use, but belonging to none of them. The thought of just what she stood for in the realm of exact definitions came upon Crissie at first with a sense of the ludicrous, but later she began to cry for just nothing at all, as women do ; and old memories stirred in her, and sobs broke up the depths of her placid exterior. She recalled her only love affair with a new shock of pain— how Salmon had broken it off with his strong, heavy hand, because Judson was poor, and he wanted Crissie to minister to his comfort ; and now Judson was dead, and she was an attachment in a rich man's house, serving on to twice seven years.

It was a few days after Crissie's tempestuous night, such a night as brings new weather in the soul, that Crissie went to church in the village with the children and the governess, and the young clergyman preached that powerful but erratic sermon about our duty to ourselves and the perfection of being. The seed fell on prepared ground and Crissie came home with her eyes so feverishly bright that Mrs. Poindexter asked her at the luncheon table if she were not well. Oh, yes, she was quite well, never better. In fact there was so much moral dynamite stored up in Crissie's brain at that moment, it is a wonder it did not explode and blow the roof off. Crissie was not absolutely dependent. Her father had left her a small portion at his death, which her brother Salmon, it must be said to his credit, had managed with excellent judgment. He was always joking her about her estate, telling her that some day it might actually amount to ten thousand dollars, and perhaps by his shrewd and skillful manipulations might yield her an interest of ten per cent.

"Of course," he would say to his wife, "Cris will never use a penny of it; I give her all the money she wants, and she is naturally economical. When she dies, it will come to the children; and it is a mere matter of form, my keeping it separate, with an account-book of its own. You see what a conscientious fellow I am."

But Mrs. Poindexter, who was always on the alert about Crissie, with her sharp feminine eyes noticed that a change had come over her sister-in-law. Her eye was brighter, her very step more energetic and purposeful. What could it mean? Had leaven got into Crissie's dough? When not engaged with her household duties, she was always busy in her own room writing out notes from some book, and footing up little columns of figures on scraps of paper. One of these fell into her sister-in-law's hands, and she could make nothing of it, but she kept it to show to Salmon, and then forgot all about it. It happened one afternoon that Crissie had written an important letter which she wished to post privately in the village. She asked for the carriage; of course she could always have it when it was not in demand for some other member of the household. But it so chanced this afternoon that Mrs. Poindexter was going to the next town for a drive, where she would meet her husband, just returned from the city.

Crissie withdrew to her own room, and with trembling, eager hands, buttoned her street-jacket and tied on her bonnet. It was the first step toward a new departure. She slipped out of the side door, and through the grounds, to evade the children. She set off along the village road in a half-run, which settled into a dog-trot, and finally lapsed into a quick, nervous walk. Crissie was naturally not much of a walker. Now the exercise became delightful to her, and she suspected that she would have aged very young if something had not come to stir her up. The sky was of a cool November blue, with streaks and patches of purple cloud sailing high. The dark hills had warm gleams upon them, and the air tingled in the nostrils and braced the system like a cordial. The naked trees, rooted in mosses, looked friendly and sympathetic; and as she went along, scattering the fallen leaves with the swish and flow of her skirts, her brain seemed to be humming some old doggerel, keeping time to the motion of her feet. First it went " Te-tum, te-tum, te-tum. I am not, I am not." Then it changed a little, " I will not be, I will not be an unearned increment."

As Crissie came back a few hours later she met the carriage with Mrs. Poindexter and her husband beside her on the back seat, looking fairly blossomed red in the face with prosperity, and with his clothes all new as if they had just come off the shop counter. They stopped the carriage and took her in. "Why, Cris," said her sister-in-law, "I thought you never walked. I thought you disliked walking."

"I thought so to," said Cris, "but I find that I do like it. I am discovering some new things about myself."

Mrs. Poindexter telegraphed with her eyes to her husband, and he returned the glance, quite puzzled.

"Well, I have made a pleasant discovery, too, Cris, and in your interest," said Salmon. "Your little fortune yields a whole thousand this year."

"I am glad of it," Cris returned demurely, though she was quaking inside. "I shall need the money."

"Don't you have sufficient pocket-money, Cris?"

"I don't mean that. I am going to live for a time on my income."

Salmon gave a scornful, incredulous laugh, and Angeline turned quite pale. She saw the moment of revolt had come.

"Bless my soul," cried Salmon, as if a musquito had

revolted against his big hand. "If our Cris isn't going to be independent, and live all alone by herself, and have nothing to do with nobody."

"That's about it," and Cris shut her mouth firmly, and then opened it again, clinching her hands under the edge of the carriage-robe to give her strength. "A woman, though she is unmarried—a dreadful old maid—has a right to some portion of her own life. She is an individual, and not an un———" She checked herself. It would be too ridiculous to betray that secret. Cris said this over with deliberate slowness, as if she had been coaching herself a long time, which, in fact, was the case. But she was really so excited she hardly knew what she was saying.

Salmon again laughed scornfully as the carriage moved slowly forward, and he sat there just opposite his sister—that ungrateful sister-worm who at last had turned. He refused to take her seriously, and yet he felt a strong impulse of rising passion. "I never knew, Cris, there was any insanity in our family, but I begin to think you are out of your mind. What do you propose to do, now you are about to assert your brand-new independence and have it all your own way?"

Cris pulled one of those little slips of paper out of her pocket she had been scribbling on so much of late and began to read. "I am going to spend the winter in New York and shall visit art galleries, listen to music, and go to the theater. The Bruces have promised to take charge of me. They have already found me a boarding-place. I should not wonder if I began to crimp my hair. In the spring I am going to Germany, living is so cheap and delightful there. I know just with whom I am going to stay—Frau Lippert, Alter Strasse, Wiesbaden. Oh, such a homelike place and such good cooking! You couldn't hire an attic in New York for what I shall pay Frau Lippert. I am enjoying it all in anticipation. You know I have never seen much of the world." The carriage now stopped at the door and the master of it descended in a rage: "You are crazy, crazy as a loon, to think of streaking off over the world alone. It is not decent or respectable, and I will never permit it. Besides, you are horribly hard-hearted to wish to leave the children when they are at such an interesting age and so attached to you."

"There is a child in my own soul that has been crying in the dark this many a year," said Cris: "and I know, Salmon A. Poindexter, and so do you, that I belong absolutely to myself." She swept out of the room looking a foot taller than usual. Salmon gazed after her with stupid, lowering wonder, and then he fell into a state of angry collapse, and for several days almost refused to speak to his sister. But his wife, in a sudden, unexpected fit of generosity, took Crissie's side.

"I am glad you are going," said she. "I respect you for it, Cris. Salmon has no business to behave as he does; and I know now that I have wronged you. Hundreds of times I have told people that you liked to be a second mother to the children—to give up every thing and stay at home, and bear my burdens. I made myself half believe it, and now I am so sorry, Crissie. Say you forgive me." Cris kissed her sister-in-law. It was just before she entered the carriage to take the train for New York. If Salmon A. had known just what part the young minister had unwittingly played in his domestic affairs, I believe he would have felt like thrashing him.

CHAPTER XLIV.

JOE ELMORE AND BOB SMARTWEED AT HOME.

YOU may have heard of the literary housewife who stewed her angels. Miss Candace has asked me for a recipe to do up villagers. She thinks she would like to can some for winter use. I can only say that villagers must never be taken in a crude state. It is bad art, and bad for the mental digestion. You must cook them a long time, letting them simmer gently over a slow fire— so to speak, in their own sauce. You must not try to make them look exactly like any body you have known, but you must put the real essence of human nature into them. You must have great regard to that invisible side of villagers which, like the shadowed hemisphere of the moon, we do not see with the naked eye. And when they come out of your preserving-kettle done to a turn, though they live just across the street or in your own house, they will not know themselves; they will believe that, like malaria, they belong to the next town. I should say that it is well to mix more of sugar than of vinegar in the confection, and the product will be a kind of sweet pickle which seems to hit the average of human nature, neither good nor bad, but a little of both.

Now we are getting ready for Thanksgiving, and the woods and hills stand so still and look so knowing these gray days, I fancy they understand it all. The old houses warm up slowly for the beloved festival, like the great bake-ovens, where pies, and turkeys, and chicken pasties all go in together. Did it ever strike you that the world is very much like a Thanksgiving bake-oven? We are all put into the heat and stress of life, but the product is not as calculable as are the viands coming out of the old oven. Some come out overdone, some underdone, some juicy and sweet, some all dried up and without substance, some with such a nice brown crust and light as a feather, others heavy as lead and bad for the digestion. Some are crisp, others are very tough. Some get just the right burn on them, but nearly all are scorched too much or not well done on the under-crust.

The mystic pre-Thanksgiving rites consist in cleaning, and brushing a great deal. Windows must be washed, rugs shaken, carpets swept with tea-leaves, and all the table-service new burnished. We show our thankfulness by trying to be very clean. The sons and daughters and grandchildren and great-grandchildren are all coming home. We seem to hear their voices afar off down the railroad track and the blue hills open their arms to take in the rovers, the world-weary exiles from the hearthstone, and the flocks of little children who make the air so sweet with their lispings. It is an autumn freshet of kindred that floods the village and leaves a high-water mark of good feeling.

Jake Small has been wondrously important and busy of late. An air of mystery has hung round him amusing to witness, and he has now absolutely no time to attend to Mrs. Small and her eight children in the way of kindlings, firewood, provisions, and the general comforts of life. Jake believes in a special providence whose business it is to take care of his family and preside over the domestic hearth, and as heaven thus far has been kind to him in the shape of good neighbors who would think it a scandal to let any one, however worthless, seriously suffer within the town limits, he finds himself quite at ease to attend to other people's affairs.

Jake has a patron to whom he is wholly subservient. This is Joe Elmore, Margaret's brother, now in his second year at college, and very high in his secret fraternity.

Jake taught Joe all he knew when a boy about woodcraft, fishing and gunning, and has always held him in the greatest respect and affection, because Joe puts him down in his place and assumes the mastery over him with a perfectly unscrupulous hand. He is as fond of Joe Elmore as he is of his ridiculous gore of land, and will follow him about like a whipped dog that loves the hand that beats it. In his high Sophomoric dignity Joe felt it was absolutely necessary to look up some nice girl upon whom he could fix his affections, some charmer to dream about and scribble bad verses to, while he kept her photograph stuck in his looking-glass and was joked about her by his chum. It would be delightful to correspond with this maiden on the sly, though there was no reason for not doing so openly. Joe had looked around for an eligible girl in the village to whom he could devote himself, and he found a very nice one in the person of Stella Withers, the eldest daughter of that Widow Withers who married " Brother," and the sister of the twins. When Joe selected his girl, much as he might have chosen the finest pippin on an apple tree, he felt himself to be a connoisseur in girls; nothing but the best could pass muster with him. What made the situation deliciously dramatic was the fact that he had a rival, and must guard his girl with Argus-eyes.

Joe had promised his sister Margaret and his aunt solemnly not to go to wine-parties. He felt it a grievance, for if there was any thing he coveted it was the reputation of being very fast while he retained his pristine innocence. He had been made very ill by smoking a few cigarettes in the privacy of his own room, so that he might tell the fellows that he did smoke sometimes. He had been invited to drink tea twice at the houses of a brace of old professors, and had been petted and praised by their very mature sisters, cousins, and aunts. He had a glorious time among those old ladies, and when he went home at about ten at night he fairly danced across the campus, hugging himself and saying inwardly: "Whew! ain't I going it, though. This is life." He told some tremendous "whoppers" to his chum as to the age and general good looks of the faculty ladies, that he might be envied of men. Joe's heart was so pure and innocent that the smallest lapse from the college discipline made him feel like a bandit from the plains. He meant honestly to be a "dig," to justify all the sacrifices Margaret and Miss Elmore were making for him. He fully expected to turn out a very brilliant scholar, to attain a high position in life, possibly to mount to the presidency of these United States. But just now Joe desired, like many another fine young fellow, to eat his cake and have it too. It was perfectly comical to see him assume the airs of a finished gentleman, copying the manners of the president of his college, even to the mode of using his handkerchief, and then lapse, in a moment of forgetfulness, into a rather slangy college boy. He never could bear the strain of fine manners very long, but Margaret particularly enjoyed their assumption in his noblest moods.

Now that Joe had set Jake Small Argus to watch his Io in the form of Stella Withers, he felt so delightfully villainous it seemed as though his rakish propensities must be seen and known of all men. This beat making mild love to the elderly ladies at professorial teas all hollow. Joe's rival was an old friend and former comrade, whom he had learned to distrust, if not to hate. He was no other than Robert Smartweed, the very "cute" young reporter on a small city paper, said daily being possessed of an immense stock of brass, assurance, and wicked inventions.

It published probably the worst-looking cuts of public people that ever were devised. The very badness and impossibleness of these cuts helped to sell the paper;

people bought it to see how far the pictorial art could sink before it touched bottom. The stock of pictures which did duty on all occasions got shuffled up like a pack of playing-cards, and the editor forgot to whom special ones belonged, and used them quite at random. A saintly philanthropist or great divine was often represented by some noted pugilist or murderer of extreme ferocity. Bob Smartweed felt very proud of his profession. There was nothing he cared to do but furnish highly-spiced matter for his journal. He was naturally of a chilly nature, and the cool impudence engendered in him by his favorite vocation had congealed and hardened until it was thought by his landlady hardly necessary to keep a refrigerator in her basement, even in summer. It hardly can be said that he never had been young, but the semblance of youth he once may have possessed was quite lost in the office of the illustrated daily. At the time of which I am writing, the Sphinx of Egypt was actually frisky compared with Bob. Tadmor in the desert would seem juvenile beside him, and as for the hills, we know the little ones sometimes skip like lambs and the great ones like rams, so it would be impossible to compare this nineteenth-century youth even to them. He might possibly fraternize with "chaos and old night," but nothing more nearly up to date. The sarcastic expression and look of universal knowledge that came over Bob when you tried to tell him any thing was very amusing. He made every body feel as green as grass, even his Grandfather Maydew, who lives in our village; and as to Grandma Maydew, she had a kind of shuddering dread and delight in Bob, such as *Gretchen* may have felt when she first encountered *Faust*.

"I feel kind of scared to have you on that paper," she said timidly to Bob, who was at home for the autumn holidays, looking up at him through her innocent old glasses while paring a pan of rosy-cheeked apples for

Thanksgiving pies. "You know all them murders, and suicides, and divorces, and babies smothered by whisky-drinking mothers, or burned to crisp on red-hot stoves. Oh, it is dretful," and she vaguely waved her hand as if she had seen a vision of these noisome things like a flock of carrion birds flying in at the windows of the editor's sanctum. "Oh, it is dretful to have you there," and the nice old lady heaved a deep, tremulous sigh. "What have I got to do with the murders and suicides?" returned Bob, brushing himself off. He was always brushing, being particularly nice about his person, even to the tips of his well-kept finger-nails.

Grandma Maydew opened her mouth to answer his question and then closed it again. She hated to betray her ignorance to the sneer of her grandson Bob, but she had always secretly felt that he was some way implicated in the murders, and suicides, and other atrocities, and it had been a subject of secret grief to her.

"I will tell you what, grandma," Bob resumed, with condescending gentleness, "you must not be frightened by head-lines double-leaded." "Head-lines double-loaded," repeated the old dame, more mystified than ever. Could he mean dynamite? She meant to ask Marthy when she came home that evening. Marthy was Bob's sister, who taught school in the village. She was sharp too, but in a different way from Bob, and she would surely know what head-lines double-leaded meant.

"Well," she resumed, with another quivering sigh, "the world is getting away from me. I can't pretend to keep track of things. We never have had a murder here in this town, though we have had 'most every thing else in my time, and I do hope we never shall have one."

"It's entirely unnecessary to get one up for me to report in our paper," returned Bob, with one of his rare laughs; "and mind what I say, granny, don't be worried by what you read. It's most of it——"

"You don't mean to say it's all a pack of lies?"

"No, not quite that; but it's cooked up—doctored to suit the public palate—a little sage, and pepper, and summer-savory, such as you put in your turkey stuffing, granny."

"Well, mind what I tell you, Robert, it's devil's cooking."

Bob took his hat and went out for an afternoon stroll, and his course lay in the direction of the big sycamore tree and Stella Withers's home. Jake Small had been on the look-out for him, and had written to Joe Elmore, who was coming home for his vacation, and, indeed, did arrive the next evening, a cabalistic note which ran thus: "The enemy have hove in sight. He is kind of laying around loose just at present; but I think he will put in some fine work before long. You had better get home immediate." This was written on a postal-card without signature, in such a terrible hand it actually amounted to a secret cipher, for it could only be made out by the one to whom it was sent.

Jake saw Bob Smartweed go into the house, and ensconcing himself in the shadow of the big tree, he watched and listened. Presently a tune was struck up on the piano, and then it stopped, and then it began again. Bob was making a long call. Jake affectionately felt of a thick stick he carried, and almost patted it in his desire to exercise it on Smartweed's head. After a while Bob came out and lingered a little at the door, with the rosy face of Miss Stella just behind him. Jake sauntered away, but not so far that he did not hear every thing that was said:

"So you think you can't go? I am very sorry."

"I'm engaged," lisped Stella, sweetly, and then Bob gave her a long, searching look, and turned and walked slowly away. Bob had been asking Stella to take a buggy-ride on Thanksgiving afternoon. Most of the young men and maidens of this part of the country seem to think Sundays and holidays were mainly invented to give them an opportunity for buggy-riding. Joe Elmore had engaged Stella in advance for this particular occasion, having in his mind's eye his Uncle Hillman's new rig—a shining buggy and excellent fleet-footed horse, which he had already arranged to borrow in order to cut as great a dash as possible in town. There was at that time but one rather poor livery-stable in the village, and Joe knew well enough that Bob Smartweed could procure nothing better than an old slouch of a horse and a very rusty rattletrap of a conveyance.

After Bob Smartweed had moved off from the door of the cottage, Stella lingered a little on the porch to pick some dead leaves from a few potted plants which stood there under cover. She was humming a merry little air which seemed to go to the words, "I will not be a reporter's bride." Jack Small crept up to the steps and put his hand to his ragged cap, and said in a loud whisper:

"If Mr. Joe knew as him was snoopin' round here, miss, he'd give him a knock on the crown, and if you says the word, miss, I'll do it myself."

Miss Stella's fancy was delightfully titillated by the fact that she had two adorers that were at daggers drawn, and might come to blows on her account, but she snubbed Jake Small, as he deserved.

"Go along," said she, quite uppishly, "and let Mr. Joe take charge of his own affairs."

"So I will, miss; he's a-coming on the eight train tomorrow night, and him will look arter his own preserve in his own way."

Joe arrived duly, so full of self-content and delightful juvenility the village seemed to grow brighter merely by his presence. It amused his sister Margaret not a little to watch Joe's maneuvers and subterfuges in getting away to see his girl. The excuses he made for his sudden disappearances and long absences were sometimes of the thinnest. He tried to meet Bob Smartweed and give him a little touch of swagger and defiance, but for a day or two without success. On the afternoon of Thanksgiving Day Joe got his Uncle Hillman's horse and buggy, as I have said, per contract, and drove round by a back way to Stella's house. He had never felt so delightfully rakish in his life as on this occasion when taking out his chosen girl with another man's horse, which he did not intend by any means to spare. If the beast just escaped laming and foundering, it was all that could be expected, considering the occasion. Joe handed his girl in with a flourish, and the young couple bowled down the pike and along the Roundabout Road in the highest glee. Stella wore a particularly becoming fall hat, and her cheeks glowed like red roses. As they neared the glen where the smoke from charcoal pits was ascending through the naked trees and the still air, they saw before them another buggy pursuing the same road. Joe knew it was one of Haines's horses, and he guessed who was in the vehicle. By speeding his very willing nag, much to the delight of Stella, who was high-spirited and courageous, he managed to come up abreast of the other buggy, and get a peep at the occupants. The driver was, of course, Bob Smartweed, and the girl beside him proved to be no other than our old acquaintance, Freddie Haven, the most popular girl in the village, who, since the marriage of Ned Buckner to Sylvia Macy, had been quite subdued, but was now again taking to the society of boys and youths of Bob's age with fresh avidity. Seeing that his old friend Joe intended to get past and give him his dust on the road, Smartweed applied the lash to the back of his lean nag with such vigor that he gave a great lurch forward, and fairly got away from the Hillman horse to the distance of some rods.

"Don't she look old and wrinkled?" asked the blooming Stella, after Bob's spurt on the road had carried them beyond ear-shot. "I should think she would be ashamed to fix herself up as she does."

Joseph was too much excited to answer Stella. He was bound to run by Smartweed if it cost his Uncle Hillman his best horse. So he laid on the lash, and amid a clatter of wheels and a great cloud of dust the nag bounded forward, while Stella emitted a series of shrill little shrieks indicative of her excitement and delight. Bob's hired horse had not much staying power, and as it turned out the livery buggy had less. Joe, with his powerful horse, soon came alongside, and the two young men glared at each other horribly. Again Bob bent forward and laid on the lash with all his might. The poor rackabones gave a high desperate leap; something cracked about the forward wheels, and in a moment the buggy-box had half slipped from the running gear, a wheel was off, and Miss Freddie was sitting in the soft part of the road quite unscratched, and Bob, equally unharmed, had fallen his full length on the turf by the side of the way.

It cost Smartweed half a month's salary to repair the damage of that deadly encounter. The story got abroad in the village, and there was a great roar of laughter. Uncle Hillman enjoyed the little tale and pardoned Joe for bringing his horse back quite wind-blown and knocked up. Joe was more bumptious than ever. He felt that he had achieved something in the fast, reckless, dissipated line worthy the hero of a penny dreadful. Smartweed had been discomfited, and poor Freddie had been obliged to walk back four miles to the village. But Bob had vengeance in his eye. He intended to do a stroke of business before leaving the village. So after a day or two he arrayed himself in his smoothest, most oily fashion, and called on John Dean. He was received in that great man's snuggery, where cigars were handed, and the two, with chairs drawn up before the open fire, fell into easy, unrestrained chat without the least suggestion of note-book or pencil.

"Of course you won't publish any thing I say here in my own house where you are received as a guest," remarked Dean, who was perfectly delighted to have a chance to unburden his mind to a reporter; "you will consider my remarks strictly confidential."

"Strictly," returned Bob with mild assurance. "We have a theory in our office that men are never interviewed unless they wish to be; and I know, Mr. Dean, you don't care to appear in print."

"Exactly," said Dean, exulting in his heart at the thought that reporters are all egregious liars, and the more they say they won't interview the more they mean to. Consequently, in the blissful hope of seeing his opinions reported in full under a vile cut, he opened the whole of his mind to Smartweed, kept his finger rotating by the half-hour together, and made even that hardened young man gasp for breath. But Dean's cigars were very good, and when Bob did escape into the open air he indemnified himself by taking a number of them. I may say here that John Dean subscribed at once for six months to the illustrated daily, and scanned its columns every morning to find the interview rehashed and dressed up in the best sensational style. But he never did find it, and no man was more disgusted with that rascally reporter, who for once had told the truth.

Bob stepped across the street to the house of Judge Magnus, and was received with much kindness by the judge himself, who happened to be in a genial mood. "I am afraid of you fellows," the judge remarked. "Among you I feel as if I must protect my secrets much as one guards one's pocket-book in a crowd of pickpockets. Your paper has lied about me up hill and down. You have misconstrued my motives and defamed my acts."

"All great men are lied about," returned Bob solemnly. "That is the penalty you pay for greatness. Lies do a man like you no harm, Judge Magnus. You are too well braced in the affection, the esteem—what shall I say?—the reverence of the people."

The judge smiled at the young fellow's coolness, but his vanity began to warm up, and as Bob wormed his way into the judge's mind, all his political secrets, his damaging opinions of his friends and associates trickled out. Bob protested entirely too much that he should never betray the judge's confidence, and thinking it over later the great man went about with an uneasy, half-nauseated feeling in his mind, until, behold, one day there appeared in the illustrated daily the whole interview, doctored, dressed up, spiced with malignity, and peppered with misconstruction, and at the head of it stood one of those dreadful grinning cuts, labeled with the name of the illustrious Judge Magnus.

I must draw the curtain. There was wailing and gnashing of teeth and tearing of hair; and the judge believes this interview has cost him the nomination for governor of the state.

CHAPTER XLV.

A BUNDLE OF LOVE-LETTERS.

THE young man named Hugh has reached a turning-point in his destiny; he is going to be married. These last days and weeks of the year he has been tramping about in wind and snow-flurries, rain and sunshine, taking a mute farewell of the places where he has so long practiced his druidical worship of nature, finding a kind of compensation for all his failures in the sense of a beautifully ordered universe—solid beneath his feet, sound in all its parts, governed by immutable laws, in themselves highest and noblest harmonies.

His joy during the years he has lived in our village has been in finding himself free—his own master. If he is proud at all, it is because he has never been bought and sold for money, reputation, or any poor or trifling ambition. If he has not added much to the bulk of the world's good, he has made his little protest against the ruling passions of men. He has injured no man, robbed no fellow-being, combined to harm no widow or orphan through legal means. He has broken no trust, never has he fled to Canada to escape punishment for embezzling other people's funds, never has he depleted a church treasury or watered the stock of a railroad, or made a corner in grain to raise the price of bread in poor men's mouths. He has simply lived his own life, held to his own inward convictions, laughed at his neighbor's weak points, not unkindly, and cultivated his natural instincts.

While most of his college classmates have grown old, turned gray, or worn their hair off in the pursuit of money or position, he has retained every spear of his hair, with his good, natural color, his bright eyes, and handsome teeth, and all the youthful spirits with which he was endowed. Hugh has done this by keeping up that nexus between himself and nature which belonged to him at birth, and taking hold of simple enjoyments with fresh idealism. Yes, Hugh is a bit of a genius, but it lies as much in his heart as in his head. He knows how to love the world unselfishly without rendering himself miserable if he can not possess a large share of its dirt and stones. His ideal ownership is immense. No one has ever lived in this part of the country who has so thoroughly possessed himself of the streams, woods, hills, the river, the mountains, every thing that lies under the sky.

Though village life is very narrowing to many minds, it has not injured Hugh. He has known how to skim the cream of existence where most folk let it mold on the pan. So he might have gone on for years without really fossilizing or becoming as crotchety as old Spengler, as tedious as Rastus B——, or as much of a piece of bank mechanism as Allibone. But the finger of fate seemed to point pretty conclusively to the fact that Hugh needed a new and enlarged sphere of life or his natural development would be arrested. He had pushed individualism to an extreme. The time had come to take up the burdens of humanity, and live for others. At that moment Oriana came, as I have told you, into the narrowed slit of the pupil of his eye, was photographed upon the retina, and thence by some mysterious process transmitted to his heart.

Hugh has not enjoyed the uninterrupted rapture of love's young dream. He has been walking all over the country in extreme agitation of mind. Now that he is committed to something else, owing to the perversity of his nature the old life seems to lie placid and serene behind him as if lapped in the valley of the Lord, and the new looks often vexed, doubtful, and uncertain. Yet do not for a moment suppose that he is not deeply in love with Oriana. He has tried to get tuned up by the company of bare trees—great oaks with the stiff leaves rattling on their branches, or pines making music with their fingers on the air strings, or cedars, hemlocks, and spruces, all so hearty, so unvexed by notions and crotchets and self-torments as they lift themselves after the summer's decay into the cold crystal air with a great sense of rejoicing at the core. The dead leaves upon the moss have spoken to him, and the brave strong limbs that in an access of new life have pushed them off to secure enlarged conditions of growth. He has tramped to all the hill-tops and looked at the clean-cut blue mountains whose faces he knows so well, now like hard gems graved with a sharp-edged tool. He has found his way to Cedar Glen Hollow and the little red schoolhouse, but the school-money ran short this year before the customary three-months' term ended, and the school is not in session. The scholars are dispersed, and the red-haired, nasal-voiced teacher has not yet begun her rule.

As the door was unlocked, Hugh entered and gazed about at the empty, cold little place, with its hacked benches and scribbled walls, the box-stove turned red and rusty, the ceiling fallen in patches, and the blackboard with its sums still remaining. Hugh peeped into Tim Long's desk in the hope of finding a stray composition left there by chance, but it was devoid of all interest, though half filled with a litter of school-boy rubbish. He sat down on one of the low benches as if he too had come there to be a learner in the school of life, and because of his shortsightedness, disobedience, and folly could only gain admittance to the primary grade. For almost the first time in his life he felt the need of perfect humility and some extraneous aid to help put away pride and inward resistance. Though he was very much in love with a charming young lady, and but partially aware of the cause of his qualms and reactionary fits, it was probably owing to the gipsy vein in him that Hugh did hesitate to give up his manly independence to take upon him the yoke of matrimony, and settle down into the rather tame, subdued barn-yard fowl, which to his vision symbolized the average domestic man.

Now that he sat in the cold little school-house, of all places best suited to his mood, he began to think over his courtship with Oriana, and its various ludicrous and tragic phases—its storms and calms, and wind-gusts, and thunder-claps and flashes of lightning, followed by sweet weather and inland quiet. It had probably been different from any other courtship on record, and necessarily so, considering the very positive and strongly marked characteristics of the two people engaged therein. I fancy that real courtships are generally very different from the novelists' conception. They are more prosaic and commonplace, or more original. Each one is a little drama quite by itself, so that your own experience, if you have had one, does not let you into that water-tight compartment where other lovers sit as secure as if they alone inhabited the planet.

Hugh's love-making had been difficult—not so much from any inherent stumbling-blocks in Oriana's nature as from the need they both felt of being absolutely generous and self-forgetful to the point of making each other miserable for life. Hugh had scruples about living on Oriana's fortune. Oriana had scruples about imposing a fetter on Hugh's free spirit. She feared he would regret the step if once he should take it. He feared she might covertly despise him in the end for his want of positive success in life. So they stumbled about in the dark, getting into deep bogs of misconception, and then floundering out the best they could. But after every misunderstanding, which caused them both nameless tortures, they felt that they were dearer to each other, more necessary to each other than ever—that life would not be worth the living unless they could spend it together.

Hugh sat in the cold school-house that November day, done up in his great-coat, with the clouds skurrying across the hills, and thought it all over. A grim kind of facetiousness suffused his mind as he realized how two intelligent, enlightened people not in the first flush of youth could ingeniously contrive to torment each other, while at the same time their whole prospect of earthly happiness lay in sharing a common life united in the tenderest and most enduring bonds. The folly, nay, insanity, of the whole proceeding presented itself to him, and he tried to probe his own mind and find out whether he were the guilty one. Surely Oriana was not to blame. With all her moral whimsicality and superfine notions Oriana was always noble, a creature of such infinite charm, such capacity for happiness and making others happy, he could only compare her to the earth and sky he loved so well, to nature in all its varying and delightful phases. Hugh felt positively ill when he recalled the pain he had given this woman. He took out all her letters and telegrams from a little letter-case he carried in his pocket and spread them out on Tim Long's desk, in order to study them for a few hours and try and make up his mind as to where the blame lay. I shall take the privilege of looking over his shoulder to copy some paragraphs from this singular correspondence. In order to make the thing complete, it is necessary to glean a part from Hugh's own memory of his wicked little notes.

She—"We can not live together, and we can not live without each other; what are we going to do! You never gave me any thing but the little black arrow-head, and I will send that by return mail, with all your letters and telegrams."

He (telegram)—"Wait—I am coming by the next train."

After three days, having thought better of the journey: "You know your taunt is most ungenerous. I have given you all I have that is of any value, and you scorn it. I will take nothing back from you. I will shed my heart's blood before I take any thing back."

She—"I knew you would not come. It is silly to talk about shedding your heart's blood. We are not acting in a cheap play at a dime museum, and you would do the *Claude Melnotte* business very badly. I do not believe we shall ever understand each other. I am high-strung and passionate; so are you, with a great many old-bachelor crotchets thrown in. I never knew so set a man at your age. We had better repent at leisure before we marry in haste. This is probably the last time I shall tell you that I think the affair had better be considered off. It is growing actually childish. I feel myself to be getting imbecile. When we have finally settled this matter, I shall try to return to a state of calm, but I fear my life will have been hopelessly spoiled."

He—"Oriana, I walked about in the woods all last night trying to get over the smart of your terrible unkindness. You are the cruelest girl in the world. You know I love you with entire, absolute devotion, and yet you will torture me like a child sticking pins into a helpless fly. When, oh, when will this cease? If it were not for the last words of your heartless letter, I should wish to shoot myself."

She (telegram)—"You had better not walk around in the woods all night, you will get malaria. Are you ill?"

He—"I might as well be dead as to be in the condition I am in. Will you marry me next month, as you once promised? A perfectly plain wedding at seven in the morning. No friends, no bride-cake, no nothing but our two selves and the parson. Answer by return mail."

She—"I do not remember ever making such an absurd promise. You are really more provoking than John Dean. He never has thrown it up to Elspeth about her money. He has always used it as if it belonged to him. Why can't you do the same with mine?"

He—"I appreciate the sarcasm of your last note, and feel it to be decidedly unhandsome. Rather than be looked upon with the contempt with which I regard J. D., I would hang myself. Could you not give your money to Mr. Bergh for the prevention of cruelty to animals? You ought to as a return for all you have inflicted on one, *i. e.*, myself. Then we might go out in the world hand in hand, like the Babes in the Wood. Telegraph me how this idea strikes you. I could get myself up as an Italian padrone; you could dance and sing to a tambourine. Do you accept my terms?"

She—"I would not telegraph an answer to any such nonsense. What would the operator think? You know you refuse to take this matter seriously. You are trifling with me, and I am just breaking my heart for nothing. Elspeth suggests by letter marked private that I had better get up a flirtation with somebody else. I send you this proposal of Elspeth's because I will not do anything underhand. What do you think of it?"

He—"I should probably, in the hypothetical case you state, come immediately and break the other fellow's head. I am half inclined to think you make the suggestion in order to throw me over. Have I ever done anything so despicable as to throw out the hint that I could ever think of another woman? Do I not adore the very ground you tread on? Am I not ready to devote my whole life to your happiness—every thought, feeling, impulse, and aspiration? When I fancy you are thinking of me, it makes me dizzy with joy."

She—"Rather late in the day for such a gush of sentiment. One would think you had not yet emerged from jackets. Please do not send me any more letters copied out of the 'Perfect Letter Writer.' I know you dread to give up your bachelor independence and roving habits. You think I will turn out a whimsical, perverse, peevish, neuralgic, headachy kind of woman, who will make a bond-slave of you, and deprive you of all liberty of thought and impulse. This is the real trouble between us. You love your old ways, and old books, and old pipes more than any thing else, and fear you may regret the change. I have felt this to be true all along, and I release you without submitting you to the humiliation of asking for your freedom. Why did we ever meet? Oh, I am a very unhappy person."

He—"You have the wickedest nib to your pen any woman ever had, and every time you use it you draw blood. If you were poor, it would be very different. You would not then feel that you have the right to tutor me. Our natural positions are reversed, and I do not see how we are ever to get over this insuperable obstacle. But do not mind what I say now; you have made me angry. Haven't you ever a kind word to fling to me? You might telegraph."

She—"I don't send love missives by telegraph or on postal-cards. You have now begun to doubt my—my feeling for you, and I think it must soon end. You will keep flinging it up in my face that I have a little money. I never knew any thing so scandalous in all the days of my life. If I were a perfect termagant, you could not talk to me much worse than you do. I do not at all know what I am made of to stand it. Ah, me, I am very miserable. How terrible it would be if we should find ourselves tied together with nothing really in common but a mutual disposition to squabble and bicker! If you should repent the step you had taken, I think I should commit suicide. I feel so snubbed by your last letter I hardly know what to say or do. I am sure you regret having written it; but you would do the same thing over again next week. We are too old to take deliberately the risk of life-long misery, and I think we had better consider this correspondence closed."

Now, as Hugh sat in the cheerless school-house at Cedar Glen, with the letters spread out before him on Tim Long's desk, he felt an emotion of intense wonder and astonishment that two sensible grown people should get into such a boggle by their own perversity and misdirected nobleness of nature. But sitting there, with almost the whole history of his unique love-affair in view, Hugh saw with a rush of repentant feeling that he had been in fault, not only through his false pride, which haggled about the bargain in taking what love offered, but also by a certain wild and nomadic streak in his nature that made it hard for him to bow and worship the domestic ideal. It was selfish doubtless, and Oriana, with her subtle woman's instinct, had felt it all out, and had doubted with perfect propriety the wisdom of the step they thought of taking.

It all came upon Hugh as a new discovery—his pride and tough-rooted independence, the sense of resistance toward yielding to an absolute self-surrender. At that moment he felt that he loved Oriana for the first time as she deserved to be loved. He resolved to burn his ships for her sake and cut loose from every yearning for the old life. He looked about for the stub of some ancient pen, an ink-bottle, and the stray blank leaf of an old copy-book, and sitting there he wrote the best and greatest, if not the first, love-letter of his life. I shall not tell what it contained further than to say that it might be expressed in Gen. Grant's immortal words, " Immediate and unconditional surrender."

And now they are going to be married, and next day sail on an Italian steamer for Naples. Hugh has said farewell to all his favorite haunts, the hills and fields, the rocks and woods, and trout-brooks, and forest walks, and lonely glens, and waterfalls, but he has slipped away just before the close of the year without taking a formal leave of any of his friends in the village except Aunt Dido. Poor Aunt Dido is heart-broken, and yet so happy to have Hugh settled in life. She laughs with one eye and cries with the other. To relieve her mind from its burden of grief for the final departure of her eccentric but charming young man she has plunged into communistic literature between her spells of cooking, and now, she says laughingly, mixes a little dynamite with her crullers and seed-cakes. She has taken up the works of Mr. Henry George, but merely as a means of distraction.

" 'Tain't Progress and Poverty," she says, that she cares about so much ; it's only to relieve the destitution and heart-ache she feels for the loss of Hugh.

CHAPTER XLVI.

LOOSE ENDS AND DROPPED STITCHES OF VILLAGE LIFE.

WITH us Thanksgiving and Christmas seem to lean toward each other, and clasp hands. Like righteousness and peace, they meet together and kiss. The sweetness of family affections has been hived in the life cells, and with the pressure of this good time the comb yields abundant store of honey. In the fall and winter holidays every body comes home, and there is a little freshet of news and gossip. Many dropped threads of village life which have strayed away into distant places can then be picked up and woven into the story without an end, with more or less of consistency in the web. The village tingles with pleasant expectations of weddings and social events.

And to begin with the news : Those two Busy Bees, the middle one and the youngest, are both soon to be married from the house of their sister, Mrs. Worldly Wiseman. The middle girl, with her turn for æsthetics and decorative art, has taken up with a rich oldish man, with grown children, who are furious because she dares to intrude into the family, and refuse to come to the wedding. The youngest, that volatile butterfly-girl, will bestow her hand on a young drummer who knows all about silks, and laces, and Lyons velvet, and goes to Paris every year to buy for his house. So it would seem that not one of these Bee marriages is ideal, only conventional and respectable. Not one of the Bees I fear has that dainty little cross which is said to lie at the base of the forefinger in the palm of every person who finds his or her true mate.

But there is a delicious little secret which I must confess has given me a great deal of pleasure, especially because I know all about it, and it has not yet leaked out and got abroad in town. We all of us love to be ensconced behind the scenes while the rest of the world are kept out in the cold; only one aches so to tell, that the pleasure is somewhat modified.

I sympathize deeply with the little sisters, Miss Henriette and Miss Sophie, who in their delight and exultation seem to be more one soul in two bodies than usual. Their tiny house is fairly bursting with the importance of what it tries to hold. The cat (I firmly believe she is an enchanted princess) sits on the little porch and licks her white fur with a knowing look. The window-panes seem to wink and the vines to wave toward me as I go past. Shall I let out the secret? I must. Miss Crayshaw has been spending a few weeks in our neighborhood, not just in the village, but with a friend some miles away, and she is going to marry Mr. Allibone, our bank cashier, that poor man who was so dreadfully scathed by the charming adventuress, Mrs. Bridgenorth. It would take too long to tell you how it came about. They were thrown together quite accidentally by a designing friend; and I think Miss Crayshaw felt that in poor Mr. Allibone's fate there was something similar to her own. And you know sympathy is akin to love; only one little step remains to be taken.

Though both are quite mature, and Miss Crayshaw seems a little affected and artificial, I should not at all wonder if they discovered that tiny cross at the base of the forefinger upon which the adepts in palmistry lay such stress. The little sisters are going to have a wedding of their own. All their predictions have come true, and who can help being a partaker in their pure, unselfish joy, although they idealize Crayshaw in the most ridiculous way, and have as much sentiment about her as if she were sweet sixteen instead of six-and-thirty?

One swallow does not make a summer. There will still remain many perpetual widows and widowers and old maids in the village. The constant Spengler still continues to shut himself up and hold a day of fasting and prayer when one of his friends or acquaintances commits the enormity of a second marriage. There are spinsters like Marcella Hildreth and Miss Candace, Melissa Tooler, and Marthy Smartweed, who might as well be one hundred and fifty as on the bright side of fifty for all practical purposes of matrimony. There are widows like Sist'r Ann and Aunt Mariar who have been too severely scorched in the ordeal to think of marrying again if they could, which is out of all question. There are others, like the Widow Holcomb and young Mrs. Holt who are too comfortable to think much of taking another mate, having a good nest already built and stocked with means sufficient to keep it in perfect repair.

As for my delightful friend Milly Grant, the milliner, I am not so certain about her. She is still on the Roundabout Road of life, and must remain there until I can take her up at a point further on. I could wish that some man, wise and good, and sensible enough to win her love, might get a peep at her through the keyhole of her bright little shop, and learn how shrewd and clever, sympathetic, and even noble, she is.

But if this never happens, Milly will do well. She will have her Spinoza and her Plato from which to draw an ideal philosophy and maxims for the higher life. She will still love folks, and laugh at their oddities and foibles with a kindly heart. She will still idolize the memory of a bad father, being of that feminine mold that must idolize something, and will go weekly, summer and winter, to put flowers on his grave. She will still take that precious MS. volume of her father's poems from the case and read some favorite verses to her intimate friends, saying thoughtfully, "When I am rich enough, these shall be published." It is something to live for. As to Margaret Elmore and many another nice girl in our village, their story lies warm and rosy in the bosom of the future. Next year, perhaps, shall be Pentecostal and bring them the perfect blessing for which their pure young hearts are waiting.

Salmon A. Poindexter is still with his family at his country-seat, the Cedars. He has written to his sister Crissie, who is now abroad, that if she will come home, he will build a new wing to the villa, with apartments for her use, which she can shut off when she wishes to be alone. He will give her a pony-carriage for her exclusive pleasure, and as they now have an excellent housekeeper, there is no need of her taking charge. She can live and do as she pleases, only he wants her back again because she is necessary to his comfort. But Mrs. Poindexter has also written. She is perfectly delighted Crissie is having a happy time abroad. Crissie's last letter contained an account of how she had learned to drink beer and eat black bread, and was very amusing, especially her account of the way she danced at the Hofrath's ball with a great red-bearded colonel in sword and spurs. Mrs. Poindexter has just nursed Beatrice through the measles. She has been getting acquainted this year with the minds and hearts of her children, and although they miss Aunt Crissie so much, still she desires her to remain abroad until she is quite satisfied, and has taken her fill of sights and impressions. As an inducement for Cris to go to Italy this winter she has forwarded a handsome sum, quite unbeknown to Salmon A., who thinks she has spent the whole amount on two evening dresses.

Just now I saw Marcella Hildreth pass the window with her uncle Jones Davis, a tall soldierly-looking man, erect as a young ash, with long silky white hair waving about his head, and an active black eye as quick to see a pretty girlish face as it ever was. Davis had always been the strong, loving friend of his brother-in-law, our heavenly-minded deacon, known among the children as the town clock, albeit a very different type of man, a man of the world, fond of jovial companions, good suppers, and all the pleasures of life, and though not a scoffer at sacred things, by no means a religionist. Still he loved the steady-going deacon, and for many years, until the war broke out, was accustomed to drive over with his wife on Thanksgiving Day from the county town where he lived to break bread with the Hildreths.

But the war came and thrust its sharp sword into many a united family circle, and Jones Davis was known as a copperhead of a very rank and offensive kind. The deacon, on the other hand, felt his heart burning for the Union cause, and gave his money to equip regiments, and sent his son to die, burned up, they say, in the Battle of the Wilderness, a year after his first colonel, Ralph Freeman, fell mortally wounded on the field. For some time after Sumter was fired on there was little or no communication between the Davis and Hildreth families, but when Thanksgiving Day came, because old habits are strong, and his wife urged him to try and heal the breach silently made, Jones Davis drove over as usual to the village with his wife and daughters. As the horses drew up before the deacon's door he came out bareheaded, and before any one knew what he meant to do, he, without saying a word, took them by the bits and turned the carriage round squarely in the road until the horses' heads pointed down the old pike. There were tears in his eyes and his lips were tremulous, but his hand was as firm as iron.

"Jones," said he, in a husky, broken voice, "don't come here until the war is over, and if it goes against the Union don't ever come," and then he stood and pointed down the pike like a mystic figure of fate, and Jones with his head dropped on his breast drove slowly away.

The families did not meet again for four years. The Davis girls grew to young womanhood, and the deacon yearned to see them, for he had been very fond of them as children. As the war had ended in a way to make him happy in spite of the memory of his dead boy, whose body he had sought for on the field of battle, but never found, the deacon's heart was suffused with a great tender glow of gratitude. He could even find some grain of tolerance for his copperhead friends and neighbors, remembering that God tolerates them, and that the rain falls and the sun shines on the just and the unjust.

The day before Thanksgiving he said to his wife: " Mother, we will drive over to Jones's to-morrow, and I will tell you what we will do. We will sit in the wagon before his door, and wait like Lazarus before the rich man's gate for some of them to come and speak to us and bid us enter, and if Jones harbors hard feeling, still at any rate we shall have shown him that we are ready to meet him more than half-way."

So they did accordingly, and after drawing up before Davis's door, and sitting there expectantly for some minutes, the door opened and the youngest Davis girl, a bright and pleasing picture of young maidenhood, flew down the steps, and, with ready wit, unhitched the traces, and led the horse away into the stable. Then she ran back, and giving her hand to her aunt, said, " Uncle, if you and aunt will walk right in and make believe there never has been any war, father will be perfectly delighted." So they did ; and now Jones Davis is an old man, and perhaps his memory is failing, but he tries to make out that he was the strongest kind of an abolitionist.

I ought to mention that St. Patty's sons, those stalwart Western men, came home this year to eat of the sacred turkey under the family roof-tree, and there was a great gathering of kindred. It was charming to see the delight those big boys took in petting their old mother and making her happy. For the first time they met the Rev. Arthur Meeker, Drusilla's husband, and I suspect they tried very maliciously to give him the moral support he needed, partially at least, to throw off the domestic yoke. That big western ex-governor has been convulsed with inward laughter during his entire visit by the state of subjection to his wife's will in which he found poor Meeker. It has leaked out in the village that under his protection Arthur has been caught smoking a mild cigar. He was at once summoned before the bureau of domestic correction, but we hope—we almost pray—he was not utterly subdued in the inquisitorial chamber. Some people say he has actually refused to live any longer on messes and Graham food. It is even confidently predicted that within a year he may swear at his wife and demand a latch-key. But as he is a clergyman, trained up to meekness and long suffering, this is of course a profane joke invented by the old enemy.

I have peeped into some of the humble homes of the village to get a glimpse of their Thanksgiving cheer. The wish of the good French king is realized. Every laborer has a fowl, not in his pot, but in his oven; even the poor-house people have been abundantly feasted. Mrs. Judge Magnus sent the Small family what Jake called " the handsome compliment of a generous dinner." Tim McCoy has taken a new wife, an excellent, clean, strong woman, and a good cook, who will see that the "childers" are cared for like her own. The hearth is bright this year, and the humble larder well stocked. Tim does not mind if his son-in-law, Wilkins, gives him the windy side of the street. The postmistress is always true to her poor relations, nor does she forget the lowly nest where she was born. As for our one colored family, Mandy and Sambo Brown and the "pickaninnies," you should see them around the board with the "tukke" as center-piece and common object of fetish worship. How the teeth gleam, and the whites of the eyes roll up, and the tight little wool takes a new kink at this happy time, when Mandy abates the rigor of her rule and allows the children to make as much noise and litter as they please.

Between Thanksgiving and Christmas there is a great deal of coming and going. Mrs. Magnus warms up her large house hospitably for some weeks before she withdraws to Washington, and Aunt Dido is busy cooking and planning for her entertainments. This year we were all in a state of quivering expectancy over the advent of a great novelist who was coming to pay a visit of some days to the Magnus mansion. The village felt itself honored in advance by the rumor of his approach. From time to time in the past there had been no lack of distinguished visitors among us, but this celebrity was of a more exhilarating and exciting kind than any we had heretofore seen. We had read his books with avidity, and there had always been a little scramble as to who should draw them earliest from the library, and thus get the first cut of the new loaf. We had enjoyed his characters and scenes, and talked them over together to see if they "jibed" with our own experience in life. Some of us felt that he would understand our secret aspirations, and that we should be conscious of a kind of flow of sweet sympathy from his soul into ours.

Our literary young lady, who writes poetry for the local papers and occasionally gets a little piece inserted in a religious journal in one of the large cities (I think the *Religious Chromo* has printed two of her pieces), had such dreams over the advent of the great genius that she actually believed he would volunteer to offer her thin manuscript volume which she calls "Soul Thrills and Heart Hunger," to his own publisher. She had always been hidden away in a corner, unappreciated and unprized, but if he deigned to smile upon her, Fame might yet breathe her name through his trumpet. Thus she dreamed early in the morning, half awake, while all the sparrows in the vines around her window seemed to twitter the name of the great novelist. If he could have imagined one-half the silly fancies and foolish expectations of his lady admirers in the village, he would have been a great man indeed.

Mrs. Magnus had sent out invitations for an evening reception to Mr. and Mrs. Fancy Penholder. The place was in a flutter from end to end. We all endeavored to furbish up our best bib and tucker, and also to invent some suitable conversation wherewith to approach the lion. We primed ourselves with beautiful things we would say to him, delicate compliments we meant to pay, and lay awake nights getting our little speeches by heart. There was a singular previousness about this proceeding which did not strike the village mind as at all funny, but then we did not confess to each other. Secretly, we all meant to be so very clever and bright that he would see at a glance we are not clodhoppers, but thoroughly instructed people, quite abreast of every thing in literature and art, and, of course, not too much overawed by the presence of any celebrity, however portentous. And yet we all secretly knew we were ready to get down on our knees and worship if he proved in the least worthy of adoration.

Mrs. Magnus had illuminated the grounds and the Doric porch of her house with Chinese lanterns, and it was very interesting to watch the people as they poured in at the hospitable door. Poor Freddie Haven had not been invited, I am sorry to say, the social prejudice against her being just now very extreme. She therefore sat by her window in the dark, and watched all who went in, as one can fancy, with a perturbed and aching heart. There was Deacon Hildreth in his black stock and well-brushed clothes, his wisp of hair combed high up on his head, and with his comfortable stout wife on his arm quite confident that she had never looked so well in her life. Behind them came that handsome old worldling, Jones Davis, who had remained over for the occasion, with his niece Marcella on his arm, looking extremely prim in her new black silk. There was Drusilla in her business suit convoying the Rev. Arthur as if he had been a charity scholar. There was the young parson, his hair "tousled," his neckcloth a little on one side, all agog for new ideas, while his pretty wife looked as if she were thankful to have the opportunity of wearing her best gown and laces once in the season. There was the doctor, with his saintly wife and blooming grandchild, and Brother George in evening dress. Miss Candace came plain as a Quaker, and without gloves. Mr. Worldly Wiseman looked as sleek as a shiny glass bottle, and his handsome wife in a city-made gown was a little overdressed.

The Busy Bees, with their chosen suitors, made quite a flutter of high fashion as they entered. The literary young lady brought the MS. of "Soul Thrills" in a little blue bead bag, which she carried on her arm. She felt almost certain he would ask to see it. "Brother" and his wife, she that was the Widow Withers, and rosy little Stella glided in just in the wake of Miss Elmore, and Margaret, and the Sophomoric Joe, who soon made it manifest to his girl that this adoration of genius was all bosh, and they two could live a romance that would beat any thing the novelist had ever written all hollow. The little sisters came in their best frisettes and false fronts, and paid their respects with many courtesies and old-time steps. Miss Crayshaw came too, trying to pretend she did not see Mr. Allibone, whose head shone like a billiard ball. Old Madam Macy entered, looking like a duchess, and Mrs. Ned Buckner on her husband's arm seemed very happy spite of the whispers that have gone round that she is much to be pitied.

They poured in and flooded the large, handsome, light

rooms, all eager to pay homage at the shrine. *He* stood upright, expressionless, by the side of his hostess. His supercilious glance ranged coldly over the crowd. He was tall and faultlessly dressed, and when he spoke it was with an affected stammer which he had cultivated at some pains and cost to himself. He bowed just so many times a minute, bending his body at exactly the same angle each time. When relieved from the necessity of bowing, he adjusted his eye-glasses, and looked around with a perfectly impersonal glance which seemed to say, "If you think I have any thing to give away, you are mistaken. My ideas are all engaged at so much a line." After a few moments, however, he did relapse into a fatigued, world-worn expression, as if his social duties weighed upon him like lead.

After the first observations, most of the people were struck with awe and crept into corners and conversed in whispers. When the doctor, and the young clergyman, and a few others approached the lion in the hope of tickling him into a mild conversational roar, they could get nothing out of him except, "Oh, ah; I fancy you are quite right"; or, "You are really very kind to say so." But Mrs. Fancy Penholder proved to be quite another style of person. She was somewhat of the Skye-terrier order, you know, great eyes and a picturesque tangle of hair; but she dressed to a charm and was really very pretty. Her frankness in talking about her husband was truly original and engaging. She spoke of him almost as if he did not belong to her, while she was merely part of his properties for getting up his novels.

"I'm less literary than I was before I married Mr. Penholder," she said with naïve frankness to Mrs. Worldly Wiseman. "I find being literary in earnest is rather tiresome. And then I have to dress up to each of my husband's characters as they form themselves in his mind. If he has a tragic woman on the carpet, I am expected to come out in a thunder-cloud polonaise with streaks of lightning cut bias, or I must wear something very lurid and fiery. If he is in a sentimental Bopeep novel, then he will not let me put any thing on but sky-blue muslin and rosebuds. You can have no idea what a time I have trying to embody all his conceptions. I have almost lost my identity. When I am allowed to be myself, I naturally seek something light and frivolous. At home Mr. Penholder refuses to let me wear any thing that does not match the furniture, and when I am buying a new gown I have to carry the wall paper, the chairs, sofas, and carpets, even the picture-frames in my eye. Sometimes I get so mixed up with his creations I am nearly wild. There is Lady Claudia—I detest that woman, she ran away with another woman's husband, and yet for a time I had to personate her. I am fast coming to the point where I shall have absolutely no character of my own. I shall only be a faint echo of Mr. Penholder's novels."

The people escaped to the library, the hall, and the front porch to laugh over Mrs. Penholder and to groan over her husband. "Are you not dreadfully disappointed?" "What a stupid man!" "Do you think he wrote his own books?" "He evidently does not mean to give himself away." "How conceited he looks!" "Perhaps he despises us." These were some of the whispered comments passed around from one to another. There was one poor joke from Jones Davis: "He may fancy Penholder, but we don't." But when the wife was mentioned, every body said, "Isn't she a little trump?" Our literary young lady kept the secret of the blue bead-bag locked in her own breast. She never thought of the silly hopes she had placed on the great genius for the publication of "Soul Thrills and Heart Hunger" without a certain sense of shame.

We have all come to the conclusion that Penholder does not write his own books, but we firmly believe his bright, animated better-half not only poses for them, but composes them.

CHAPTER XLVII.

CHRISTMAS IN THE VILLAGE.

THE first real snow-storm of the season came in loose large flakes, like white feathers or tufts of wool cast down from the shearing of the heavenly sheep. It has remained with us for the Christmas festival, and has brought the genuine Christmas cheer and jollity. It lies downy and pure upon the fields, and gently rounds the valleys and clings to all the inequalities of the hills. Virgin purity breathes over the village and makes it to shine like the palace of Baldur, the Norse god of light, which knew no grain of dust or touch of defilement. The roads lead through a spotless world, softly laced and printed with the shadows of naked trees and the delicate blues and violets of the hills. The villagers look more picturesque than their wont in fur hoods and cloaks; the cheeks of the young glow lustily, and the old are beautified by the snow-frame with its interfoliations and arabesques; the sleighs are out with tinkling bells; and the sleds are out, manned by boy crews; the sunshine glides into old rooms through speckless windows, and touches old faces and antique furniture with a new charm of expression. Like a dove the snow has come and perched on the house-tops, and the evergreeens are burdened with tufted white, the Christmas roses of our northern clime.

In these last sad sweet days of the year, when the longest story without an end must needs come to a period for the time being, I have been going round in the village like an old Diogenes, with a tallow dip in my hand, to find one perfect character. There is the doctor's wife, there is Miss Candace, old Deacon Hildreth, St. Patty, and a dozen others who are often spoken of as just perfect—saints upon earth ; but when we look closely we detect little flaws and specks of narrowness and old habits, the hardening of opinions and prejudices, tag-ends of folly and vanity and human weakness, small lapses from the highest ideal, such as mark too many repentant crosses in our own life experience.

There is not one perfect, no, not one. But going about with my candle in the still twilight of the old year, when the trees stand so gray and motionless, I see, strange to say, a shadowy figure stealing along beside every human being—that other self so strange and mysterious even to its owner. On reflection I am sure Styles Garth saw that other self in his shadow, and its potentiality of evil may have frightened him when he caught sight of it in the sunlight. It is the shadow-self that makes every human being interesting and worthy of study. The village, quiet, humdrum, and sleepy, with its faded old houses and steady habits, is still full of this subtle, mysterious, creeping life, which we do not comprehend and only discover by flashes of true insight. The quiet air often tingles with the radiation of thought and feeling as a blue column quivers over the glow of flame.

You may have remarked that my village has increased strangely in size for so small and unimportant a place. But its story does not embrace so much of what is as what has been. The past is still intact with us. It accompanies the village as an aggregate shadow self, a village ghost ; often to be seen looking white and wan like the pallid moon before sunset. It takes in the whole of Burying-Ground Hill ; for the dead are not so dead as they seem, nor are the living so much alive. The dead walk about here at all hours. A dead hand sticking up out of a grave on the hill often points the finger of destiny to the new-born, and shapes the lives of creatures who come even a hundred years after it was put away in earth. Have I not said that powerful, sound-headed, large-hearted Dr. Abijah Manners, though he died some half century ago, seems alive and active to the children who play in our street? Much more is he alive to-day than many a torpid creature maimed and deformed by disobedience to the laws of his own being, and broken on the wheel of life, not strictly as punishment, but because of the inevitableness of the laws of the universe.

It is an odd thing, but only yesterday I saw "Dr. Jekyll and Mr. Hyde" walking close together through the village street, not interchangeable, but existing in a semi-detached state. For Hyde, however ugly he may be, carries Jekyll's features, and Jekyll, though a prosperous, handsome man, is still marked by Hyde as by the small-pox, nor can he get rid of him while wearing his own proper form.

I have a curious fancy on Christmas Eve I have never confessed before. It comes to me while the evergreen and holly are going up in the church. The young clergyman likes these beautiful old heathenish customs, and encourages the boys and girls to make the church look as lovely as possible in its verdant garniture. Many houses, too, are wreathed with Christmas green, notably the doctor's. For days before the blessed eve, he and Effie are abroad in the woods gathering ground-pine and lusty branches of spruce and hemlock. All the pictures look out of leafy setting, and the hearth is wreathed with boughs and red berries.

When the church and the village homes begin to deck themselves on Christmas Eve, I have the strange fancy that all the dead come home to keep the holiday—old and young, white-haired people, beautiful maidens, bands of little children, all bearing the Christmas rose and palm. In they glide, with no pushing or crowding, such as happened in Mrs. Oliphant's "Beleaguered City," but they make the place only the more homelike to those who remain, and sweeten the air as if they had poured upon it the essence of violets.

It is a strange fancy, but I can not shake it off, and I steal about in the dusk of this gracious eve, the fairest of all the year, and seem to see the departed friends troop in over worn thresholds of old homes. They carry gifts in their hands, and as they go in they all turn and smile at me, sometimes roguishly. The dear children look back with their starry eyes through floating sunny curls. I wonder if the mothers whose constant hearts still ache for their little ones, no matter how long they have been what we call dead, do not feel the warm kisses and the little clinging hands while tender heads nestle upon their bosoms. Shall I tell them their little ones have all come home to-night? Before I can speak or move the vision vanishes—perhaps it was only a dream.

It is the custom of our good doctor to celebrate Christmas Eve with a little gathering of friends and neighbors about the holly-decked hearth, and though he offers but the simplest entertainment—nuts and apples and sweet cider—no occasion is ever awaited with more impatience and delight by the few who are privileged to come together there.

The doctor has a peculiar sentiment connected with this eve. He feels for all the children who are so restless and happy in their little beds, dreaming of Santa Claus, while the stockings dangle around the chimney-piece. It is a holy night, sacred to childhood, when, according to the old traditions, witches have no evil power, only good elves and fairies can come into homes with the evergreens, and blessed influences rain in star showers over every crib and cradle. While Drusilla and the First

Church ladies give out fat turkeys to all who are too poor to buy them, the doctor sees to it that no poor child, not even a little Irisher, shall go without some gift in the stocking. He stole away the other day to the nearest large town, not even taking Effie with him, as he coveted the luxury of buying cheap toys all by himself, and when he came back his wagon was full of mysterious, odd-shaped parcels. Not one of Jake Small's bantlings, nor Sambo Brown's pickanninies, nor Tim McCoy's children were forgotten; and out of his overcoat pocket protruded an eye-winking, real-hair doll for Chippie, cheek by jowl with a fine dog-collar for her dog, Zip Coon.

This Christmas Eve of which I am writing has been a joyous one to the doctor, for his brother George was still with him, and the friends who came were taken into a warm hospitable embrace. The judge and Mrs. Magnus are now in Washington, where he has been corresponding immensely in the newspapers, to try and soften down and explain away the interview with Bob Smartweed. As this brings him so much before the public the judge feels with a little inward, pious self-justification that there is balm in Gilead. The judge, therefore, could not beam upon the doctor's little party, but he had Milly, and Aunt Dido, and Miss Candace, and John Dean and his wife, and the clergyman and his pretty mate, and Drusilla and the Rev. Arthur Meeker, and Deacon and Mrs. Hildreth, and the Elmores, and others of our friends who need no particular mention.

The company played games and sang old songs at times to Effie's accompaniment on the piano, and again they gathered about the hearth and told old tales, some of them of a weird and ghostly nature, as seemed to befit the occasion. I know the doctor spoke of a patient of his who once lived on the other side of Saddleback, indeed was a neighbor to the man Hayrick, who came to such an awful end about the time of President Lincoln's assassination. This old man Sawyer was something of a hermit, and entertained peculiar religious views. The old man had been unfortunate with his children, most of whom died young, and the only boy who grew to manhood went into the war and was carried off by camp fever in hospital. In a few years Sawyer's wife had passed away, and he was left alone, a solitary, slim old body, creeping noiselessly about the mountain world where he lived. His religious oddities troubled none of the few and widely-scattered neighbors. They consisted in certain rites and ceremonies peculiar to himself, among others the placing of plates and chairs at the table for all his dead family on Sundays, Thanksgiving, Christmas, and at the New Year festival. Silently on those days he seemed to sit down and break bread with the departed in a strange invisible communion, and the country children spread the rumor abroad that "Miss" Sawyer often appeared at a certain window of the house, looking out with wan, shadowy presence at the place where she had been accustomed to sit in life to watch the "passing," of which there was but the least. Old Sawyer is dead and the place has new occupants, but the haunted window where "Miss" Sawyer's ghost used to sit and gaze is still pointed out, and idlers have scratched their names all over the glass.

This purely local tale called forth from George Rivington a little story which he had heard from an ex-confederate officer in the south-west. It was narrated to him at a large hotel in St. Louis some ten years after the close of the war. After the capture of Lee's army, twelve officers who had served together in the same army-corps in the confederate ranks formed themselves into a little club. They had scattered away to various parts of the South and West, but they agreed to meet on Christmas Eve of each year at a large hostelry in one of our western cities for a late supper. Exactly as the bell chimed the hour of midnight they were to rise, and solemnly, and in silence, pledge the memory of their dead comrades. Moreover, as one after another the members of the club were taken by death, the covers were still to be laid for the entire twelve, and the memory of these comrades was but to swell the aggregate of honor and sorrow paid to all the confederate dead. When the agreement was first made, all the club members were comparatively young, strong, vigorous men. But in a few years death had singularly reduced their ranks, and each season, as the survivors met around the board, the occasion became more melancholy and the midnight ceremonies more solemn and impressive. Six or seven years after the club was formed there were but five surviving, and they, sitting with the seven empty seats, seemed to be attending their own funerals. Four years later the gentleman who told this tale to George Rivington was the sole survivor of the club.

On Christmas Eve he repaired to the place of meeting as usual, and ordered the table laid for twelve. Alone he seated himself in full uniform at the head of the board, and strove to go through the ceremony of dining. As the clock struck twelve, the waiter having left the room, he slowly rose from his chair, glass in hand, and with suffused eyes, drank to the memory of the departed. At that instant, by some strange illusion, every place was filled. He saw his dead friends exactly as in life, with the light glancing off epaulet and sword-hilt, each holding his glass as he rose to his feet to drink the solemn pledge to the confederate dead. With a groan he sank back in his chair. The glass was dashed from his hand. The sound of his fall brought the people of the house, who found him insensible, apparently in a fit. They put him to bed and procured a doctor, and it was long before his confused brain could recall the exact occurrences of that night. But when he regained strength and memory, the dread of the next Christmas Eve, when he was pledged again to meet his eleven comrades, affected him with superstitious terrors. However, before the time came round he too had passed over to the great majority.

When Mr. Rivington had finished this strange little Christmas tale, it was drawing on toward the witching hour, and a kind of awed hush fell on the company, as if they expected to see a ghostly troop enter the room. Effie stole to the piano and struck some notes of Auld Lang Syne, and just as the clock chimed twelve, and Christmas Day was born the whole company broke into the grand, inspiring old song, the uncanny feeling was at once dispelled, and the lamps which had seemed to burn blue, brightened the room.

The good doctor, knowing Milly's weakness, asked her before they parted to recite one of her father's little poems. Not for their merit did Milly choose the following simple lines, but because they seemed to breathe a spirit of hope and courage toward the great dim unknown future upon whose threshold they were standing:

> Brave hearts rejoice to meet the summer's gold,
> Brave hearts still gladden in the winter's cold,
> Blow high, or low the winds on land and sea,
>   They bring no ill to me.

> The sun but sinks to lead the new-born day,
> Its red rose blossoms out of misty gray.
> Blow high, or low the winds on land and sea,
>   They bring no ill to me.

> In youth, dear Nature decks the sunny brow,
> In age, she wreathes anew the frosty pow.
> Blow tempests wild, or breathe a southern gale,
>   All winds shall fill my sail.

Good wishes and merry quips had flown about like little birds in all directions. A few simple gifts were exchanged, and then the guests poured forth into the cold night air, where the winter sky sparkled resplendently with ten thousand stars over the snow, and a trace of sweetness seemed to linger, as if the herald angels, with their new song of "Peace on earth, good will to men," had just passed that way. And because a child was born and laid in a manger—the symbol of infancy's closeness to nature, and her creative powers—the old earth seemed happier than her wont.

As the season brings its pleasant tokens fraught with love and kindness, so would I send you a present, though of a humble, homely sort; and I therefore slip into the hamper of Santa Claus, as he makes his midnight rounds, a bundle of *Village Photographs*.

THE END.

www.ingramcontent.com/pod-product-compliance
Lightning Source LLC
Chambersburg PA
CBHW051851300426
44117CB00006B/351